The GOSPEL of HEALTH

D0672778

The A *to* Z GUIDE *to*
VIBRANT HEALTH...GOD'S WAY

VALERIE
SAXION, N.D.

Strength
& Honor

BRONZE BOW PUBLISHING
MINNEAPOLIS, MINNESOTA

The Gospel of Health

Copyright © 2004 Valerie Saxion

All rights reserved. No part of this book may be
reproduced in any form or by any means without
written consent of publisher/author.

ISBN 1-932458-10-7

Published by Bronze Bow Publishing Inc.,
2600 E. 26th Street, Minneapolis, MN 55406

You can reach us on the Internet at
www.bronzebowpublishing.com

Literary development and cover/interior design
by Koechel Peterson & Associates, Inc.,
Minneapolis, Minnesota.

Manufactured in the United States of America

The Gospel of Health

goes to the Originator!

He knew us before we were
in our mother's womb.

He knew what our bodies needed
before they were birthed.

So I thank Him

for giving me a glimpse from
the Owner's manual as to
what it takes for our
vehicles to run properly.

I thank my God

for showing me practical
applications in healthy living
and for allowing me to share
what I have learned
with others.

CONTENTS

CONDITION-SPECIFIC HELP

ABOUT *the* AUTHOR

DR. VALERIE SAXION IS ONE OF AMERICA'S MOST ARTICULATE CHAMPIONS OF NUTRITION AND SPIRITUAL HEALING. A twenty-year veteran of health science with a primary focus in naturopathy, Valerie has a delightful communication style and charming demeanor that will open your heart, clear your mind, and uplift you to discover abundant natural health God's way. Her pearls of wisdom and life-saving advice are critical for success and survival in today's toxic world.

As the co-founder of Valerie Saxion's Silver Creek Labs, a premier manufacturer and distributor of nutritional supplements and health products that cover a wide range of healing modalities, Dr. Saxion has seen firsthand the power of God's remedies as the sick are healed and the lame walk. "It's what I love most about what God has called me to do," she says.

Valerie Saxion is the host of TBN's *On Call*, which airs twice weekly across America. The program is dedicated to bringing the most up-to-date health and nutritional information to the viewing audience. Dr. Saxion is one of TBN's favorite speakers and can be seen quarterly on the flagship show, *Praise the Lord*. The audience is nationwide as well as international, with a potential 33 million broadcast households.

She is also seen on the Daystar Television Network and Cornerstone Television Network. Dr. Saxion has been interviewed on numerous radio talk shows as well as television appearances nationwide and in Canada. Hosts love to open the line for callers to phone in their health concerns while Dr. Saxion gives on-the-air advice and instruction.

She has also lectured at scores of health events nationwide and in Canada. She has advised international government leaders, professional athletes, television personalities, and the lady next door. "All with the same great results," she says, "if they will only follow the recommendations."

After attending one of Dr. Saxion's lectures, you may have cried, you may have laughed, you may get insight, but one thing is sure: You will leave empowered with the tools to live and love in a healthy body!

Dr. Saxion is also the author of *How to Feel Great All the Time, Super Foods for Super Kids,* and *Every Body Has Parasites* as well as four very practical, life-changing booklets, including *How to Stop Candida and Other Yeast Conditions in Their Tracks, The Easy Way to Regain and Maintain Your Perfect Weight, Conquering the Fatigue, Depression, and Weight Gain Caused by Low Thyroid,* and *How to Detoxify and Renew Your Body From Within.* She is currently a monthly columnist for BeautyWalk.com, hosted by Peter Lamas, famous makeup artist and hair designer for the rich and famous.

Married to Jim Saxion for twenty-plus years, they are the parents of eight healthy children, ages toddler to mid twenties.

To schedule Dr. Saxion for a lecture or interview, please call 1-800-493-1146, or fax 817-236-5411, or email at valerie@drval.tv.

JUMP START

WHAT IS *THE GOSPEL OF HEALTH*? WE RECOGNIZE THE WORD *GOSPEL* AS "GOOD NEWS," AND THE WORD *HEALTH* AS RELATING TO A PERSON'S PHYSICAL FITNESS OR LEVEL OF WELL-BEING.

From a Christian perspective, we have certain reference points made throughout the Bible that direct us to God's idea of physical health, spiritual health, and emotional health. One familiar and comprehensive verse reads: "Beloved, I pray that you may prosper in all things and be in health, just as your soul prospers" (3 John 2). While I am not a theologian and won't try to plumb the depths of this scripture, I know that God is saying, "I yearn for My people to do well and live out their lives in a way that will satisfy them and please Me, knowing they have accomplished My plan for the precious gift I call life."

When I'm out speaking, I often point out that we have to keep our "vehicles" running well to finish the race. God calls this life a race, and the vehicle is our body. The apostle Paul said, "Do you not know that those who run in a race all run, but one receives the prize? Run in such a way that you may obtain it" (1 Corinthians 9:24). If our body is not performing well, we have a problem.

Using the racing analogy, we could be demolished, end up in the pit, finish last or somewhere in between, or we could be the winner. You know where God wants you to finish, and even better than an automobile manufacturer He's given us the vehicle, the manual, the fuel, the diagnostic computer, the tools, the intuition, the Instructor, and something that no human has come up with, a self-correcting mechanism called healing.

HEALTH *and* HEALING

Let's talk about healing for a moment. The Bible says, "But He was wounded for our transgressions, He was bruised for our iniquities; the chastisement for our peace was upon Him, and by His stripes we are healed" (Isaiah 53:6). That's a good place to start, an indisputable place to start. Jesus paid for our healing at Calvary, and so it belongs to you. Theologians may dispute what this verse means. I just believe what the Bible says. If you're wise, you will, too. If you have an illness, believe you are healed through Jesus' death and resurrection. That's an excellent place to start, because it gives you a distinct advantage on your path to whole health.

We all realize that this life is full of obstacles to sound health. For some, it starts at birth, while others encounter conditions, symptoms, problems, or issues as they age. Very few people make it through to one hundred twenty-five years without running into a health problem. I don't know of one, do you?

Our paths are different; we come from different backgrounds, cultures, ethnicities. In many ways, we live in different worlds even though we live on the same planet and maybe even in the same nation, state, county, or city. Our air, food, water, soil, insects, elevation, housing, hygiene, genetic makeup, and many other factors make our individual pathways unique. We all have opportunities to conquer one health hurdle or another. So let's look at our options.

When I look at health and healing, I always see God's grace. Healing is in our DNA. If we get cut, we heal naturally. And healing happens on innumerable levels, and my opinion is that it boils down to the individual and where they can meet God's provision for their situation. Consider two people who have the same deadly disease. One goes through radical surgery and is healed; the other person is miraculously healed. "God is no respecter of persons" (Acts 10:34), so what happened? I think He met each person on his or her own level. To one He gave a surgeon; to the other a miracle. Both were healed by God, but by different means. Therein lies the Gospel of

Health. He provides whatever you need to be healthy and finish your course on the stage where you live.

I have a doctoral degree in Naturopathy, which means that my healing path and the path that I lecture on is a natural one. God made nature, it belongs to Him, and in it we find amazing natural products that have a wondrous ability to aid our health. Look around at what He has made—the herbs, roots, barks, plants, leaves, stems, fruits, vegetables, water, minerals, and the list goes on and on. These contain the natural blueprint for patentable drugs. But the common denominator is that God designed the blueprint—the portion of the plant that heals—and He understands how to remedy anything and everything. He created it all for our use, for our health. Think about it, in everything natural there's something that can help a human being in one way or another. For thousands of years we've seen these natural products work. Their uses are chronicled in ancient documents and confirmed today by scientific research.

However, nature's way isn't the first healing choice for most Americans. We have been trained to use a medical system that usually treats health challenges with pharmaceutical drugs. These drugs are usually synthetic, which means they are a copy or imitation of something, and that something is…nature. Yes, nature or natural products, or parts thereof. Keep in mind, though, that I said God meets us on different levels. And one of those levels could be a surgeon, an M.D., a D.O., an OBGYN, etc. It is not my intention to circumvent the wisdom and knowledge of the medical profession but to work together for the highest health achievement—wholeness of spirit, mind, and body.

No statements made in this book should be construed as a claim for a cure, treatment, or prevention of any disease. The Bible says that there is wisdom in a multitude of counselors, so read this book and consult a qualified health-care professional.

The good news, the gospel, is that help is available. There are answers. Thousands of men and women over the centuries have devoted their lives to understanding the correlation between the problems and the natural answers.

In this book I endeavor to share some of these principles for the most common problems we may run into during the course of this race on earth. You'll see lives changed by simple, natural methods. Discover easy, natural strategies created for you by God. Maybe for the first time in a long time you'll identify hope for a happy, successful life. That's some good news!

WHERE HEALTH BEGINS

As a child, perhaps you recall hearing these words: "You are what you eat." "Breakfast is the most important meal." "Drink more water." "Eat your vegetables." And the wisdom of your mother went on and on. Right? If not, you missed out on some of the best free medicinal insight available.

But we start where we are today, and no one knows where you are better than you. Let's take a look at the quality of fuel you're putting in your vehicle. The food and drink you consume have a direct correlation upon your mood, behavior, energy, and overall wellness. Unfortunately, for many people, the old adage couldn't be more true: "Garbage in, garbage out."

I've dedicated several chapters of this book to directing you to the purest, freshest foods, and God has provided us with an abundance of healthy foods to consider. You may be surprised that the quality of the most basic fundamentals of life—air and water—are crucial to your health. Just because you're drinking plenty of water doesn't mean that it's doing your body good, if it's the wrong water.

By way of introduction, if you believe any liquid you drink—such as coffee, tea, or a soda—gives you the benefits of water, you're believing a myth. I commend you if you carry a water bottle—your body absorbs and makes use of a maximum amount if you drink a little bit constantly rather than guzzling it down. In a chapter to come I'll discuss exactly how much water you need daily and a specific water that I believe is the best to hydrate the body and promote proper cellular communication.

THE GOSPEL OF HEALTH

FOUNDATIONS

———— ❧ ————

*"He is like a man building
a house, who dug deep and laid
the foundation on the rock.
And when the flood arose,
the stream beat vehemently
against the house,
and could not shake it;
for it was founded
on the rock."*

LUKE 6:48

———— ❧ ————

FOUNDATIONS *to the* GOSPEL *of* HEALTH

THERE ARE CERTAIN FOUNDATIONS FOR LIVING THE GOSPEL OF HEALTH, and without them you'll miss out on the health God intended for you to enjoy. They are the cornerstones of what I call "supernatural health" and vital to supernatural living. Even if you're not looking for "super natural," perhaps you're just looking for the best natural life you can have—if so, these are still monumentally important details.

Life is full of problems—physical, mental, emotional, and spiritual. At home, at work, and even in our kitchens, life seldom goes the way we want it to go. And there's no lack for those who claim they can help. Everywhere you turn you bump into counselors, therapists, self-help books, magazine articles, and radio and TV talk shows shouting for your attention. Even though I participate in these venues, I can see the problem.

Unfortunately, most of the messages we hear only deal with the inception of the problem—endless explanations for why you feel unhappy and which cruel early life experience made you powerless to get along with your family. While all of that might be interesting, it is ultimately useless and sometimes destructive. So listen very carefully. At the end of the day, there's only one thing that makes a difference—how to make the problem disappear!

Only one thing matters—you want solutions, not explanations or excuses. That's the Gospel of Health, your key to change. Remember: a problem is a recurring pattern that you don't like...the same situation with its unpleasant feelings comes up over and over again. The solution is to take a different action, and to do it one step at a time.

In Chapter 18, "Quick Weight Loss for Anyone Who Wants to Take Charge of Their Health," you'll read how my husband had numerous physical problems. He took one action step...and it literally changed everything! Gone was the pain, the anxiety, fear, lethargy, disease, and distress. Would you believe that most of these symptoms vanished in the first 10 days?

FOUNDATION #1:
PRAYER *and the* GOSPEL *of* HEALTH

I've always been amazed that God hears us and cares about the smallest detail of our lives. I suppose it shouldn't be surprising, in light of the fact that we were created to communicate with Him as Adam and Eve did in the Garden (Genesis 3:8). We are children of God, made into the very likeness of our elder brother, Jesus; so there, too, we should have the same open communication with our Father as Jesus did.

So why is it amazing that God would hear and answer prayer? I think it comes down to simply trusting and believing. Some people must be brought to the end of themselves to understand it. They say there are no atheists in foxholes. Why? All other cares of the world have been eliminated, and there's only time to engage in the most serious of thought—life, and life eternal. So they cry out to God, He hears them, and one way or another the prayer is answered.

On the other hand, I know people who stay in touch with God all day long, seven days a week. They talk to God, He talks to them; they ask, He answers; problems come, and problems are solved; and when this life is at an end, they're fully prepared to go to the next, for it's just like going home. Because they spent so much time in God's presence, they know He can be counted on in every situation and with every need.

These brothers and sisters are careful about what they ask God for, because they really believe it will come to pass. It's just as real as asking the best daddy in the world for something you already know he is going to do for you. Prayer is that simple.

We never see Adam or Jesus trying to wrangle something out of God. No, they asked, He answered. The Bible is full of this advice for us, too. "Whatsoever ye shall ask in prayer, believing, ye shall receive" (Matthew 21:22). "If ye abide in me, and my words abide in you, ye shall ask what ye will, and it shall be done unto you" (John 15:7).

My amazement in this is based on the fact that God is so good. His goodness is better than life. He surpasses our wildest dreams of goodness. He delights in His people living in health and never intended for us to die! But mankind's fall into sin happened, and God was prepared. Jesus came and fixed things up for us to have that same communication—so if you want it, it's available. But you have to ask—that's prayer.

And not only is prayer good for the soul, it's good for the physical body. Even science backs up the power of prayer and verifies the Bible as the final word.

Study #1. Between August 1982 and May 1983, 393 patients in San Francisco's General Hospital Coronary Care Unit participated in a double-blind study to assess the therapeutic effects of intercessory prayer. Patients were randomly selected by computer to either receive or not receive intercessory prayer. All participants in the study, including patients, doctors, and the conductor of the study himself, remained blind throughout the study. To guard against biasing the study, the patients were not contacted again after it was decided which group would be prayed for and which group would not.

It was assumed that although the patients in the control group would not be prayed for by the participants in the study, family members and friends would likely pray for the health of at least some of the members of the control group. There was no control over this factor. Meanwhile, all the members of the group that received prayer would be prayed for by not only those associated with the study but by others as well.

The results of the study are not surprising to those who believe in the power of prayer. The patients who received prayer as a part of the study were healthier than those who had not. The prayed-for group had less need of having CPR (cardiopulmonary resuscitation) performed and less need for the use of mechanical ventilators. They had a diminished necessity for diuretics and antibiotics, less occurrences of pulmonary edema, and fewer deaths. Taking all factors into consideration, these results can only be attributed to the power of prayer.

Study #2. A study conducted by Duke University Medical Center in Durham, North Carolina, had over 4,000 participants over the age of 65. The study found that those who pray and attend religious services on a weekly basis, especially those between the ages of 65 and 74, had lower blood pressure than their counterparts who did not pray or attend religious services. They found that the more religious the person, particularly those who prayed or studied the Bible weekly, the lower the blood pressure. According to the study, these people were 40 percent less likely to have high diastolic pressure or diastolic hypertension than those who did not attend religious services, pray, or study the Bible.

Dr. David B. Larson, president of the National Institute for Health Care Research in Rockville, Maryland, who co-authored the study, also says that prayer can lower high blood pressure.

Study #3. A study done at the Virginia Commonwealth University Medical College of Virginia in Richmond, which studied 1,902 twins, found that those who were committed to their spiritual lives tended to have less severe depression and a lower risk of addiction to cigarettes or alcohol. The healthful lifestyles of the spiritually rich and faithful clearly contribute to their well-being. They tend not to smoke or drink or not do either excessively. Their marriages are more stable, and their spiritual communities form a network that can support people when they are ill.

These studies have shown conclusive evidence of the power of prayer. Time after time the outcomes of these tests have shown the reality of the force of God and our ability to communicate with Him.

We have also learned from viewing the results of these studies that the expectations we have while praying factor into the outcome of our prayers. Though the faithful will always believe that there need not be any physical evidence of the power and effects of prayer, science has come a long way toward showing just that—prayer is real, and it works.

FOUNDATION #2:
FORGIVENESS *and the* GOSPEL *of* HEALTH

Driving to work one morning, a motorist encountered another driver who cut him off in heavy traffic. The motorist bitterly shouted expletives to the other driver accompanied by passionate hand signals. Other extreme but unseen actions underscored his anger—his blood pressure soared, his heart raced, adrenaline poured, sweat glands produced, and chemicals raged as his brain released them. When he arrived at work, he relived this experience with his coworkers, and later that night he repeated the details to his wife. Then, just before going to sleep, he dreamily rehearsed what he would have done if he had only been driving an eighteen-wheeler instead of his Volkswagen Bug.

Meanwhile, the other driver went merrily on his way, never noticing he had accidentally cut the motorist off.

Kenneth Hagin tells the story of a woman who traveled a great distance to attend healing services he was holding. As always, he encouraged people to hear the Word of God and let it build up before coming to the prayer line. Furthermore, he instructed them to forgive others along with other helpful guidelines that would be of assistance prior to prayer.

The woman listened intently to the sermon and followed every instruction. She knew she needed to forgive her brother for a twenty-five-year feud they had, during which time they had not spoken. After the service she called her brother, told him that the Lord had forgiven her, and apologized for the fight, taking all the blame on herself.

After resting in her motel room, she went to the evening meeting. She again listened to the preaching and couldn't wait until the prayer line formed, feeling she was ready for what the Lord would do for her. When it finally came time, Brother Hagin gave the instructions and added, "Check yourself for your problem." When she did, her physical problem was gone. She had been healed before anyone could pray for her because she had been obedient and forgiven.

I've seen this same thing happen over and over with people whom I counsel. Disease can take many shapes and comes under numerous titles, but often has the same root of unforgiveness. Once that forgiveness is released, healing occurs.

Listen to these amazing words from Herbert Benson of the Harvard Medical School: "To be angry is not good for your health…. Hatred is a banquet until you recognize you are the main course." I'll go a step farther and include all sickness and disease with this. Dr. Benson goes on to say that "60 to 90 percent of all the business that comes to physicians is stress-related, and forgiveness reduces anger and stress."

Recent research shows that holding on to anger increases your likelihood of a heart attack as well as cancer, high blood pressure, high cholesterol, and other illnesses. Forgiveness boosts your sense of worth and lowers your blood pressure and heart rate, experts say. Forgiveness also helps you sleep better at night and promotes a positive change in your attitude.

David R. Williams, a sociologist, says, "We found a particularly strong relationship between forgiveness of others and mental health among middle-aged and older Americans." People who reported higher levels of this type of forgiveness were more satisfied with their lives and less likely to report symptoms of psychological distress, including feeling nervous, restless, or sad.

Dr. Robert Enright, a professor of educational psychology at the University of Wisconsin at Madison, conducted a study in which he measured people's emotional states before and after they forgave someone who had hurt them. His study found that those who forgave no longer had feelings of anxiety and depression and felt better about themselves.

Forgiveness and loving your enemies is where the rubber of Christianity hits the road, and you can experience the Gospel of Health when you follow this advice.

FOUNDATION #3: FREEDOM FROM FEAR *and the* GOSPEL *of* HEALTH

As I'm writing, I'm concerned about how many readers will get to this point and wonder how or why fear relates to health, especially the Gospel of Health. Someone once said, "There can't be good news without bad news." If this is correct, fear is the bad news of health. The Bible says, "Fear involves torment" (1 John 4:18). Here are a few synonyms for torment—anguish, suffering, distress, pain, affliction, aching, hurting, stiffness, throbbing. Sounds like sickness and disease, doesn't it?

I'm going back to what I said in the introduction: God meets us on many levels. Wherever you're at, that's where He will meet you. Later on I'm going to discuss major diseases that might qualify as legitimate fear factors. But first, there are a lot of people reading this book who don't have a major disease but are fearful. I need to tell you that to remain fearful is to position yourself to receive things you don't want. Sickness and disease are two of them. As powerful as the Word of God is, as powerful as Jesus' name and the stripes He took for us on Calvary, one thing can prevent the Gospel of Health from working for you—and that's *fear*.

We are told to "be strong and of good courage" (Joshua 1:6). "Fear not" appears 110 times in Scripture, and we are also commanded to "be not afraid." God would not tell us these things if it weren't possible. He wouldn't waste the words if there wasn't a good reason for these instructions. But there is a good reason, and it's apparent to everyone who's been afraid at one time or another. Fear is destructive.

Sickness, disease, plague, illness, and hospitals frighten people. The common cold may not send shivers down your spine, but what about the C word or AIDS. Colon cancer is fairly common and bound to stop you in your tracks if the hint is given that you might have it. Say the word lump, and I know that the next thought you have probably won't be peaceful. Just the thought that your family has a history of heart problems can cause your brain to release numerous chemicals that can really have a negative effect on you. But remember, Jesus already paid for your healing, and Satan is just trying to put something on you that doesn't belong to you.

Fear is the mother of every disease and ailment. Fear will take and nourish a simple virus or bacteria that your immune system would normally conquer naturally and blow it up into the most brutal case of "whatever" possible. Fear can turn nerves of steel into a quivering bowl of Jell-O and make the strongest of men weak. When weak, the immune system may not be up to the task, and you open the door to new ailments or exasperating ailments that already exist.

So what's the solution? Franklin D. Roosevelt summed it up this way: "Let me assert my firm belief that the only thing we have to fear is fear itself—nameless, unreasoning, unjustified terror which paralyzes needed efforts to convert retreat into advance."

We must convert retreat into advance. When God commands us to "fear not" and to "be not afraid," there's more to this. Here's the key: each time God says fear not, the command is followed by "I." "Fear not for I am with you." And other mentions of His divine presence that incapacitate fear. It doesn't matter whether the problem is big or small, He is there and He can handle it!

"Casting all your care upon him; for he careth for you" (1 Peter 5:7). God told us to do that, so we are able to. To make this point, my husband would always toss an object to the person he was talking with and say, "It's out of my hands now. You control it." When we give the fear to the Lord, He takes and controls it and then gives us joy in return.

Joy brings love, and love casts out fear (1 John 4:18)—what a beautiful circle. Because when you're in love, you're at peace, happy and content that the outcome will be healthy for you regardless of how the situation may appear. God's got it.

If you want to be a little more aggressive and really give fear a black eye, forcefully resist it. Resist fear, sickness, disease, and sadness. To resist means to "oppose, defy, refuse to accept, stand firm." And the Bible tells us we are to "Submit to God. Resist the devil, and he will flee from you" (James 4:7). That means fear has to flee as well.

Step two in the complete overthrow of fear is to be proactive and start helping other people who are facing similar trials. To pray for people and visit people in the hospital initiates an all out attack against fear.

Finally, know that each time you rely on God, He sees you and takes notice of your actions. When you believe and trust, God is pleased, and you will feel His pleasure.

The Gospel of Health says stop fear at all costs. Listen to wisdom concerning your health and take the steps that lead to victory.

FOUNDATION #4:
LAUGHTER and the GOSPEL of HEALTH

"A happy heart is good medicine," said King Solomon, "and a cheerful mind works healing" (Proverbs 17:22). Laughter stimulates circulation, produces a sense of well-being, exercises the face and stomach muscles, stimulates the production of endorphins (the body's natural painkillers), provides more oxygen to the brain, and is fun on top of it. One study revealed that the healing power of humor can reduce pain and stimulate the immune function in children who have cancer, AIDS, or diabetes and in children receiving organ transplants and bone marrow treatments.

Laughter is to the soul what soap is to the body. Researchers suggest that we need a minimum of twelve laughs a day just to stay healthy. It can affect our brain chemistry and immune system in very positive ways. We've long known that the ability to laugh is helpful to those coping with major illness and the stress of life's problems. But researchers are now saying laughter can help do a lot more—it can basically bring balance to all the components of the immune system, which helps us fight off diseases.

Twenty-one children ages 8 to 14 were asked to put their hand into cold water, and the study found that the whole group tolerated the temperature longer while watching a funny video. Those who laughed most remembered less of the pain, and hormone tests on their saliva showed their stress levels were lower after laughing.

A study by doctors at the University of Maryland found that people who fail to smile in stressful or uncomfortable situations may be more likely to develop heart problems. Research suggests that laughing and having a good sense of humor can protect against heart disease.

Laughter reduces levels of certain stress hormones. In doing this, laughter provides a safety valve that shuts off the flow of stress hormones and the fight-or-flight compounds that swing into action in our bodies when we experience stress, anger, or hostility. These stress hormones suppress the immune system, increase the number of blood platelets (which can cause obstructions in arteries), and raise blood pressure. When we're laughing, natural killer cells that destroy tumors and viruses increase, as do Gamma-interferon (a disease-fighting protein), T-cells (which are a major part of the immune response), and B-cells (which make disease-destroying antibodies).

Researchers estimate that laughing 100 times is equal to 10 minutes on the rowing machine or 15 minutes on an exercise bike. Laughing can be a total body workout! Blood pressure is lowered, and there is an increase in vascular blood flow and in oxygenation of the blood, which further assists healing. Laughter also gives your diaphragm and abdominal, respiratory, facial, leg, and back muscles a workout. That's why you often feel exhausted after a long bout of laughter—you've just had an aerobic workout!

Laughter may lead to hiccuping and coughing, which clears the respiratory tract by dislodging mucous plugs. Laughter also increases the concentration of salivary immunoglobulin A, which defends against infectious organisms entering through the respiratory tract.

Laughter provides a way for emotions such as anger, sadness, and fear to be safely released. Laughter is healing. That's why some people who are upset or stressed out go to a funny movie, so they can laugh the negative emotions away (these negative emotions, when held inside, can cause biochemical changes that affect our bodies).

Figure out what makes you laugh and do it (or read it or watch it) more often.

Surround yourself with funny people—be with them every chance you get.

One doctor said, "The recommendations for a healthy heart may one day be exercise, eat right, and laugh a few times a day."

WHAT YOU NEED
to KNOW

———— ❧ ————

"My people are destroyed
for lack of knowledge."

HOSEA 4:6

———— ❧ ————

PROTEINS, CARBOHYDRATES, and FATS

IF WE COULD EVEN REMOTELY GRASP HOW WONDERFULLY OUR BODIES ARE MADE, and how totally interconnected they are, we would never struggle with our worship of the Creator God. With all its amazing complexities, the human body and soul is easily the most amazing creation on earth. And it is well equipped to keep itself in perpetual health through a powerful immune system that can meet most challenges without outside help.

However, our bodies require that we carefully supply them with all they absolutely require for health, whether by nutrients or exercise. God designed that radiant health reign over every aspect of our body and that we would feel great physically and emotionally. But if we fall short, if we deprive our body of nutritional Top Natural Aids or abuse our body with what we know or don't know is harmful, we will suffer a breakdown in our health, and that specific symptom will negatively affect our whole person.

Twenty-four hours a day the millions of cells in our body require the right nutrition to function at optimal levels. If the nutrition is incomplete, it is an inescapable fact that it will lead to malfunction and eventual breakdown. All our energies will be burned in trying to cope with the disease, and it will significantly limit all we wish to do as God's people.

THE CHOICE IS OURS

If you hope to maintain your health, the quality of your nutrition directly influences your biochemistry as well as your immune system. Health and nutrition go hand in hand. Whether it involves bacteria, viruses, or fungi, there are many harmful microorganisms that constantly work to suppress the immune system. This can leave you more vulnerable to getting sick and make you susceptible to many diseases. The prevalence of the flu and colds and mononucleosis and bronchitis and yeast infections represent but a fraction of the problem we face today. It is said that by eating just 3 tablespoons of sugar you compromise your immune system up to 6 hours.

Where does the breakdown start? Again, it doesn't require a doctor to figure it out. Statistics from the United States Department of Agriculture show that as many as one out of every two Americans is not getting the minimum RDAs (Recommended Dietary Allowances) from their current diet. Keep in mind that these guidelines were established as a minimal level, not for maximizing your health! Meanwhile, other statistics show that fat consumption has increased by 30 percent and sugar consumption by 50 percent in the past several decades. It's a formula ripe for disease.

There are four basic nutrients that your body requires to maintain its health—water, protein, carbohydrates, and fats. I will deal with water in a subsequent chapter of its own, but here I want to cover the basic components of a healthy diet.

PROTEIN

Next to water, protein is your body's most plentiful substance. Proteins exist in every cell and are essential to life. Along with carbohydrates and fats, protein is one of the three main classes of nutrients that provide energy to the body. You need proteins for building and repairing body tissues, and for producing hormones, enzymes, and nerve chemicals. They are vital for sustaining a healthy immune system and to building the brain's messengers—the neurotransmitters. They need to be taken in daily, because your body cannot store them. We must obtain most of them from the foods we eat.

Proteins are large, complex molecules made up of small units called amino acids. The amino acids are linked together into long chains called polypeptides. Twenty amino acids are assembled into the thousands of different proteins required by the human body. To assemble the proteins it needs, the body must have a sufficient supply of all these amino acids. Some amino acids, called essential amino acids, cannot be produced by the body and must be supplied by various foods. Humans require nine essential amino acids. The remaining acids, called nonessential amino acids, can be manufactured by the body itself.

When protein is eaten, your digestive processes break it down into amino acids, which pass into the blood and are carried through out the body. Your cells can then select the amino acids they need for the construction of tissue repair and new body tissue (especially bone cartilage and muscle), antibodies, hormones, enzymes, and worn-out and dead blood cells. Every cell needs protein to maintain its life. When you consider that most white blood cells are replaced every 10 days and skin cells are replaced every 24 days, you get a sense of the high demand for protein that is occurring within you.

Your muscles, hair, nails, skin, and eyes are made of protein. So are the cells that make up the liver, kidneys, heart, lungs, nerves, brain, and your sex glands. The body's most active protein users are the hormones secreted from the various glands—thyroxin from the thyroid, insulin from the pancreas, and a variety of hormones from the pituitary—as well as the soft tissues, hardworking major organs, and muscles. They all require the richest stores of protein.

The complete proteins that contain the essential amino acids come from meat, poultry, fish, eggs, milk—all dairy products. Cereal grains, nuts, legumes (peas and beans), and vegetables contain some but not all of the essential amino acids.

Insufficient protein in the diet may cause a lack of energy, stunted growth, and lowered resistance to disease. If the body does not receive enough proteins from the food eaten, it uses proteins from the cells of the liver and muscle tissues. Continued use of such proteins by the body can permanently damage those tissues.

The body is not able to store protein, and if excessive amounts are being consumed, they will be converted into sugars and fats. Most Americans, not surprisingly, eat too much protein, particularly through diets that are high in meat and dairy products. The idea that it is less fattening to eat lots of protein instead of carbohydrates is wrong. A balanced diet is the only way to ensure that you are getting all the nutrients you need.

CARBOHYDRATES

Carbohydrates are the major source of energy in our diet and are found in grains, legumes, fruits, vegetables, sugar, and alcohol. They have beneficial effects on the way we absorb and use our nutrients. During the digestion of food, carbohydrates in the food are broken down into smaller sugar molecules such as fructose, galactose, and glucose. These are the body and the brain's favorite fuel because it helps to maintain concentration, keeps us mentally sharp, and provides the power for all the brain's functions. Children especially need sufficient levels of carbohydrates not only because they are so active but because they need energy to grow.

You need to keep in mind that carbohydrates are divided into two classes. Some carbohydrates release their energy slowly and provide long-lasting sustenance to the body and the brain. These are the ones you want—primarily the brown grains and rice, fruits, or leafy green foods with all their fiber intact. One value of the fiber is that it prolongs the carbohydrate's energy release for hours after you've eaten. These foods are more "complex" than simple carbohydrates.

Then there are the "simple" carbohydrates that release quickly— the refined white starchy foods, sugars, and alcohol. They deliver a burst of energy by the quick breakdown into glucose and release into the bloodstream, but they leave you soon exhausted and unable to concentrate. Bad carbs such as processed sugary snacks, chips, breads, muffins, and candy pick you up quickly and drop you like a lead balloon. The effects of a drop in blood sugar levels can also include nervousness, hyperactivity, confusion, depression, anxiety, forgetfulness, headaches, palpitations, dizziness, and insomnia.

Researchers have also discovered that the constant insulin "highs" produced by fluctuating blood sugar levels lead to an increase in body weight. Insulin stimulates an enzyme called lipoprotein-lipase, which directs circulating fatty acids into fat-cell storage, which increase body weight. Children who are allowed to snack on cookies, ice cream, candy, cakes, and potato chips will put on the weight.

Sugar is the most addictive substance in our diets, and food manufacturers know it. You'll find sugar in almost every processed or packaged food, and the cumulative effect is reflected in bulging waistlines and poor health. You have to cut out the heavy intake of sugar.

Excellent carbohydrate sources are vegetables of all kinds (raw whenever possible), fruits, legumes, milk, whole grains, and whole wheat pasta. The good news is that foods containing complex carbohydrates, such as bread and pasta, are usually rich in vitamins, minerals, and trace elements.

FATS

Despite the unrelenting warnings, fat is as essential to our diets as any other component. Fat supplies the body with its most concentrated source of energy, providing nine calories per gram of energy compared to four calories per gram from carbohydrates or protein. Fat helps to build cell membranes in every cell in the body. Good fats, essential fatty acids, affect the brain so much that every area of sensory and motor skills either improves or declines through what you eat. In my book, *Super Food for Super Kids*, I stressed that during infancy and childhood, fat is an absolute requirement for normal brain development. These fats ensure that the nervous system functions properly. Sixty percent of the brain is made up of good fats, and we must have these good fats for proper brain function and increased memory. Children can develop ADD or ADHD at a very early age because of the lack of essential fatty acids or an imbalance of Omega 3/6/9 combined with the increased sugars that are in the foods we give our children.

While it's true that we eat far too many *saturated* (usually hard or solid at room temperature) and *hydrogenated* fats from sources such as meat, dairy products, margarine, cooking oils, and packaged food, certain fats are needed for good health. *Unsaturated* fats (usually soft at room temperature and often called oils) are divided into *monounsaturated* fats and *polyunsaturated* fats.

Monounsaturated fats appear to provide some protection from heart disease and are the best for cooking, as they do not tend to undergo chemical changes when they are heated. These fats are rich in fatty acids and important for normalizing prostaglandin levels.

Polyunsaturated fats are prone to changes when they are exposed to light, heat, the air, and other chemicals. If they are processed, such as in the manufacture of margarine through hydrogenation, chemical changes can occur, leading to the production of *trans fats*. These are fats that the body cannot easily break down and often lead to blocked arteries and heart disease. Trans-fatty acids are contained in foods such as ice cream, potato chips, tortilla chips, burgers, chicken nuggets, French fries, fried foods, candy, cookies, cakes, donuts, margarine, shortening, mayonnaise, partially hydrogenated oils, puffed cheese snacks, and dressing—the common menu for many Americans.

Two *polyunsaturated* fatty acids, linoleic acid and alpha-linolenic acid, are known as "essential fatty acids" because our body does not produce them. These come mainly from the Omega family of fats and are necessary for cell membrane function, metabolic processes, and balanced prostaglandin production. Good Omega-3 fats include flaxseed, hemp seed, pumpkin seed, soy, wheat germ, walnuts, leafy green vegetables, borage seed oil, fish oil, salmon, trout, mackerel, herring, blue fin, sardines, anchovies, and white albacore tuna. Good Omega-6 fats include walleye, carp, pike, haddock, sesame oil, borage seed oil, evening primrose oil, unrefined sunflower oil, walnuts, chicken, rice bran, black current seeds, fresh unroasted and unsalted nuts and seeds, and eggs. Good Omega-9 fats include extra virgin olive oil, avocados, and meats.

If you go on a low-fat diet, be sure you are working with a counselor to ensure you are getting enough unsaturated fatty acids and a balance of the Omega oils. For optimal behavior and mood function, there must be a balance. Dr. Michael Schmidt, an Applied Biochemistry and Clinical Nutritionist at Northwestern College, has shown that an imbalance contributes to depression, postpartum depression, OCD, problems with MS patients, winter blues, fears and phobias, chronic fatigue, attention problems, hyperactivity, violence and aggression, schizophrenia, stress response, mood swings, and behavioral problems. He also noted that cultures that eat lots of fish (high in Omega 3 and 6) show little to no depression problems.

Dr. E. A. Mitchell and his colleagues studied ADD and ADHD in children. They found continually low levels of Omega 3 and 6—the two key brain fats. Hyperactive children were shown to have higher levels of Omega 6 and lower levels of Omega 3. When Omega 6 is higher than Omega 3, there is lower brain function. He also showed that breast-fed children are less likely to have ADHD due to high contents of essential fatty acids in the milk.

3

GOOD FOODS, BAD FOODS

> *Thy food shall be thy remedy.*
>
> —HIPPOCRATES

HIPPOCRATES SPOKE THOSE WORDS TO HIS GREEK MEDICAL STUDENTS ABOUT TWENTY-FIVE HUNDRED YEARS AGO. It seems remarkable that we have drifted so far from the importance of food as the central component of health. God gave us food as the original source of sustained health, and the various components of the food we eat profoundly influence us either toward health or illness.

For instance, it's a simple fact that eating certain foods raises our risk of heart disease. Some foods help prevent cancer while others seem to cause it. Published reports show that improving our diets and lifestyle may reduce the incidence of colon cancer by 70 percent. Certain foods trigger hormones and form addictions that act like drugs. Foods can cause insulin imbalances while others cause neurotransmitter dysfunction that contribute to depression and ADD.

If you want to enjoy the health God means for you to experience, it begins with an attitude that considers every piece of food we put in our mouths as contributing to our long-term health or to illness. Seeing food for its medicinal value and honoring our bodies with the good foods God meant for us to enjoy is a practical decision that starts and stops with us. Making the right decision here has the power to prevent countless illnesses as well as to heal others that may have crept in.

FRUITS *and* VEGETABLES

Fruits and vegetables are so packed with minerals, vitamins, chlorophyll, and enzymes that they're well worth turning into your main-dish meal rather than merely side dishes. These enzyme-rich foods make it possible to convert food into body tissue and the fuel to keep you going, and they are at the top of my list of healing foods. In addition, these foods contain phytochemicals or phytonutrients ("phyto" means "plant"). A single fruit or vegetable may contain several hundred phytochemicals, and many of these have been proven to promote health. They work with your body so it can use its built-in health abilities. Eating raw fruits and vegetables or juicing them delivers the full benefits to your system.

Fresh fruit contain comparable amounts of fiber, minerals, vitamins, and phytonutrients as vegetables and have an alkalizing effect in the body. Its natural water and sugar content are quickly converted to energy and speeds up our metabolism to burn more calories. To gain the maximum benefit, fruits should be eaten alone or with other fruits. Citrus fruits possess over fifty known anticancer compounds—more than any other food.

Vegetables are also loaded with healing qualities, whether eaten raw or lightly cooked. The chlorophyll and plant enzymes offer amazing health benefits you can't get from any other source. How you cook your vegetables will make a huge difference in preserving their nutrients and texture. Steam them or cook them in as small amount of water as possible, and you will preserve the water-soluble nutrients such as vitamin C. You can cut down the nutrient loss by not adding your vegetables until the water is boiling, thus reducing your cooking time. When the vegetable's color has intensified and they're tender-crisp, they are ready to eat.

With the prevalence of pesticides used on fruit and vegetable crops, which are designed to kill a variety of pests by damaging their brains and nerves, has come residue that interacts with the chemicals in our bodies. Because children are still growing, they are the most at risk from pesticide contamination, and some experts see a direct correlation between hyperactivity and pesticides.

Organically grown fruits and vegetables eliminate the concern over pesticides and have more vitamins and minerals than conventionally grown produce. Because organic farmers use natural fertilizers, which contain a wide variety of minerals that help maintain the balance of minerals in the soil, their fruit and vegetables contain more minerals such as calcium, iron, manganese, magnesium, and more protein and vitamins. They may be a bit more expensive, but they're well worth it.

Fruits and vegetables must always be washed thoroughly. Green leafy vegetables should be washed leaf by leaf. If your vegetables are not organic, root vegetables such as carrots and fruits such as apples and pears should always be peeled before eating or cooking because of the pesticides. It's always best to eat fresh fruits and vegetables, but convenience, season, and price may make that difficult. Keep frozen and canned goods on hand to make certain you're eating plenty of fruits and vegetables every day.

You want to eat at least five servings daily—fresh, fresh, fresh! Organic, if possible. Remember: We started in the Garden of Eden. Hint…hint!

FISH

Fish has become a popular source of healthy protein, and for good reason. According to Leviticus 11:9, fish without scales is considered to be a clean food. Jesus had fishermen on staff, which should tell us something. Fish is high in protein but low in saturated fats. Almost all fish are naturally low in calories and rich in health-giving oils as well as essential vitamins and minerals. Fish contain important Omega-3 fatty acids, which have been proven to lower cholesterol, inhibit blood clots, lower blood pressure, improve mental function, and reduce the risk of heart attack and stroke. According to David Siscovick, M.D., a professor at the University of Washington School of Medicine, eating fish once a week or more often provides a 44 percent lower risk of having a fatal heart attack.

For years cod liver oil has been used as an immune system booster and tonic to cure any number of ills. Today, medical experts are seeing the wisdom that has been in God's plan from the beginning of time. Researchers at Rutgers University have shown that fish oil is also an effective cancer fighter, reducing your risk of breast, pancreatic, lung, prostate, and colon cancers. Migraine sufferers also find great relief with Omega-3 fish oils, according to studies at the University of Cincinnati. Another study there showed that people who suffer from psoriasis were helped tremendously after taking Omega-3 fatty acid.

Many fish are delicious and quick-serving—a real convenience food. The best fish sources, which are naturally low in calories, are salmon, mackerel, and halibut. By way of comparison, 4 ounces of salmon contain up to 3,600 mg of Omega-3 fatty acids, while 4 ounces of cod (a low-fat fish) contain only 300 mg. Shellfish and fish without scales are high in cholesterol and considered high-stress foods. Stay away from these.

If you don't like fish, learn! Eat fish meals at least two to three times per week. To get the best fish, the freshest fish, look for a fish vendor with a high turnover. Make sure the whole fish is covered in ice. The fish eyes should be bright and clear, not sunken, and the skin should be shiny and unblemished. Fillets or steaks should have a moist, almost translucent sheen. Avoid any fish that has dried out or gaping flesh.

MEATS

Chicken has replaced beef as America's favorite meat, and turkey is right behind. That's a healthy trend, since poultry is one of the leanest meats available, and it's a trend that you need to make sure is true in your family.

With poultry, the leanest meat is the breast, followed by the drumstick. The fattiest parts are the wings, which have a lot of skin and little meat, and the thighs. Always remove the skin to cut out the fat.

Whether it's a juicy hamburger or tender lamb chop, red meat holds a strong appeal among Americans. The fact remains that most of us need to cut down our red meats because they are a primary source of saturated fat and cholesterol. It is true that meat producers are providing leaner beef and lamb. Always look for the lean cuts and keep your portions small. Trim off all the visible fat before cooking, and think 2 to 3 ounces as the serving size. I stay away from all pork meat because it is an unclean food, a non-Kosher food, according to biblical definitions.

Because of the crowded conditions and the antibiotics that are used routinely in most conventionally farmed poultry and livestock, if at all possible buy free-range poultry and organic meats. Look for it at your local health food store or check out this web site, www.eatwild.com, for comprehensive, up-to-date, accurate information about grass-fed and organic beef, pork, lamb, bison, dairy products, and poultry. "Free range" ensures that the poultry was given a minimum of indoor and outdoor space. "Organic" means that the animal was raised outdoors, was fed organic food, and is free of antibiotics. I also highly recommend Kosher meats because their slaughtering methods are far more humane, which keeps hormones from being released in the animal's bloodstream and then spilling into the flesh.

Keep in mind that most steers are given a synthetic steroid hormone designed to cause rapid, substantial, weight gain. Beef cattle became 20 percent heavier on 15 percent less food per pound than genetically similar cattle not given the drug, and the residues of the drug remain in the meat. Members of the European scientific community were so convinced of the dangers of hormonal beef that in 1989 they banned the import of U.S. beef into their countries. In 1998 the World Trade Organization ruled the ban illegal, citing a lack of evidence that the hormones are dangerous. Today the European Union, comprised of 15 countries, states it now has scientific evidence to justify the ban.

The residues of these drugs in meat, our government assures us, are so small as to be insignificant, except when some careless or greedy factory farmer continues feeding a drug until shortly before the animal is slaughtered. There is no question that there are all kinds of drug residues in meat and dairy products. And there can be no question that these residues, over time, have become insidiously incorporated into our environment and food chain.

Go for the organic, hormone free meats…or stay away!

GRAINS, SPROUTS, NUTS, *and* BEANS

In biblical times, including the days of Jesus, bread was the staple food. When Jesus taught us to pray for "our daily bread," He meant just that. People ate bread at every meal, most from whole grain wheat or barley. It was not uncommon to eat fresh kernels of grain right from the field.

Grains are excellent sources of protein, fiber, vitamins, minerals, and unsaturated fatty acids. In choosing breads, choose whole grain. These contain the wheat germ, the bran, and the starch. Through processing, white flour has approximately 80 percent of its nutrients removed, and the high temperatures used in processing the grains create lipid peroxides, which cause free radical reactions.

Sprouts are baby plants that have just begun to grow from their seeds. They are loaded with trace minerals that are not so easily found in other foods. During germination all the nutrients needed by the young plant are mobilized from storage, which makes it highly nutritious. For instance, alfalfa sprouts are up to 30 percent protein by dry weight and are an excellent source of chlorophyll, bioflavonoids, and carotenes. Almost as good as seaweed as a mineral source, alfalfa contains iron, sulfur, silicon, chlorine, cobalt, magnesium, calcium, potassium, and zinc. It is by far the most common sprout to be in salads or sandwiches. They are very tasty but should be eaten fresh so that they do not ferment.

Nuts should be eaten raw. Genesis 43:11 specifically mentions pistachios and almonds. That's interesting in that those are particularly low in fat and calories. Nuts in general are a great snack food, with the exception of peanuts, which are really not a nut! Peanuts are high in fungus and the number one cause of allergic reactions in children. Nuts are naturally rich in zinc, copper, iron, calcium, magnesium, and phosphorus, as well as being high in protein. Dr. Walter Troll of New York University says that nuts are among the top cancer-fighting foods in the world, containing cancer blockers. Nuts also help to keep blood sugar levels steady so you don't get those bothersome hunger pangs that can lead you to grab the first snack you can find, which is normally high in sugar and carbohydrates.

Beans are high in protein, free from the saturated fats you get in animal sources of protein, and easy on your food budget. They are also less likely to contain heavy concentrations of pollutants. Soy in particular is an excellent health-enriching food and can be found in numerous meatless items such as soy burgers. Ask the Okinawans, the longest living people in the world, what the role of soy is in their diet, and you'll find it is a staple.

FIBER

One significant factor among good foods is the fiber they deliver. Fiber comes from the cells walls and other parts of plants, with fresh, live foods being the best source. It is a key to a low glycemic diet and essential for good health. A diet rich in fiber can help fight obesity, heart disease, diabetes, and cancer. It slows down the digestive process and helps regulate the release of insulin into the bloodstream, which allows for a steady supply of energy over a longer period of time. Beyond that, fiber speeds the transit time of fecal matter out of the body, which makes it highly valuable.

While Americans eat an average of 12 to 17 grams of fiber daily, the American Dietetic Association recommends an intake of 20 to 25 grams, and some experts say that for optimal health a person should get 40 to 60 grams a day.

Fiber comes in two forms: soluble and insoluble. Soluble fiber, which is present in legumes, brans, fruits, vegetable, whole grain products, seeds and nuts, and psyllium seed, helps to reduce cholesterol and to balance blood sugar levels. Insoluble fiber, found in whole wheat products, brown rice, kidney beans, skins of fruits, and many vegetables, reduce the risk of constipation as well as help prevent bowel cancer.

BAD FOOD

"Junk food" is a general term that has come to encompass the bad foods that offer little in terms of protein, minerals, or vitamins, and lots of calories from sugar or fat. We're talking about high-sugar, low-fiber, and high-fat foods that attract us and our children like magnets and put enormous stress on our healing system. While there is no definitive list of junk foods, most authorities include foods that are high in salt, sugar, or fat calories, and low in nutrient content. The big hitters on most people's lists include fried fast food, salted snack foods, carbonated beverages, candies, gum, and most sweet desserts. The term "empty calories" reflects the lack of nutrients found in junk food.

According to a study in the *American Journal of Clinical Nutrition*, one-third of the average American's diet is made up of junk foods. Because junk foods take the place of healthier foods, these same Americans are depending on the other two-thirds of their diet to get 100 percent of the recommended dietary intake of vitamins and nutrients. Studies show that the average American gets 27 percent of their total daily energy from junk foods and an additional 4 percent from alcoholic beverages. About one-third of Americans consume an average of 45 percent of their energy from these foods. Researchers are certain that such patterns of eating may have long-term, even life-threatening, health consequences.

If you have any question about the nutritional value of a food, judge it by the list of ingredients and the Nutrition Facts label found on packages. That label will list the number of calories per serving, grams of fat, sodium, cholesterol, fiber, and sugar content. If sugar, fat, or salt show up as one of the first three ingredients, you can probably consider that food to be a nutritional risk.

Steer clear and don't give in to junk foods! "Do not crave [the king's] delicacies, for that food is deceptive" (Proverbs 23:3). Food with no nutritional value can only cause harm.

4

CAN WE GET *the* NUTRITION WE NEED FROM *the* FOODS WE EAT?

I HAVE NO DOUBT THAT THE NUTRITION IN THE GARDEN OF EDEN WAS PERFECTLY ESTABLISHED TO GIVE ADAM AND EVE AN ABUNDANCE OF EVERY NUTRIENT OUR BODY REQUIRES. But access to the perfect garden was shut a long time ago, and the quality of the food chain has suffered enormously.

Most soils have produced food for hundreds of years. That our soils have been depleted of essential, trace, and rare minerals so vital to health is no secret. Nearly 70 years ago, in 1936 the United States Department of Agriculture issued U.S. Senate Document 264, stating "that virtually all soils in the United States were mineral deficient.... It is bad news to learn from our leading authorities that 100 percent of the American people are deficient in minerals, and that a marked deficiency in any one of the more important minerals actually results in disease.... Sick soil means sick animals and sick people. We have sick soil." Scientists at the 1992 Earth Summit in Brazil submitted documentation that soils worldwide were depleted of minerals. The United States soils rated as one of the most serious with 85 percent of essential minerals depleted.

Farmers today cannot afford to set aside their fields for a year in order to let the soil recoup lost minerals as God directed in the Old Testament. Every crop grown and harvested from farmers' fields depletes the precious nutrients—especially minerals—that are required to keep you healthy. Now depleted, the produce grown is less nourishing and healthy. Rather than allow the soil to recoup naturally, farmers add synthetic fertilizers and chemicals—not so their crops are nutritious, but so they grow.

Twice a Nobel Prize winner, Dr. Linus Pauling categorically stated: "You can trace every sickness, every disease, and every ailment to a mineral deficiency." If you read the "Short Course on Vitamins," you'll note that vitamins absolutely require minerals in order to work. Every cell within you must have minerals to live and function. Enzymes, hormones, immune system, and almost every biological activity demands a wide variety and amounts of minerals. However, if minerals are not in the soil, they can't be in the food. If they're not in the food, they can't be in you!

Here's another simple reality as stated in the *Prescription for Nutritional Healing*: "Data compiled by the U.S. Department of Agriculture indicate that at least 40 percent of the people in this country routinely consume a diet containing only 60 percent of the RDA of each of ten selected nutrients. This means that close to half of the population suffer from a deficiency of at least one important nutrient. A poll of 37,000 Americans conducted by Food Technology found that half of them were deficient in vitamin B6 (pyridoxine), 42 percent did not consume sufficient amounts of calcium, 39 percent had an insufficient iron intake, and 25 to 39 percent did not obtain enough vitamin C."

Simply put, to get the correct amount and balance of nutrients you have to supplement.

ORGANIC FOODS

While we must supplement for nutrition, we must first make wise food choices reflected in the One Perfect Diet (Chapter 16). Not only must we choose the right foods, but they must be healthy right foods—organic foods that are completely free of harmful additives and artificial ingredients. Unprocessed foods that have had nothing taken away and nothing added. Raw produce. And you want the freshest foods, for fruits and vegetables lose nutrients every day after they are picked.

Here's an interesting fact. According to a new study by researchers at the University of California, Davis, fruits and vegetables grown without synthetic chemicals have higher levels of flavonoids than produce treated with chemicals. Food scientists compared corn, blackberries, and strawberries and found that those grown without synthetic chemical pesticides had consistently more flavonoids. Another thing they noted was that frozen fruit and vegetables retained their flavonoids better than fresh. When frozen fresh off the vine, fresh foods retain their values.

Buying organic food helps, but when you add that to the amount of time from the field to your dinner table, you realize that even fresh isn't fresh anymore, and what should be the healthiest food isn't necessarily the case. For the best possible results, grow food at home. A window box of herbs, a fruit tree, zucchini squash, tomatoes, or carrots. Take the time and see how good fresh grown food tastes. Your body will reward you for it.

BUY OR RAISE PASTURE-FED, HORMONE-FREE MEAT

In his book *21 Days to a Healthy Heart*, Alan L. Watson states: "Starting in the 1950s, the meat industry began taking animals off pasture and grass and putting them into feedlots and on grain. Grass is high in Omega 3. In humans and in cattle, Omega 3 promotes leanness. Grains are high in Omega 6. In humans and cattle, Omega 6 promotes obesity.

"More Omega 6 and less Omega 3 is a recipe for obesity and inflammatory conditions such as blood vessel damage and cancer. Cattle put on weight more rapidly on a high-grain diet than they will in the pasture, even when they consume exactly the same number of calories. The Omega-6 rich grain diet creates more fatty acid synthetase, an enzyme that promotes fat production.

"Meat from grain-fed animals contains as much as 20 times more Omega 6 than Omega 3. Grass-fed beef has an n-6/n-3 ratio of 3:1, ideal for human health. When we exceed a ratio of 4 (4 times more Omega 6), diseases such as cancer and diabetes get their start. The excess Omega 6 we are eating has increased our ratio of Omega 6 to Omega 3 from 3:1 to as high as 20:1.

"Getting Omega 3 directly from grass-grazing animals contain dramatically more Omega 3 than grain-fed cattle. In fact, pasture-raised beef provides all healthy fats, including Omega 3, monoun-saturated Omega 9, and stearic acid, a saturated fat. In addition, meat from pasture-raised animals is more abundant in beta-carotene, vitamin A, vitamin E, and conjugated linoleic acid (CLA).

"Our Native American and pioneer ancestors ate meat from ruminant animals. Our bodies are superbly adapted to this type of food. Grass-fed meat was the only meat available for thousands of years. In the last 50 years, all of us—humans, cattle, and chicken—have made an abrupt shift away from grass-fed in favor of grain-fed.

"Over the years, our bodies have come to expect the kinds and amounts of fat found in grass-fed food. Our hearts love the Omega 3 and the balance of fats found in the grazing animal. When we switch from grain-fed back to grass-fed, our bodies immediately respond and function better—optimally—once again."

Look for pasture-fed, hormone-free meat at your local health food store or check out this web site, www.eatwild.com, for com-prehensive, up-to-date, accurate information about grass-fed and organic beef, pork, lamb, bison, dairy products, and poultry.

5

A SHORT COURSE
in VITAMINS

VITAMINS CONSTITUTE ONE OF THE MAJOR GROUPS OF NUTRI-ENTS, WHICH ARE FOOD SUBSTANCES NECESSARY FOR GROWTH AND HEALTH. They stimulate or are catalysts on the cellular level and as such regulate chemical reactions through which the body converts food into energy and living tissues. Thus they have a key role in producing energy for each and every cell in the body. Vitamins also help to manufacture enzymes, which do wide-ranging tasks within the body from digesting food to making neuro-transmitters. Of the thirteen vitamins we need, five are produced by the body itself. Of those five, only three can be produced in sufficient quantities to meet the body's needs. Therefore, vitamins must be supplied in a person's daily diet.

Some vitamins are water soluble, and others are oil or fat soluble. Water-soluble vitamins (vitamins C and B-complex) must be taken into the body daily, as they cannot be stored. Oil-soluble vitamins (vitamins A, D, E, and K) can be stored for longer periods of time in the body's fatty tissue and liver.

We tend to think that any vitamin will do, but this is not the case. Every vitamin has a specific function that nothing else can replace. And, if you lack any vitamin, it can actually hinder the function of another. Vitamin deficiency diseases, such as beriberi, pellagra, rickets, or scurvy, are the result of an ongoing lack of a vitamin.

A well-balanced diet from all the basic food groups is the best way to obtain these essential vitamins. However, not one dietary survey has shown that Americans eat anywhere near the RDA amounts in their normal diets. A recent USDA survey of 21,500 people over a three-day period showed that not a single person got 100 percent of the RDA nutrients. If you take supplements, always take a food-based multivitamin capsule as well as specific nutrients to help them work more effectively. Do not exceed the Servings printed on the packaging.

Vitamin A is found both in animal sources (retinol) and in plants (beta-carotene). It is essential for healthy vision and promotes healthy skin, bones, teeth, gums, urinary tract, and lining of the nervous, respiratory, and digestive systems. Derivatives of vitamin A are used to treat acne and renew aged skin. It is found in full-fat dairy products, fish liver oil, liver, eggs, butter, sweet potatoes, cantaloupe, and yellow and green vegetables.

Vitamin B1 (thiamine) is required for carbohydrate metabolism and the release of energy from food. It assists in the production of hydrochloric acid, which is the key for proper digestion. It helps your heart and nervous system function properly. Beriberi is a rare nervous system disorder that can result from a thiamine deficiency. Thiamine is found in whole grains and whole grain breads and cereals, eggs, fish, brown rice, nuts, sunflower seeds, peas, potatoes, soy, poultry, and most vegetables.

Vitamin B2 (riboflavin) promotes healthy hair, skin, nails, and tissue repair and helps body cells use oxygen. It plays a necessary role in red blood cell formation. Riboflavin is found in liver, full-fat milk, yogurt, cheese, eggs, liver, fish, poultry, mushrooms, almonds, legumes, and leafy green vegetables.

Vitamin B3 (niacin) helps to maintain healthy skin and digestive trace and hormone production. It is essential for cell metabolism and absorption of carbohydrates and can lower cholesterol. Niacin is found in lean meat, liver, fish, whole grain, eggs, milk, nuts, potatoes, almonds, avocados, bananas, sesame seeds, tomatoes, and soy flour.

Vitamin B5 (pantothenic acid) promotes healthy skin, hormone production, muscles, and nerves. It helps convert carbohydrates, fats, and proteins into energy. It is known as the "anti-stress vitamin" because it is vital to proper adrenal activity and is an aid to natural steroid synthesis. Pantothenic acid is a stamina enhancer found in nuts, eggs, meat, whole grain cereals, brown rice, yams, soy products, royal jelly, mushrooms, legumes, and green vegetables.

Vitamin B6 (pyridoxine) is involved in more bodily functions than almost any other single nutrient. It is important for healthy teeth and gums, blood vessels, nervous and immune systems, and red blood cell regeneration. Pyridoxine is found in whole grain cereals, liver, poultry, fish, meat, brown rice, wheat bran, eggs, avocados, most vegetables, bananas, soy, walnuts, and sunflower seeds.

Vitamin B12 (cyanocobalamin) helps prevent infection and anemia through the proper development of red blood cells. It aids the nervous system and is critical to DNA synthesis. It is found in fish, dairy products, meats, whole grain breads, sea greens, and eggs.

Biotin assists the circulatory system, aids in cell growth, and promotes healthy skin and hair. It is found in eggs, milk, poultry, soy, liver, nuts, kidneys, and most fresh vegetables.

Vitamin C (ascorbic acid) is a powerful antioxidant vital for the immune system as well as for skin, bone, teeth, cartilage formation, and for wound healing. It safeguards against heavy metal toxicity and is essential in the formation of collagen tissue. It is found in citrus fruits, tomatoes, raw cabbage, cauliflower, leafy green vegetables, peppers, broccoli, potatoes, strawberries, and cantaloupe.

Vitamin D (cholecalciferol) helps calcium to be utilized for bones and teeth and promotes a healthy heart and nervous system. It can be found in fish liver oils, salmon, tuna, leafy green vegetables, mushrooms, eggs, full-fat milk, butter, and sunlight.

Vitamin E (tocopherol) is an antioxidant that promotes healthy cell membranes by helping to prevent the oxidation of polyunsaturated fatty acids in those membranes and other body structures. It aids fertility, stamina, and combating changes of old age. It can be found in leafy green vegetables, wheat germ oil, olive oil, eggs, tomatoes, sweet potatoes, soybeans, brown rice, fresh nuts and seeds, and whole grains.

Vitamin K (phytonadione) is needed for normal blood clotting, healthy bones and teeth. It is found in leafy green vegetables, sea greens, cheese, liver, molasses, eggs, fish, full-fat milk, oats, safflower oil, kelp, and raspberry leaf tea.

Folic acid is a B vitamin needed for the production of red blood cells and helps in the prevention of anemia, heart disease, and congenital abnormalities. Because it functions as a coenzyme in DNA and RNA synthesis, it is important for healthy cell division and replication. It is found in leafy green vegetables, fruit, whole grains, liver, meat, poultry, fish, and full fat milk.

DAILY OPTIMAL VITAMIN SUPPLEMENTATION

The following recommendations for daily intake levels of vitamins are designed to provide an optimum intake range for maintaining good health. If possible, buy natural, organic vitamins, preferably labeled as not having sugar, preservatives, lactose, yeast, or starch. Also follow instructions regarding storage and recommended serving. Some vitamins are toxic in high Servings, and the safe Serving can be exceeded if you take supplements from more than one source.

VITAMINS	SUPPLEMENTARY SERVING RANGE
Vitamin A (retinal)	5,000–10,000 IU
Vitamin A (from beta-carotene)	10,000–75,000 IU
Vitamin D	100–400 IU
Vitamin E (d-alpha tocopherol)	400–1,200 IU
Vitamin K (phytonadione)	60–900 mcg.
Vitamin C (ascorbic acid)	500–9,000 mg.
Vitamin B1 (thiamine)	10–90 mg.
Vitamin B2 (riboflavin)	10–90 mg.
Niacin	10–90 mg.
Niacin amide	10–30 mg.
Vitamin B6 (pyridoxine)	25–100 mg.
Biotin	100–300 mcg.
Pantothenic acid	25–100 mg.
Folic acid	400–1,000 mcg.
Vitamin B12	400–1,000 mcg.
Choline	150–500 mg.
Inositol	150–500 mg.

6

A SHORT COURSE
in MINERALS

MINERALS ARE NUTRIENTS THAT FUNCTION ALONGSIDE OF VITA-MINS AS COMPONENTS OF BODY ENZYMES. While they are needed in small amounts, they are absolutely essential for the biochemical processes of the body to work. Without your minerals in adequate supply, you can't absorb the vitamins. Minerals are needed for proper composition of teeth and bone and blood and muscle and nerve cells. They are important to the production of hormones and enzymes and in the creation of antibodies. Some minerals (calcium, potassium, and sodium) have electrical charges that act as a magnet to attract other electrically charged substances to form complex molecules, conduct electrical impulses (messages) along nerves, and transport substances in and out of the cells. Magnesium and manganese are essential to convert carbohydrates into energy for the brain.

According to the U.S. Department of Agriculture, the average American consumes only about 60 percent of the essential minerals their bodies need. And without sufficient amounts of minerals, you can't absorb your vitamins! Which is why I'm stressing them here. Here are 10 minerals you can't be healthy without:

Calcium is absolutely vital for strong bones and teeth and for the battle against osteoporosis. It helps the body maintain a regular heartbeat, aids in the transmission of nerve impulses, lowers bad cholesterol, helps prevent cardiovascular disease, and wards off muscle cramps.

Copper aids in the formation of bone, hemoglobin, and red blood cells. It's also involved in the body's healing process and energy production and is required for healthy nerves and joints.

Iodine is so essential for mental and physical development that if children are lacking in it, they can end up mentally challenged. Sufficient iodine is necessary for a healthy thyroid, and in trace amounts iodine helps to metabolize excess fat.

Magnesium is a vital catalyst in enzyme activity, particularly those involved in the production of energy. It helps the body absorb calcium and potassium and helps prevent muscle weakness and twitching, while maintaining the body's proper pH balance. A deficiency of magnesium interferes with the transmission of nerve and muscle impulses, resulting in irritability and nervousness. If you suffer from PMS or depression, this mineral could be your magic bullet.

Manganese is a must-have for iron. Minute quantities are required for the metabolism of protein and fat, healthy nerves, a healthy immune system, and proper regulation of blood sugar. The body also uses it to produce energy, and it's required for normal bone growth, reproduction, the formation of cartilage, and the production of synovial fluid, which lubricates the body's joints and tendons.

Phosphorus assists the body both in utilizing vitamins and converting food to energy. It's needed for bone and teeth formation and cell growth and helps both heart and kidney function. Deficiencies can lead to anxiety, bone pain, fatigue, irregular breathing, irritability, numbness, skin sensitivity, trembling, and weakness.

Silicon is a mineral superhero! It helps the body absorb calcium and plays a major role in the prevention of cardiovascular disease. Since it counteracts the effects of aluminum, it is essential in the prevention of Alzheimer's disease and osteoporosis. It also stimulates the immune system and inhibits the aging process in tissues.

Sodium assists in regulating the body's water balance and blood pH. It helps maintain normal heart rhythm and is necessary for proper stomach, nerve, and muscle function.

Sulfur is not only necessary for the formation of collagen for bones and connective tissue but promotes healthy nails, skin, and hair. It also disinfects blood, helps the body resist bacteria, and protects the protoplasm of cells. Sulfur slows down the aging process by protecting us from the harmful effects of radiation and pollution.

Zinc is essential for the normal growth and development of reproductive organs and is required for normal prostate gland function. It protects the liver from chemical damage, promotes a healthy immune system, and assists in the healing of wounds. Symptoms of a deficiency include acne, fatigue, hair loss, cracking or peeling fingernails, recurring colds and flu, and slow healing of wounds.

If the thought of taking handfuls of minerals pills each day is a bit daunting, there are many ways to get your daily Serving of minerals. One of the easiest methods is to simply drink them down in a liquid supplement. My strongest recommendation is for you to immediately start a liquid Colloidal mineral on a daily basis and continue to take it the rest of your life.

DAILY OPTIMAL MINERAL SUPPLEMENTATION

The following recommendations for daily intake levels of minerals are designed to provide an optimum intake range for maintaining good health. Always follow instructions regarding storage and recommended serving. Some minerals are toxic in high Servings, and the safe Serving can be exceeded if you take supplements from more than one source.

MINERALS	SUPPLEMENTARY SERVING RANGE
Boron	1–2 mg.
Calcium	250–750 mg.
Chromium	200–400 mcg.
Copper	1–2 mg.
Iodine	50–150 mcg.
Iron	15–30 mg.
Magnesium	250–750 mg.
Manganese (citrate)	10–15 mg.
Molybdenum (sodium molybdate)	10–25 mcg.
Potassium	200–500 mg.
Selenium (selenomethionine)	100–200 mcg.
Silica (sodium metasilicate)	200–1,000 mcg.
Vaadium (sulfate)	50–100 mcg.
Zinc (picolinate)	15–30 mcg.

7

A SHORT COURSE
in HERBS

FOR THOUSANDS OF YEARS, NOT JUST HUNDREDS OF YEARS, HERBS HAVE PROVIDED A CONSTANT SUPPLY OF HEALING AGENTS TO PEOPLE. Herbs are medicinal plants. Records from many ancient cultures show that herbs have been used to cure practically every known illness and that herbs have been considered man's first line of defense. I believe herbs were given by God to bring healing to the body!

Whether from the roots, leaves, stem, bark, flowers, or berries of plants, herbs have been scientifically proven to be nature's pharmaceutical agents as well as very effective in the prevention of illness. They are powerful, though usually gentle, and are a safe and natural alternative to drugs when used properly. My personal experience is that while they tend to move slower than pharmaceutical medicine, the harmful side effects are not attached. The use of herbs should be considered as broad-based for overall support or specific for a particular problem.

Commercial herbal preparations are available in numerous forms. You will find herbs packaged as essential oils, teas, salves, tinctures, capsules, tablets, plasters, compresses, poultices, syrups, vinegars, and concentrated extracts. Always follow the manufacturer's advice regarding the serving.

ESSENTIAL MEDICINAL HERBS

While a comprehensive list of the most commonly used medicinal herbs is beyond the scope of this book, here are what I call the Top Natural Aids that you should bring into your home so as to begin to enjoy the health-enriching effects they bring:

Aloe Vera is used externally to treat skin problems, particularly for burns and wounds. It stimulates healing and is antiviral, anti-fungal, antibacterial, and an emollient. You'll find it in many skin lotions and shampoos. Internally, it is used as a laxative, increases blood-vessel regeneration, and soothes stomach irritation.

Bilberry, which is also known as **blueberry** or **huckleberry**, has long been used for better eyesight, and studies show that it helps prevent diabetic retinopathy, macular degeneration, cataract, and glaucoma. It keeps blood vessels flexible and thus is effective for varicose veins. It can be found in extracts, capsules, and tablets.

Bromilene is used for inflammation, sports injuries, respiratory tract infections, menstrual cramps.

Burdock is a mild internal cleanser that promotes the production of urine and sweat, which promotes the health of the kidneys, lungs, and liver. It has antibacterial and antifungal properties and acts as an antioxidant, and thus is also used to treat chronic skin problems. Can be taken as a tea.

Chamomile can be used as a relaxing tea that aids digestion and the production of urine and helps induce sleep. A traditional remedy for stress and anxiety and insomnia. It is also used as an ingredient in herbal salves to treat skin problems and soothe the skin.

Dandelion has long been used to strengthen the liver as it cleans the blood and increases bile production. It also helps improve the function of the spleen, kidneys, pancreas, and stomach. Useful for water retention and obesity. Good source of potassium. Dandelion greens are eaten like spinach and also comes as a dried herb for teas.

Dong Quai is a favorite Chinese herb that is effective for menopausal and premenstrual symptoms as it nourishes the reproductive system. It comes as tablets, capsules, concentrated drops, tinctures, and extracts.

Echinacea works to fight viral infections and inflammation. It boosts the immune system as it stimulates certain white blood cells and aids in wound healing. Good for use on colds, flus, and allergies. Can be used in tincture or as a standard infusion. A freeze-dried form or alcohol-free form is recommended. Should not be used for more than two weeks at a time.

Fennel is used to relieve cramps and gas and as a digestive aid. As a tea, it can be applied with an eyedropper as a soothing eyewash. It can be found in extracts, concentrated drops, essential oils, capsules, and tinctures.

Feverfew works to fight inflammation and muscle spasms. Noted to be effective for migraine headaches. As an anti-inflammatory, it is used to treat arthritis, and as a febrifuge, it can help reduce fever. It comes dried and in capsules, extracts, tinctures, and concentrated drops.

Flaxseeds or **linseeds** boost the liver with Omega-3 oils. Also promotes strong bones, nails, and teeth as well as healthy skin. Soaked flaxseeds are excellent fiber that help the colon.

Garlic has antibacterial, antiviral, and antifungal properties. It helps cleanse the body, especially the liver, and protects against infections by strengthening the immune system. Helps with elevated cholesterol levels, high blood pressure, and diabetes. It is actually thought to be good for any illness or infection.

Ginger as a tea helps reduce nausea and vomiting with pregnancy as well as motion sickness. It has been shown to reduce inflammation, especially in those people who suffer with arthritis. It also helps to keep the blood from sludging, which is one of the factors that contributes to heart attacks and strokes. Take it as a tea or as a garnish on your vegetables.

Ginkgo Biloba helps improve brain function and boost memory by increasing the blood supply to the brain and may slow the progression of Alzheimer's disease. Also beneficial for ringing ears, dizziness, impotence, asthma, and varicose veins. It comes in tablets, capsules, extracts, tinctures, and concentrated drops.

Ginseng is a very popular herb that aids in the recovery from illness, stress, fatigue, diabetes, improvement of mental and physical performance, and sexual function. It strengthens the immune system and is used by athletes for body strengthening. It comes as a powder or whole root as well as in tablets, capsules, teas, tinctures, and extracts.

Goldenseal is one of the most effective of all the herbs and is used to fight infection and inflammation. It is effective against parasitic infections of the gastronomical tract, against all forms of yeast infections, and infection of mucous membrane. Effective in stopping flus, colds, and sore throats if caught at the onset.

Gotu Kola has long been used for wound healing, varicose veins, and scleroderma. Overall, it is used to increase energy and endurance, to improve the memory, and alleviate depression and anxiety. You can purchase it as dried and in tinctures, extracts, capsules, and concentrated drops.

Gugulipid is a plant extract that has been shown to lower elevated cholesterol and triglyceride levels and have no adverse effect on the liver or blood sugar. It is also used for arteriosclerosis and hypothyroidism. Comes in concentrated preparations.

Hawthorn contains active flavonaids that prevent the constriction of blood vessels, thus lowering blood pressure. It also strengthens the heart muscle and helps against congestive heart failure and angina. Helps to lower cholesterol and reverse arteriosclerosis. Sold in tinctures, dried plant parts, and solid extracts.

Hops is a digestive stimulant that helps relieve cramps and gas. It is also a mild sedative that relieves anxiety. You can get it dried and in tinctures, extracts, and concentrated drops.

Lapacho or **Pau d'arco** or **Taheebo** fights bacterial and viral infections, and particularly *Candida Albicans*. The tea extract can be taken orally or applied topically for bites and stings, infections, and inflammation. Look for it as dried, shredded bark, or as capsules and liquid extracts.

Licorice Root fights viral, bacterial, and parasitic infections. It is good for the vocal cords and is also used to relieve coughs, asthma, and bronchitis as well as to treat peptic ulcers, premenstrual tension syndrome, and low adrenal function. Licorice comes in powders, extracts, tinctures, capsules, and concentrated drops.

Lobelia acts in a similar way to nicotine and has been used as a smoking deterrent. It acts as an expectorant in asthma, bronchitis, and pneumonia.

Milk Thistle or **Silymarin** or **Mary Thistle** is a traditional liver remedy as it boosts the liver's ability to filter blood and prevents damage from toxins. It may help treat hepatitis, cirrhosis of the liver, and psoriasis. Comes in an extract, capsule, and concentrated herbal drop.

Psyllium is a laxative and demulcent that also works to lower cholesterol.

Rosemary has long been a popular cooking herb that relaxes the stomach and promotes digestion. It helps relieve migraines, tension headaches, exhaustion, and fatigue. Try a few drops of this essential oil in a bath and feel it relax you. You can find it dried and in essential oils, tinctures, and concentrated drops.

Sage is a liver stimulant that promotes the flow of bile. Also stimulates the digestive tract and central nervous system. Helpful for hot flashes and other symptoms of estrogen deficiency.

Sarsaparilla is an anti-inflammatory and tonic used for treating skin problems such as psoriasis and eczema.

Saw Palmetto has shown positive clinical results in treating prostate enlargement. May also effect male sex hormones and function. You can find it in tablets, extracts, tinctures, and concentrated drops.

Slippery Elm is used as a gentle laxative that soothes the inflamed mucous membranes of the bowels, stomach, and urinary tract. It is also used in lozenges for relief of sore throats, coughs, and colds. It is sold in tablets, powders, lozenges, and extracts.

St. John's Wort is good for depression, anxiety, stress, sleep disturbance, and aids in healing nerve damage.

Tea Tree Oil is a topical antiseptic that is good for acne, athlete's foot, boils, and wound healing.

Turmeric has antibiotic, anticancer, and anti-inflammatory qualities. It is good for arthritis as well as protecting the liver against toxins. It restricts blood platelet aggregation, thus protecting the heart.

Uva Ursi is good for urinary tract infections and helps the spleen, liver, pancreas, and small intestine. Promotes the excretion of fluids and thus helps fight water retention.

Valerian is a strong nerve tonic and sedative that helps with insomnia, anxiety, high blood pressure, and intestinal spasms. Best as a water-soluble extract.

GREEN TEA

The benefits of drinking green tea have been lauded over the past few years, and for good reason. For more than 30 years, researchers have known that the frequency of solid tumor cancers (lung, gastrointestinal, and breast cancers) is far lower in countries where populations consume large amounts of green tea. The questions has been why this is so.

In the May 24, 2004 e-Alert titled "Envy with Green" from the Health Science Institute (www.hsibaltimore.com), Jenny Thompson highlights recent research that points the way to the answer. About one third of the dry weight of green tea leaves is made up of a flavonoid called catechin. And the most abundant of the four types of green tea catechins is epigallocatechin gallate (EGCG), which is the component of green tea that is thought to inhibit tumor cell growth.

A recently published Japanese study from researchers at Kyushu University indicates what makes EGCG effective to protect against several cancers. The researchers focused on a cancer receptor cell known as 67 LR. Many cancer tumors produce large amounts of this cell, and scientists believe it is one of the key agents that promotes the spread of cancer throughout the body. Using lung cancer cells, the Kyushu researchers observed that cell growth was inhibited by exposure to EGCG *at concentrations that would equal just three cups of green tea.* They believe that EGCG binds to 67 LR cells and prevents them from prompting tumor growth.

A second recent study of EGCG was reported in the journal, Blood, by researchers from the Mayo Clinic. They examined the interaction between EGCG from green tea and cancer cells taken from 10 patients diagnosed with the most common type of leukemia: B-cell chronic lymphocytic leukemia (CLL). This research also involved a receptor cell, called VEGF, which nurtures growth in leukemia. Researchers found that EGCG suppressed the VEGF mechanism, inhibiting the growth of new blood vessels necessary for cancer proliferation. In 8 of the 10 samples, EGCG prompted the death of cancer cells. Mayo researchers hope their study will eventually lead to a non-toxic way to treat early stage CLL.

Another recent study yielded some promising results concerning the prevention of breast cancer. Researchers from the Department of Preventive Medicine at the University of Southern California interviewed almost 1,100 Asian American women (aged 25 to 74) living in Los Angeles. 501 women had been diagnosed with breast cancer, and 594 were cancer-free. Between 1995 and 1998, each subject was interviewed in person to determine a wide variety of factors—from personal medical history to general lifestyle details. The data showed that women in the non-cancer group were much more likely to be regular green tea drinkers. In fact, on average, those who drank at least 8.5 milliliters (less than half a cup) of green tea each day had a reduced breast cancer risk of nearly 30 percent. Those who consumed more than that reduced their risk even more. This benefit was found only with green tea consumption.

I hope this convinces you to change your coffee habit and make green tea your healthy brew of choice. Your body will love you for it.

8

A SHORT COURSE *in* ANTIOXIDANTS, ENZYMES, *and* AMINO ACIDS

ANTIOXIDANTS

IN THE PROCESS OF METABOLISM OR OXIDATION, OUR BODY CELLS PRODUCE MOLECULES CALLED FREE RADICALS. They are unstable molecules that attempt to steal electrons from any available source, such as our body tissues. Free radicals cause mutations and cellular damage and are partly responsible for a wide range of illnesses, including all the degenerative diseases such as arthritis, cardiovascular disease, Alzheimer's, and cancer.

Antioxidants are nutrients in foods and herbs that reverse the free radical process. These nutrients donate electrons to atoms and stop the breakdown of cells and tissues. Antioxidants, such as beta-carotene, vitamins A, E, and especially C, and selenium, work to neutralize these unstable chemicals and protect us from them. Think of them as free radical scavengers. The more antioxidants we get in our diets, the more we are able to stop these damaging effects. Any shortage of antioxidants can become catastrophic to one's health. When our antioxidants are low, energy is not available and internal cleansing cannot take place in a normal fashion. Therefore, toxins accumulate or are stored until they can be processed.

The main sources of antioxidants are fruits, vegetables, nuts, grains, and cold-pressed plant oils. Other excellent sources of antioxidants are found in bioflavonoids, grape seed extract, ginseng, garlic, molybdenum, DHEA, wheat and barley grass, Echinacea, manganese, carotenoids, Ginkgo Biloba, melatonin, L-Cysteine, acetyl-l-carnite, Coenzyme Q10, milk thistle, and B-vitamins.

ENZYMES

Enzymes are energized protein molecules that have a major impact on your health and internal cleansing. They are involved in practically every biochemical activity that is going on inside of you. They help digest and absorb proteins, carbohydrates or starches, lipids or fats. Absorption is absolutely crucial to your health. They also clean up dead tissues, enhance your own enzyme capacity, and help the bowels in cleansing, because they liquefy the bowel content and make for a quicker passage. The quicker the toxins are out of your system, the better your health is, and the better you feel!

While vitamins and minerals get significant attention, don't minimize the role of enzymes. Vitamins and minerals are used to activate enzymes, but enzymes do the hard work of detoxifying toxins and supporting the metabolism of the body through the prompt oxidation of glucose, which creates energy for the cells. If it were not for the catalytic action of enzymes, most of these reactions would be too slow to sustain our life.

Enzymes are often divided into two categories: digestive enzymes and metabolic enzymes. Metabolic enzymes such as proteases repair cells and help us heal faster. They also catalyze the chemical reactions within cells, such as energy production and cleansing. Go to any cell, tissue, or organ in your body and you will find metabolic enzymes hard at work.

Digestive enzymes are secreted along the gastrointestinal tract and assimilate our food nutrients. Although there are three categories of digestive enzymes with very specific tasks, know that from the moment food contacts the saliva in your mouth until it is digested in your stomach, enzymes are at work converting the nutrients into a state that the body can use.

Fatigue, premature aging, and weight gain are the first signs that a person is short of enzymes. Most of the nutrient-deficiency problems that we face as we age are not from a lack of nutrients but from a lack of enzymes to absorb the nutrients. Enzyme depletion as we age must be compensated for by the plant enzymes we eat as well as the supplements we take.

The best source of plant enzymes is fresh raw fruits and vegetables, which can be supplemented with multi-digestive enzymes. Unfortunately, enzymes are easily destroyed by processing and cooking. If you eat a high proportion of processed foods, you lose out on these vital ingredients. By eating a wide range of foods, as close to their raw state as possible, you can enjoy all these benefits.

The liver is the source of most detoxification enzymes, which it either makes or stores. To aid the liver in removing and eliminating wastes and toxins, enzymes are best taken with meals. This way they aid in digestion.

Enzyme Therapy is showing a positive research, especially as regards anti-aging. See Appendix B.

AMINO ACIDS

While amino acids were included in the discussion of proteins, more needs to be said. Amino acids are the building blocks of protein in the body. Twenty amino acids are assembled into the thousands of different proteins required by the human body. Essentially, the amino acids are linked together into long chains called polypeptides. To assemble the proteins it needs, the body must have a sufficient supply of all these amino acids. And without these amino acids, health is not possible.

There are approximately twenty-eight common amino acids that are combined in a multitude of ways to create the different types of protein. The liver produces 80 percent of the amino acids you need, and the rest must come via the foods you eat. Some amino acids, called essential amino acids, cannot be produced by the body and must be supplied by various foods. Humans require nine essential amino acids: histidine, isoleucine, leucine, lysine, methionine, phenylalanine, threonine, tryptophan, and valine.

The remaining acids, called nonessential amino acids, are manufactured by the body: alanine, arginine, asparagine, aspartic acid, citrulline, cysteine, cystine, gamma-aminobutyric acid (GAMA), glutamic acid, glutamine, glycine, ornithine, proline, serine, taurine, and tyrosine. To label these as nonessential simply means that they need not be obtained through our diet—they are just as essential as the "essential" group.

If you review the crucial role that proteins play in every area of the human body, it is clear that even one amino acid shortage will reduce the body's ability to produce the vital protein it needs. And a lack of proteins can cause problems ranging from indigestion to depression to stunted growth. The key remains to eat a well balanced diet as well as to maintain the enzyme levels that will enable the nutrients to be absorbed into the body.

The complete proteins that contain the essential amino acids come from meat, poultry, fish, eggs, milk—all dairy products. Cereal grains, nuts, legumes (peas and beans), and vegetables contain some but not all of the essential amino acids.

9

LIFE-ENRICHING
WATER *and* OXYGEN

ALONG WITH CARBOHYDRATES, PROTEIN, AND FATS, WATER IS AN ESSENTIAL NUTRIENT THAT IS LITERALLY INVOLVED IN EVERY FUNCTION OF THE BODY. Every life process—from taking in food to digestion to absorption to getting rid of wastes—requires water. Without water, there can be no life.

The human body is composed of from 65 to 70 percent water. Even our bones are 10 percent water. Water maintains homeostasis, or balance, in the cells, where everything is working correctly. Watery solutions help dissolve nutrients and carry them to all parts of your body. Through chemical reactions that can only take place in a watery solution, your system turns nutrients into energy or into materials it needs to grow to repair cells. Water is used for every enzyme process that governs the nerve chemicals, and therefore every thought and action, every chemical process, and therefore every function in the body. And water is required to maintain normal body temperatures.

Think of these benefits the next time you drink a glass of sparkling pure water with ice and a slice of lemon. That water flushes the kidneys and liver, enabling them to remove toxins from your body, and reduces feelings of hunger. It helps maintain energy levels, increases the efficiency of your immune system, and keeps your skin looking good and feeling soft. And it reduces the risk of developing kidney stones and gallstones as well as headaches.

Water, water, water! You can't get enough! As an adult, you should be drinking half of your body weight in ounces of water daily. For example, if you weigh 150 pounds, you should drink at least 75 ounces (a little more than two quarts) of water daily. If you are in hot weather or exercising or sweating for whatever reason, you need to increase these levels. Children need to drink more than adults, and the smaller they are, the more they need to drink. A boy between the ages of 11 and 14 needs to drink around 100 ounces of water daily, and a girl the same age needs eight 8-ounce glasses of water daily. Dehydration has been shown to contribute to poor concentration and memory.

I constantly stress that the quality of the water we drink is crucial to the maintenance of our health. Much has been written about the quality of tap water, which is usually chlorinated, fluoridated, and treated. Not only is it vulnerable to many different types of impurities, including parasites, but it may be full of harmful pollutants and inorganic minerals.

I am a strong proponent of drinking only steam-distilled water. Our family has been drinking distilled water for over twenty years. Our eight kids have had very few cavities and have been extremely healthy. I know there is controversy over steam distilled, but I think it's the best water for your body. Some medical authorities think it throws off our biochemical/electrical balance and prefer regular, purified water. Obviously, I don't agree. Because of its lack of minerals and flat molecular structure, distilled water draws other particles (nutrients and toxins) to it, which actually pulls out the toxins that build up in the body. Yes, you urinate more, but it's simply the bladder dumping more as the water pulls out unwanted substances. That's a good thing.

Here's another benefit of drinking distilled water. It helps rid the body of those awful cravings for junk foods. As the water flushes out your system, it cleanses the remainder of the junk food you may have eaten. Remember the last food eaten will be the next food craved. So if you've loaded up with junk, you will continue craving it if you do not get it flushed out of your system.

Need more reasons to drink steam-distilled water? Well, it has a pH level of 7.0, meaning it will help bring up your pH so that you are not acidic, but more on the alkaline side. Doctors and scientists agree that by keeping the body more alkaline, you are more likely to remain free from disease. (See Acid and Alkali Imbalance in the Condition-Specific Helps.)

Our family also drinks Clustered Water in the morning and throughout the day, for its wonderful properties. Dr. Lorenzen's Clustered Water is probably the greatest breakthrough in health science product development in this century. Clustered Water, produced at home using one ounce of concentrate to one gallon of steam-distilled water, replenishes the most vital support for all cellular DNA and the 4,000 plus enzymes that are involved in every metabolic process in your body. It increases nutrient absorption by up to 600 percent, which means your vitamins and organic foods will deliver far more vital nutrients to your body. Essentially, it replicates the powerful healing waters of the earth and is excellent for cleaning out lymphatic fluids.

Thirst is not necessarily a reliable sign that our body needs water. When you feel thirsty, you are probably already in the initial stages of dehydration. And from early adult age our sense of thirst begins to dull. Which is why we need to drink water regularly, whether we feel thirsty or not.

Drinks that contain alcohol and caffeine, such as coffee, teas, or soft drinks, do not count the same volume as water, because they increase the loss of water from the body in urine. This leaves the body dehydrated. Replace these drinks with herb and fruit teas or coffee substitutes made with barley or rye, chicory, or dandelion. Substitute diluted fruit juices or herbal cocktail drinks for alcoholic drinks.

OXYGEN, *the* BREATH *of* LIFE

I am constantly amazed by the lack of attention given to the role of oxygen as it regards our health. Many of the major books on natural and nutritional healing barely touch on its importance. Even water runs a distant second in importance to oxygen's number-one role for our health. We can live for weeks without food. We can even live for a few days without water. But we can only live for minutes without oxygen. Since the creation of the world, oxygen has been and continues to be the very breath of life that keeps every one of us functioning for our allotted space of time upon this planet (Genesis 2:7).

Oxygen is your greatest and first source of energy. It is the fuel required for the proper operation of all your body systems. Only 10 percent of your energy comes from food and water; *90 percent of your energy comes from oxygen.* Oxygen gives your body the ability to rebuild itself. Oxygen detoxifies the blood and strengthens the immune system. Oxygen displaces or burns deadly free radicals, neutralizes environmental toxins, and destroys anaerobic (depleted of oxygen) bacteria, parasites, microbes, and viruses.

Oxygen greatly enhances the body's absorption of vitamins, minerals, amino acids, proteins, and other important nutrients. Oxygen enhances brain power and memory. Oxygen can beneficially affect your learning ability. The ability to think, feel, and act is all dependent on oxygen. It also calms the mind and stabilizes the nervous system. Oxygen heightens concentration and alertness. Without oxygen, brain cells die and deteriorate quickly. As you age, and oxygen deficiency increases, it takes longer to learn, and your retention span is decreased. Oxygen strengthens the heart. Increased oxygen lowers the resting heart rate and strengthens the contraction of the cardiac muscle.

Maintaining proper oxygen levels in the body is an essential ingredient to health, vitality, physical stamina, and endurance. You must have a means of replenishing your oxygen level. Researchers, scientists, molecular biologists, nutritional specialists, and others have reported phenomenal health benefits from increased oxygen uptake.

PROBLEMS WITH TODAY'S OXYGEN

There are two very big problems concerning oxygen that may be killing you ever so slowly. According to Dr. Carl Baugh, noted archeologist, author, and creationist, in pre-flood conditions the oxygen saturation levels in the earth's atmosphere were 35 percent, and carbon dioxide was probably less than 1 percent. Today in "country living" you may get 21 percent oxygen. In "big city" pollution, we do good to get 17 to 18 percent oxygen with 25 percent carbon dioxide. The truth is that there is much less oxygen in the air to breathe, and what is there brings chemical pollutants and other harmful substances into our bodies.

The other major problem is that most people are starving the body of vital oxygen through shallow breathing. It is reported that people in Western cultures barely use one-fifth of the lung's capacity to increase the oxygen flow to their bodies. In conditions in which there is insufficient oxygen being carried by the blood to our body tissues, oxygen is to be used in cases of severe anemia, shock, circulatory collapse, pulmonary edema, pneumonia, and many others. It also can contribute to headaches, muscular aches and pains, stiff joints, constipation, indigestion, aching backs and feet, poor eyesight, poor hearing, sore throats, and respiratory ailments such as emphysema, asthma, sinus infections, and bronchitis.

Commenting in an article in the *Journal of Longevity* that was titled "Oxygen Decrease Leading to Worldwide Increase in Disease," Dr. Philip Stavish said, "Oxygen deficiency results in a weakened immune system, which can lead to viral problems, damaged cell growth, toxic buildup in the blood, and premature aging—among other ailments." According to Norman McVea, M.D., Ph.D., in *Wellness Lifestyle* magazine, "More than anything else, good health and well-being is dependent on the maximum production, maintenance and flow of energy, which is produced by oxygen.... It contributes to proper metabolic function, better circulation, assimilation, digestion, and elimination. Oxidation is the key to life."

First, there are heart-related problems due to the lack of oxygen in our systems. Virtually all heart attacks can be attributed to a failure to deliver oxygen to the heart muscle. Dr. Richard Lippman, renowned researcher, states that a lack of oxygen (hypoxia) is the prime cause of 1.5 million heart attacks each year.

Second, there are also *cancer*-related problems that arise. According to Dr. Otto Warburg, noted researcher and Nobel Prize winner in 1952, "Once the level of oxygen available in a cell drops below 60 percent of normal, the cell is forced to switch to an inferior method of energy production—fermentation. The cell can never be returned to the proper oxidation system and produces alcohol and lactic acid. If a parasite moves into the area and begins to feed on the alcohol, its waste products inhibit the suppressers of enzyme growth factor (EGF). The anaerobic cells are flooded with EGF and begin to replicate themselves wildly. This condition, we call cancer."

Dr. Warburg also pointed out that any substance that deprives a cell of oxygen is a carcinogen, if the cell is not killed outright. He stated that it is useless to search out new carcinogens, because the result of each one is the same—cellular deprivation of oxygen. He further stated that the incessant search for new carcinogens is counterproductive because it obscures the prime cause, a lack of oxygen, and prevents appropriate treatment. The National Cancer Institute endorsed Dr. Warburg's findings in 1952.

Dr. Harry Goldblatt published similar findings in the *Journal of Experimental Medicine* in 1953. His research confirmed that a lack of oxygen plays the major role in causing cells to become cancerous. "Disease is due to a deficiency in the oxidation process of the body, leading to an accumulation of toxins." Keep in mind these toxins are ordinarily burned in normal oxidation.

A third major health concern regards the burning of fat. In Dr. Heinerman's *Encyclopedia of Nature's Vitamins & Minerals*, he states that oxygen is the key to burning stored fat. "If you want help in losing weight, stoke your biological furnace with more oxygen. The oxygen you take in is carried directly to cell mitochondria, where energy is created and preserved. Your body's internal combustion gets accelerated to the point that more stored fat is chemically burned off." This is because the highest grade fuel in the body is fat, or lipids. Additional oxygen that is brought into the body helps to burn that high-grade fuel.

INCREASING YOUR BODY OXYGEN

- If you smoke, stop. Smoking robs you of 50 percent of the oxygen your body needs. The chemicals in the cigarettes eat up that oxygen from your system. Smoking also delivers two deadly poisons to your system—arsenic and carbon dioxide. The nicotine also poisons your system and immediately affects your lung function and constricts your cardiovascular system.

- Consider your diet. Whether our bodies are sufficiently oxygenated to eliminate toxins and prevent disease depends greatly on our diets. Junk food, food additives, and sugar all deplete the body of oxygen. I recommend eating God's way, the One Perfect Diet, the Levitical Diet! Calcium balance in the cells is critical in allowing oxygen into the body. Calcium absorption from digestion depends on vitamin D, and most diets are deficient in it. Coenzyme Q10 and vitamin C and E help the cell use its oxygen as well. Make a habit of eating five fresh fruits and vegetables a day. Not only will you get oxygen into your body, but you slash your risk of getting cancer by 30 percent, according to the American Cancer Society. A good liquid mineral supplement helps the body keep everything working in perfect harmony. Keeping your body in a healthy balance starts with a healthy diet, just as God designed it to do!

- Circulation of clean, oxygen-carrying blood is a basic requirement for healthy living. The first place to start is to daily practice deep-breathing techniques. This is the quickest way to increase oxygen levels. Starting right now, sit up straight so that you can get full lung capacity. Breathe in deeply through the nose and fill your lungs with oxygen, hold the breath for a few seconds, and slowly release the carbon monoxide out through the mouth. Do this several minutes each day!

- An ozone generator is a great investment and will give you rapid results.

- Good clean water is a must. Tap water loaded with chlorine, fluoride, and iodine deplete your oxygen levels. I choose steam-distilled water and make certain that I get my minerals from my fresh fruits, veggies, and liquid minerals.

- Exercise is absolutely essential. You must exercise, even if you just start with walking in place. Start somewhere. Practice your deep-breathing techniques while you walk. Set your goal to exercise a little each day, 10 to 15 minutes, or 3 or 4 longer programs a week.

- Cut out all food chemicals. Read the labels on your foods, drinks, and even on your hair, skin, and personal items.

- Treat yourself once a week to an oxygen bath. The oxygen is absorbed through the pores, and oxygen levels are increased. Remember that your skin is the largest organ of your body. Oxygen bars are also now available in some areas. You have a seat, and they will hook you right up. I highly recommend my product, Body Oxygen™. The testimonials are endless of those who had deficient oxygen levels but were able to raise it to healthy levels after using it, as well as those just needing an extra pick-me-up.

- It is important to remember that fear, worry, and depression all interfere with free breathing and thus reduce oxygen uptake. God has not given us a spirit of fear, but of power, love, and a sound mind (2 Timothy 1:7).

10

HEALTHY METHODS
of COOKING

MY FIRST GOAL IS TO GET YOU COMMITTED TO BUYING OR GROWING FOODS THAT ARE HEALTHY. How food is grown, treated, processed, and handled makes a world of difference. And how it's been stored, packaged, prepared, or cooked will influence how well your body processes and assimilates its nutrients. And it's common sense that you can't have healthy eating without healthy cooking methods. The wrong cooking methods will consistently neutralize or ruin the best foods in the world.

That doesn't mean you have to choose between food that tastes good and food that's healthy. No one wants to eat tasteless nutrients, and few people will stick with eating healthy if it isn't appetizing. It's important that we enjoy what we eat, and there's no reason why healthy meals can't be delicious. And you don't have to go to chef school and refurbish your kitchen with special cookware to do it. Healthy cooking is as simple as using basic cooking methods to prepare foods in healthy ways.

IS RAW BETTER THAN COOKED?

In a perfect world, as in the Garden of Eden, we would only eat raw foods. It is an idea that's returned to our culture through the Raw-Food Vegan diet, and we're seeing more raw food preparation even in restaurants. Depending on where you live, this may be somewhat easier for you than others. I enjoy eating this way, but even in my house we're probably only 20 to 25 percent raw. We do have a higher percentage of organic consumption, but these are things that do not require much (if any) preparation. Ideally, 80 percent of the food you eat would be raw.

Before I detail healthy cooking methods, I first need to discuss the raw-foods philosophy. It is built upon the belief that cooking any food weakens the potency of the minerals and vitamins and destroys enzymes. Some advocates go so far as to say that cooking introduces toxins.

There is much that I appreciate about this diet, just as there is much that I appreciate about a vegetarian diet. I hope you become convinced to shift your diet to eating lots of raw organic vegetables and fruits and nuts. To increase the amount of antioxidant rich foods will give your body an immediate health boost. A study published in the May 1998 issue of the journal *Epidemiology* showed that a diet laden with fruits and vegetables will reduce your chances of getting breast or colon cancer. And the *British Medical Journal* reported in September 1996 that a diet that included daily fresh fruit reduced heart attacks and related problems. As a general rule, raw vegetables and fruits retain the most nutrients.

However, it's not the food enzymes that are the key to our digestion, as the raw-food advocates insist. It's the enzymes our body generates that do the work. And it is primarily the antioxidants and fiber from the vegetables and fruit that make the difference. Raw is still better, but for a different reason than the enzyme argument.

Nancy Lee Bentley, the coauthor of *Dr. Mercola's Total Health Cookbook & Program*, sheds some light on the role of cooking from history. She notes that "throughout history all cultures have modified, cooked, or altered their foods in some way. This is one of the eleven fundamental Characteristics of Traditional Diets, based on extensive research on so-called primitive cultures throughout the world by Dr. Weston Price in the 1930s.... Whether through the application of heat (boiling, baking, frying, etc.), microorganisms (fermenting or pickling), mechanics (juicing, chopping), activations (sprouting), or preservation (canning, freezing, salting, drying, milling, or other processing), cooking or altering food is invariably a form of predigestion."

The fact remains that some foods are simply easier to digest and

deliver their nutrients when cooked properly, and it is the assimilation of nutrients that counts. Taiwanese researchers and the Rutgers
University recently showed that the body more easily absorbs iron
from 37 of 48 vegetables tested when they're boiled, stir-fried,
steamed, or grilled. For instance, the absorbable iron in cabbage
jumped from 6.7 percent to 27 percent with cooking and broccoli
flowerets rose from 6 percent to 30 percent.

I am concerned for those who follow the Raw-Food Vegan diet
because of its missing proteins, minerals, vitamins, and essential
fatty acids. The only reliable sources for certain nutrients are animal
products, and to be without them for the long term is dangerous.

I should note that sprouting seeds, grains, and beans is a mag-
nificent way to eat and improve your health. The process of sprouting makes the nutrient content you ingest higher than eating their
fully developed brothers. Sprouts deliver the highest protein of its
kind available. Sprouting is also fun to do and can involve the whole
family. All the products you need are available from your local health
food store, and it's inexpensive. By the way, if your health food store
doesn't carry these seeds, beans, grain, or the sprouting canister,
most stores will gladly order them for you if you ask.

Along with the raw foods our family uses, we also us a raw organic
food supplement, Creation's Bounty, that delivers unprocessed goodness
in our morning smoothies. Since I implemented this blend of whole,
raw organic herbs and grains several years ago, I've seen my children's
school grades improve and overall thought process develop.

HEALTHY COOKING METHODS

How you prepare your foods can have a profound effect on their
nutrient content as well as the flavors captured in the process. Any
cooking of vegetables or fruits causes the loss of nutrients, but the
amount varies according to the time food is heated and how long it
is in contact with water. Using a timer will help ensure you hold to
the shortest possible time, and eating food as soon as possible after
it is cooked makes a difference.

Utilizing the right cooking strategies can help retain and, in some cases, improve the nutritional value of your most popular dishes. The following cooking methods tend to produce lower saturated fat levels: baking, broiling, braising, searing, poaching, roasting, steaming, stir-frying, sautéing, and grilling.

Steaming is one of the simplest and healthiest cooking methods for retaining flavor and maximizing the nutrients in foods. Steamed vegetables in a perforated basket suspended above simmering liquid allows you to get them crisp on the inside and tender on the outside in a minimal amount of time. A tight lid conserves nutrients by holding in steam and heat. This shortens cooking time and reduces the amount of water needed. Vegetables are often steamed for much too long, causing them to lose their flavor, color, and nutrients. Be sure to note the time for steaming in your recipe.

Steaming cooks the vegetables with the even moist heat of the vapors. So the heat is consistent throughout cooking time, make sure the water is just below the level of the basket and at a rapid boil before adding your vegetables to the steamer basket. Once your water is at a rapid boil, turn your heat to a moderate temperature and place your vegetables in the steamer basket. If you are steaming more than one vegetable at a time, place the vegetables in the steamer basket in layers, with the densest vegetable on the bottom. If you use a flavorful liquid or add seasonings (such as fresh herbs, lemon, and olive oil) to the water, you'll add a potentially delightful flavor to the food as it cooks.

Try steaming a variety of vegetables with a nice piece of salmon or halibut on top. You can make a simple dressing and drizzle it over everything when done. It is the perfect way to make a healthy meal in one pot in a very short amount of time. When you have eight children as I do, less messy and shortened times are real plusses!

Boiling with a little water can have good results as it is quicker than steaming. Boiling heats foods more quickly to the cooking temperature at which a vitamin C-destroying enzyme is killed. When boiling, use only a one-inch depth of water. Retrieve lost nutrients by using the cooking water as stock.

Baking and **roasting** really describe the same function. Baking usually refers to the cooking of foods made from batter or dough—breads, cakes, cookies, and pastries. It is also used to cook uniform-sized pieces of vegetables, fruit, seafood, poultry, or lean meat. Place food in a pan or dish surrounded by the hot dry air of your oven. You may cook the food covered or uncovered. Baking generally doesn't require that you add fat to the food.

Roasting is used to describe the baking of certain kinds of meat. For example, a turkey or leg of lamb is roasted, but a ham is baked. For poultry, seafood, and meat, place a rack inside the roasting pan so that the fat can drip away during cooking.

Braising. This method involves browning the ingredient first in an open or covered pan on top of the stove, and then slowly cooking it with a small quantity of liquid. In some recipes, the cooking liquid is used afterward to form a flavorful, nutrient-rich sauce. Salmon and most quality fish are superb when braised. Try braising chicken thighs with vegetables and you'll be pleased with how tender the thighs get and how succulent the broth is.

Searing is an oil-free technique used in grilling, roasting, braising, and sautéing that cooks the surface of the food (usually meat, poultry, or fish) at high temperature so that a carmelized crust forms. It is commonly believed that this acts to "lock in moisture," resulting in a juicier end product. However, it has now been scientifically shown that searing results in a loss of moisture. Nonetheless, it remains a healthy way to cook meat as the contrast in taste and texture between the crust and the interior makes the food more interesting to the palate.

Typically in grilling, the food will be seared over very high heat and then moved to a lower temperature area of the grill. In braising, the seared surface acts to flavor, color, and otherwise enrich the liquid in which the food is being cooked.

For an easier clean up, heat a non-stick pan over medium high heat for about 2 to 3 minutes, then season your meat or fish and place in the hot pan. The fish or meat will sear and cook rather quickly, then turn the heat to medium so it doesn't burn while cooking through. If the piece of fish or meat is very thick (one inch), this is not the best method of cooking to use.

Grilling and **broiling**. Both of these cooking methods expose fairly thin pieces of food to direct heat and allow fat to drip away. To grill outdoors, place the food on a grill rack above a bed of charcoal embers or gas-heated rocks. Keep open-flame grilling of meats to a minimum as this practice produces cancer-promoting compounds. Always avoid eating charred food.

To broil, place food on a broiler rack below a heat element. To quick broil, preheat the broiler on high for most recipes. Let the pan get very hot under the heat, then place your seasoned meat or fish on the hot pan. You do not need any oil in the pan. Because it is so hot, it immediately seals the meat on the bottom and keeps the meat from sticking. The meat or fish cooks rapidly from both sides, so it does not need to be turned. For fish, the cooking time can be as quick as 1 to 2 minutes, depending on the thickness.

Sautéing allows you to quickly cook relatively small or thin pieces of vegetables without using heated oils. The key is using a good-quality nonstick pan. Depending on the recipe, use broth, juice, wine, nonstick cooking spray, or water in place of oil. If you must use oil, use extra virgin olive oil, safflower oil, or sesame oil. Use half the suggested amount of oil and add a little water. If you start with onions, they release their own oil that allows them to be sautéed without adding any. Don't worry if your onions start to stick to the pan. Just keep stirring, and when you add liquid to your pan it will release what little is stuck to the pan. This actually adds extra flavor.

Stir-frying quickly cooks small, uniform-sized pieces of food while they're rapidly stirred in a wok or large nonstick frying pan. You need only a small amount of oil or nonstick cooking spray or none at all. A small amount of broth (one tablespoon) in place of the oil makes it healthier and better tasting. The food is cooked over medium-high heat, which requires the food to be stirred constantly to allow the ingredients to cook quickly, keeping them crisp without burning. Begin by adding onions to the wok to release moisture and any ginger as the second or third ingredient. The moisture from the onions and other ingredients gives the ginger the opportunity to cook briefly to release its flavor.

Do not microwave your food. Microwave cooking results in the greatest loss of nutrients of all methods of cooking and does not kill salmonella or other bacteria that might be present in the food. Microwave cooking changes the molecular structure of the food. It has been shown to convert the naturally occurring cis-fatty acids into the harmful trans-fatty acids found in hydrogenated fats. It also causes "structural, functional and immunological changes" in the blood and the cells of the body.

Spice it up. Creating meals that use spices (such as cinnamon, nutmeg, pepper, and paprika) and herbs (such as oregano, basil, cilantro, thyme, parsley, sage, and rosemary) is one of the best ways to add color, taste, and aroma to foods. Choose fresh herbs that look bright and aren't wilted. Add them toward the end of cooking. Add dried herbs in the earlier stages of cooking. When substituting dried for fresh, use about one-third the amount.

Try these low-fat flavorings during preparation or at the table: reduced fat or nonfat salad dressing, mustard, reduced fat or nonfat sour cream, reduced fat or nonfat yogurt, reduced sodium soy sauce, salsa, lemon or lime juice, vinegar, horseradish, fresh garlic, fresh ginger, red pepper flakes, and sprinkles of parmesan cheese.

GENERAL COOKING TIPS

- Trim all visible fat from meats before cooking.
- Refrigerate all stocks, stews, and soups and remove the congealed fat before reheating.
- Bake foods using non-fat marinades to retain moisture.
- Switch to sea salt immediately. Table salt is artificial and responsible for increasing blood pressure and heart problems. Sea salt, however, contains many health-promoting minerals such as magnesium, calcium, potassium, sodium, chloride,

sulfate, phosphate, and many trace minerals. These trace minerals are absolutely vital in the electrolytic activity of the whole body, and without them you simply cannot function. Sodium helps convey energy and is the electrical charge that enables nerve impulses and muscle contraction. Every day our body loses these vital minerals that must be replaced.

- Cut the salt in half in your favorite recipes. Most of the time this will not produce a noticeable taste change. Consider replacing part of the salt with an herb or spice, flavored vinegar, citrus juice or peel. Garlic or onion powder (not garlic or onion salt) work well in meats, soups, and sauces. Make your own mix of garlic, onion, paprika, and parsley flakes.

- Add vegetables whenever possible to ensure your five-a-day intake. Experiment with more veggie variety in salads, try new vegetable mixes, include some shredded vegetables in casseroles, and add different vegetables to soups and stews. Use chopped red or yellow peppers to "pep" up the flavor. Try vegetable salsas and fruit chutneys as accompaniments to meat or poultry in place of heavy gravies or sauces.

- Reduce the fat in home baked goodies by substituting applesauce, pureed prunes, mashed bananas, or yogurt. It works! The end result is moist and the fat content is reduced.

- Substitute whole grain products for all-purpose flour in your cooking. Try whole wheat flour, oatmeal, or flax in bread and muffins, or add some bran or wheat germ to your meatloaf. Try using some soy flour in biscuits and breads.

- Remember that cold-pressed, unrefined oils retain more nutritional value and flavor. For high-temperature cooking, used olive, canola, and sesame oils. For low-temperature cooking, use sunflower, hazelnut, and canola oils. For cold dishes, use sunflower, hazelnut, wheat germ, walnut, and olive oils.

11

SWEETENERS

I HOPE THAT YOU'RE NOT AMONG THE AVERAGE AMERICANS WHO CONSUME AN APPROXIMATE 120 TO 150 POUNDS OF SUGAR PER YEAR. Sugar is the most addictive substance in our diets, and food manufacturers know it. You'll find sugar in almost every processed or packaged food.

Sugar offers a quick energy lift to the brain that just as quickly lets you down, but lower than when you started. Refined sugar is sucrose and brings no nutritional benefits. It adds nothing but calories to the body. And as you should be aware of if you listen to any news at all, eating lots of sugary foods raises your production of insulin, which contributes to problems associated with diabetes, hypoglycemia, high triglycerides, and high blood pressure. Pile on the added problems of the fluctuation of blood sugar levels and its affect on one's feelings of well-being, as glucose is the main sugar in the blood and brain, and you see the major affect it has on one's health.

If you haven't gotten the message by now, you have to cut the heavy intake of sugar.

Here are some safe sweeteners I recommend. Other natural sweeteners are available, but these are the most common.

- **Stevia** is an herb in the chrysanthemum family, which grows wild in parts of Paraguay and Brazil and has also been successfully cultivated commercially in Uruguay, Central America, the U.S., Israel, Thailand, and China. Technically, FDA restrictions state it can't be called a "sweetener." However, it has been used for hundreds if not thousands of years similar to table sugar and is now proving to be beneficial with adult-onset, or type II, diabetes and high blood pressure. It can be processed into powder form like table sugar or into a liquid extract and is found in most grocery stores and health food stores. Stevia has zero calories, zero grams of sugar, and is about 25 times sweeter than sugar! Only use a tiny bit or the taste overpowers the food or drink you are sweetening.

- **Honey** has been used since the beginning of time! Not only does it taste great, it has bioactive, antibiotic and antiseptic properties. Honey contains all the vitamins, minerals, and enzymes necessary for proper metabolism and digestion of glucose.
- **Turbinado** is unprocessed sugar cane or the raw sugar.
- **Barley Malt** is a mild, natural sweetener made from barley sprouts that releases slowly into the bloodstream because it is a complex carbohydrate. We use it in our Creation's Bounty.
- **Blackstrap Molasses** is the liquid sludge after sucrose is extracted from the cane sugar refining process. It is an excellent source of minerals and vitamins.
- **Sucralose** is a low-calorie sweetener made from sugar used around the world as an ingredient in low-calorie processed foods and beverages, and as a tabletop sweetener available to consumers in supermarkets and other consumer outlets. In studies on rodents given the equivalent of 1,500 soft drinks daily, no cancer-causing effects were found.

CONTROVERSIAL SWEETENING AGENTS

- **Sorbitol, mannitol,** and **lactitol** are made from a sugar alcohol base. They commonly cause diarrhea and other gastrointestinal side effects.
- **Mycoprotein** is a fungus base sweetener. It has shown that up to 90 percent of the cases studied had gastrointestinal discomfort. This is most likely due to the fact that it is a fungus and the mycoprotein feeds the fungus.
- **Saccharin** is made from petroleum and toluene, a solvent used to stop knocking in gasoline engines. Said to be 300 times

sweeter than sugar and calorie free. After a Canadian study in 1977, saccharin was connected to bladder cancer in rats. The FDA proposed a ban on saccharin, which was blocked by Congress, although saccharin is now sold with a cancer-causing warning label.

- **High Fructose Corn Syrup** is a highly refined, commercial glucose made from chemically purified cornstarch. It uses up 32 percent of your fat burning ability and makes you sluggish, which makes you gain weight! One study stated that since the 1970s when HFCS was introduced, our belts have expanded by 250 percent.

SWEETENERS BANNED FROM MY HOUSE

Avoid using artificial sweeteners at all costs. There is research that suggests the use of these sweeteners may result in numerous negative consequences.

Aspartame and its brand names, NutraSweet and Equal, are banned from my house! Realize that it is in everything from instant breakfasts to soft drinks to instant teas and even yogurt. In his book, *Aspertame (NutraSweet): Is It Safe?* renowned diabetes expert Dr. H. J. Roberts reported a link between aspertame and increased incidence of brain tumors, seizure disorders, chronic headaches, and hyperactivity in children. There are over 92 different health side effects associated with aspartame consumption. For some individuals, the symptoms are gradual, and for others the symptoms are immediately severe.

- Eye: Blindness, blurring, bright flashes, squiggly lines, tunnel vision, night vision problems, dry eye, bulging eyes.
- Ear: Tinnitus—ringing in the ears, buzzing, intolerance to noise, hearing impairment.
- Neurological problems: Epileptic seizures, headaches, migraines, dizziness, confusion, drowsiness, sleeplessness, numbness in the limbs, severe slurring speech, hyperactivity, restless legs, facial pain, severe tremors.

- Psychological or psychiatric problems: Severe depression, irritability, aggression, anxiety, personality changes, insomnia, phobias.
- May trigger or mimic: Chronic fatigue, Epstein-Barr syndrome, Lyme disease, Graves' disease, Alzheimer's, MS, Lupus, Lymphoma, ADD, ADHD, hypothyroidism, fibromyalgia.

Aspartame has been shown to change the ratio of amino acids in the blood, blocking or lowering the levels of serotonin, tyrosine, dopamine, norepinephrine, and adrenaline.

Anyone who exhibits the symptoms above should cut out all aspartame immediately and consider conducting an internal organ cleanse. You need to restore your nutrients, eat raw food and digestive enzymes, and drink lots of water.

12

HOW to EAT OUT HEALTHY

YES, IT'S TRUE THAT THE AVERAGE RESTAURANT MEAL CONTAINS 1,000 TO 2,000 CALORIES AND 50 TO 100 GRAMS OF FAT. Did I mention that that's without the appetizers, bread, drinks, or dessert? And, yes, the USDA found that restaurant foods are about 20 percent fattier and 15 percent higher in saturated fat than good old home cooking. And, as you might expect, most restaurants are more concerned with the way food tastes than the size of your waist. To eat out healthy presents a challenge to us all.

But don't let the savory smells and large portions and visual stimulation and luscious desserts discourage you from your goal to eat healthy. The good news is that many restaurants offer sufficient options that allow you to eat healthy when you're away from home. Research shows that more restaurants are satisfying the ever-changing tastes and preferences of their customers by providing flexibility in food preparation methods, portion sizes, and expanded menu offerings.

I should know. As much as I travel and end up dining in restaurants, I've had countless opportunities to learn how to make wise meal choices when dining out. There are simple steps you can take to beat the restaurant diet traps. Once you recognize them, you'll have no problem avoiding the pitfalls…if you're committed to walking in health.

TIPS for EATING OUT

- If you know the name of the restaurant ahead of time, call and ask what healthy items they serve on the menu. They'll be happy to help you, and if they're not, pick a restaurant that is. Having made your choices before you arrive goes a long way to beating the temptation to order a high-fat entrée that the server declares is "to kill for." Look for descriptions that indicate low-fat preparation or ingredients—such as baked, broiled, grilled, poached, roasted, steamed, sautéed or stir-fried in a small amount of oil, broth, or water. Avoid items that are described as a la king, au gratin, basted, breaded, buttered, broasted, creamed, fried, hollandaise, and sautéed or stir-fried in heavy oil.

- Read through the item descriptions on the menu. If none is available, ask your server what's in the meal and how it's prepared. Learn to identify the hidden fat language. Chefs use phrases such as "lightly breaded" to cover the real meaning: "submerged in a tub of butter." Ask your server, who is your ally, how an item is prepared. He or she wants to meet your needs, if for no reason other than your tip. Don't be afraid to ask for special preparations of menu items.

- Choose appetizers with vegetables, fruits, or fish. Avoid fried or breaded appetizers, despite the urges you feel.

- Broth-based or tomato-based soups are better choices than creamed soups, chowders, and pureed soups, which often contain heavy cream and buckets of calories. Ask for the soup's ingredients. Know what it is that you're swallowing.

- Order a spinach salad with dressing on the side, preferably a low-fat or fat-free version. Be aware that Caesar, Greek, chef, and taco salads tend to be higher in fat and calories.

- Choose whole-grain breads. Muffins, garlic toast, and croissants stack up the calories and fat. If you have a bread basket at your table, take one piece and ask your server to remove the basket. You don't need the yeast. Use only small amounts of butter or olive oil.

- Ask for rice or vegetables as side dishes that come without butter or cream sauces. Stay away from the golden French fries, onion rings, or mayonnaise-based salads. You know they're killers.

- Ask the server which entrées have a lower-fat preparation. You can't go wrong with lemon-baked fish, broiled shish kebabs, grilled chicken breast, or London broil. Steer clear of high-fat foods, such as filet mignon with béarnaise sauce, fried chicken, fried rice, prime rib, shrimp tempura, veal parmigiana, stuffed shrimp, or fettuccine Alfredo. Choose pasta primavera or linguine with red tomato sauce and pass on the pasta with meat or cheese stuffing.

- Always consider splitting an entrée with a companion, particularly when you know the restaurant serves large portions. Or request a to-go container and immediately place half of the food into the container when the meal arrives. Seventy percent of restaurant customers say they often order larger portions to turn the evening's dinner into the following day's lunch.
- Try something new such as seasoning a baked potato with Picante Sauce rather than the traditional butter and sour cream. Or a potato covered with cottage cheese, salt, and pepper. You don't necessarily need to avoid your favorite foods, but you can alter the preparation in order to cut the fat.
- Finish the main meal and let it settle before ordering dessert. You may not even want dessert. If you are craving dessert, opt for something low-fat, such as sorbet, fresh berries, or fruit. And split it with your companions or take half of it home.
- Order unsweetened iced tea or sparkling water or mineral water with a twist of lemon. For a hot drink, try green tea minus the sugar and other extras. Many beverages contain a staggering amount of totally wasted calories. For example, a large soda (32 ounces) has about 400 calories!
- Stop eating when you are full. Listen to your body, and you'll be rewarded. If you're tempted to clean your plate, ask your server to remove the dishes.

BUFFETS

Buffets loom in front of us with an added challenge. When we are trying to eat smaller portion sizes, the freedom to go back for a second or third helping of sumptuous, gorgeous food easily opens the door to excess. And buffets have a mysterious ability to demand that we must get our money's worth by eating as much as we can stuff down.

To limit the amount of food you eat, you need to approach it with a plan. Survey the entire buffet line, then decide what you want and take only that. Make a colorful salad without the high-fat dressings and toppings, such as cheese and croutons, your first course. Then go back for an entrée. Fill up on plenty of fruit and vegetables that don't have added butter, margarine, or sauces.

Make wise choices. Be in charge. You can do it!

FAST-FOOD MEALS

There are times when the fast-food franchises are your only option. Fortunately, many of them now offer several lighter-fare items, such as salads and grilled chicken. But watch for dressings, sauces, and other condiments that can boost your meal's fat and calorie content. Take your time and be selective. Don't rush because the servers are in a rush. Make sure that what you're paying your hard-earned dollars for is worth it. These guidelines can help:

- For breakfast, consider fresh fruit, unsweetened fruit juice, cereal, fat-free muffins, or pancakes and a small amount of syrup.
- Choose unbreaded poultry items, such as broiled or grilled chicken or sliced turkey sandwiches. Or order a veggie sandwich minus the high-fat condiments.
- Request sandwiches on whole wheat bread or pita bread.
- Stay away from the fried items—period. Don't cheat.
- Go for the fresh fruits and vegetables if the restaurant has a salad bar. Look for low-fat or fat-free dressings, and if you can't find any, ask.
- Cut back on the ketchup, mustard, sauces, and pickles. They're loaded with salt.
- I shouldn't have to say this, but avoid milk shakes and dessert items such as fruit pies and sundaes with syrup. Try fresh fruit or a flavored coffee instead.

EATING OUT *at a* FRIEND'S HOUSE OR DINNER PARTY

If you are going to a friend's house for dinner, call and ask what you can bring. That affords you the opportunity to bring a healthy item and to be courteous, and there's a good chance you'll discover what's being served without being impolite. If you're going to a large dinner party, call ahead and ask what the menu is (if they ask why, simply tell them you're eating healthy and want to plan ahead). If the menu is unhealthy, I suggest you eat something healthy about an hour before the meal. That will reduce your hunger and allow you to eat very small portions. But remember this advice: It is better to occasionally offend your diet for one meal or a treat than to offend a friend for a lifetime. Taking charge of your eating habits and lifestyle may provoke some jealousy at first, but God says, "Love always wins."

WHAT YOU
NEED *to* DO

*Beloved, I wish above all
things that thou mayest prosper
and be in health,
even as thy soul prospereth.*

3 JOHN 2

13

CLEANSING YOUR SYSTEMS

> *Do not be deceived.*
> *God cannot*
> *be mocked.*
> *A man reaps*
> *what he sows.*
>
> —GALATIANS 6:7

IF YOU ARE EXPERIENCING A DECLINE IN HEALTH OR A SPECIFIC HEALTH PROBLEM, IT USUALLY HAS COME ON GRADUALLY AND PERHAPS HAS BEEN NEARLY UNDETECTABLE. What is happening is that your body is sending you a signal that your body cells are in disease. You have stepped out of homeostasis, "the state of being in health." Disease is associated generally with the absence or lack of some substance from our system, and/or a buildup of toxins in the body that needs to be eliminated.

Too often we have been doing and are doing things to our bodies that cause the problems, and if these are left unresolved, our problems will persist or get worse. Years of poor diet habits and lack of exercise bring us to these points, and a quick and easy fix won't mend what's broken. Your body may have been able to cope for a lack of a specific nutrient for a while, but you can only cheat for so long and not reap the harvest you've sowed.

For thousands of years, body purification has consistently been found at the foundation of health rituals. Today, this is more important than ever. Besides the harm we may be doing to our bodies, there are other factors constantly warring against us. The effects of breathing in smog and cigarette smoke, exposing our bodies to increasing levels of UV rays, and contact with chemical products as well as their fumes have shown to cause damage to the cells of our bodies. We are surrounded by pesticides, asbestos, formaldehyde (in particleboard, plywood, paints, and plastics), vinyl chloride, radioactivity, and X-rays—all of which are dangerous.

Add to that the preservatives and chemical additives to food, agricultural pesticides and hormone-enhancing drugs, chemical sprays, food processing, cured and processed meats, even our deodorants and shampoos, and the tremendous amounts of sugar added to our food. Then there are the daily stresses that take their toll on our energies and health—emotional traumas, physical injuries, antibiotics (that kill both bad and good bacteria in the body), and the fluctuations between hot and cold surroundings. All these negatively affect us over time.

No one escapes toxins. A toxin describes the chemicals in your body that have not been made harmless or "detoxed." Toxicity occurs on two primary levels. First, toxins are taken in from our environment. Second, your body produces toxins naturally all the time. Biochemical, cellular, and bodily activities generate waste substances that need to be eliminated. Free radicals, for instance, are biochemical toxins. When these are not removed, they can cause tissues and cells to become irritated or inflamed, blocking normal functions on a cellular, organ, and whole-body level. Yeasts, intestinal bacteria, foreign bacteria, and parasites produce metabolic waste products that we must process and eliminate from our bodies. Even stress creates a toxic state, if we allow it to dominate our mind and emotions.

INTERNAL CLEANSING

There is good news, though, despite the bleak picture. God is a God of restoration. He made your body in such a wonderful way that it is ceaselessly trying to make and keep you well. Your body is making billions of new cells right now. There is hope for every situation. Cleansing your body of impurities and renewing your body from within is simple, and it is wonder-working. The purpose is to rid your body of the cause of disease before it makes you sick. It is totally doable, and you can start right where you are today.

There is a cleansing process going on inside your body every second of your life. Your body was designed by God to eliminate toxins, but over time these chemicals can build up in your system and overwhelm your ability to remove them. Or you yourself might be overpowering your system by the amount of toxins you are taking in physically, emotionally, or spiritually. Some drugs and many pesticides produce immediate, dramatic toxic symptoms. Others take a long time to develop into a manifest disease, such as asbestos exposure that invisibly leads to lung cancer. It is no surprise that toxicity diseases such as cardiovascular disease and cancer have increased as our world has become more toxic. Many skin problems, allergies, arthritis, and obesity are others. In addition, a wide range of less frightening symptoms, such as headaches, fatigue, pains, coughs, constipation, gastrointestinal problems, and problems from immune weakness, can all be related to toxicity.

CLEANSING YOUR TOTAL SYSTEM

You were given five central systems that work together moment by moment to eliminate toxins. It is your responsibility to maintain their health. These systems include the *respiratory*—lungs, bronchial tubes, throat, sinuses, and nose; *gastrointestinal*—liver, gallbladder, colon, and whole GI tract; *urinary*—kidneys, bladder, and urethra; *skin and dermal*—sweat and sebaceous glands and tears; and *lymphatic*—lymph channels and lymph nodes.

The liver filters out foreign substances and wastes from the blood, metabolically altering the toxins and making them easier for the organs to eliminate and less harmful to the body. It also dumps wastes through the bile into the intestines, where much waste is eliminated. The kidneys filter wastes from the blood into the urine, while the lungs remove volatile gases as we breathe. We also clear heavy metals through sweating. Our sinuses and skin may also be accessory elimination organs whereby excess mucus or toxins can be released, as with sinus congestion or skin rashes.

A cleansing program is designed to safely and gently enhance your body's own natural processes. It can be done at several levels. Anything that promotes elimination can be said to help us detoxify. Drinking more water will usually help you eliminate more toxins.

Eating more cleansing foods, such as fruits and vegetables, and less meat and dairy products creates less congestion and more elimination. Some programs are directed toward specific organs, such as the liver or kidneys or skin. The secret to great health is to combine these cleansing programs into a lifestyle program that works for you.

Is it possible to go overboard? Certainly. Some people go to extremes with fasting, laxatives, enemas, colonics, diuretics, and exercise, and begin to lose essential nutrients from their body. Some people push it to the point where they experience dangerous protein or vitamin-mineral deficiencies, even becoming paranoid to the extent of bondage! But the vast percentage of our health concerns result from the opposite of going overboard.

It is proven that many common serious and chronic diseases may be diminished or eliminated by a program of cleansing. You will feel better when your system gets rid of the unchanged or partially changed toxins that cause negative symptoms. Your immune system will be strengthened in its relentless battle against infections, and you may also reduce the risk of developing cancer. Many of the poisons (toxins) that we take in or make are stored in the fatty tissues. Obesity is almost always associated with toxicity. When we lose weight, we reduce our fat and thereby our toxic load.

Fasting is the most effective and practical and quickest way to cleanse your system, which my husband, Jim, will discuss in Chapter 18. When you read Jim's experience, you'll see why fasting is so fundamental to good health. Yet I recognize that it is a more extreme form.

CLEANSING STARTS HERE

Step #1—start eating and drinking right. If you cut your toxic intake, you cut your need for cleansing. If you don't correct a bad diet and the quality and amount of water you're taking in, you drastically reduce the effectiveness of any other cleansing methods you use. That is nothing more than common sense.

My preference is called the Levitical Diet which you can read about in Chapter 16 and the use of steam-distilled water as I detailed in Chapter 9. Following this diet will eliminate the foods that commonly trigger problems with digestion and elimination, and your body does not have a better detoxifying friend than water. Refined, processed, and junk foods are out for any cleansing program to work. Sugar is drastically cut because of its "empty calories" and tendency to produce hypoglycemia as well as feed cancer cells. Meats are cut back or eliminated because they may contain hormones, antibiotics, and require many enzymes for digestion.

Natural vegetarian diets are cleansing and bring the body several benefits. You get plenty of fiber to stimulate the bowels as well as generous amounts of vitamins to feed and nourish all the eliminative organs. They also include a valuable source of enzymes, since most vegetarian diets are eaten raw. However, even vegetarians can be very off balance due to a lack of good protein and essential salts.

CLEANSING *the* BOWELS

Cleansing the bowels consistently is a vital key to good health. When the bowels slow down, the bad news begins. First, there is an increase of bad bacteria in the small intestine and putrefaction in the large intestine. The battle ensues when the bad bacteria weaken your immune system (which is located in the small intestine) and can result in digestive complications. When only partly digested proteins and bacterial toxins cross the intestinal wall, they can cause allergies.

Untreated, the walls of the bowels become weak and deformed, as with diverticulitis, and hard crusts cover the intestinal walls and restrict movement within the bowels. In severe cases, the products of putrefaction cross the weakened walls of the large intestine and enter the bloodstream. The whole body may become poisoned, and it is possible to seriously damage your body. Enemas and colonics may be needed to break up and cleanse the bowel encrustation.

Reabsorbed toxins are carried back to the liver for recycling and elimination, causing stress to the liver, which then produces extra bile salts that are linked to increased cholesterol levels. Also, when the bowels constipate and toxin levels increase, the bad bacteria grow to outnumber the normal flora and cause dysbiosis. Every part of your nervous system may be affected, and sometimes the heart or brain takes the brunt of the damage.

Niacin (100 mg per day) cleanses the skin from within and lowers bad cholesterol.

The easiest way to correct these intestinal problems is a diet of predominately raw foods. A high-quality fiber diet of fresh fruits and vegetables gets the bowels moving and strengthens the bowel walls. You may want to add extra fiber by drinking a glass of water (juice) with psyllium husk powder or 1/2 cup of oat bran daily to speed up the process. But it's unwise to become dependent on herbal laxatives. There is no substitute for an excellent fibrous diet to cleanse the bowels as well as bring down bad cholesterol naturally.

CLEANSING the SKIN

The skin is the largest organ and one of our best eliminative organs of our body. Skin cleansing is therefore a vital part of the cleansing process, particularly when it comes to the heavy metals (aluminum and mercury) that are eliminated through the skin's pores when we sweat. Consistent exercise, steam rooms, and sauna baths are excellent ways to remove toxins from the skin and maximize your health.

Basic skin care is a daily matter, beginning with using natural soaps when you bathe. Skin care products made from chemicals may be cheaper, but remember that those chemicals will be absorbed into the bloodstream. Though the amount may be small, it is the cumulative effect of the chemicals that damages your health over the long run. If your body has a toxicity problem, you will notice the difference when you move to natural products on your body. Especially stay away from the ingredient sodium laurel sulfate—a known carcinogen.

Dry skin brushing is easy to do and helps in removing the outer dead skin layers and keeps the pores open. You will need to buy a natural bristle brush or bath mitt and expect to spend five minutes for brushing your skin. Use light pressure and a circular motion, then shower and moisturize your skin. Another good technique for cleansing the skin is to towel off roughly until the skin gets slightly red. It will only take you a few minutes more than usual.

Food grade hydrogen peroxide baths are excellent for energy and cleansing. Epsom salts baths are also very good. For each bath you will need between 8 to 16 ounces of Epsom salts and 3 ounces of sea salt. Run comfortable warm water and add the salts and dissolve them. Soak for 10 to 20 minutes and then scrub the skin gently with soap on a natural fiber. Within a few minutes the water will turn murky. The darkness to the water is because of heavy metals coming out of the skin. Get out of the bath carefully, as you may feel light-headed. Then wrap yourself in several towels (you may sweat heavily afterward) and go to bed. Make sure you have water at your bedside because you will be thirsty. Do this once a week during a cleansing program, but once a month is sufficient normally.

Niacin (100 mg per day) cleanses the skin from within and lowers bad cholesterol.

Good skin care also requires good nutrition and an abundance of water. Since your skin is mainly fat, you need high-quality fats and oils from natural sources to keep your skin healthy. Olive oil is an excellent source as well as evening primrose and vitamin E, and combinations of essential fatty acids.

CLEANSING *the* DIGESTIVE TRACT

A key to improving our digestive functions, the immune system, and overall health is the constant restoration of healthy intestinal flora ("friendly" bacteria). It is such an important part of the cleansing process that I devoted an entire chapter on *"Candida Albicans"* in my book, *How to Feel Great All the Time*. I go into detail on the essential role of the normal flora of our gastrointestinal track to defend our body from the pathogenic species of bacteria and to perform many vital functions, one of which is rid the system of toxic chemicals. When our normal flora are present, they secrete mediators in which the pathogenic forms cannot grow.

However, antibiotics kill off the good bacteria as well as the bad and allow the bad to repopulate and develop antibiotic resistance. Natural forms of antibiotics are better, since they do not kill off the good bacteria with the bad and do not allow drug resistance to take place. Fresh, raw garlic, for example, has strong antimicrobial power and is more effective against pathogens than most antibiotics today. Herbal antiseptics and antibacterial tonics are far better and less dangerous to our health than antibiotics.

Replacing our natural flora is a good step for preventing disease and keeping our bowels healthy. Eat fresh and raw vegetables, which will help to restore the normal intestinal flora in your body. Eat yogurt (no aspartame) daily, as much as possible, with live active cultures that are documented on the label. Natren Probiotics, daily, creates a good terrain for aerobic bacteria (good bacteria) to live and thrive in.

HERBAL CLEANSING

Herbs have been used medicinally for centuries to supplement the cleansing of the blood and tissues or strengthening the function of specific organs. Many herbs have been proven as powerful neutraceutical agents that can support or even cause detoxification. There are hundreds of possible medicinal herbs, and they also provide vitamins, minerals, and enzymes for excellent nutrition. I have a short course on herbs (Chapter 7) that will help direct you in this area. It includes a list of essential medicinal herbs and specific concerns about herbs.

Herbal teas are an easy way to start to enhance your health throughout the day. They are a delicious substitute to break the coffee habit and a potent source of health modulators.

Many people utilize herbal cleanses. For example, first thing in the morning they may drink a glass of steam-distilled water with a teaspoon of blackstrap molasses and a teaspoon of apple cider vinegar added. During the morning they drink a glass of water with psyllium husk powder, which they follow with a second glass of water. During their meals they take digestive enzymes. Between meals they may take liver herbs and drink herbal teas that specifically help support the liver.

CLEANSING OUT FREE RADICALS

See my short course on antioxidants (Chapter 8) to see how essential they are to any internal cleansing program. In the process of metabolism or oxidation, our body cells produce molecules called free radicals. They are unstable molecules that attempt to steal electrons from any available source, such as our body tissues. Antioxidants work to neutralize these unstable chemicals and protect us from the destructive effects. The more antioxidants we get in our diets, the more we are able to stop the damage.

ENZYMES *and* CLEANSING

Enzymes have a major impact on your health and cleansing. They help digest and absorb proteins, carbohydrates or starches, lipids or fats. Absorption is absolutely crucial to your health. They also clean up dead tissues, enhance your own enzyme capacity, and help the bowels in cleansing, because they liquefy the bowel content and make for a quicker passage. The quicker the toxins are out of your system, the better your health!

The liver is the source of most cleansing enzymes, which it either makes or stores. To aid the liver in removing and eliminating wastes and toxins, enzymes are best taken with meals. This way they aid in digestion.

An excellent way to stimulate the liver to detoxify itself is with coffee enemas. We refer to this as a "Liver Cleanse." They are not for the function of cleansing the intestines. This enema is most often used in metabolic cancer therapy and is extremely valuable in many successful cleansing programs. See Appendix A for more on the coffee enema.

CLEANSING OUT MERCURY TOXICITY

The dangers of mercury toxicity related to dental fillings are well documented, and the fact is that silver-mercury amalgam comprises about 50 percent of the most common filling in the world. This amalgam also contains copper, tin, silver, and zinc. There are many factors that can increase the release of mercury emissions into your system, but the fact that mercury is released at all is scary. Many experts feel that the amount of mercury released is adequate to contribute significantly to disease processes.

Where does all the mercury go? Into your body. Absorption of mercury occurs the fastest from the area under your tongue and the insides of your cheeks. Being in such close proximity to the fillings, the efficiency of absorption is great. From these tissues, the mercury can destroy adjacent tissues or travel to the lymphatic drainage system and directly into the bloodstream. From the bloodstream, mercury can travel to any cell in the body, where it can either disable or destroy the tissues. Mercury can also travel directly from the fillings into the lungs, where it then enters into the bloodstream, and every cell in the body becomes a potential target.

The ability of mercury to travel throughout the body and its accompanying destruction are what define mercury toxicity. It may favor nerve tissue for a destruction target, but the kidney is high up on its hit list. After these two areas, it can wreak havoc in any tissue that gets in its way. It can alter almost anything in the body; therefore, mercury should not be allowed to enter for any reason.

This is especially problematic if someone has a tooth or teeth that have leached a significant amount of mercury into the body. A cleansing program will not help to any great extent until the mercury is taken out. Another aid would be EDTA Chelation whether by suppository or IV.

THE HEALING CRISIS

Even during mild cleansing programs, it is possible for your body to detoxify too rapidly and have toxins released faster than the body can eliminate them. When this occurs, you may suffer from headaches, nausea, vomiting, depression, and even old aches and pains you forgot you had! This is a good thing! It means your body is working. If this occurs, back off the program and proceed at a slower pace. Forcing a cleansing process too quickly can have negative results.

According to naturopathic theory, any symptoms of the disease that have previously been experienced may also be experienced transiently during cleansing. However, sometimes it's difficult to know what is going on inside. Should you treat the problems that come up or simply watch them? Since my basic approach is to allow the body to heal itself and support the natural healing process whenever possible, that is what I try to do unless it becomes intolerable.

For many of us, especially the new or inexperienced, it is wise to begin any special program, diet, or lifestyle changes with a few days at home or possibly over a weekend. In time, experience will tell you what is best. Most of us can maintain a regular work schedule during a cleanse (you'll probably feel great), but it may be easier to begin a program on a Friday, as the first few days are usually the most challenging.

14

GETTING *the* BUGS OUT

WHENEVER I TALK ABOUT PARASITES, THE FIRST REACTION I GET IS: "THIS CANNOT BE TRUE INSIDE OF ME!" I wish I could agree, but the statistics are not in their favor, and my professional experience points dramatically in the opposite direction. Many outstanding doctors in the United States believe that 80 to 90 percent of the American public has parasites. Millions of people are suffering needlessly from chronic diseases that are primarily caused by parasites.

It is a lot easier to become a parasitic host than you think. Just because we don't live in a Third World country and our sanitation methods are advanced has not stopped parasites from being a formidable though often hidden problem. Dr. Frank Nova, Chief of the Laboratory for Parasitic Disease of the prestigious National Institute of Health said, "In terms of numbers, there are more parasitic infections acquired in this country than Africa."

Parasitic experts estimate that there are between 100 to 130 common parasites being hosted in the American populace today. They vary from a microscopic amoeba that destroys the lining of the intestines of human beings and produces the painful disease called amoebic dysentery to several feet-long tapeworms that are the stuff of our most horrific nightmares. Just the thought of looking down into the toilet and seeing a mass of pinworms that have been passed puts most of us straight into denial.

A parasite is an organism that feeds and lives on another organism. A host is any animal that harbors a parasite. Parasites look for suitable habitat where they can thrive inside us, and most of the time they remain there uncontested. Some parasites not only live in us but also reproduce offspring that live in us, creating the potential for a serious parasitic infestation. There is no part of a human's body that is immune to parasites—not your organs, muscles, blood, brain, or lungs.

Anne Louis Gittleman is a nutritionist and international lecturer who has written the book, *Guess What Came to Dinner? Parasites and Your Health*. She has this to say: "You may be the unsuspecting victim of the parasite epidemic that is affecting millions of Americans. It is an epidemic that knows no territorial, economic, or sexual boundaries. It is a silent epidemic of which most doctors in this country are not even aware."

One would think that in a country where 50 to 55 million children are estimated to be hosts to some type of worms, regular screening for parasites would be a part of every medical checkup. But few health-care providers are taught to suspect, diagnose, or treat parasitic infections. If, for instance, you are suffering from diarrhea or fever and you go to your doctor, it is highly probable that he or she will treat the symptoms without even checking into a possible parasitic cause. And if a parasite is suspected, many of the test procedures for parasites are extremely inaccurate. If a parasite is found, an imprecise treatment may only cause the parasite to move to another spot, or it may kill that specific parasite while leaving others behind that were not detected. In the case to the tapeworm, if your treatment only expels the body and not the head, the whole worm will grow back—not what you want to hear.

Dr. Ross Anderson says, "I believe the single most undiagnosed health challenge in the history of the human race is parasites."

NOT *a* BELIEVER YET?

In the spring of 1993, the National Institute of Allergy and Infectious Disease reported 100 deaths and more than 400,000 people having fallen ill from the parasite *cryptosporidium*, a protozoan (a one-celled organism) that had infected the city of Milwaukee's water system. In October 1994, NBC's *Dateline* reported *cryptosporidium* as the cause of deaths and illnesses in New York City.

That was followed in September 1998 by the same parasite causing widespread water contamination in Sydney, Australia.

If you were in the Pacific Northwest in 1993, you will recall the deeply feared E. *coli* bacteria outbreak in which 477 people were infected and two children died from contaminated, undercooked hamburger. Many additional E. *coli* bacteria outbreaks have occurred in the United States, and some of them from non-beef sources, including lettuce and salad bars where foods were contaminated by improperly cleaned utensils, working surfaces, and infected food handlers. In addition, outbreaks have occurred in people who have consumed garden vegetables fertilized with animal manure, unpasteurized apple cider, and homemade venison jerky.

While some parasites are thought to cause little or no harm to their host, many cause great harm. For example, the protozoans that cause malaria are parasites that invade and destroy red blood cells and consequently take the lives of 3 million people worldwide every year. Some parasites are content to feed on the host's food supply while others go deeper and consume body tissues and cells, occasionally even burrowing through into the kidneys, muscles, corneas, and brain. A tapeworm can grow within us to a considerable size, and it's highly likely we will not be aware of it. Waste products from the parasites may be toxic and are released directly into the host's body. Infections from parasites wreak havoc in our immune systems.

WHAT *to* LOOK FOR

The symptoms caused by parasites will often mask themselves effectively beneath other ailments, and therefore often go undiagnosed. Many of the symptoms are subtle because they are experienced commonly by people without parasites. Thus, many doctors may correctly and consistently note their patients' fatigue, diarrhea, or irritability, but incorrectly attribute those symptoms automatically to wrong causes. For instance, a diagnosis of a peptic ulcer may rather be an infection from roundworms, or a case of giardiasis (an infection in the gut by water-borne microscopic protozoan *giardia*) may be misdiagnosed as chronic fatigue syndrome.

The following list, while by no means exhaustive, reflects some of the common symptoms of parasites. See if you can relate to any of these:

- Allergies
- Anemia
- Apathy
- Asthma
- Bedwetting
- Bloating
- Blood in stools
- Blurry or unclear vision
- Chronic fatigue
- Constipation
- Depression
- Diabetes
- Diarrhea
- Dizziness
- Eating more than usual but still being hungry
- Excess weight
- Fatty tumors, especially on feet
- Fevers
- Forgetfulness and mental slowness
- Gas
- Immune dysfunction
- Intestinal obstruction
- Irritability and nervousness
- Irritable bowel syndrome
- Itchy ears
- Itchy nose
- Itchy anus
- Lethargy
- Lips dry during the day and moist at night
- Nervousness
- Nutrient deficiencies, especially Vitamin B12 and folic acid
- Pain or aches in the back, joints, or muscles
- Problems with menstruation
- Sensitivity to touch
- Sexual dysfunction in men
- Sleep disorders
- Swollen glands
- Teeth clinching
- Teeth grinding
- Toxicity
- Unpleasant sensations in the stomach
- Various skin problems

As noted previously, parasites are not necessarily the cause of any of these symptoms, but they should not be dismissed. Perhaps what you're experiencing is just a case of poison ivy, but if the signs appear on a regular basis and the itching isn't somehow connected to a walk in the woods, you should pay attention to the signs. Unfortunately, parasitic causes are almost never even considered. Remember, 80 to 90 percent of us have parasites and don't know it, so perhaps the best thing to do is go with the numbers, act as if you do, and make the decision to do something about it.

I recommend that you keep a journal of your symptoms, and particularly note symptoms that persist over time. It is vital to note any treatments you have received for a diagnosed problem that were not effective. This information could prove invaluable when you talk with your physician or naturopath. If you remove the cause, the symptoms will cease, and vice versa.

SOURCES

Because the range of parasites is so extensive, the range of sources is equally extensive. There is no way to avoid all contact with parasites, but there are common sources that you should be aware of.

Animals, particularly wild animals and farm animals, carry parasites. Small children tend to be especially exposed to parasitic contamination, including roundworms, through contact with animal feces in their yards or play areas. But pets also pose a formidable problem. Think of the multiplied millions of dogs and cats that are played with, slept with, and allowed to lick faces and snuggle, and then consider the potential parasitic roundworms and hookworms they carry, or the toxoplasmosis transmitted to humans by cats. While the routine deworming of pets is absolutely vital, that does not make your pet parasite-proof—reinfections can and do occur.

Fruits and vegetables. Whether it is contamination at the growing site or at the handling stage, most of us are aware that fruits and vegetables can carry a host of parasites. Billions upon billions of tons of food are imported every year, and some of those fruits and vegetables have been fertilized with human feces. For instance, contaminated raspberries imported from Guatemala caused almost 1,000 laboratory-confirmed cases of the *cyclospora* parasite to be reported to the Centers for Disease Control and Prevention (CDC) between May 1 and mid July 1996. But we're foolish to think similar contaminations are not happening in the fruits and vegetables grown and marketed locally. It happens all the time.

And while parasites are by no means limited to immigrant workers, the huge influx of immigrants who come from parasite-infected areas of the world and find jobs in the food service industry has increased the risk of parasite transmission exponentially. Add to that the fact that sanitation conditions in some food service facilities are abysmal, and it's no secret that we should avoid eating raw fruits and vegetables that have not been thoroughly cleansed. Soak your fruits and vegetables in a dilution of food grade peroxide available at your health food store or from Silver Creek Labs.

Meats. Anyone who thinks that our supplies of beef, chicken, pork, and seafood are parasite-free is living on another planet. Despite the best efforts of the FDA to safeguard our food supplies, it is very possible that undercooked pork, fish, and beef carry tapeworms that will infect you if you partake of them. Raw meats and raw fish, however delicious and appealing, are a wide open door to the transmission of parasitic larvae from worms. Be aware that wherever undercooking takes place within meat of every kind, the potential for transmission of parasites increases.

Infected drinking water. I've already noted the outbreaks related to *cryptosporidium*, a water-borne parasite, which are not unusual, even within the United States. *Giardia lamblia* is another parasite that has found its way into American water supplies and is not killed by chlorination. Wherever you have water systems that are exposed to infected human sewage or polluted watersheds, such as in rural America, you bring in the element of parasites. And the reality is that swimming pools, lakes, and rivers are easily contaminated. The next time you inadvertently gulp down a mouthful of water while swimming, realize that no matter how clear and pure it appears, it may be contaminated and primed to infect your system.

Day-care centers. If a child in a day-care facility has become infected with a parasite, it is an ideal environment for being passed along from one child to the next as well as to the day-care staff. For instance, giardiasis (a parasitic infection of the gut by the single-cell protozoan giardia) is spread through direct contact with infected feces, and changing diapers facilitates the transfer.

Overseas travel. The more you travel internationally, especially to Third World nations, and the more remote your destinations, the more you have the chance of encountering malaria or blood flukes or other serious parasitic infections.

Basic hygiene. When it comes to parasites, one cannot stress enough the importance of washing your hands after touching and handling anything that might be contaminated—whether you've changed a diaper, gone to the bathroom, or handled food, especially raw meat or fish. And make certain that the toilet seat is clean before you sit on it; and if you can't do that, then squat over the toilet and don't touch it. Pinworm eggs from infected people may be on the seat, although you can't see them.

Sexual practices. Connected to basic hygiene, there is no question that today's careless attitudes of multiple sexual partners and practices have increased the transmission of parasites. The more that nonstandard contact is practiced, the proportional increase in infections that are spread to the hands, mouth, and body through fecal contamination. Anyone who believes that the use of a condom or a latex barrier in any type of sexual contact means complete protection is foolish.

SPECIFIC PARASITES

I recommend that you get a copy of my book, *Every Body Has Parasites*, to gain a comprehensive understanding of the major parasites that you are facing and may be hosting. In my book I detail several species within the various classes of roundworms, tapeworms, flukes, and protozoans, and I also cover another subtle parasite that has a major impact on millions of people, Candida. To treat them with any detail here is beyond the scope of this book.

CLEASING OUT PARASITES

Cleansing your bowels is a key part in this process of the elimination of parasites. The intestines provide parasites with an abundance of food and very little interference to their activities. The

Royal Academy of Physicians of Great Britain states that "90 percent of all disease and discomfort is directly or indirectly related to an unclean colon (due to impacted fecal matter)."

Regular elimination during a parasite cleanse is vital. A cleanse that does not include ingredients that will help establish a regular pattern of three or more bowel movements a day should be reconsidered. If you are one of those people who wonders how many times a day your bowels should move, you need only think of a newborn baby. With each feeding, the baby's bowels will generally move. Adults, too, should be that regular.

If you are not that regular, you must take action involving the elimination process. It is imperative that if you are going to go through the parasite cleanse that it include a product that will gently guide you back into a regular cycle of waste elimination. We tell everyone who uses our ParaCease cleanse that we hope they will have three movements a day, on their own, after 90 days on the program.

So where can we enlist the best defensive force in this war on parasites? First, the parasite cleansing product needs to be superior. It should include natural ingredients that assist your colon's natural movement. If not, it's going to be up to you to investigate and find a natural product that will accomplish this goal. It takes time and must be proven effective for long-term results.

DIGESTIVE ENZYMES *and* PROBIOTICS

During a cleanse you should take digestive enzymes to dissolve the protective shell that surrounds some parasitic cysts. And whenever you have completed an intestinal cleanse, always follow it with a good probiotic, and do it daily. It creates a good terrain for aerobic bacteria (good bacteria) to live and thrive in and is a first line of defense against any intruders.

FOODS *to* HELP DEFEAT *the* BUGS

- Consider the ParaCease program that's described in the Silver Creek Labs in the back of the book. It comes with a dietary program.

- Use apple cider vinegar with each meal.
- Almond oil
- Increase protein intake
- Cranberries and cranberry juice
- Garlic
- Pomegranates
- Pumpkin seeds
- Drink only distilled water

AVOID THESE IF YOU THINK YOU HAVE PARASITES

- White potatoes
- Egg plant
- Tomatoes
- Red peppers
- High carbohydrate diets can make parasitic infections worse, so limit the carbs, and that includes breads.
- Be careful with the purity of your flour. If you knew the bugs and other stuff that makes their way into the flour you use, you would inspect it carefully.
- No matter what, always avoid water that may be infected. This includes tap water, well water, spring water, mountain water, etc. Remember, if you order drinks in a restaurant, the coffee, tea, and soft drinks probably are made using tap water and may contain these unwanted elements.
- Never eat raw or undercooked beef, pork, chicken, or fish. Shrimp alone can contain 60 types of parasites.
- Unwashed fruits or vegetables
- Water chestnuts and watercress

THREE POWER BOOSTERS *to* YOUR IMMUNE SYSTEM

A weakened immune system is an open door that parasites are quick to pass through. The best security system that one can employ is to strengthen one's internal defenses to them. The Levitical Diet described in this book will go a long way to helping you restore your immune system to health as well as maintain it. Foods rich in vitamins and minerals and proteins and fiber give you more than a fighting chance against parasites.

But it is also possible for individuals to be deficient in single or multiple nutrients that need to be supplemented. You can indemnify the health of your immune system by the supplementation of vitamins and minerals and herbs that improve your immune function. I have three supplements in particular that I want to bring to your attention as true power boosters to your immune system.

THYMIC FORMULA

The thymus gland plays an instrumental role in the immune system of our body. The thymus aids in the development of white blood cells called lymphocytes, which help the body fight diseases. Lymphocytes travel to the thymus, where they are changed into T cells by a substance produced by the thymus that is called thymosin. Those T cells leave the thymus and inhabit the blood, lymph nodes, and spleen. From there they attack bacteria, cancer cells, fungi, viruses, and other harmful organisms.

God placed the thymus within us to defend against all these problems. But many of us are in such poor shape that there's not even a guard at the door of our immune system to hinder invaders, whether it's parasites or hepatitis B, hepatitis C, rheumatoid arthritis, psoriasis, multiple sclerosis, or systemic lupus.

Through years of experimentation and analysis, Dr. Carson Burgstiner came up with a specific combination of nutrients, including extract of thymic glandular tissues, that appeared to stimulate his patients' malfunctioning immune systems and reverse even supposedly incurable conditions. Independent laboratory tests prove that his thymic protocol created marked increases (up to 700 percent) in immune-system activity, as measured by the levels of thymic hormones in the blood.

Dr. Burgstiner felt that his thymic formula produced an immune-regulating effect. That is, in hyper-immune conditions, such as rheumatoid arthritis and multiple sclerosis, it would turn the overactive immune response down. In hypo-immune conditions, such as cancer, it would turn the immune response up. His patients reported that, in general, they experienced a significant improvement of a functional immune system within 30 days. Naomi Judd was a patient of Dr. Burgstiner, used this formula, and is now free from hepatitis C.

LACTOFERRIN

Lactoferrin is a type of cytokine—an immune chemical that helps coordinate the body's cellular immune response, defending against invaders such as bacteria and viruses that some parasitologists also classify as parasites. In particular, it functions as a type of border guard and shield against infection. This potent, natural immune booster has been reported to hinder tumor growth and metastasis, and protect the immunologically vulnerable from deadly viruses and bacterial infections. In healthy individuals, it can mean near-total immunity from colds, influenza, microbial parasites, and infectious bacteria. Its healing powers appear to be unrivaled.

In a healthy individual, Lactoferrin is found in secretions such as tears, perspiration, the lining of the intestinal tract, and the mucous membranes that line the nose, ears, throat, and urinary tract—in short, any place that is especially vulnerable to infection. But by far the highest concentrations of Lactoferrin are found in a substance called colostrum (or "first milk"), produced by a new mother in the first few hours after she gives birth. For the newborn, Lactoferrin provides crucial immune-system stimulation, helping the new baby to survive in its new germ-laden environment outside the womb.

Recently, scientists have discovered that using Lactoferrin in the form of a nutritional supplement can significantly boost the immune system and greatly enhance the body's ability to withstand and recover from infection and other illness. Many Lactoferrin supplements are produced using bovine colostrums from cows that have not been fed antibiotics or hormones. Research has documented a long list of remarkable benefits, especially against retroviruses and malignancies.

Lactoferrin supplementation may be your key to developing an immune system that is strong enough to knock the bugs out before they take hold in your body. Lactoferrin increases both the number and the activity of at least a half-dozen different types of specific immune cells that help your body fight infection. The most distinguishing characteristic of Lactoferrin is its ability to bind to iron in the blood, denying tumor cells, bacteria, and viruses the iron they need to survive and multiply.

OLIVE LEAF

You may not believe it now, but infectious "smart bugs" are going to be the No. 1 threat to your health. Back in the golden age of antibiotics, doctors could destroy these disease-causing bugs with powerful drugs. But today, as fast as we create new antibiotics in our laboratories, deadly bacteria are developing resistance to the potent but limited drugs. There is one way, however, to stop these super-bugs. We can outsmart them, using the tremendous protective power of nature.

Nature's most promising antibiotic, antiviral, and antifungal agent is a compound derived from the olive leaf, called calcium elenolate. This plant extract not only helps your body battle the dangerous bugs that cause infectious disease, but also cleanses your entire system, enhances your energy, improves your circulation, activates key components of your immune system, and has beneficial effects on cholesterol and blood-sugar levels.

Treatments made from the olive-leaf extract have been around for at least 150 years, with records dating back to 1827, when it was used as a treatment for malaria, which is a parasite. In 1906, the olive-leaf extract was reportedly far superior to quinine for the treatment of malaria, but quinine, because it was easier to administer, became the treatment of choice. From 1970 to the present, a hydrolyzed form of oleuropein has been tested and found effective against dozens of different viruses and many strains of bacteria.

Now in capsule form, olive-leaf extract is making a comeback. Because it is a natural substance, olive-leaf extract has a much wider range of actions than man-made antibiotics. It contains a maze of chemicals harmless to us that lie in wait for invading bacteria. It directly stimulates phagocytosis—your immune system's ability to "eat" foreign microorganisms that don't belong in your body.

God's creation has provided germ killers far more potent than any that laboratory scientists can invent. The olive-leaf extract is one of these germ killers.

Thymic Formula, Lactoferrin, and Olive Leaf are all available from Silver Creek Labs.

15

DIET FACTS, FADS, *and* FALLACIES

POPULAR WEIGHT-LOSS APPROACHES ABOUND TO THE TUNE OF AN ESTIMATED $40-BILLION-A-YEAR INDUSTRY. And with the hundreds of diets backed by slick advertising campaigns bursting with remarkable life-transforming testimonies and spectacular promises to those who will follow, doesn't it seem as remarkable that the problem of overweight and obesity continues to climb? According to the U.S. Department of Agriculture, 70 percent of Americans are overweight or obese. Obviously, there's a growing problem that the multitudes of today's popular and fad diets aren't fixing.

I am frequently asked whether I think the South Beach diet is better than the Atkins' diet, or if I think the Beverly Hills diet is healthy, or whether I've ever tried the Grapefruit diet, or why the no-fat diet left them fatter than before they started. With so many diets to choose from, some that promise and deliver weight loss on steaks and fried bacon while others do the same on baskets laden with cabbages or high-fiber vegetarian plans, most people have no idea of what is best, let alone what is healthy for them. And, sadly, many of them get so frustrated trying to figure it out that they end up tossing in the towel and do nothing while their waistline continues to expand. Or they've tried one diet after another, with varying degrees of initial success, only to fail and end up gaining back whatever they had lost plus a few more pounds on top of it. As a last resort, the extremely obese get the famous gastric bypass surgery and lose one hundred pounds or more. And sadly, some lose their life.

All you have to watch is one diet infomercial or even a 30-second ad to understand the appeal of most popular diets—quick, effortless weight loss in exceedingly short windows of time. With 200 million overweight or obese adults in the U.S. desperate to find a fix for their problem (that's not counting the epidemic among today's children), just about any diet will find a market if it's given the right spin and a couple "before and after" photos. My point is not to argue whether that initial weight loss is possible, but whether the weight loss is long term or not and whether the person is left healthy. It's not a secret that for the vast majority who buy into most diets, the results are short-lived.

Sifting through the hundreds or even thousands of diets that I've heard or read about, I've given up on attempting to analyze the intricacies of diets. Rather, I've found it far simpler to look for a pattern or a category that the particular diet fits into and view it from a more comprehensive perspective. Many of these supposed new diets have in fact been around for years with various alterations, and when you boil them down, there are patterns that makes them fairly easy to understand.

But before we look at the patterns, let me explain why you shouldn't get too excited by the testimonials you hear.

THE SECRET IS SIMPLE: LOW CALORIE INTAKE

Here's a scenario you may find yourself in. One of your friends has been on a high-protein/high-fat, low-carbohydrate diet for several months and is thrilled to have shed 30 pounds and dropped several dress sizes. Another friend was persuaded to try a high-carbohydrate, low-fat vegetarian diet and is equally thrilled to have lost the same amount of weight and is feeling great. How do you explain that such differing approaches could work equally well?

Without exploring whether one approach is healthier than another, you need to understand that when it comes to simple weight loss, it's not about the nutrients being offered by a diet plan. It's about the calories you're consuming. Nothing changes the fact that if you are burning more calories every day than you are taking in, you should lose weight. And vice versa. That's the bottom line, whether the calories come from protein or fat or carbohydrates.

While one marketer tells you that their diet plan works because you have eliminated sugars and refined carbohydrates, and another marketer points to the reduced carbohydrates and the increased proteins as the success of their diet, the reality is that through following their plan you have reduced your calorie intake and not even noticed. Don't get caught up in the spin. For instance, if you follow the Atkins' diet, you'll take in between 1,200 and 1,800 calories a day, or if you prepare the Sugar Busters menus, you'll consume around 1,200 calories a day—which will result in the loss of weight.

Another factor to consider is that often the weight that is being lost is not necessarily fat. The scale may be going down, but those increments may only represent water and muscle that's being shed. While this is most often true of crash diets, it is a part of most popular diets as well. Without the establishment of a balance of the proper nutrition and exercise, a diet can be far more detrimental in the long term than any temporary celebration through a change in wardrobes.

HOW *to* RECOGNIZE *a* FAD DIET

While there is no absolute definition of a fad diet, the American Heart Institute offers the following list of characteristics that you should be aware of:

Magic or miracle foods that burn fat. Foods don't burn fat. Your body converts calories—units of food energy—from food into fat when you take in more calories than your body needs to burn. Fat is burned by increasing your physical activities or by decreasing the amount of calories consumed.

Bizarre quantities of only one food or type of food, such as eating only tomatoes or beef one day or unlimited bowls of cabbage soup or grapefruit. These foods are fine as part of an overall healthy diet, but to eat large quantities of them could lead to unpleasant side effects, such as intestinal gas, bloating, flatulence, and bad breath, as well as nutritional imbalances that could have a serious impact on your health.

Rigid menus. Many diets set out a very limited selection of foods to be eaten at specific times. Frequently, these limited diets don't address the widely varied taste preferences of our diverse American population.

Specific food combinations. Although some foods taste good together, there is no scientific evidence that eating foods in certain sequences or combinations has any scientific or medical benefit.

Rapid weight loss of more than two pounds a week.

No warning for people with either diabetes or high blood pressure to seek advice from the physician or health-care provider. Some fad diets could raise blood pressure or blood glucose, even if you lose weight. Diets high in fat can lead to heart disease and cancer. In addition, high-protein diets can worsen kidney or liver function in people with moderately advanced liver or kidney disease. Some of the high-fat, high-protein diets wreak havoc on the gallbladder.

No increased physical activity. Simple physical activities, such as walking or riding a bike, are one of the most important tools to losing and maintaining weight loss. Yet many fad diets don't emphasize these easy changes. Any increase in physical activity will help you burn more calories.

BASIC CATEGORIES *of* DIETS

Leslie J. Bonci, M.P.H., R.D., is director of the Sports Nutrition Program at the University of Pittsburgh Medical Center and the author of *The ADA Guide to Better Digestion*. She explains that the majority of popular diets fall into four basic categories that I found extremely helpful. My comments are meant to be general as regards the category rather than specific to a particular diet.

HIGH-PROTEIN/FAT, LOW-CARBOHYDRATE DIETS

The Atkins', South Beach, Protein Power, and the Carbohydrate Addict's diets are some of the more popular ones. Based upon the notion that we are carbohydrate crazy and carbohydrates make you fat, these diets restrict fruits, vegetables, and whole grains while putting a major emphasis on foods with high protein and high saturated fat. While these diets represent varying degrees toward being balanced and can show at least short-term weight loss, the lack of important vitamins and minerals and fiber found in carbohydrates has the potential for long-term health problems. The American Dietetic Association states that the body need about 150 grams of carbohydrates a day to maintain its health. There are also concerns about whether it promotes heart disease (high fat damages arteries), stroke, and cancer. People with kidney or liver problems have the potential for troubles with these diets, because high protein, especially animal protein, causes the organs to work hard to remove the waste products of protein metabolism.

HIGH CARBOHYDRATE, MODERATE PROTEIN/LOW-FAT DIETS

Dr. Dean Ornish's Eat More, Weigh Less diet, the F-Plan, and Pritikin diet are among the noted ones. Based upon the premise that calories from fat cause one to become fat, these diets push down the fat (10 to 15 percent of the total calories) and up the consumption of foods with high fiber, vitamins, and minerals—grains, fruits, and vegetables. While these diets tend to be favored as healthy by the medical community for their low-fat content, the vegetarian slant make these diets less appealing to those reared on an Western diet, and many people won't stick with it for the long term. Studies by the National Weight Control Registry indicate that the majority of people who lose weight and keep it off ate a diet comprised of 55 percent carbohydrates, 20 percent protein, and 25 percent fat. Don't forget that dietary fat (good fat) is also essential for the transportation of vitamins as well as the simple pleasure of eating.

FOOD COMBINATIONS

Among the more popular are The Zone, Sugar Busters, Eat Right for Your Blood Type, Fit for Life, and Suzanne Somers's Get Skinny diets. While these diets vary on many levels, there is a commonality of eliminating certain foods from your diet while combining others to accelerate calorie and fat burning. However, there is no scientific evidence that eating foods in certain sequences or combinations has any scientific or medical benefit. And whenever there is a heavy restriction on a category of food (Sugar Busters emphasizes sugar as "toxic"), it leads to imbalance and won't work for the long term because it is not the real way we eat. The Zone regards food as a medicine prescription and takes the pleasure out of eating by making you concentrate on food all day long. And look out for diets that simply have no scientific research to support them.

GIMMICKS

The Cabbage Soup Diet, The Grapefruit Diet, Beverly Hills Diet, and the 5-Day Miracle Diet are based on the "fat-burning" potential of certain foods. Again, while these vary significantly in approach, the commonality is rapid weight loss. And though the "fat-burning" aspect gets the attention, the reality is that the plans restrict dieters to such low calories that they border on being unsafe. The dramatic weight loss tends to be water and lean body tissue, which means that a weight rebound is inevitable and maintenance of the weight loss is nearly impossible.

FAD DIETS VERSUS *the* ONE PERFECT DIET

So where do you turn? I highly recommend that you turn to the One Perfect Diet that God gave the Jewish people after they were brought out of bondage in Egypt. Why not learn to eat the way God set forth in the Old Testament? It only makes sense that God gave them a specific dietary plan that provided them with everything they needed to keep themselves in vibrant health. It's a plan that has worked for thousands of years, so why not start on your way to success today?

While I will not go into great detail on how much you should eat every day or specific combinations of foods, realize that the secret to this Levitical diet is first of all in the quality of the foods and in keeping your diet balanced. My favorite diet is about 70 percent fruits, vegetables, nuts, and grains; 25 percent cold-water fish and hormone-free chicken; and about 3 to 5 percent hormone-free red meat. By knowing your body, you will know what you need. If you have any questions regarding your diet, consult a professional nutritionist, naturopath, or physician.

16

THE ONE PERFECT DIET

"*Fruit trees of all kinds will grow on both banks of the river. Their leaves will not wither, nor will their fruit fail. Every month they will bear, because the water from the sanctuary flows to them. Their fruit will serve for food and their leaves for healing.*"

—EZEKIEL 47:12

IT ONLY MAKES SENSE THAT GOD HAD A PLAN FOR HEALTHY EATING FROM THE VERY BEGINNING. After the Jewish nation was brought out of bondage in Egypt, God gave them a specific dietary plant for everything they needed, including what to eat to keep themselves in vibrant health and with a strong immunity system. Those who follow it walk in health, and those who don't are left to struggle with malnutrition, obesity, and disease. Need proof? Studies show that Israel is the healthiest nation on the earth, while the United States is ranked a dismal 96. That statistic alone should make you stop and take notice of what God has to say about your diet.

To fulfill the Word of God, the Jews observe the laws of Kashrut (keeping Kosher) as established in the Old Testament—an awesome testimony of faithfulness and obedience to God! So many times we think of the Old Testament as a lot of do's and don'ts, but we fail to realize that God never does anything without a purpose. Those do's and don'ts have meaning! Although we will probably never know all the intricacies of the full benefits from eating God's way, I want to explore a few.

Hosea 4:6 says, "My people are destroyed from lack of knowledge." That's where most people stop reading. Let's finish the verse, though! God says, "Because you have rejected knowledge, I also reject you. . .because you have ignored the law of your God." Does that mean you're not going to heaven if you do not follow the dietary laws of the Old Testament? No, of course, not. The early church made it clear that it was not a mandatory part of the Christian faith (Acts 15). But I do believe that when we disregard the wisdom that God has already provided, we lose—in this case, our health.

God's plan is that we be submitted to Him in every area of our lives. He wants us to be free from other controls and dominion (Romans 6:14), including being in bondage to food. We've been redeemed from all bondages by the death and resurrection of Jesus Christ our Lord. I believe that He alone should have authority over our spirit, soul, and body.

We need to bring our eating under submission to God. We are spiritual beings who live in physical bodies. We are the temples of the Lord. Our body is merely a vehicle for fulfilling His purpose on the earth. Once you get that perspective, you'll eat to live, not live to eat. So before you read the following plan for eating God's way, take a moment to pray and submit yourself to God. Ask the Lord to show you areas where you can enhance your daily living by making dietary changes. He will show you, because He wants you to have victory in this area of your life.

Psalm 103:1–5 says, "Praise the Lord, O my soul; all my inmost being, praise his holy name. Praise the Lord, O my soul, and forget not all his benefits—who forgives all your sins and heals all your diseases, who redeems your life from the pit and crowns you with love and compassion, *who satisfies your desires with good things so that your youth is renewed like the eagle's.*" So many times we only look at the fact that we want our youth renewed, and we overlook the prerequisite, which is satisfying our desires with good things. Not things that just taste good, but things that are good for us!

We all need to submit to God's plan so that we can enjoy the true blessings of God, whether it is in spiritual warfare or in our eating. God's plan is that we treat our body as the temple of the Lord and feed it the right sustenance so that we walk in health every day of our lives.

KASHRUT TERMS

Kosher—properly prepared or ritually correct under Jewish law.

Milchik—food that is or contains milk or milk derivatives.

Fleischik—food that is or contains meat or meat derivatives.

Pareve—food that has none of the above properties (neutral foods such as fish, fruits, or vegetables).

KASHRUT PROCEDURES

Do not mix dairy and meat products. The traditional Jews will not even use the same dishes or cookware; much less eat them at the same meal.

Meat and fowl must be slaughtered correctly to be Kosher.

Fruits and vegetables are considered pareve (neutral) and may be served with either milk or meat foods.

Fish that has both fins and scales is considered Kosher and pareve. However, fish is not to be cooked together with meat.

FUNDAMENTAL RULES

Only the meat and milk of certain animals is permitted. This restriction includes the flesh, organs, eggs, and milk of the forbidden animals.

Of the animals that may be eaten, the birds and mammals must be killed in accordance with the Jewish law.

All blood must be drained from the meat or boiled out of it before it is eaten.

Certain parts of permitted animals may not be eaten.

Meat (the flesh of birds and mammals) cannot be eaten with or cooked with dairy. Fish, eggs, fruits, vegetables, and grains can be eaten with either meat or dairy. (According to some views, fish may not be eaten with meat.)

Utensils that have come into contact with meat may not be used with dairy, and vice versa. Utensils that have come into contact with non-Kosher food may not be used with Kosher food. This applies only if the contact occurred while the food was hot.

Grape products made by non-Jews may not be eaten.

According to Leviticus 11:3 and Deuteronomy 14:6, you may eat any animal that has cloven hooves and chews its cud. This includes cattle, sheep, goats, buffalo, and deer. It specifically excludes the hare, pig, camel, and the rock badger (you probably won't have a problem staying away from the latter two animals).

In Leviticus 11:9 and Deuteronomy 14:9, shellfish such as lobsters, oysters, shrimp, clams, and crabs are all forbidden. Fish such as tuna, carp, salmon, and herring are all permitted.

For birds there is less criteria. Leviticus 11:13–19 and Deuteronomy 14:11–18 list birds that are forbidden but does not specify why. However, they all are birds of prey and/or scavengers, which is why the rabbis said they were set apart. Birds such as chicken, geese, ducks, and turkeys are all permitted.

SOME EXAMPLES *of* NON-KOSHER FOODS

Pork, rabbit, and horse meat; fowl, such as owl and stork; fish, such as catfish, eels, shellfish, shrimp, and octopus; and insects are all non-Kosher foods according to biblical definitions.

Even processed food can be non-kosher. This is because all ingredients and sub-units in a product must conform to the dietary laws in order for the food item to be considered Kosher. Even one non-Kosher ingredient can render the entire product unsuitable. Soda may contain a flavor enhancer called castorium, which is extracted from beavers. Cookies may contain a non-Kosher emulsifier, which is derived from animal fat. Potato chips may be fried in animal oil. So read your labels carefully.

The important point is not to get into the bondage of having to look for everything marked "Kosher," but to realize that God has given us a very clear plan for the foods we should eat. For example, the laws regarding Kosher slaughter are so sanitary that Kosher butchers and slaughterhouses have been exempted from many USDA regulations. And there is no comparison between the manner of operation in Kosher slaughterhouse and in a non-Kosher slaughterhouse. In Kosher slaughtering the method is that of slicing the throat, which causes unconsciousness within two seconds, and is widely recognized as the most humane method of slaughter possible. There is no pain or fear in the animal, with no chemical releases, whether natural or synthetic. In this method, there is also rapid and complete draining of the blood. The Bible specifies that we do not eat blood because the life of the animal is contained in the blood. Today we know that disease is found in the blood, and if it is not drained properly, you can ingest it into your system.

SEPARATION *of* MEAT *and* DAIRY

The Torah says that meat and dairy should never be consumed together. Spiritually, the Jews believe that it is callous to take an animal's life in order to satiate their own appetites. So they don't drink milk, which represents the nurturing of animal life, when they eat meat, which represents the destruction of life.

Once again, God had a dual purpose for a waiting time between eating meat and dairy. First, there is evidence that the combining of meat and dairy interferes with digestion. It's important to realize that the key to losing weight naturally and living healthy is dependent on good digestion and the absorption of nutrients. Whatever inhibits digestion needs to be avoided.

Plus, it is no coincidence that it takes approximately three hours to digest fish and fowl and anywhere from six to eight hours to digest meat. Why extend that time with milk? No modern food preparation technique can reproduce the health benefit of the Kosher law of eating them separately.

Remember that anything from an animal is high in fat, so eat more fowl and fish and less red meat. They take less time to digest, which means more energy for you and less energy devoted to processing a large piece of meat. Stick with Kosher if possible. If Kosher is not available, go for the hormone-free.

THE EXCELLENCE *of* FISH

According to Leviticus 11:9, fish is a clean food. It is naturally low in calories and rich in health-giving oils as well as essential vitamins and minerals. For the ordinary person in Israel, fish was far more than meat. Meat was considered a luxury reserved for special celebrations. Many of the meals that Jesus ate featured fish as the main course.

Fish contain important Omega-3 fatty acids, which have been proven to lower cholesterol, inhibit blood clots, lower blood pressure, and reduce the risk of heart attack and stroke. The best fish sources, which are naturally low in calories, are salmon, mackerel, and halibut.

Shellfish and fish without scales are high in cholesterol and considered high-stress foods. Stay away from these. And stay away from fish that is not immediately put on ice—parasites that would be normally contained in discarded parts are allowed to travel up into the flesh where infestations occur.

TIPS ON FOODS

- Extra virgin olive oil is by far the best oil you can use! It has been proven to be the healthiest for your heart as well as lowering your cholesterol level instead of clogging your arteries the way the saturated fats found in your typical grocery store oils and margarinated butter does. It is far more versatile and can be used for just about anything. Medicinally speaking, olive oil has proven to be a natural antibiotic as well as antiviral. It tastes great and is good for you!

- Eat as many fresh fruits and vegetables a day as possible. By eating five daily, according to Johns Hopkins University, you can cut your risk of cancer by 30 percent and lower your systolic blood pressure by 5.5 points and the diastolic pressure by 3.0 points. Their researchers concluded that you could reduce your risk of heart disease by 15 percent and the risk of a stroke by 27 percent.

- Go for Bible snacks instead of the processed foods. Fresh fruits, fresh veggies, nuts, raisins, granolas, yogurts, unrefined crackers, and flat breads—get creative! Genesis 43:11

specifically mentions pistachios and almonds. That's interesting in that those are particularly low in fat and calories. Nuts in general are a great snack food, with the exception of peanuts, which are really not a nut!

- A good rule of thumb is to stay away from processed foods. Then you don't have to be concerned about those hidden ingredients labeled as "natural flavoring." Try to eat foods that are as close to the way that God created them—chemical free!

- Researchers at Loma Linda University in California have shown scientifically that Kyolic® (a brand of garlic capsules found in any health food store) reduces the dangerous LDL levels of the blood and increases the beneficial HDL levels. A study in India showed that garlic has the ability to reduce blood clotting as well as serve as an anticancer agent.

- Go to your local health food store and get a good powdered kelp to use for your seasoning. This is a great additive to your food as well as a plus to the thyroid, which controls your entire metabolism. A liquid bladder wrack—an old herbal remedy used for low thyroid—is also excellent when on a weight-loss program. It's very natural to the body and excellent for weight loss by speeding up the metabolism with no harmful side effects.

- Water is vitally important to your body. Following my instructions in Chapter 9 will make a big difference in your weight loss and health.

- Think about sprouting at home. It's easy, it's fun, it's cheap, and it tastes good! Even the kids love them and love to grow them! They're great on sandwiches and salads, and they can be used as snacks as well. The rewards are great. They are loaded with trace minerals that are not so easily found in other foods. You can get everything you need at your local health food store to sprout.

- Go for foods rich in color! Stay away from the white deadly things! White sugar, white flour, white salt, even white potatoes. Choose red potatoes instead of white. Choose a dark lettuce or spinach instead of iceberg.

- Yogurt, or fermented milk, isn't mentioned in the Bible, but according to history we know that it was a mainstay at that time. Yogurt has been attributed to longevity in many civilizations. It is the ideal diet food for folks who want to add flavor and health benefits to their diet. Stay away from yogurts with artificial sweeteners or added sugars. Yogurt is a natural antibiotic that keeps your digestive system healthy by replacing the good flora in the intestinal track. This is needed for a healthy immune system. You can use yogurt in a variety of ways with salad dressings. It's a healthy snack—my favorite is my Creation's Bounty shake with yogurt in the mornings! Those who are lactose-intolerant typically do fine with a good yogurt.

TIPS ON EATING

- Remember: the ball of your fist is the size of your stomach when it is empty. Open up your palm. That should be the portion size you eat at each meal. More than that at a time, and you are overeating!
- Before meals, eat 4 or 5 almonds. This will help to curb your appetite by sending a signal to the brain that you are full.
- A good oat bran is a great way to end your day instead of a heavy meal at dinner. A half-cup a day has also been proven to cut your risk of cancer by 30 percent. It is very effective in the elimination of waste from the bowels, acting like a broom that sweeps away the breeding ground of accumulated waste and disease. The bran fiber is an effective bulking agent that absorbs toxins and other wastes as it passes through.
- Wait 10 to 15 minutes before having a second helping. This is how long it takes to get the signal to the brain to tell you you're full. In doing this, you usually won't want a second helping.
- A study was done of men from all around the world.

Surprisingly, the healthiest men over all were French! Considering the typical heavy, sauce-covered French foods, this fact is quite shocking. The three things that made the difference in their diet were the following: a little red wine, which aids in digestion; lots of fresh foods and fresh herbs; and, most important of all, they ate their salad last. The living enzymes in the fresh vegetable eaten last works to break down all the other foods just eaten. With all your food being broken down more efficiently, you get better absorption of all your nutrients, you feel better, and you have more energy.

- If you can avoid it, never eat past 6:00 p.m. in the evening! The later you eat, the less likely you are of burning the new calories. If you are having a smoothie, the time is not important because it is easily digested and absorbed.
- After your dinner, take a brisk walk. If your health does not allow it yet, start with walking in place for 5 to 10 minutes and increase as you can. If you're past that, go for it. Schedule in a daily exercise. Remember there will never be a good time to exercise. You have to create one. At least 20 to 30 minutes is a good place to start. As with all changes in diet and exercise, consult with your physician first.
- Don't drink anything with your meals. If you must drink, have water with a slice of lemon. Sodas, teas, and coffees interfere with the stomach acids and enzymes vital for digestion.
- If you have a problem with poor digestion, try a glass of steam-distilled water with a teaspoon of raw honey, a fourth of a fresh lemon, and two tablespoons of organic apple-cider vinegar. This mixture can be taken with each meal and has been proven to increase your digestive ability. Many of those with chronic upset stomach, acid indigestion, and gaseous problems find themselves being relieved with this inexpensive home remedy.

PRACTICAL APPLICATION

Putting the One Perfect Diet into your daily living is actually very easy once you get in the swing of things. The important key is to get the body back into a place of homeostasis, which is a happy, healthy body, and the proper foods will make a world of difference. The rewards of healthy living, an energetic body, and sound, clear thinking will cause you to never want to turn back.

Remember that God's way works!

17

WALK YOUR WAY *to* HEALTH *in a* FEW MINUTES *a* DAY

DESPITE THE FACT THAT EXERCISE PLAYS AS SIGNIFICANT A ROLE IN OUR HEALTH AS DOES NUTRITION AND WEIGHT MANAGEMENT, FEW OF US ARE AS PHYSICALLY FIT AS WE COULD OR SHOULD BE. The National Center for Chronic Disease Prevention and Health Promotion estimates that 60 percent of American adults exercise only once in a while, and 25 percent never exercise. Nearly half of American youths 12 to 21 years of age are not vigorously active on a regular basis. Add to that the fact that the average American consumes 300 calories more today than he did 30 years ago, yet burns 260 less calories each day, and it's no surprise that every other person you meet is overweight.

According to a report of the Surgeon General on "Physical Activity and Health," millions of Americans suffer from illnesses that can be prevented or improved through regular physical activity. And exercise does not need to be strenuous or overly time-consuming. The walking program I am suggesting is easy to perform, represents a realistic level of activity for most people, and minimizes the risk of musculo-skeletal injury.

If you are among the 50 percent of us who are totally sedentary, I have a word for you. You were not designed by God to come home at the end of the day and plop down in front of the television for the last hours of the day after having sat at a desk for 8+ hours. Your body was not made for inactivity while you pour in the calories with a poor diet. The human body was created perfectly by God for walking, and He wants you to break the lethargy syndrome that seems to bind so many people to an unhealthy lifestyle.

10 HEALTH BENEFITS *of* EXERCISE

Regular physical activity (30 minutes of walking) reduces the risk of developing or dying from some of the leading causes of illness and death in the United States. Regular physical activity improves health in the following ways:

1. Exercise increases the calories you burn and accelerates your weight loss while it decreases your appetite. It will develop lean muscle and build and maintain healthy bones and joints. How's that for starters?

2. Exercise reduces symptoms of anxiety and depression and fosters improvements in mood and feelings of well-being. Physical activity also causes the release of endorphins, which in layman's terms are the body's natural feel-good hormones. Exercise has the marvelous ability to remove the adrenaline that gets pumped into our bloodstream through stress, and thus it helps keep stress under control. Stress is a huge contributor to heart problems.

3. Exercise reduces the risk for heart disease and stroke. A good physical workout improves the strength of all the muscles in your body, particularly your heart muscle.

4. Exercise lowers your blood pressure, lowers triglyceride levels, and raises HDL (good) blood cholesterol levels.

5. Exercise reduces the risk of developing diabetes, as it lowers the blood sugar level.

6. Exercise increases a person's sex drive.

7. Exercise reduces the risk of developing colon cancer. It also increases the motility of the colon and clears away constipation—just go for a walk in the morning and see!

8. Exercise delays the development of osteoporosis.

9. Exercise increases the body's internal cleansing systems as well as the cellular turnover.

10. Exercise helps normalize women's hormone levels. And there is evidence to suggest that women who exercise regularly have significantly fewer problems with PMS, menopause, and breast cancer when compared to women who do not exercise.

Those are ten fantastic reasons to start to exercise today, no matter how badly you are out of shape. How we think about exercise will determine how faithful we are to do it. Understanding the value of exercise can positively affect our attitude toward it. I've watched people who could barely lift 5 pounds move up to 30 pounds in just a couple weeks. You can do it! You must do it!

WHERE *to* START?

There are countless ways to begin exercising. There's walking, jogging, cycling, swimming, calisthenics, dance, hiking, skating, tennis, basketball, aerobics, martial arts, Rollerblading, and on and on. Some find that a membership at a health club keeps them motivated as well as provides all the equipment they like to use. Others prefer to set up a home gym, while others stick more with an aerobic program that requires little or no equipment.

I recommend that you consider walking as a great starting point for exercise. It brings all the health benefits listed previously, and it is a very doable exercise that costs almost nothing. Recent studies have shown that a brisk walk provides strenuous enough exercise for cardiovascular training in most adults. And unlike running, it puts little strain on your knees and legs.

By way of comparison, a healthy woman of 140 pounds burns around 80 calories per hour while sitting. She'll burn 240 calories an hour if she's doing a light activity such as cleaning the house. If she is on a brisk walk (3.5 mph) or vigorously gardening, she'll burn 370 calories per hour. And if she's advanced to jogging (a 9-minute mile), she'll burn 580 calories per hour. A healthy man of 175 pounds will burn slightly more calories than a woman while doing the same activity.

The point is to get up and start burning some extra calories. Take your spouse's hand and head out the door for a comfortable walk, burn some calories, and perhaps put a little spark of romance in your day. Depending on the distance to your job, consider walking. Park your car at the farthest end from the store entrance and take a little stroll before going inside. Something as simple as climbing five flights of stairs every day significantly lowers your risk of heart disease.

BEFORE YOU START

Check with your doctor regarding any form of exercise program you intend to begin. If you are over 40 and in poor health, a treadmill test is highly recommended. A physician or exercise specialist can provide this test that checks blood pressure and uses an electrocardiogram to monitor heart performance. These tests should be repeated every three years or as often as your doctor recommends. If you ever have symptoms such as chest pain or pressure, heart irregularity, or unusual shortness of breath, call your doctor immediately.

Get the right equipment to help you facilitate your exercise. For instance, if you are going to walk or run, go to a shoe store that specializes in running and talk with trained personnel who know what you'll need. Saving $30 on a cheap pair of shoes isn't worth it.

Start out slowly. If you are really out of shape, it will take time to restore your health. Begin your physical activity program with short sessions (5 to 10 minutes) of physical activity and gradually build up to the desired level of activity (30 minutes). Don't overdo it. Pushing too hard can lead to damage. You don't have to run marathons for your health to reap significant benefits. The same moderate amount of activity can be obtained in longer sessions of moderately intense activities (such as 30 minutes of brisk walking) as in shorter sessions of more strenuous activities (such as 15 to 20 minutes of jogging). You just need to be consistent.

Consider weather conditions. Excessive heat or cold must be seriously considered. Never put yourself at risk.

Drink water—before, during, and after exercise, especially during warm weather. Replacing water lost by sweating is crucial.

Always warm up for 3 to 5 minutes before stretching. Then stretch out for 3 or 4 minutes before exercising. Stretching the Achilles tendons and the hamstrings should always be included in a warmup.

Properly stretching your muscles lessens the likelihood of any muscles being damaged and increases your flexibility. If you are over 60, it's good to walk for about one-quarter mile before stretching.

Cool down for five minutes after working out. Just keep walking around slowly. Don't lie down or sit. And never go directly into a sauna or steam room after exercising. The heat increase can cause heart problems right after exercise.

AEROBIC EXERCISE
and YOUR HEART RATE

Aerobic exercise is any activity requiring oxygen that uses large muscle groups, is rhythmic in nature, and can be maintained for a period of time. Done consistently, aerobic activity trains the heart, lungs, and cardiovascular system to process and deliver oxygen in a more efficient manner. Therefore, an aerobically fit person can work longer and harder during an exercise session than someone who is not. Whether your goal is weight loss or general health, the longer the duration of your exercise, the more calories you will burn.

Most experts agree that 3 to 5 aerobic sessions per week for a duration of at least 20 minutes at 60 to 85 percent of your age-specific maximum heart rate is a good place to start. Beginning exercisers would start lower in their target zone. Advanced exercisers will exercise at the higher end of their target zone.

As you set goals for how long you are going to exercise, keep in mind that it's okay to be a bit out of breath, but not so much that you can't talk. Pace your workout so that you push without overdoing it. If you are still tired an hour after the exercise, you should back off a bit and build up slower.

If you prefer to be more scientific about it, measure your heart rate by taking your pulse. Aim for a heart rate between 70 and 80 percent of the maximum for your age group. If you need to lose weight, you can achieve the greatest loss if you aim for about 60 percent of your maximum heart rate and exercise for 45 to 60 minutes 3 to 5 times a week.

AGE	70–80% OF MAX RATE	60% OF MAX RATE
20	140–160	120
30	133–152	114
40	126–144	108
50	119–136	102
60	112–128	96
70	105–120	90

THE COOPER 40-PLUS PROGRAM

Dr. Kenneth Cooper, the "Father of Aerobics" and founder of the Cooper Aerobics Center (www.cooperaerobics.com), has developed a six-week walking program for men and women over the age of 40 that I recommend. It sets simple goals, and it works.

WEEK 1: Walk one mile in 24 minutes, five times a week.
WEEK 2: Walk one mile in 22 minutes, five times a week.
WEEK 3: Walk one mile in 20 minutes, five times a week.
WEEK 4: Walk one-and-a-half miles in 30 minutes, five times a week.
WEEK 5: Walk one-and-a-half miles in 29 minutes, five times a week.
WEEK 6: Walk two miles in less than 40 minutes, five times a week.

Obviously, at the end of the sixth week, you can continue to challenge yourself by increasing your speed. You'll like how you feel when you're walking two miles in less than 35 minutes!

STRENGTH TRAINING

Studies tell us that between the ages of 20 and 30, without weight-resistant exercise, we begin to lose muscle. As we age, the rate at which we lose seems to increase slightly. As we lose muscle, our basal metabolic rate slows down, which means we are burning fewer calories. This change in metabolism generally means a gain in fat. Let's say that between the ages of 30 and 40, we have lost 10 pounds of muscle and gained about 10 pounds of fat. That means that in 10 years, we would have a 20-pound body composition change and still weigh the same amount.

No wonder as we age it is so easy to gain fat simply by not exercising. Many people are frustrated by the fact that they eat just as they always have, but now they are gaining weight, not realizing that each year without resistance exercise, their metabolisms are slowing down. Exercise is the only way to reverse this effect of aging.

There is another interesting aspect to muscle. Did you know that one pound of muscle burns 35 calories a day, whereas one pound of fat burns a paltry 2 calories? Just think, by increasing your muscle, or your lean body mass by 10 pounds, you would increase your metabolic rate by about 350 calories a day. Just gaining 5 pounds of muscle would increase your calorie expenditure by 175 calories a day. That's 63,875 calories or 18 pounds a year! And muscle is denser and takes up much less space than fat. You could therefore maintain the same weight you are now and be 2 sizes smaller by gaining 10 pounds of muscle and losing 10 pounds of fat.

Dr. Cooper states that if you are in your 40s, you should spend 70 percent of your weekly exercise regimen doing aerobic activity and 30 percent of the time doing strength training. In your 50s, the ratio moves to 60/40. And in your 60s and 70s, it moves to 50/50.

As much as I love walking, and you will too, strength training does not come through walking. I strongly recommend what I consider the best strength-training system that's available today. For men, you'll find it in John Peterson's *Pushing Yourself to Power*; and for women, you'll find it in Wendie Pett's *Every Woman's Guide to Personal Power*. I've used the Transformetrics™ Training System, and I love it that I don't have to go to a gym or buy any expensive exercise equipment to do it. It can be done anytime and anyplace, and it will help you achieve your body's natural, God-given strength and fitness potential. Each book also has a wonderful introductory program for people who are weak and obese that you won't find anywhere else. Check it out at www.bronzebowpublishing.com.

18

QUICK WEIGHT LOSS *for* ANYONE WHO WANTS *to* TAKE CHARGE *of* THEIR HEALTH

TWO OF THE PREVIOUS CHAPTERS, "THE ONE PERFECT DIET" AND "FADS, FACTS, AND FALLACIES," DEAL WITH DIET, BUT IN THIS CHAPTER I WANT TO BRING YOU INTO MY LIFE. I have a husband who has endured my telling of his personal health challenges for years now, and he's never complained. He has told me that the Lord showed him that our family (four boys and four girls) is a microcosm of the world.

A microcosm is a small version of something larger. We have seen both good and bad in our family, and Jim's health is no exception. It began with feelings of sluggishness, an occasional bout with depression, and days when he didn't seem quite as sharp as normal. Sound familiar? In Jim's case, shortly after he started noticing these symptoms he was diagnosed with Hepatitis C—a disease that's found a home in a large percentage of Americans, many who have no idea they have it although they show all the symptoms.

So, using the platform God has given me, I share his story with you to bring the hope and answers God has shared with us. I think it's so powerful because when Jim applied God's principles to his problems, the results were amazing. And what God did for Jim, He'll do for you. Here's what happened.

In November 2002, Jim began using a prescription steroid called Prednisone for an upcoming eye surgery. One of the side affects of this medication was added weight. This wasn't especially pleasing to him since his thyroid gland had virtually stopped working twenty years before, and weight had been an ongoing battle ever since. As time progressed, the surgery eventually took place, the medication continued, and the weight mounted.

My husband is a good-looking man. We met in the church I attended for most of my life and where Jim came to faith in Jesus Christ in 1980. We were married after dating only three months, and over the years we've had eight children together. As you might imagine, we've seen the best and the worst over these years together. One thing I've noticed as the years progress is that you see and appreciate the inner beauty in a person more than the outer beauty that may have originally attracted you to that person.

That was the case here. Until I started preparing to write this book, I really didn't realize how overweight he was. I saw the pictures that you're looking at and couldn't believe my eyes. They were taken on our vacation eight months after he began the medication. After the photos

came back from being developed, he kept them away from us, but he gave his permission to use them now, hoping to help others.

Vacation was in July 2003, which Jim made it through, but he was almost at the end of his rope and no one knew it. He had had the eye surgery in December, but continued to add excess weight. Along with this came depression, fatigue, pain, lethargy, and finally complete exhaustion. He stopped coming into the office around the end of May but did what work he could from home, which was good and beneficial to our company. If you could have seen him, you would realize that that was a miracle in itself.

August came. It was almost time for the kids to return to school, my schedule was busy, and Jim was worse. One evening he was sitting in the den and I asked him how he was doing. I'll never forget the response. He said, "You will never know how it feels to know you will never feel good again."

I wasn't even sure how to respond, but I tried to encourage him, and I prayed. If you skipped the section on Prayer in the "Foundations to the Gospel of Health," go back and read it now. Prayer works, guys!

Jim prayed, too, but he's quick to say "you better be prayed up before you get sick, because after you are, it's very difficult."

His answer came this way. He said to me, "Honey, God has given me a plan. I'm going to let all my organs rest as much as I can by only taking in liquids. I'll keep my nutrition levels as high as possible, but I think the Lord has something for me here."

"If ten days can change your life forever, imagine what 100 will do!"

—JIM SAXION

He started immediately, and in only 10 days most of his numerous problems had vanished. In 40 days he had lost 45 of the 60 extra pounds he was carrying. Here's what he did for 100 days that totally reversed his health and removed 65 pounds of unhealthy toxins and excess flesh.

HOW JIM TURNED HIS LIFE AROUND

6:00   Upon waking, drank one glass of Clustered or distilled water with thyroid supplement and one ounce of Body Oxygen.

6:30   Glass of water with the juice of half a lemon and a tablespoon of apple cider vinegar.

7:00   Liquid Minerals, one or two ounces in apple juice.

8:00   Creation's Bounty blended with 10 ounces of apple juice, ice, and a banana.

9:00   16 ounces of protein drink.

10:00   Coffee (I did not approve).

11:00   12 ounces of unsweetened grapefruit juice with 3 tablespoons of lecithin or the equivalent in capsule form.

12:00   Creation's Bounty blended with 10 ounces of apple juice and a teaspoon of local bee pollen.

1:00   Soup Hearty, but liquids only, no solids.

2:00   12 ounces of unsweetened grapefruit juice.

4:00   V8 juice.

5:00   Soup broth with kelp.

6:00   6 to 8 ounces of blueberry or Concord grape juice.

7:00   One cup of hot herbal tea with a little honey to taste.

9:00   One tablespoon of liquid Collagen with a glass of water.

A good night's sleep of 8 to 9 hours was very important.

There was no sugar, no soft drinks, no milk, and he limited his coffee to one cup (none is better). A glass or cup of green tea or water is good anytime—as much as you like.

Once a week Jim would have a colonic done by a colon therapist. However, if you don't have a colon therapist in your area or would like to save the money, I suggest you do one coffee enema, each day of the diet, in the morning if possible (see Appendix A). If doing enemas, be sure to take blackstrap molasses to put back lost potassium in your system. Put 1 tablespoon in 4 ounces of organic milk or rice or almond milk.

In addition, drink as much good water as possible. I recommend using distilled or Clustered water and drink half your body weight in ounces daily (example: if you weigh 128 pounds, drink 64 ounces of water, which is 2 quarts).

Your body cannot manufacture its own vitamins, so I suggest supplementing the above with the following:

Beta-carotene—at least 4,000 IU
Vitamin C—18,000 grams with rosehips
Vitamin E—1,200 IU
Liquid minerals are essential, one to two ounces a day
B-complex vitamins, food based
Vitamin A—25,000 IU
Sunlight—one hour if possible
Smart Oil Cap

THE IMPORTANCE *of* FASTING

Jim was on a liquid fast. Fasting is a period of restricted food intake that detoxifies the body, giving the organs a rest and bringing natural healing by cleansing the body. A whole meal according to the FDA constitutes 250 calories per meal. Smoothies are actually more than that in calories.

But fasting is not only excellent for the body, it is also breath to the spirit as well. God says in Isaiah 58 that He has a chosen fast that is redemptive for every area of your life. Your spirit, mind, and body are included so that no disease will come upon you! Fasting facilitates this divine freedom. "Then your light will break forth like the dawn, and your healing will quickly appear." Your fast can be a time to be restored to a right relationship with Him! He will go before you as your righteousness, and His glory will be your guardian.

Fasting has been proven to be the most effective means of getting the body into a natural healing process. It is also an instrument to literally reset the body's odometer and help reverse the aging process. Disease and aging begin when the normal process of cell regeneration and rebuilding slows down. This slowdown is caused by the accumulation of waste products in the tissues, which interferes with the nourishment and oxygenation of cells. This may happen at any age, and when it occurs, the cells' resistance to disease diminishes and various ills start to appear. Given the fact that at any given moment one-fourth of all our cells are dead and in replacement, it is of vital importance that the dying cells are decomposed and eliminated from the system as efficiently as possible. Quick and effective elimination of dead cells stimulates the building and growth of new cells.

If you have never fasted before, I recommend starting with several one-day fasts before moving on to a three-day fast. In general, three- to ten-day fasts are recommended for health and longevity. For a complete guide to fasting, I recommend that you read my "Fasting" chapter in *How to Feel Great All the Time*.

FROM JIM

God gave me a simple plan that changed my life for good. It's been a long time now since I finished my 100-day program. I haven't gained any of the weight back, and the dis-ease and ailments have vanished. People tell me I look great, and I feel that way, too. When I started I never dreamed I could feel this good.

Around the 50th day I started walking on a treadmill, and that exercise has become a way of life. About day 70, I added strength training with my son's weight set. It feels strange to say that I now look and feel somewhat athletic. It's amazing, but it only goes to show God really will meet us where we're at.

I hope you'll write to Valerie and me. If you've adopted this or a similar weight-loss program, send your pictures and we'll praise the Lord with you as you regain and renew your healthy life.

God bless you, and thank you, Lord Jesus,

Jim Saxion

CONDITION-SPECIFIC HELP

*So do not fear, for I am with you;
do not be dismayed, for I am your God.
I will strengthen you and help you;
I will uphold you with my
righteous right hand.*

ISAIAH 41:10

19

CONDITION-SPECIFIC HELP

IN THIS SECTION, YOU'LL SEE FOUR OR FIVE SECTIONS IN EACH CRITIQUE:

1. **Description of the ailment,** personal observations, and hints.

2. **Top Natural Aids.** Here you'll find the best overall supplement suggestions for the ailment.

3. **Important Aids.** This list of supplements could be next in importance. I say "could be" because something in this category may play an even larger role in your personal progress than an item in the "top" list. Because you have now taken charge of your health, it will be up to you to identify what is best.

4. **Other Potential Aids.** This section rounds out the balance of possible supplemental aids. This book brings a complete list of alternative specific natural health assistance available today, but it's you who must ultimately decide what's best for you.

5. **Some topics** contain food, herbal, and alternative recommendations.

☞ ACID AND ALKALI IMBALANCE

ACID AND ALKALINITY are measured according to the pH scale. Water has a pH of 7.0 and is neutral. Anything below 7.0 is acidic; anything above is alkali. The ideal pH for the human body is between 6.0 and 6.8, slightly alkaline. If we become too acidic, we are out of balance and eventually death will occur.

Check your pH today. Diseases thrive in an acidic environment—cancer, viruses, bacteria, Candida, fungus, and much more! We know its important or God would not have put us in a garden! Remember the fresh things keep us balanced!

Some symptoms of imbalance are:
- Frequent sighing
- Insomnia
- Water retention
- Recessed eyes
- Arthritis
- Migraine headaches
- Abnormally low blood pressure
- Acid or strong perspiration
- Dry hard stools
- Burning sensation in the anus when having a bowel movement
- Altering constipation/diarrhea
- Difficulty swallowing
- Halitosis
- Burning sensation in the mouth or under the tongue
- Sensitivity of the teeth to vinegar and acidic fruits
- Bumps on the tongue or the roof of the mouth

While acidosis may be caused from specific disorders, most are caused by improper diet. You can get pH strips and self-test to see where you are on the scale. If you are too acidic, here's what you do.

TOP NATURAL FOODS

- Eat a diet of 50% raw foods. They will help to correct the balance. Specifically: apples, avocados, bananas, grapefruit,

grapes, lemons, pineapple, strawberries, and all vegetables.
- Fresh fruits, especially citrus, reduce acidosis. Start small and work your way up.
- Avoid animal protein.
- Drink potato broth every day.
- A good rule of thumb is 80% alkali-forming foods and 20% acid-forming foods.

ALKALINE-FORMING FOODS

All vegetables, especially raw vegetables, balance the acidity and alkali levels in the blood.

- Avocados
- Corn
- Dates
- Fresh Coconut
- Fresh Fruits (most)
- Fresh Veggies
- Honey
- Horseradish
- Maple Syrup
- Molasses
- Mushrooms
- Onions
- Raisins
- Soy Products
- Sprouts
- Umeboshi Plums
- Watercress

LOW-LEVEL ALKALINE-FORMING FOODS

- Almonds
- Blackstrap Molasses
- Brazil Nuts
- Chestnuts
- Lima Beans
- Millet
- Soured Dairy Products

ACID-FORMING FOODS

- Alcohol
- Asparagus
- Beans
- Brussels Sprouts
- Buckwheat
- Catsup
- Chickpeas
- Cocoa
- Coffee
- Cornstarch
- Cranberries
- Eggs

- Fish
- Flour
- Flour-based Products
- Legumes
- Lentils
- Meat
- Milk
- Mustard
- Noodles
- Oatmeal
- Olives
- Organ Meats
- Pasta
- Pepper
- Plums
- Poultry
- Prunes
- Sauerkraut
- Shellfish
- Soft Drinks
- Sugar and All Sugary Foods
- Tea
- Vinegar
- Drugs—aspirin, tobacco, and most drugs

LOW-LEVEL ACID-FORMING FOODS

- Butter
- Canned or Glazed Fruit
- Cheeses
- Dried Coconut
- Dried or Sulfured Fruit
- Grains
- Ice Cream
- Ice Milk
- Lamb's Quarters
- Nuts
- Seeds
- Parsley

TOP NATURAL AIDS

- Tri-Salts bring balance.
- Digestive enzymes break foods down and gets them out of your system more efficiently.
- Body Oxygen provides stamina and nourishes cells with added oxygen while reducing high acid content in the body.
- Potassium—take black strap molasses
- Vitamin B-complex is needed for proper digestion.
- MSM—sulfur helps to maintain proper pH

Practice deep breathing and chew your food slowly.

☞ ADD

ATTENTION DEFICIT DISORDER is a syndrome characterized by the inability to focus one's attention and periods of hyperactivity, commonly exhibited in children but also affecting adults. ADD is believed to occur as a result of insufficient development of the Corpus Callosum of the brain—this component of the brain is responsible for the interhemispheric flow of information.

ADD is more prevalent in males than in females. Estimates of the ratio between males to females range from 3:1 to 5:1. ADD is the common childhood psychiatric disorder. It has been estimated that 2–20% of schoolchildren in the U.S. are afflicted with ADD. ADD patients commonly have inner ear infections as children.

According to Dr. Michael Schmidt of Northwestern University, the author of *Good Fats Bad Fats*, all those diagnosed with ADD and ADHD have a deficiency and imbalance of Omega 3, 6, and 9. Nowhere in the world are the statistics as high as the U.S.

My own children could have worn this label if we had been traditional. But we supplemented with essential fatty acids and watched their diets carefully.

One child I met with appeared to have ADD, but the real problem was periods of low blood sugar. With a simple explanation I was able to help him understand what it was and what to do, and now at age eight he will say, "I have low blood sugar," and he knows he may not be thinking or acting right. With a quick nutritious snack or meal he is back on target.

I remember Dr. James Dobson saying that by age eight most children level out. Some are not ready to read at age six or seven. Out of my own eight children I have seen that to be true with three of them. Thank God for Dr. Dobson!

Staying away from sugars, dyes, and harmful chemicals is essential. Also make sure the child does not have an overgrowth of Candida Albicans, which can come with use of antibiotics. Children diagnosed with ADD may have had multiple ear infections, generally treated with antibiotics. This means the antibiotics may have depleted good flora from the GI tract. When good bacteria are depleted, so are B-vitamins as well as other nutrients that are essential to the central nervous system as well as good brain function. To check a child's neurotransmitters, see Appendix A.

European studies show that children and adults alike can improve school grades and behavior by simple getting one more hour of sleep a night. The study showed performance levels improved and average class grades went up an entire grade point.

TOP NATURAL AIDS

- Omega 3, 6, and 9
- Gamma-Linolenic Acid—200 to 600 mg daily
- Phosphatidylserine—100 mg two to three times daily
- Calcium—1,500 to 2,000 mg daily
- Magnesium—200 mg daily
- Zinc—30 to 50 mg daily
- Gamma Aminobutyric Acid (GABA)—750 mg daily
- Vitamin B6 facilitates the production of serotonin in ADD. 50 mg daily, best taken with other B vitamins, as in the form of a B-complex supplement.
- Ginkgo Biloba—40 to 80 mg three times daily of a 50:1 extract standardized to contain 24% ginko-flavone glycosides
- SAMe—400 mg three to four times daily (not for children under 12)
- Valerian eliminates the anxiety, fear, restlessness, and aggressiveness associated with ADD and improves motor coordination in ADD patients. 2 to 3 grams twice daily.

IMPORTANT AIDS

- DHA essential fatty acids—good sources include tuna, salmon, and herring
- Choline—400 to 550 mg daily
- Vitamin C with bioflavonoids—1,000 mg three times daily
- Vitamin E (d-alpha-tocopherol form)—600 IU daily

- American Ginseng may help memory. Take as directed on label.

OTHER POTENTIAL AIDS

- Amino Acids
- 5-HTP—100 to 200 mg three times daily
- Glutamine—250 to 1,000 mg daily
- Phenylalanine—600 mg daily
- Tyrosine—up to 5,000 mg daily
- Exposure to full spectrum fluorescent light prevents ADD: Optimal exposure to sunlight. Children who attend schools where shielded full spectrum fluorescent light is provided are less prone to hyperactivity than those working under other forms of fluorescent light.
- Dopamine is a neurotransmitter (brain chemical) that helps regulate behavior. Eating high protein foods promotes the production of Dopamine, which tends to promote alertness.
- Serotonin is a neurotransmitter that eases tension. Eating complex carbohydrates raises the level of tryptophan in the brain, which in turn raises the level of serotonin.
- Oils (dietary oils)

☞ AGING

STUDIES SHOW that we age because we are toxic; we don't get toxic because we are aging. We must keep these toxins out and away from our bodies. That requires cleansing or detoxifying on a regular basis and putting living foods and water back into our bodies. An excellent way to accomplish this is through juice extraction and juice fasting on a regular basis. Exercise, pH-balancing, and Chelation Therapy are valuable keys as well.

TOP NATURAL AIDS

- Collagen liquid—take 1 tablespoon with 1,000 mg vitamin C at bedtime
- Vitamin A—15,000 IU daily
- Liquid Colloidal Minerals—one to two ounces daily
- Bilberry helps strengthen small blood vessels. It's excellent for the eyes. Take 20 to 40 mg daily of a product containing 25% anthocyanidins.
- Potassium—100 to 200 mg daily
- Selenium—300 mcg daily
- Zinc—50 mg plus 3 mg copper daily
- Ashwagandha helps the body handle stress. Take as directed.
- Ginkgo Biloba helps memory. Take 40 mg three times daily of a product containing at least 24% ginkgo heterosides.
- Green Tea contains powerful antioxidant agents not available in black tea. Drink it daily.
- Grape Seed extract—take as directed on label
- L-Carnitine assists the cardiovascular system and improves physical endurance. Take 500 mg twice daily.
- Cysteine, especially the N-Acetyl-Cysteine (NAC) form of cysteine—take 250 mg daily
- L-Tyrosine—500 mg twice daily on an empty stomach
- Beta-carotene (use natural form)—25,000 IU daily
- Superoxide Dismutase (SOD) is a potent antioxidant that destroys the free radicals that contribute to premature aging. It's found in vegetables such as broccoli, cabbage, cauliflower,

and Brussels sprouts, or can be taken as a supplement according to label directions.

- Glutathione fights premature aging. Foods such as garlic and onions stimulate the production of glutathione, or it can be taken as a supplement in amounts of 500 mg twice daily on an empty stomach.
- Coenzyme Q10—100 mg daily
- Vitamin B3 (niacinamide form)—2,000 to 3,000 mg daily
- Vitamin B5—50 mg three times daily
- Vitamin C with bioflavonoids—4,000 to 10,000 mg daily in divided portions
- Vitamin E—start with 200 IU daily and slowly increase to 800 IU daily. If you take blood-thinning medication, consult your physician before increasing amount.

IMPORTANT AIDS

- Ginseng has antioxidant properties. Take according to label directions.
- Boron—3 to 6 mg daily
- Calcium—1,500 to 2,000 mg daily
- Magnesium—750 mg daily
- Melatonin possesses life-extension properties when regular supplementation is commenced over the age of 40 to 45. Melatonin aids sleep and reportedly slows the aging process. Take 1.5 to 5 mg daily, 2 hours or less before bedtime.
- Phosphatidyl Serine improves brain function. Take 1,000 mg three times daily.
- Vitamin D3—600 to 1,000 mg daily
- Chromium Picolinate—400 to 1,000 mcg daily
- Lecithin—1,200 mg three times daily with meals
- Deoxyribonucleic Acid (DNA)—use a sublingual form and take 100 mg daily
- Ribonucleic Acid (RNA)—use a sublingual form and take 100 mg daily
- Bee Pollen

OTHER POTENTIAL AIDS

- Thymus Extract
- Velvet Deer Antler
- Charcoal—30 grams daily for two days of the week counteract some of the cellular changes that are associated with the progression of the aging process.
- Garlic
- Chelation Suppositories with Ethylene-Diamine-Tetra-Acetate (EDTA), which is a synthetic amino acid used in chelation therapy, possess life-extension potential.
- L-Dopa
- Dehydroepiandrosterone (DHEA) slows the aging process. Take as directed on label. Women shouldn't take more than 15 mg daily except under medical supervision.
- Human Growth Hormone (hGH) is a naturally occurring hormone that strengthens the immune system. It requires a doctor's supervision.
- Pregnenolone—start with 10 mg daily, then gradually increase to 30 mg daily. Take it 3 weeks on, 1 week off.
- Phosphatidylcholine
- Carnosine
- Fo-Ti can help ease arthritic pain and inflammation. Take 500 mg twice daily.
- Blueberries
- Blackcurrants
- Chaparral fights free radicals and dissolves heavy metals.

☞ AIDS

AN AUTOIMMUNE DISORDER caused by infection with the retrovirus HIV, which destroys certain white blood cells and is transmitted through blood and bodily secretions such as semen. Patients lose the ability to fight infections, often resulting in death from secondary causes such as pneumonia and Kaposi's sarcoma.

TOP NATURAL AIDS

- Probiotic supplement—take as directed on label
- L-Carnitine can help prevent toxic overload from some drugs used to treat AIDS. Some HIV patients have experienced improvement in their immune function. Take a minimum of 1,000 mg three times daily and discuss larger amounts with a physician.
- Liquid Collodial Minerals—1 or 2 ounces daily
- Alpha-lipoic Acid helps with fatigue. Take 100 mg three times daily.
- Ozone therapy
- Infrared Sauna
- H_2O_2 IV from a medical doctor
- Clustered water
- Dimethylglycine (DMG) has antiviral and anticancer properties. Use a sublingual form and take as directed on label.
- Vitamin B-complex—at least 50 mg of every major B vitamin three times daily
- Vitamin B12—1,000 mcg daily of sublingual form
- Vitamin E—start with 200 IU daily and gradually increase until taking 400 IU twice daily
- Vitamin C with bioflavonoids—3,000 mg and up in divided portions
- Bromelain helps with respiratory problems. Take 400 mg three times daily between meals.
- Vitamin D3—400 IU daily
- Zinc—50 mg with 3 mg copper daily

- Selenium—200 mcg daily
- Raw Thymus Glandular enhances T-cell production. Glandulars from a lamb source are reportedly the best. Take according to label directions.
- Quercetin—1,000 mg daily
- Coenzyme Q10—320 mg daily
- Colostrum (Bovine Colostrum)—take according to label directions
- Colloidal Silver—take according to label directions
- Aloe Vera juice consumed orally. Aloe Vera contains carrisyn, which appears to inhibit the growth of HIV. Take 2 cups twice daily of a pure food grade product.
- Astragalus supports the immune system. Take 350 to 500 mg before first two meals of the day. Note: Don't take astragalus if you have a fever or any other acute infection.
- Licorice root helps endocrine gland function. Take 500 mg twice daily. Don't take licorice for more than a week at a time.
- Siberian Ginseng supplies energy and helps strengthen the endocrine system. Take 200 mg twice daily, 30 minutes before first two meals of the day. Use a standardized extract containing 0.5 % eleutheroside E.
- Silymarin extract helps protect and repair the liver. Use as directed on label.
- Grapefruit Seed extract—4,000 mg three times daily

IMPORTANT AIDS

- Spirulina helps maintain energy and may prevent the AIDS virus from attaching to cells. Take 3 tsps. daily or mix into juice.
- Egg Lecithin—20 grams daily in divided portions. Take on an empty stomach.
- Barley Grass
- Boxwood—1,000 mg daily of an extract of boxwood leaves and stems

- Cat's Claw has shown to be helpful for people with AIDS and related cancers.
- Goldenseal—take as directed but not for more than one week at a time

OTHER POTENTIAL AIDS

- Garlic fights all forms of infection. Take 4,000 mcg three times daily. The most effective form is fresh or as an essential oil.
- Red Algae
- Bee Propolis
- Clustered Water
- Free-form amino complex—take according to label direction
- Folic Acid helps with mouth sores. Take 400 mcg up to three times daily in chewable tablet form.
- American Ginseng
- Chaparral has antibiotic, anti-inflammatory, and antioxidant properties. Take 1 capsule three times daily or 10 to 30 drops of extract three times daily.
- Echinacea should be avoided by people with AIDS. It appears to assist in replicating the virus.
- Essiac
- European Mistletoe
- Green Tea helps protect against cancer.
- Hawthorn helps raise immunity.
- Hyssop is good for circulatory and congestion problems.
- Korean Ginseng
- Neem leaf extract or tea consumed orally.
- Nettle acts as a pain reliever, expectorant, and tonic.
- Pine Bark extract or Grape Seed extract help fight inflammation. Take 50 mg three times daily of either one.
- Olive Leaf extract fights bacteria, viruses, fungi, and parasites.
- Shark Cartilage (pure dried shark cartilage) inhibits tumor growth. Take as directed on an empty stomach.
- Terminalia Bellerica

- Carnivora
- Maitake, Reishi, and Shiitake Mushroom have antitumor and antiviral properties. Take according to label directions.
- Coconut Milk (Coconut Cream)
- Coconut Oil
- Flaxseed Oil helps the nervous system and the skin. Take 1 to 2 tbsp. daily or 500 to 1,000 mg twice daily in capsule form. If diarrhea develops, discontinue until it improves.
- Vinegar (white or brown)
- Rye Sprouts
- Bitter Melon (unripened)
- Hyperbaric oxygen therapy can help overcome opportunistic infections.

People with AIDS should consume as many fresh fruits and vegetables as possible. Approximately 75% of the diet should consist of raw organic foods, plus lentils, nuts, seeds, and whole grains. Fresh live juice is recommended, especially juice containing leafy greens such as spinach, beet juice, carrot, and kale. Drink live juices three times daily, if possible.

☞ ALLERGIES

AN ALLERGY is an unusual sensitivity to a normally harmless substance that, when breathed in, ingested, or brought into contact with the skin, provokes a strong reaction from the person's body. The body is sensitized by the immune system's response to the first exposure to the substance and mobilizes white blood cells to fight the nontoxic invaders, creating more damage to the body than the invader. Thus, the allergic response becomes a disease in itself. Try a lemon and watermelon fast for a few days—this has helped many people reduce allergies. Read Chapter 14.

TOP NATURAL AIDS

- Local Bee Pollen (locally harvested)—start with a few granules and gradually work up to 2 tsp. daily. Discontinue if you experience any negative reaction.
- Vitamin B-complex—50 mg of each major B vitamin twice daily
- Vitamin E—400 IU daily
- Digestive Enzymes
- Vitamin C with bioflavonoids—5,000 to 20,000 mg daily in divided portions
- Probiotic supplement supplying acidophilus—take as directed on label
- Calcium—1,500 to 2,000 mg daily
- Magnesium—750 mg daily
- Methylsulfonylmethane (MSM) may help reduce severity of an allergy attack. Take 500 mg three to four times daily with meals.
- Quercetin—500 mg twice daily
- Bromelain—100 mg twice daily
- Raw Adrenal Glandular—500 mg twice daily
- Raw Spleen Glandular—500 mg twice daily
- Raw Thymus Glandular Extract—500 mg twice daily
- Vitamin B5—100 mg three times daily
- Vitamin B6—50 mg three times daily

- Vitamin B12—300 to 1,000 mcg three times daily
- Nettle leaf heals mucous membranes. Take 400 to 800 mg every four hours.

IMPORTANT AIDS

- Vitamin A—10,000 IU daily
- Selenium—50 to 100 mcg daily during allergy season
- Coenzyme Q10—100 mg daily
- Coenzyme A—take as directed on label
- Potassium—100 mg daily
- Licorice Root can help allergic inflammation. Do not use for more than 5 days in a row.
- Flaxseed Oil—500 to 1,000 mg twice daily

OTHER POTENTIAL AIDS

- Evening Primrose Oil—1,000 mg three times daily
- Spirulina may help counter allergic reactions.
- Reishi Mushrooms
- Vitamin D3—400 IU daily
- Rice Bran
- Wheat Grass juice
- Proteolytic enzymes aid digestion. Take on an empty stomach, as directed on label. Note: don't give these enzymes to children.
- Aloe Vera juice consumed orally.
- Cat's Claw—take according to label directions
- Eucalyptus and/or Thyme Leaves inhaled as steam can help with congestion.
- Eyebright tea can reduce watery eyes and runny noses in children.
- Ginkgo Biloba is beneficial for asthma.
- Grape Seed extract—take as directed on label
- Holy Basil
- Indian Lobelia
- Neem oil applied topically or leaf extract consumed orally.
- Olive Leaf fights bacteria, fungi, parasites, and viruses.

- Perilla seeds
- Rosemary Oil can provide relief from an allergic rash. Use 1 tbsp. of oil in 1 cup of water and apply topically.
- Shark Liver Oil
- Oregano Oil consumed orally.
- Rye Sprouts
- Turmeric helps with the fatigue that can accompany allergies. Take 500 mg three times daily.
- Aged Garlic Extract

☞ ALZHEIMER'S DISEASE

THE FOLLOWING THERAPIES are normally available over-the-counter from health food stores and supermarkets. This condition may relate to a reduced flow of blood in the body, which affects the brain and produces corresponding symptoms. Check for high levels of heavy metal toxicity and vitamin B12 deficiency as well as essential fatty acid deficiency.

TOP NATURAL AIDS

- Beta-carotene—5,000 IU twice daily
- Coenzyme Q10—300 mg daily taken in three 100 mg servings
- Ginkgo Biloba increases brain circulation and oxygenation.
- Liquid Colloidal Minerals
- Selenium—100 mcg twice daily
- Vitamin B-complex—100 mg three times daily
- Vitamin B6—100 mg daily
- Vitamin B12—if at all possible, 3 to 4 mg (3,000 to 4,000 mcg) daily of the methylcobalamin form consumed sublingually (under the tongue) in order to maximize absorption
- Vitamin C—3,000 mg daily taken in three 1,000 mg servings
- Lecithin—25 gram (25,000 mg) daily or more
- American Ginseng—1,000 to 3,000 mg daily (1 to 3 grams) for unstandardized products and 600 to 2,000 mg for products that have been standardized to contain 10.28% ginsenosides. The therapeutic long-term (more than 3 months) serving of American Ginseng is 500 to 1,500 mg daily for unstandardized products and 400 to 800 mg for products that have been standardized to contain 10.28% ginsenosides.
- Panax Ginseng—short-term (up to three months) serving for unstandardized Asiatic ginseng is 1,000 to 2,000 mg daily. If standardized Asiatic ginseng (i.e. 7–32% ginsenosides) is used, this serving can be lowered to approximately 300 to 400 mg daily.
- Phosphatidylserine—300 mg daily for twelve weeks, followed

by 100 mg daily
- Zinc—25 mg twice daily
- Evening Primrose Oil or Flaxseed Oil—500 to 1,000 mg twice daily
- Magnesium—1,000 mg daily, preferably in the magnesium citrate, magnesium diglycinate, magnesium fumarate, magnesium malate, magnesium orotate, or magnesium glycinate forms
- Chelation EDTA

IMPORTANT AIDS

- Folic Acid—400 to 800 mcg daily
- Huperzine A—100 mcg daily
- Calcium—1,600 mg daily at bedtime
- Vitamin E—2,000 IU daily
- Melatonin—10 mg taken at bedtime
- NADH—10 mg daily consumed 30 minutes prior to breakfast
- RNA—1,000 to 1,500 mg daily
- SAMe—400 mg twice daily

OTHER POTENTIAL AIDS

- Arginine—3,000 to 6,000 mg daily
- Alternatives: CDP-choline, Lecithin, DMAE, and Centrophenoxine "work" via similar mechanisms to choline. CDP-choline, DMAE, and Centrophenoxine are likely to be more potent than Choline.
- Creatine Monohydrate—2 to 5 grams daily divided into 2 to 3 servings
- DHA—600 to 2,200 mg daily
- Alternatives: Fish Oils are a good source of DHA. Flaxseed Oil and Perilla Oil both contain high levels of the Omega-3 fatty acid, alpha-linolenic acid that is converted within the body to form DHA. Oily fish such as herring, salmon, mackerel, trout, and sardines contain high levels of DHA—3,600 mg daily.
- Flaxseed Oil contains high levels of the Omega-3 fatty acid,

alpha-linolenic acid, which is converted within the body to form DHA—2 to 4 tablespoons daily

THESE PRODUCTS MAY BE HELPFUL

- Glutamine—2,000 mg daily
- Inositol—50 to 200 mcg daily
- Lycopene—6.5 mg daily
- Silicon—30 to 50 mg of the orthosilic acid form of silicon daily
- Taurine—2 grams three times daily
- Tyrosine—2,000 to 10,000 mg daily
- Vitamin A—10,000 to 50,000 IU daily
- Vitamin B1—150 to 1,500 mg daily taken as three 50 to 500 mg servings
- Whey Protein—20 grams daily
- DHEA—50 mg daily for men; 5 mg daily for women
- Glutathione—100 to 1,000 mg daily
- Malic Acid—1,000 mg of the magnesium malate form of malic acid daily
- Perilla Oil—6,000 mg (6 grams) daily
- Phosphatidylcholine—3,000 mg (3 grams) daily
- Pregnenolone—minimum of 30 mg daily
- Thyroid Extract—taken as directed
- Vitamin K—10 mg of the vitamin K1-form daily

☞ ANEMIA

ANEMIA is an ailment involving a reduction in the oxygen-carrying capacity of the blood resulting from a deficiency in the quantity of red blood cells or hemoglobin in the blood.

It's urgent to find out why one is anemic. Bleeding with a bowel movement can be a sign of cancer. Where there is fruit, there's a root.

It's a good idea to stay away from refined foods and anything white, such as sugar, salt, flour, etc. Exercise and deep breathing help. Read the Exercise Chapter 17.

TOP NATURAL AIDS

- Raw Liver Extract contains all the elements essential for the production of red blood cells. Take 500 mg twice daily.
- Black Strap Molasses contains iron and essential B vitamins. Take 1 tbsp. twice daily for adults; 1 tsp. added to milk for children and infants.
- Biotin—300 mcg twice daily
- HCL or Apple Cider Vinegar in water before meals
- Folic Acid—400 mcg two to three times daily
- Vitamin B12 (the sublingual form is best)—2,000 mcg twice daily
- Vitamin C with bioflavonoids—3,000 to 10,000 mg daily in divided portions
- Spirulina—12,000 mg daily
- Bee Pollen
- Wheat Grass juice
- Nettle tea is rich in iron and is very effective for treating iron deficiency anemia.

IMPORTANT AIDS

- Zinc—30 mg with 2 mg copper daily. Copper is needed for the production of red blood cells, and zinc is needed to balance the copper.
- Vitamin B-complex—50 mg three times daily

- Vitamin B5—50 mg three times daily
- Vitamin B6—100 mg three times daily
- Vitamin E prolongs the life of red blood cells. Take 600 IU daily. Take vitamin E separately from any iron supplements.
- Vitamin A—10,000 IU daily; with natural beta-carotene, 15,000 IU daily
- Yellow Dock contains bio-available iron. Take 500 mg twice daily for six weeks.

OTHER POTENTIAL AIDS

- Carnitine, especially for forms of anemia that occur in persons undergoing dialysis treatment.
- Glutamine
- Lysine
- Anemia can occur as a result of iron deficiency. If your physician determines that iron supplementation is necessary, iron should be taken in an organic form, such as ferrous gluconate and iron-fed yeast in iron tonics.
- Ferritin (Iron Deficiency)
- Deoxyribonucleic Acid (DNA)
- Carnosine
- Alfalfa—take as directed on label
- Dandelion—as tea or juice
- Chinese (or Korean) Ginseng helps revitalize the body and is often used for anemia. Take 100 mg twice daily for 2 to 3 weeks. Don't use if you have high blood pressure, heart disease, or hypoglycemia.
- Dong Quai is often used to treat anemia. Take 500 mg twice daily for three weeks.
- Beet (Beetroot) juice
- Lettuce

☞ ANOREXIA

ANOREXIA NERVOSA is an ailment caused by the malfunction of the lateral hypothalamus (which normally generates the hunger sensation) that is characterized by self-inflicted starvation (purportedly in order to achieve weight loss). Check neurotransmitters (see Appendix A) as well as seek spiritual counseling. This ailment is usually accompanied by a lack or an imbalance of essential fatty acids.

TOP NATURAL AIDS

- Evening Primrose Oil—1,000 mg three times daily
- Multivitamin and mineral complex
- Beta-carotene—25,000 IU daily
- Vitamin A—10,000 IU daily
- Calcium—1,500 mg daily
- Magnesium—1,000 mg daily
- Potassium—100 to 200 mg daily
- Selenium—200 mcg daily
- Vitamin E—600 IU daily
- Vitamin D3—600 IU daily
- Vitamin B-complex—100 mg three times daily
- Zinc—80 mg daily with 3 mg copper
- Vitamin C with bioflavonoids—5,000 mg daily in divided servings
- Milk Thistle—200 mg two to three times daily of extract standardized to contain 70% silymarin
- Probiotic

IMPORTANT AIDS

- 5-HTP—100 to 200 mg three times daily
- Vitamin B1—50 to 100 mg daily
- Siberian Ginseng—100 mg twice a day

OTHER POTENTIAL AIDS

- Iron—18 to 30 mg daily
- Biotin—400 to 800 mcg daily
- Kelp—2,000 to 3,000 mg daily

☞ ANXIETY

ANXIETY is also known as Generalized Anxiety Disorder or worry and is a mood disorder characterized by a feeling of vague, unspecified harm, apprehension, or distress, often about the future, without an apparent cause. Psychiatrists often distinguish between anxiety that can be thought of as a reaction to an indistinct or imagined danger, and fear, which is a response to a real threat.

Approximately 10% of adults in Western nations have experienced an anxiety disorder in the preceding six months. Approximately 27% of adults in Western nations experience an anxiety disorder during their lifetimes.

Anxiety is all too common. The primary culprits seem to be emotional stress, physical stress, lack of rest, drugs, and a poor diet. *But the most common culprit is elevated blood lactate levels.* Sugar, caffeine, alcohol, B-vitamin deficiency, calcium or magnesium deficiency, and food allergens are strong factors for this ailment. Check for heavy metals.

Below you'll see supplements recommended for anxiety, but digging a little further may pay great dividends. I suggest an at-home neurotransmitter test to see what, if anything, is out of balance (see Appendix A), and then use natural supplements to bring the brain chemicals back into balance.

You must look truthfully at your diet! See what needs to be removed, such as chemical-laden foods, drinks, additives, sugars, bad fats, fast foods, and more. Check to make certain your essential fatty acids are in balance.

A good fast is a great place to start, cleansing the body from toxic overload, and then begin to add the right things back into your diet. Look at chapter 18 for this information.

Make sure you are getting proper amounts of rest, and that your sleep gets into the Delta stage to obtain proper recovery in the body. Reduce stress.

Also check adrenal function.

TOP NATURAL AID

- Kava Kava—300 mg daily divided servings
- High Potency Multivitamin daily
- Collagen at bedtime
- Magnesium—320 to 600 mg daily
- Selenium—50 to 200 mcg daily
- Vitamin B3—15 to 50 mg daily
- Calcium—2,000 mg daily
- Vitamin B6—50 mg three times daily
- Vitamin B12 administered concurrently with folic acid alleviates anxiety. B12—200 to 400 mcg daily. Folic Acid—800 mcg twice daily for first month, then once daily for second month. Maintain at 400 to 800 mcg daily.
- Potassium—200 mg daily
- Flaxseed Oil—1 tablespoon daily
- Vitamin C—500 to 1,000 mg daily in divided servings
- Vitamin E—400 to 600 IU daily
- Zinc—30 to 50 mg daily
- Passionflower—In tea form, tinctures, or pills should be taken according to label directions.
- St. John's Wort—300 mg three times daily of an extract standardized to contain 0.3% hypercin
- Valerian—2 to 3 grams twice daily
- Bilberry—120 to 240 mg twice daily of extract standardized to contain 25% anthocyanosides

IMPORTANT AIDS

- Tyrosine (L-Tyrosine)—500 mg three times daily on an empty stomach
- Melatonin—3 mg at bedtime
- Vitamin B1—50 mg three times daily with meals
- Vitamin B3 (niacinamide form)—1,000 to 6,000 mg daily
- Chromium Picolinate—200 mcg daily
- Ginkgo Biloba—80 mg twice daily

- Chamomile—In tea form, tinctures, or pills, should be taken according to label directions.

OTHER POTENTIAL AIDS

- 5-HTP—100 to 200 mg three times daily
- Theanine
- Threonine—6 grams daily
- Enzymes
- Pyruvate—22 to 44 grams daily
- DHEA—50 to 200 mg daily
- Pregnenolone—30 mg daily
- Iron—To correct iron deficiency, supplement with 100 to 200 mg daily. Once corrected, reduce to lowest level that maintains iron balance, typically 10 to 15 mg daily.
- Methylsulfonylmethane (MSM)—3,000 to 9,000 mg daily
- Inositol—12 grams daily
- GABA—750 mg twice times daily in conjunction with Inositol

FOODS *and* HERBS THAT IMPROVE ANXIETY

- Fungi Mushrooms
- Reishi Mushrooms alleviate anxiety—2 to 6 grams daily of raw fungus or equivalent serving of concentrated extract taken with meals
- Ashwagandha—1 teaspoon of powder twice daily boiled in milk or water
- Black Cohosh—1 to 2 tablets twice daily of standardized extract containing 1 mg of 27-deoxyacteine per tablet
- Brahmi
- Damiana—2 to 4 grams taken two to three times daily or take as directed
- Gotu Kola—20 to 60 mg taken three times daily of extract standardized to contain 40% asiaticoside, 29–30% madecassic acid, and 1–2% madecassoside. Note: Gotu Kola takes a minimum of four weeks to work.

- Green Tea—100 to 150 mg three times daily of extract standardized to contain 80% total polyphenols and 50% epigallocatechin gallate
- Hops—0.5 grams one to three times daily

Other helps: Aerobic Exercise

☞ ARTERIOSCLEROSIS/ ATHEROSCLEROSIS

BOTH INVOLVE THE BUILDUP OF DEPOSITS on the inside of the artery walls, causing the arteries to thicken and harden. In arteriosclerosis, the deposits come mostly from calcium. In atherosclerosis, the culprit is fatty substances, and the artery walls lose their elasticity and harden. Both hamper circulation, raise the blood pressure, and lead to angina, heart attack, stroke, and/or sudden cardiac death.

TOP NATURAL AIDS

- Magnesium—750 mg daily taken at bedtime.
- L-Carnitine—500 mg daily on an empty stomach
- Evening Primrose Oil—500 mg three times daily
- Chelation Suppositories with Ethylene-Diamine-Tetra-Acetate (EDTA) help to prevent the deposit of calcium and cholesterol in the atherosclerotic plaques that occur during the progression of atherosclerosis and also help to remove existing calcium and cholesterol from atherosclerotic plaques.
- Beta-carotene (natural form)—15,000 IU daily
- Superunsaturated Fatty Acids lower triglycerides in the blood. They are available in flaxseed oil and fish oils. Fish oils contain the important Omega-3 fatty acids EPA and DHA. Therapeutic servings include 1,800 mg of EPA and 900 mg of DHA daily. Flaxseed oil—1 to 2 tbsp. daily.
- Coenzyme Q10—100 mg daily
- Choline—50 to 200 mg daily
- Vitamin B3—100 mg three times daily
- Tocotrienols have powerful antioxidant properties. The form most readily accepted by the body is D-alpha-tocopherol, a form of Vitamin E.
- Vitamin A—25,000 IU daily
- Vitamin C with bioflavonoids—5,000 to 20,000 mg daily in divided servings
- Vitamin E—start with 200 IU daily and increase by 200 IU each week, until taking 1,000 IU daily (with mixed tocopherols)

- Ginkgo Biloba—40 to 80 mg three times daily of a 50:1 extract standardized to contain 24% ginkgo-flavone glycosides
- Green Tea—as tea, 3 cups daily; or as extract, 100 to 150 mg three times daily of green tea extract standardized to contain 80% total polyphenols and 50% epigallocatechin gallate
- Garlic has significantly slowed the development of atherosclerosis—900 mg daily.

IMPORTANT AIDS

- Lecithin—2,400 mg three times daily with meals
- Chondroitin Sulfate (CSA)—400 mg three times daily
- Bromelain—500 mg three times daily between meals
- Phosphatidylcholine helps to prevent and treat atherosclerosis. Take as directed on label.
- Chromium—1,000 mg daily
- Selenium—200 mcg daily
- Vitamin B6—100 mg three times daily
- Vitamin B12—200 to 400 mcg daily
- Germanium—200 mcg daily
- Melatonin—2 to 3 mg daily, taken 2 hours before bedtime
- Zinc (chelate form)—50 mg daily
- Copper—2 to 3 mg daily
- Horsetail contains silica, which helps maintain elasticity in the arteries. The best form is a liquid capsule, taken as directed on label.
- Hawthorn leaves and blossoms reduce cholesterol levels. Take 100 to 300 mg three times daily of an extract standardized to contain 2–3% flavonoids.
- Gugulipid has two active components, Z- and E-guggulsterone, that have been shown to reduce both cholesterol and triglyceride levels. Take as directed on label.

OTHER POTENTIAL AIDS

- Calcium—1,500 mg daily taken at bedtime

- L-cysteine—500 mg daily on an empty stomach
- L-methionine—500 mg daily on an empty stomach
- Amino Acids
- Arginine—take as directed on label
- Lysine—500 to 2,000 mg daily
- Taurine—2 grams three times daily
- Pangamic Acid
- Chitosan—3 to 6 grams daily taken with food
- Dextran Sulfate
- Glucosamine—500 mg three times daily (it usually takes weeks to work)
- Grapefruit Pectin helps lower cholesterol and reduces the risk of heart disease. An average serving is 50 to 100 mg daily.
- Ribose—60 grams daily
- Crocetin
- Lutein—5 to 30 mg daily
- Lycopene—3 mg twice daily
- Regular exposure to adequate (but not excessive) amounts of sunlight.
- Brinase
- Lipases are digestive enzymes that break down fat. They are available in an enzyme complex and should be taken as directed.
- DHEA—50 to 200 mg daily, also available in a cream containing 10% DHEA, follow label directions
- Micronized progesterone may be taken orally in amounts of 200 to 400 mg daily or applied topically using cream in amounts approximating 20 grams daily.
- Thyroid Hormones
- Conjugated Linoleic Acid (CLA)—3 to 5 grams daily
- Policosanol—5 to 10 mg twice daily
- Silicon—take as directed on label
- Vanadium—10 to 30 mcg daily
- Folic Acid—400 to 800 mcg daily

- Inositol—50 to 200 mg daily
- Lipoic Acid—20 to 50 mg daily
- Vitamin B1—100 mg three times daily
- Vitamin D—400 IU daily
- Vitamin K—100 to 500 mcg daily
- Vitamin D3—400 mg daily

FOODS, HERBS, OR BEVERAGES

- Cayenne (capsicum) has been shown to lower cholesterol levels. It has improved chest pain and circulation in some people suffering from angina. Cayenne (or capsicum) may be used in cream form or taken orally according to label directions.
- Curcumin (Turmeric)—take in a form standardized to curcumin content to provide 400 to 600 mg of curcumin three times daily.
- Velvet Deer Antler
- Royal Jelly—use as directed on label
- Bilberry—120 to 240 mg twice daily of an extract standardized to contain 25% anthocyanosides
- Alfalfa Leaf juice—take as directed on label
- Grapefruit
- Pineapple
- Rice
- Barley Grass is a potent antioxidant that helps protect the body from free radical damage. Take as directed.
- Reishi Mushrooms—2 to 6 grams daily of raw fungus or an equivalent serving in concentrated extract form
- American Ginseng—1,000 to 3,000 mg daily (1 to 3 grams) for unstandardized products and 600 to 2,000 mg for products that have been standardized to contain 10.28% ginsenosides. The therapeutic long-term (more than 3 months) serving of American Ginseng is 500 to 1,500 mg daily for unstandardized products and 400 to 800 mg for products that have been standardized to contain 10.28% ginsenosides.

- Cat's Claw—take as directed on label
- Ginger—in powdered form, 1 to 4 grams divided into 2 to 4 servings
- Saffron
- Lentils
- High consumption of Peanuts
- Cod Liver Oil, a natural source of Vitamin D—take as directed on label
- Extra Virgin Olive Oil
- Lecithin—10,500 mg daily divided into 3 portions with meals
- Grape Seed extract—take as directed on label
- Gotu Kola—20 to 60 mg three times daily of an extract standardized to contain 40% asiaticoside, 29–30% asiatic acid, 29–30% madecassic acid, and 1–2% madecassoside. Gotu Kola normally takes at least 4 weeks to work.

☞ ARTHRITIS

ARTHRITIS is a general term for several ailments involving inflamed, thickened, painful joints. Rheumatoid arthritis is the second most widespread kind of arthritis and also classified as a form of rheumatism. Rheumatoid arthritis is regarded as an autoimmune disease and involves chronic inflammation of the joints—typically the joints of the fingers, wrists, feet, and ankles and often the hips and shoulders—and causes devastation of cartilage, bone, and other adjacent tissues.

Arthritis is one of the conditions my husband had. Read Chapter 18 to see what he did.

Gout. A few years ago my then eleven-year-old daughter broke her leg. While the nurse was attending her, I noticed the nurse could hardly walk. She told me she had gout, and none of the prescriptions she tried worked for her. We discussed the foods that contributed to this problem, and also that black cherry juice sometimes worked wonders. When I visited the hospital a few days later, I saw her and she was dancing and showing me how quickly the black cherry juice and diet worked. So many times we are aggravating or causing the ailment by what we eat.

Osteoarthritis. Many have found great relief by cleansing the body as well as putting the right nutrients back in. Often these ailments are related to high protein intake. Seventy to eighty percent of the diet should be vegetables, raw foods with grains, and some fish and chicken.

Physicians often prescribe aspirin to counteract the pain associated with the various forms of arthritis. This can be toxic in that aspirin does not inhibit the damage to the joints associated with arthritis, and arthritis patients may subject their already damaged joints to further (injurious) activity when using aspirin to alleviate their pain.

Oddly enough, it's the foods people eat most that they may be allergic to that may cause this ailment. Dust, mold, pollen, pesticides, dyes, and preservatives are other considerations. Chlorine and fluoride in water and metal toxicity, heavy metals, dental amalgams, and Candida overgrowth may also contribute to this debilitating disease.

See recommended professional services in Appendix B for more help with arthritis.

TOP NATURAL AIDS

- Cleansing or Detoxifying
- No red meats
- Get lots of rest
- Clustered Water
- MSM—5,000 to 9,000 mg daily
- Green-Lipped Mussel extracts—1,000 mg daily
- Selenium—200 mcg daily
- Cox 2 Enzyme Inhibitors
- SAMe—400 mg twice daily
- Glucosamine Sulfate—500 mg three times daily (this takes about 6 weeks to work)
- Infrared sauna
- Evening Primrose Oil—500 mg three times daily
- Chondroitin Sulfate—500 to 1,000 mg daily
- Vitamin C with bioflavonoids—2,000 to 10,000 mg daily in divided portions
- Bromelain—1,200 to 1,800 mg daily taken between meals
- Gamma-Linolenic Acid (GLA) is the active ingredient in essential oils such as borage, black currant, and flaxseed oil.
- Linoleic Acid (LA), an Omega-6 fatty acid. Good sources are evening primrose oil, borage and blackcurrant oil.
- Superunsaturated Fatty Acids and Alpha-Linolenic Acids (LNA) (Omega-3 fatty acids) include flaxseed oil and some fish oils.
- EPA—1,800 mg daily
- DHEA—50 to 200 mg daily
- Devil's Claw—400 mg three times daily for 4 to 6 weeks
- Blackcurrant Seed—500 to 1,000 mg twice daily
- Borage Seed Oil—500 to 1,000 mg twice daily
- Evening Primrose Oil—500 to 1,000 mg twice daily

- Fish Oils—18 grams daily
- Flaxseed Oil ingested orally or applied topically—1 to 2 tbsp. daily or 500 to 1,000 mg twice daily
- Chelation Suppositories with Ethylene-Diamine-Tetra-Acetate (EDTA) help to prevent the deposit of calcium and cholesterol in the atherosclerotic plaques that occur during the progression of atherosclerosis and also help to remove existing calcium and cholesterol from atherosclerotic plaques.

IMPORTANT AIDS

- Trimethylglycine (TMG)—500 to 1,000 mg in the morning
- Pancreatic Enzymes
- Boswellic Acid is a phytochemical found in boswellia, an herb. It has anti-inflammatory and anti-arthritic properties. Boswellia can be used topically as a cream for pain relief or can be taken orally in capsule or tablet form as directed. Product should contain 150 mg of boswellic acid per capsule or tablet.
- Boron (Sodium Tetraborate Decahydrate form)—6 to 9 mg daily
- Vitamin B3 (Niacinamide form)—100 mg three times daily
- Vitamin B5—500 to 1,000 mg daily
- Vitamin B6—at least 50 mg daily
- Silica lessens inflammation and is useful for arthritis.
- Shark Cartilage—1 gram for every 2 pounds of body weight, divided into 3 servings
- Alfalfa juice—take according to label directions
- Feverfew—250 mg daily
- Ginger—in powdered form, 1 to 4 grams divided into 2 to 4 servings
- Nettle leaf—300 mg twice daily
- Turmeric in form standardized to curcurmin content—400 to 600 mg three times daily
- Yucca—1,000 mg twice daily
- Capsaicin from cayenne pepper

OTHER POTENTIAL AIDS

- Creatine—2 to 5 grams daily
- Cysteine—500 to 1,500 mg daily
- Histidine—1,000 to 6,000 mg daily
- Hyaluronic Acid
- Proteases
- Chymotrypsin, especially when used in combination with other Proteases
- Papain
- Trypsin, a proteolytic enzyme that helps restore circulation in body tissue. Take as directed on label.
- Superoxide Dismutase (SOD)—take as directed on label
- Pregnenolone—500 mg daily
- 10-Hydroxy-2-Decenoic Acid, a component of Royal Jelly
- Prostaglandins are hormone-like substances that can trigger inflammation. Consuming Gamma-Linolenic Acid helps suppress the production of prostaglandins.
- Germanium—100 to 300 mg daily
- Manganese—5 mg twice daily for 4 weeks
- Potassium—100 to 500 mg daily
- Zinc—50 mg daily
- Vitamin A—10,000 IU daily
- Vitamin C and supplemental vitamin C—1,000 to 3,000 mg daily
- Vitamin E—400 IU three times daily (with mixed tocopherols)
- Vitamin K—100 to 200 mcg daily
- Horsetail—take as directed on label
- Bovine Cartilage—take as directed on label
- Thymus Extract—take as directed on label
- Velvet Deer Antler
- Royal Jelly—take as directed on label
- Pineapple
- Karawatake Mushrooms
- Aloe Vera

- Comfrey ointment applied topically.
- Cat's Claw—take as directed on label
- Green Tea—as tea, 3 cups daily; as extract, 100 to 150 mg three times daily of green tea extract standardized to contain 80% total polyphenols and 50% epigallocatechin gallate
- Dandelion reduces pain and strengthens connective tissue. Take as tea or juice twice daily or 3 capsules twice daily.
- Juniper Berry—250 to 500 mg twice daily
- Deglycyrrhizinated licorice is the safest product—available in many forms, follow label directions
- Olive Leaf helps inflammatory arthritis.
- Sarsaparilla helps rheumatoid arthritis.
- Celery Seeds alleviate muscle spasms.
- Grapefruit Seeds
- Rye
- People with the highest consumption of vegetables have a lower risk of rheumatoid arthritis compared to people with low consumption of vegetables.
- Lettuce juice
- Rhubarb juice
- Sea Cucumbers are actually marine animals that have been used for centuries by Asians to treat arthritic conditions. They contain chondroitins, which are often lacking in those suffering from arthritis and related conditions. Take supplement as directed on label.

Exercise is essential.

☞ AUTOIMMUNE DISEASES

AUTOIMMUNE DISEASES are a group of otherwise unrelated disorders that are caused by the inflammation and destruction of tissues within the body by the body's own antibodies (auto-antibodies) and T-Lymphocytes. Autoimmune diseases are more prevalent in women than in men.

Rheumatoid Arthritis. While counseling a woman with RA, I asked her if she had any bitterness or unforgiveness in her life. She replied that she didn't. I explained that the reason I asked was that many times I found that autoimmune diseases such as RA and lupus have spiritual roots associated with unforgiveness. She began to weep and said that when she was first diagnosed years before, she was married to a very abusive husband. After we talked more, she forgave him and within two weeks relief came and her joints began to normalize. (Read "Foundations to the Gospel of Health.")

TOP NATURAL AIDS

- Vitamin C with bioflavonoids—5,000 to 20,000 mg daily in divided portions
- Cysteine and Glutamine should be supplemented together.
- Glutathione within the body is poorly absorbed orally. Take 500 mg twice of L-Cysteine on an empty stomach, and Glutamine as directed on label.
- Enzyme Therapy (i.e. involving multiple enzymes, especially proteolytic enzymes) break up the immune complexes that are mixed up in autoimmune diseases. Specific enzymes that are commonly utilized during enzyme therapy are: Amylase, Bromelain, Chymotrypsin, Lipases, Pancreatin, Papain, and Trypsin. Take as directed.
- Wobenzyme N (a proprietary formula of various enzymes) alleviates some types of autoimmune diseases. Take 3 to 6 tablets two to three times daily between meals.
- Selenium—200 mcg daily
- Supplemental Vitamin E

- Thymus Extract normalizes the helper T-Cells—take as directed on label
- Fish Oils contain the important Omega-3 fatty acids Eicosapentaenoic Acid (EPA) and Docosahexaenoic Acid (DHA). Therapeutic servings include 1,800 mg of EPA and 900 mg of DHA daily.
- Astragalus generates anticancer cells in the body.
- Coenzyme Q10—100 mg daily
- Garlic—2 capsules of extract
- Zinc—50 to 80 mg three times daily with copper

IMPORTANT AIDS

- Milk Thistle
- Vitamin B-complex—100 mg three times daily
- Vitamin B12—1,000 to 2,000 mg daily
- Vitamin B6—50 mg three times daily
- Vitamin A—10,000 IU daily
- Grape Seed extract—take as directed

OTHER POTENTIAL AIDS

- Natural Progesterone cream applied topically alleviates many autoimmune diseases in women. Use 1/2 tsp. daily per label directions.
- Alpha-Linolenic Acid (LNA) suppresses the autoimmune response that may help to prevent autoimmune diseases.
- Magnesium Bicarbonate—1.5 liters of magnesium bicarbonate-containing water daily for at least six weeks
- Methylsulfonylmethane (MSM)
- Vitamin D—400 mg daily
- Diet Restriction alleviates autoimmune diseases by normalizing the body's production of B-Lymphocytes.
- Ligustrum supports the thymus and spleen.
- Spirulina supplies a wide assortment of nutrients that protect the immune system. Use according to label directions.
- Red Clover enhances the immune system.

☞ BACKACHE

BACKACHE is pain in the back of any cause or description. It can occur as a constant aching pain or as a sharp, stabbing, boring, or burning pain that is worsened when twisting, turning, or bending. Many backaches are caused by muscle weakness, and it is also often regarded as a form of rheumatism.

While there are many reasons one may have back pain, I have to say that a good percentage of the time it is from weak kidneys, overactive thyroid, and being overweight. If someone is overweight, the front of the body is so heavy that it pulls the back out of whack. Often this pain will disappear with weight loss and exercise. Be sure to seek the advice of a qualified medical professional to rule out serious disorders that require their attention prior to self-treatment. Chiropractic adjustments can be invaluable.

TOP NATURAL AIDS

- Calcium—1,500 to 2,000 mg daily
- Magnesium—700 to 1,000 mg daily
- Glucosamine Sulfate—500 mg three times daily
- Horsetail (or silica)—three times daily as directed on label
- Vitamin C with bioflavonoids—3,000 mg daily or more
- Clustered Water
- MSM—5,000 mg daily
- DMSO applied topically
- Chiropractic adjustments
- Massage Therapy

IMPORTANT AIDS

- DL-Phenylalanine (DLPA)—take daily every other week. Use as directed on label.
- Vitamin D—400 IU daily
- Evening Primrose Oil—1,000 mg three times daily
- Vitamin E—400 to 800 IU daily
- Vitamin A—15,000 IU daily

- Boron—3 mg daily
- L-Proline—500 mg daily on an empty stomach
- Vitamin B12 administered intramuscularly by physician or 2,000 mcg daily in lozenge or sublingual form.
- Zinc—50 mg plus 3 mg copper daily
- Bovine Cartilage—take as directed on label
- White Willow Bark works as a pain reliever.
- Manganese—2 to 5 mg daily

OTHER POTENTIAL AIDS

- Molybdenum—400 to 500 mcg daily
- Pine Bark extract or Grape Seed extract help fight inflammation. Take 50 to 75 mg three times daily of either one.
- Devil's Claw relieves pain and inflammation.
- Beetroot juice

✍ BEDWETTING

BEDWETTING is a form of incontinence that involves the unconscious passing of urine while asleep.

Several years ago I received an e-mail from a woman concerning a six year old who still wet the bed. She was wondering if I would suggest something natural because the family lived in a small town in Ireland, and they were unable to find help.

"Easy," I said. "Eliminate all sugars and dyes and add essential fatty acids to the diet."

The dear lady immediately ordered the supplements from our office. Within two weeks the child had stopped wetting the bed. Later I learned that it was common in Ireland for children to wet the bed well into their adolescence. Obviously, there was something in common missing in their diet—the good fats. It was very rewarding to receive a letter from the father, expressing his gratitude for the monumental change in his child's life, naturally.

TOP NATURAL AIDS

- B-complex vitamins as directed on label.
- Essential Fatty Acids. See Chapter Two for "Fats."
- The following five supplements are procedures for adults; for kids 12 to 17, reduce the serving to three-quarters the amount; for kids 6 to 12, use half the amount; and for kids under 6, use one-fourth the amount.
  1. Free-form amino acid complex—take as directed on label
  2. Calcium—1,500 mg daily
  3. Magnesium—350 mg daily
  4. Potassium—100 mg daily
  5. Vitamin A—5,000 to 10,000 IU daily

IMPORTANT AIDS

- Silica—take as directed

OTHER POTENTIAL AIDS

- Iron (iron phosphate form) helps to prevent bedwetting. You should take supplemental iron only if your physician determines you have an iron deficiency.
- Zinc helps to prevent bedwetting—10 mg daily for children, 80 mg daily for adults
- Oils (dietary oils)
- Pumpkin Seed Oil helps an irritable bladder. Take as directed.
- St. Johns Wort (said to help heal nerve damage)—300 mg three times daily of an extract standardized to contain 0.3% hypercin

LIKELY CAUSES *of* BEDWETTING

- Sugars
- Food dye
- Stress
- Neurotransmitter imbalance
- Compromised immune system
- Low-grade bacterial infection in the bladder
- Allergies can be the underlying cause

☞ BIPOLAR MOOD DISORDER/ MANIC-DEPRESSIVE DISORDER

MANIC DEPRESSION is a severe type of primary depression characterized by recurring episodes of depression alternating with mania— either full blown mania or hypomania. A person may go from feelings of unrealistic invincibility and elation to the depths of misery and despair. Both depression and mania will vary in length and severity, and how long the cycles will last can vary between days and months. The sufferer is usually psychologically healthy during the intervals between attacks.

Bipolar may be worsened by an overgrowth of yeast and by nutritional deficiencies. This is a serious disorder and no one should self-medicate. The symptoms of bipolar disorder can be severe and life threatening.

These aids are only suggested as natural supportive supplements with the supervision of a qualified physician or psychiatrist. Eliminate all processed and refined foods from the diet.

TOP NATURAL AIDS

- High Potency Food-Based Multivitamin
- L-Tyrosine—500 mg three times daily. Do not take if taking an MAO inhibitor.
- Vitamin B-complex—100 mg of each major B three times daily
- Magnesium—250 to 300 mg one to two times daily combined with calcium, 500 to 600 mg one to two times daily
- Fish Oils—3,400 mg of DHA and 6,200 mg of EPA
- 5 HTP—25 to 50 mg at bedtime
- Vitamin E—400 to 800 IU per day
- Water. Read Chapter 9.

IMPORTANT AIDS

- Taurine—500 mg three times daily on an empty stomach
- Vitamin C—3,000 mg daily

OTHER POTENTIAL AIDS

- Cysteine
- Phenylalanine—up to 4,000 mg daily
- DHEA—30 to 90 mg daily
- Pregnenolone—take as directed on label
- Triiodothyronine—25 to 30 mcg daily
- Flaxseed Oil—1 to 2 tbsp. daily
- Oat Straw—500 mg two to three times daily

☞ BLADDER INFECTIONS

THE BLADDER stores and periodically expels urine produced by the kidneys into the urethra for discharge.

Many years ago a friend's elderly mother was staying with them. She had had two surgeries to repair her bladder, but the trouble remained. She had daily problems with leakage. During her stay she began to take the daily supplement her son took, Body Oxygen. Within days the bladder leakage stopped completely. The underlying factor was a low-grade bacterial infection. Unfortunately, 10 to 20 percent of women have urinary tract discomfort at least once a year. Also, see the Candida Section for cleansing. There is a growing concern that antibiotic therapy may actually promote recurrent bladder infections.

TOP NATURAL AIDS

- Probiotic—as directed
- Distilled water, see Chapter 9
- Garlic—2 capsules twice a day
- Vitamin C—4,000 to 5,000 mg with 1,000 mg bioflavonoids taken in divided servings
- Zinc—50 mg taken with 3 mg copper daily
- Bearberry (also known as Uva Ursi)
- Cranberry—8 to 16 ounces of pure cranberry juice daily or 300 to 400 mg twice daily of dry cranberry juice extract
- Goldenseal—250 mg four times daily. Do not take if pregnant or more than one week at a time.
- Uva Ursi Leaf tea—as directed
- Vitamin A—50,000 IU daily for up to 2 days (not if pregnant)
- Goldenseal
- Cranberry extract

IMPORTANT AIDS

- Potassium—100 mg daily
- Vitamin E—600 IU daily
- N-Acetylcysteine—500 mg twice daily on an empty stomach

OTHER POTENTIAL AIDS

- Magnesium—750 to 1,000 mg daily
- Silicon has anti-inflammatory and disinfecting properties. It can be found suspended in a liquid gel or as an aqueous organic vegetal silica extract (of the herb Horsetail) and should be taken as directed.
- Calcium—1,500 mg daily
- Vitamin B-complex—50 to 100 mg of each major B vitamin twice daily

FOODS AND HERBS THAT MAY HELP

- Blue Vervain
- Chamomile acts as a diuretic.
- Cornsilk acts as a diuretic.
- Lovage (in bath water) is a healing herb that refreshes and cleanses.
- Rosehips tea benefits bladder infections.
- Beetroot, especially Beetroot juice
- Oregano—75 mg extract three times daily

Caution: Do not drink caffeinated products when and if you have bladder problems.

✍ BRAIN

THE BRAIN is the enlarged and highly developed mass of nerve tissue that forms the upper end of the central nervous system (CNS). The brain is composed of various distinct regions and is comprised (on a cellular level) primarily of glial cells and neurons. It is directly attached to the spinal cord.

THESE SUBSTANCES MAY HELP THE PROVISION *of* ENERGY *to the* BRAIN

- Asparagine is created from the amino acid aspartic acid and helps maintain balance in the central nervous system.
- Glutamine—5 to 6 grams daily divided into separate servings
- Pyroglutamate
- Carbohydrates. Glucose (or glucose can be produced within the body from glycerol) is a source of energy for the brain.
- Clupanodonic Acid
- Eicosapentaenoic Acid (EPA)—5 to 15 grams daily
- Docosahexaenoic Acid (DHA)
- Curcumin—400 to 600 mg three times daily
- Coenzyme Q10—100 mg daily
- Folic Acid—400 mcg daily
- Vitamin B-complex—50 to 100 mg of each major B vitamin twice daily
- Clustered Water
- Oxygen, Body Oxygen
- Malic Acid
- Lipoic—20 to 50 mg daily

THESE SUBSTANCES MAY IMPROVE *the* FUNCTION *of the* BRAIN

- Acetyl-L-Carnitine (ALC)—500 mg twice daily (avoid the D form)
- Glutamic Acid is derived from L-glutamine, the only amino acid that passes easily through the blood-brain barrier. Take 2 grams daily.

- Taurine—2 grams three times daily
- Hyaluronic Acid is a major component of the extracellular matrix of the brain.
- DHEA—50 to 200 mg daily
- Progesterone—20 mg daily in cream form
- Alpha-linolenic Acid is essential for brain development. It can be found in flaxseed and some fish oils.
- Boron—3 to 6 mg daily
- Chromium—200 to 600 mcg daily
- Potassium—200 to 400 mg three to four times daily
- Selenium—100 to 200 mcg daily
- Copper—3 mg daily
- Selenium—200 mcg daily
- Panaxic Acid
- Choline—500 mg daily for therapeutic use, 1,000 to 1,500 mg daily
- Inositol—500 to 1,000 mg daily
- Vitamin B1—100 mg daily
- Vitamin B3—50 to 100 mg daily
- Vitamin C—6 to 8 grams daily

THESE HERBS IMPROVE the FUNCTION of the BRAIN

- Ginkgo Biloba—60 to 100 mg two to three times daily
- Ginsengs (Panax Ginseng—200 mg daily of an extract standardized to contain 4–7% ginsenosides)
- Golden Root

BEWARE!

- Detergents or shampoos such as sodium lauryl sulfate (ingested orally or applied topically) accumulates in and damages the brain. This is a common ingredient in almost every shampoo.
- Minerals such as aluminum and mercury accumulate in the brain. Excess copper is toxic to the brain.

☞ BREAST CANCER

BREAST CANCER is the most common cancer among women. The numbers say 1 in 8 women will get it. Most breast cancer estrogen dominance. Estrogen promotes cellular growth and reproductive organs. Studies show that synthetic hormones can increase a woman's chance of breast cancer by 80%. No chemicals of any kind should be used on or in the body. Some studies show that 76% of all cancers in this country are chemically driven. No cleaning chemicals should be used or sodium laurel sulfate in shampoos.

An internal body cleanse is very important. Nothing works like a good fast. Chelation is helpful to pull out the chemicals already in the body. An old Indian concoction called black salve is said to be effective. IPT therapy from alternative medical doctors shows great promise. Regular consumption of fish oils helps to prevent breast cancer and the further growth and metastasis of existing breast cancer and prolong survival. Rid yourself of unforgiveness and bitterness. Do not wear underwire bras.

For more information go to Fibrocystic Breast.

TOP NATURAL AIDS

- Selenium—800 mcg daily has been shown to stop breast cancer from metastasizing to other areas. Take throughout the day, not all at once.
- Soursop in aloe vera base
- Probiotics
- Clustered Water Cats Claw formula
- Chelation EDTA IV or suppository
- High potency multivitamin and mineral complex without iron
- Coenzyme Q10—100 mg daily
- Selenium—200 to 400 mcg daily
- Vitamin B12—2,000 mcg daily
- Vitamin B6—associated with reduced discomfort from breast tenderness.
- Folic Acid—400 to 800 mcg daily

- Vitamin E—start with 400 IU daily, gradually increase to 1,000 IU daily
- Liver cleanse to metabolize estrogen—see Appendix A.
- Alpha Lipoic Acid to cleanse fat cells, where toxins are stored.
- Colostrum—promotes healing and boosts immunities
- Calcium D-Glucarate—primary evidence suggests it indirectly helps the body lower estrogen
- Vitamin A—25,000 IU daily
- Vitamin C with bioflavonoids—5,000 to 20,000 mg daily in divided servings
- Shark Cartilage—1 gram for every 2 pounds of body weight, divided into 3 servings; for prevention, 2,000 to 4,500 mg three times daily
- L-Cysteine—combines with L-Gutamine to promote the synthesis of gluathione, a naturally occurring detoxifier and antioxidant
- Milk Thistle—200 mg twice daily of extract containing 80% flavonoids
- Flaxseed Oil—1 to 2 tablespoons daily
- Cabbage Family Vegetables help to prevent breast cancer.
- Garlic—2 capsules twice a day
- No meats that are not organic and hormone free.

IMPORTANT AIDS

- Astragalus—250 to 500 mg twice daily
- Iodine from kelp is an excellent detoxifier
- Thyme Extract—500 mg twice daily
- SOD—taken as directed
- Kelp—1,000 to 1,500 mg daily
- Black Cohosh—1 to 2 tablets twice daily of a standardized extract containing 1 mg of 27-deoxyacteine per tablet
- Chaste Berry—20 to 40 mg daily
- Red Clover—choose extract providing 40 to 160 mg of isoflavones daily

- High in isoflavones and and antioxidants
- Tea (especially Green Tea) helps to prevent breast cancer—for Green Tea, drink several cups daily or take 300 to 400 mg daily of a standardized extract containing 90% total phenols
- Maitake Mushrooms—4,000 to 8,000 mg daily
- Grape Seed extract is a potent antioxidant. Take as directed on label.
- Fish oil contains the important Omega-3 fatty acids EPA and DHA. Therapeutic servings include 1,800 mg of EPA and 900 mg of DHA daily.
- Diindolylmethane—a substance found in cruciferous vegetables that increases the metabolism of excess estrogen

OTHER POTENTIAL AIDS

- Natural Beta-carotene—10,000 IU daily
- Dunaliella
- Bovine Cartilage—9 grams daily
- Bee Propolis is available in many forms for topical application and in tablets, capsules, and extracts. Follow label directions for use.
- High consumption of Yogurt helps to prevent breast cancer.
- High consumption of Fruit reduces the risk of developing breast cancer. Grapefruit, oranges, and tangerine inhibit the growth of the cells involved in breast cancer.
- Whole grains such as brown rice, millet, wheat, and oats are beneficial.
- Wheat Bran—5 to 10 grams daily
- Hops—0.5 grams taken one to three times daily
- Rosemary has anticancer properties. Take as directed.
- Schizandra
- Suma—500 mg twice daily
- Olive Oil helps to prevent breast cancer.
- Flaxseeds—1 tablespoon of seed two to three times daily taken with plenty of liquid

- Psyllium Seeds—take as directed on label
- High consumption of Vegetables reduces the risk of developing breast cancer by approximately 46%. Brussels sprouts, cabbage, cauliflower, kale (and collards), radish (seeds applied topically to the breast as a heated poultice), rutabaga, turnip, watercress, and carrots.

Aerobic Exercise: Even moderate exercise may lower breast cancer risk.

☞ BRONCHITIS

BRONCHITIS is a respiratory system ailment involving the inflammation of the mucous membranes of the bronchial tubes caused by infection by viruses or detrimental bacteria (and also, occasionally by other antigens) and usually accompanied by excessive mucous production, coughing, pain (in the chest and/or back), and shortness of breath. Low vegetable intake may increase your risk of bronchitis. Avoid smoke. Detoxify or cleanse the body quarterly.

TOP NATURAL AIDS

- Colloidal Silver
- Candida Cleanse
- Enzymes
- Probiotics
- Natural Beta-carotene—50,000 IU daily
- Zinc—60 mg with 3 mg copper
- Vitamin A—7,500 IU daily
- Selenium—200 mcg daily
- Vitamin C with bioflavonoids—3,000 to 10,000 mg daily divided into several servings
- Horsetail—follow label directions
- Goldenseal—150 to 300 mg four times daily for acute infection (don't take longer than 2 weeks)
- Siberian Ginseng promotes lung function.
- Mullein Leaf tea—1 cup 3 or 4 times daily

IMPORTANT AIDS

- Pycnogenol is a potent antioxidant—take as directed on label
- Vitamin E—minimum of 400 IU daily
- Coenzyme Q10—60 mg daily
- Methylsulfonylmethane (MSM)—take as directed on label
- Cysteine, especially the N-Acetyl-Cysteine (NAC) form—200 mg three times daily (discontinue when symptoms disappear)

- Licorice Root—1 to 2 grams three times daily for no more than 7 days
- Mullein clears congestion.
- Thyme is a natural expectorant that eliminates mucus and reduces fever.
- Oregano Oil consumed orally
- Pine Tree Oil vapors inhaled
- Tea Tree Oil vapors inhaled—acts as disinfectant
- Garlic—500 mg of fresh garlic four times daily for acute infection
- Allergies are the underlying cause of some cases of (chronic) bronchitis.

OTHER POTENTIAL AIDS

- Proteolytic Enzymes with Bromelain—take as directed on label
- Fish Oil contain the important Omega-3 fatty acids EPA and DHA. Therapeutic servings include 1,800 mg of EPA and 900 mg of DHA daily.
- Irish Moss acts as an expectorant.
- Caterpillar Fungus
- Aniseed tea helps loosen and expel phlegm from bronchial tubes.
- Black Cohosh in tea form helps loosen and expel phlegm from bronchial tubes.
- Borage helps the adrenal glands.
- Dong Quai—10 to 40 drops of tincture one to three times daily or 1 standard capsule three times daily
- Hot Mustard Baths relieve the congestion associated with bronchitis, and mustard plaster applied topically to the chest also alleviates the congestion associated with bronchitis.
- Neem leaf extract consumed orally—take as directed on label
- Wild Cherry—usually available in syrup form, follow label directions
- Reishi—2 to 6 grams daily of raw fungus or an equivalent amount of concentrated extract

☞ CANDIDA

CANDIDA ALBICANS is one of 70 different types of Candida yeasts. It is a yeast-like fungus that normally lives in healthy balance in the body. It is found mostly in the intestines, genital tract, mouth, and throat. When the balance is upset, infection results. This is known as Candidiasis, and the fungus travels to all parts of the body through the bloodstream. It affects men, women, and children. In the mouth it is called thrush, in the vagina it is called vaginitis, on the man's groan area it is called jock itch, and on the feet it is athlete's foot. Approximately 33% of people have this overgrowth and over 60 million Americans will suffer with it this year.

What makes this condition bad is that the overgrowth produces rhizoids. Rhizoids are long and root-like and have components that are able to pierce the walls of the digestive tract and break down the protective barriers between the intestines and the blood.

Therapies that successfully treat *Candida Albicans*, by causing the rapid death of large numbers of the yeasts, can cause a "die-off" reaction known as the Herxheimer Reaction, during which great amounts of toxins are released from the dead *Candida Albicans* microorganisms. Some people hastily desert their therapy under the mistaken belief that this "die-off" reaction and its associated allergic reactions are an indication that their condition is worsening rather than diminishing.

WHY CELLULASE IS IMPERATIVE *in* ELIMINATING CANDIDIASIS FOREVER!

1) In individuals with overgrowth there is often a large amount of undigested fiber in the large intestine. It is believed that the mucous that the body produces due to the difficulty of digesting this fiber (cellulose) may protect the Candida from our body's natural ability to attack and prevent Candidiasis. Cellulase is the enzyme that breaks down fiber. It is the only digestive enzyme that our body does not make. By adding cellulose to the diet, this fiber can be more easily removed along with mucous, and our body is able to achieve balance.

Remember: *only raw foods* contain cellulase. Of all the enzymes, this deficiency carries with it the most categories of problems.

The symptoms of cellulase deficiency can best be described as malabsorption syndrome—impaired absorption of nutrients, vitamins, or minerals from the diet by the lining of the small intestine. Symptoms of malabsorption include lower abdominal pain, lower abdominal gas, bloating, and problems associated with the pancreas.

2) Fungi (Candida) are a group of organisms formerly regarded as plants lacking chlorophyll. They can either exist as single cells or make up a multi-cellular body called a mycelium, which exist of filaments known as hyphae. The cell contains some fungal cellulose or a compound called chitin. Chitin is a polysaccharide, or carbohydrate, which is structurally very similar to cellulose. For the same reason cellulose may help remove undigested fiber in the colon, it has been used in breaking down this "cellulose-like" chitin.

3) The inside of the cell of yeast is mostly protein. The enzyme protease has the ability to hydrolyze (digest) protein. Protease has been used in clinics all over the world to break down this fungus and prevent its overgrowth.

TOP NATURAL AIDS

- Candida Cleanse
- One Perfect Diet
- Evening Primrose Oil—3,000 mg three times daily
- Vitamin C—3,000 to 15,000 mg daily in divided servings
- Vitamin-B Complex—50 to 100 mg with each meal
- Garlic
- Silica
- AloeVera
- Colon Therapy

IMPORTANT AIDS

- Parasite Cleanse
- Pancreatic Enzymes and Proteolytic Enzymes (such as Pancreatic Amylase, Bromelain, Chymotrypsin, Lipases, Papain and Trypsin) lessen these symptoms.
- Charcoal—20 to 30 grams daily absorbs the toxins often neutralizing any distress.

☞ CARDIOVASCULAR DISEASE

CARDIOVASCULAR DISEASE is a generic term for many disorders of the cardiovascular (circulatory) system including the heart and is the leading cause of death worldwide—actually estimated to be responsible for 50% of all deaths.

When we consider "women's diseases," most of us think about breast cancer, reproductive cancers, and autoimmune disorders such as fibromyalgia and chronic fatigue syndrome that affect predominantly women. But heart disease? That's more of a man's health problem...right? Unfortunately, heart attacks kill six times as many women as breast cancer does. Heart disease is the chief cause of death of American women.

Research shows the "male" heart-helper, lycopene, has recently been studied in female subjects, and its benefits in lowering the risk of heart disease have been proven to cross genders. Lycopene is a carotenoid found primarily in tomatoes, and in lower concentrations in watermelon, guava, rosehip, and red grapefruit. Lycopene has also been connected with a reduced danger of prostate cancer, which is probably the main reason why the recommendations for lycopene may have been directed more toward men. But there is also first round research showing it may also protect against breast cancer and cervical dysplasia, a precancerous condition in women. Lycopene is of great benefit to men and women alike.

TOP NATURAL AIDS
- Lycopene is a powerful antioxidant. Take as directed on label.
- L-Arginine—take as directed
- Superunsaturated Fatty Acids
- Magnesium—750 to 1,000 mg daily
- Coenzyme Q10—50 to 100 mg three times daily
- Vitamin C—1,000 to 3,000 mg daily
- Vitamin E (d-alpha-tocopherol)—400 to 600 IU daily
- Clustered Water
- Hawthorn dilates coronary blood vessels and restores heart muscle.

- Fish Oils contain the important Omega-3 fatty acids Eicosapentaenoic Acid (EPA) and Docosahexaenoic Acid (DHA). Therapeutic servings include 1,800 mg of EPA and 900 mg of DHA daily.
- L-Carnitine—500 mg three times daily
- Calcium (chelate form)—1,500 to 2,000 mg daily
- Coenzyme A—use as directed
- Chelation Suppositories with Ethylene-Diamine-Tetra-Acetate (EDTA)

IMPORTANT AIDS

- Selenium—100 to 200 mcg daily
- Potassium—100 mg daily

OTHER POTENTIAL AIDS

- Bromelain is a collection of protein-digesting enzymes that can help with circulatory problems. Take as directed on label.
- DHEA—50 to 200 mg daily
- Progesterone is most effective applied topically. Use the equivalent of about 20 mg daily.
- Thyroid
- Chromium—150 to 400 mcg daily
- Quercetin—70 to 140 mg daily
- Folic Acid—400 to 800 mcg daily
- Vitamin B6—50 to 100 mg daily
- Vitamin B12—400 to 1,000 mcg daily

Fallacy—Despite its high cholesterol content, statistics exonerate the egg from the blame for cardiovascular disease, including strokes.

☞ CARPAL TUNNEL SYNDROME

CARPAL TUNNEL SYNDROME is a disorder characterized by the compression of the median nerve where it enters the palm of the hand. You may be told that there is no other way to deal with it except through surgery, but I urge you to try supplementing before surgery. Studies show that everyone with carpal tunnel is lacking vitamin B6. Try 100 mg along with a good vitamin B-complex. St. Johns Wort has been beneficial in that it helps to heal nerves. Finally, if at all possible, stop doing what you're doing that started that inflammation or rearrange your work space and hand patterns.

TOP NATURAL AIDS

- Glucosamine—500 mg three times daily
- Coenzyme Q10—30 to 90 mg daily
- Lecithin—1,200 mg three times daily before meals
- Zinc—50 mg daily
- Ginkgo Biloba helps improve circulation. Take 40 to 60 mg of a product that contains 24% ginkgo heterosides.
- Vitamin B6—100 to 200 mg daily for approximately three months
- Bromelain—250 to 750 mg three times daily between meals
- Evening Primrose Oil—1,000 mg three times daily
- Vitamin C with bioflavonoids—1,000 mg four times daily

IMPORTANT AIDS

- Vitamin E—400 IU daily
- Grape Seed and Pine Bark extracts are both excellent at relieving inflammation. Take 25 to 30 mg of one of them three times daily.
- Kelp—take as directed on label
- Horsetail helps rebuild connective tissue. Take capsules as directed or 3 cups of juice or 3 cups of tea daily.

OTHER POTENTIAL AIDS

- Selenium—200 mcg daily

- Vitamin A—25,000 IU daily
- Vitamin D—400 IU daily
- Methylsulfonylmethane (MSM) lotion applied topically.
- Vitamin B2—15 to 50 mg daily
- Capsicum (cayenne) reduces pain.
- Skullcap reduces muscle spasms.
- Turmeric contains curcumin, which helps with inflammation. Take 500 mg three times daily.

☞ CHRONIC FATIGUE SYNDROME

CHRONIC FATIGUE SYNDROME involves regular disabling exhaustion that is not helped by bed rest. Many people with CFS have an overgrowth of Candida and/or are plagued with parasites.

I will never forget as long as I live my first experience with chronic fatigue syndrome. I came out of the church service to check on my baby, and there was a 30-something woman in the lobby in tears. She was so weak she could hardly stand and was at her wits end. She had fever, muscle weakness, swollen lymph nodes, headache, joint pain and depression. All classic signs of this ailment.

I talked with her, and she started a supplement program with a simple cleanse, oxygen baths, and the appropriate supplements. She had Candidiasis from taking so many antibiotics, but within two weeks her husband came to me and thanked me for giving his wife back. That is the power of God and His way of doing things.

There are a number of other serious ailments that can cause CFS, such as diabetes, heart disease, cancer, liver disease, prescription drugs, birth control pills, tranquilizers, stress, and depression.

TOP NATURAL AIDS

- Candida Cleanse
- Body Oxygen
- Acidophilus—take as directed on label
- Evening Primrose Oil—1,000 mg three times daily
- Vitamin C with bioflavonoids—1,000 mg three times daily
- Thymus Extract—750 mg twice daily
- Vitamin C—1,000 mg 3 times daily
- Collodial Minerals—1 or two ounces daily
- Beta-carotene—30,000 IU daily
- Lecithin—1,200 mg three times daily with meals
- Malic Acid—300 mg three times daily, 20 minutes before eating
- Manganese—5 mg daily
- Vitamin B-complex—100 mg daily
- Combination of Fatty Acids (linoleic acid, gamma-linolenic

acid, eicosapentaenoic acid (EPA), and docosahexaenoic acid (DHA)) at a total serving of 4,000 mg daily.

- Magnesium (aspartate form)—1,000 mg daily
- Coenzyme Q10—300 mg daily
- Vitamin B12—2.5 to 5 mg daily administered via injection or 5 to 10 mg administered orally
- Vitamin E—800 IU daily for one month, then slowly reduce to 400 IU daily
- Astragalus strengthens production of white blood cells. Take 250 mg three to four times daily.
- Echinacea (Echinacea purpurea) helps prevent bacteria and viruses from entering. Take 15 to 20 drops in liquid three times daily for two days.
- Korean Ginseng—1,000 to 3,000 mg daily of dry powdered root or 300 to 400 mg daily of concentrated extract in capsule form. Note: Don't use Korean Ginseng if you have heart disease, high blood pressure, or hypoglycemia.
- Olive Leaf extract helps fight infection. Take 250 mg of standardized extract two to three times daily.
- Siberian Ginseng—2,000 to 3,000 mg daily of dry powdered root or 300 to 400 mg daily of concentrated extract in capsule form
- Valerian helps with relaxation. Take 200 to 300 mg 30 minutes before bedtime of a standardized extract containing 0.5% isovalerenic acids.

IMPORTANT AIDS

- Bromelain—500 mg twice daily between meals
- Chromium Polynicotinate—200 to 300 mg daily
- Vitamin A with mixed carotenoids—25,000 IU daily for one month, then slowly reduce to 10,000 IU daily
- Glucosamine Sulfate helps relieve joint pain. Take 500 mg three times daily. It may take several weeks to see results.
- Carnitine—1,000 to 3,000 mg daily

- Acetyl-L-Carnitine (ALC)—1,000 to 2,000 mg daily
- Melatonin helps with restful sleep. Take 0.5 to 3 mg daily, 1 to 2 hours before bedtime.
- Zinc—50 mg daily
- Lipoic Acid—500 to 800 mg daily
- Vitamin B6—100 mg daily
- Maitake Mushrooms strengthen the immune system. Take 3 to 7 grams as food or the equivalent in capsule or tablet form daily.
- Reishi Mushrooms helps restore normal immune function. Take 2 to 6 grams daily of raw fungus or the equivalent amount in a concentrated extract. Take with meals.
- Shiitake Mushrooms—400 to 1,800 mg daily
- Licorice Root (2,500 mg daily) increases cortisol levels. Don't use licorice for more than seven days in a row, and avoid it completely if you have high blood pressure.
- St. John's Wort helps with depression. Take 300 mg three times daily of a product containing 0.3% hypericin.
- Dandelion tea helps cleanse the blood and lymphatic system. Drink 4 to 6 cups daily.
- Red Clover tea cleanses the blood and lymphatic system. Drink 4 to 6 cups daily.
- Gingko Biloba improves brain function.

OTHER POTENTIAL AIDS

- 5-hydroxy L-tryptophan (5-HTP) helps with depression and muscle tension.
- S-adenosylmethionine (SAMe) works as an antidepressant.
- Galanthamine—16 mg daily
- Clustered Water
- Cysteine
- Phenylalanine—1,500 mg daily
- Serine—2,000 mg daily
- Tyrosine—1,500 mg daily

- DHEA—50 to 200 mg daily orally or apply topically in cream form, 3 to 5 grams daily of a cream containing 10% DHEA.
- Thyroid Hormones
- Neurotransmitters—see Appendix A.
- Succinic Acid
- Lactoferrin—300 mg daily
- Thymic Protein A
- Folic Acid—400 mcg daily
- Vitamin B1—300 mg daily
- Vitamin B2—50 mg daily
- Caterpillar Fungus
- Aloe Vera consumed orally
- Cat's Claw—start with 250 mg three times daily of standardized extract and gradually increase amount over four weeks to 1,000 mg three times daily. Note: Don't take Cat's Claw if you're pregnant or nursing, or if you are an organ transplant recipient. Use caution if you're taking blood thinner medication.
- Maca—2,800 to 5,600 mg daily
- Neem leaf extract consumed orally—take as directed on label
- Valerian Root helps with sleep. Take 200 to 400 mg 30 minutes before bedtime of a standardized extract containing 0.5% isovalerenic acids.
- Burdock Root tea—4 to 6 cups daily

Massage
Exercise is very important.

☞ CIRCULATORY PROBLEMS

CARDIOVASCULAR DISEASE is a generic term for many disorders of the cardiovascular (circulatory) system, including the heart. Cardiovascular diseases are the leading cause of death worldwide— estimated to be responsible for 50% of all deaths.

I have seen phenomenal results from chelation therapy in various people with poor circulation. My own father-in-law is first on the list. Because of injuries during WWII, he nearly had his feet amputated. But he did have various circulatory issues from that point on in his life. After he started chelation, they vanished!

Getting in the sun for half an hour to an hour a day converts bad cholesterol to vitamin D, without which you cannot absorb all those calcium supplements. So lower your bad cholesterol and strengthen your bones and get a tan. It's a win-win!

TOP NATURAL AIDS

- Ethylene-Diamine-Tetra-Acetate (EDTA), the synthetic amino acid used in chelation therapy, helps prevent many types of cardiovascular diseases.
- Chelation Suppositories
- Body Oxygen
- Superunsaturated Fatty Acids lower harmful blood triglyceride levels. Good sources include flaxseed oil and some fish oils.
- Coenzyme Q10—minimum of 100 mg daily
- Clustered Water
- L Canatein—500 mg twice daily
- Phosphatidylcholine—100 mg daily
- Vitamin C—1,000 mg three times daily
- Vitamin E—400 to 800 IU daily. Limit to 400 IU if you have high blood pressure, and consult your physician if taking a blood thinner.
- Hawthorn lowers blood pressure. Take 100 to 300 mg three times daily of an extract standardized to contain 2–3% flavonoids.
- Fish Oils contain the important Omega-3 fatty acids EPA and

DHA. Therapeutic servings include 1,800 mg of EPA and 900 mg of DHA daily.

- Essential Fatty Acids, including black currant seed, borage, flaxseed, and evening primrose oil

IMPORTANT AIDS

- Magnesium—750 mg daily in divided portions with meals
- Vitamin B6—50 mg daily
- Vitamin B12—400 to 1,000 mcg daily
- Calcium (chelated form)—1,500 to 2,000 mg daily in divided portions after meals
- Gingko Biloba

OTHER POTENTIAL AIDS

- Bromelain—300 mg daily
- DHEA (Dehydroepiandrosterone)—50 to 200 mg daily, also available in a cream containing 10% DHEA, follow label directions
- Micronized progesterone may be taken orally in amounts of 200 to 400 mg daily or applied topically using cream in amounts approximating 20 grams daily.
- Underactive thyroid can put a person at increased risk for heart attack. A blood test can determine whether the thyroid is working properly.
- Thyroxine
- Triiodothyronine
- Chromium—150 to 400 mcg
- Selenium—200 mcg daily
- Quercetin—70 to 140 mg
- Folic Acid—400 mcg daily
- Kelp—1,000 to 1,500 mg daily with meals
- Melatonin—2 to 3 mg daily taken 2 hours before bedtime
- Potassium—100 mg daily

- People who live in areas with hard water have a lower mortality rate from cardiovascular diseases than those in areas with soft water.

Exercise: Regular exercise helps to prevent various cardiovascular diseases.

✒ COMMON COLD

THE COMMON COLD is caused by any one of over 200 different viruses (including 113 types of rhinoviruses). It is so prevalent that we now give it its own season, "the cold season." But you don't have to take advantage of this seasonal opportunity. Rather, you can fortify your immune system and do as I have done for the past 20 years, not participate. If you do get a cold before you've enhanced your immune system, try fasting. It speeds healing. Get plenty of sleep.

TOP NATURAL AIDS

- Vitamin C with bioflavonoids—5,000 to 20,000 mg daily in divided portions
- Zinc lozenges containing 13.3 mg of zinc every two hours reduces the recovery time from the common cold from an average of 7.6 days to 4.4 days.
- Vitamin A—50,000 to 150,000 IU daily for three to five days
- Goldenseal helps boost the immune system and keep the virus from multiplying. Use as directed on label in combination with echinacea for best results.
- Elderbery—as tea or standardized extract
- Garlic is a potent detoxifier. Take 500 mg three to four times daily for a week or substitute 1 clove of fresh garlic for each garlic capsule.
- Stanley Burroughs Cleanse for 3 to 10 days. See Appendix A.

IMPORTANT AIDS

- L-Lysine helps destroy viruses and prevent cold sores. Take 500 mg three to four times daily for up to one week. Take Lysine on an empty stomach with water or juice, not milk.
- Pantothenic Acid is beneficial for cold symptoms. Take 250 mg three times daily for up to one week.
- Andrographis—400 mg three times daily with meals

- Colloidal Silver fights viruses and bacteria. Take as directed on label.
- Echinacea helps boost immune system and keep virus from multiplying. Use as directed on label in combination with goldenseal for best results. Use for up to two weeks.
- Ginger root relieves fever and soothes aching muscles. Take as tea every four hours when symptoms are acute.
- Grape Seed extract is a powerful antioxidant. Take 500 mg daily of a standardized extract containing 90% proanthocyanidins.
- Sage inhaled as steam reduces inflammation. Gargling with sage tea helps disinfect the mouth. Or drink as tea.
- Siberian Ginseng strengthens adrenal glands. 300 to 400 mg daily may prevent the cold.

OTHER POTENTIAL AIDS

- Capsaicin acts as an expectorant for the common cold.
- Alliin (a derivative of cysteine present in garlic)
- Iron deficiency may allow colds in. Take supplemental iron only if your physician confirms you have an iron deficiency.
- Thymic Protein A
- Quercetin—70 to 140 mg daily
- Allyl Isothiocyanate acts as an expectorant for the common cold.
- Methylsulfonylmethane (MSM) may help to prevent the common cold.
- Chlorella
- Bee Propolis lozenges
- Grapefruit
- Lemon
- Aloe Vera helps fight infection. Take it as juice three times daily.
- Astragalus supports the proliferation of white blood cells necessary for fighting infection.
- Bayberry acts as a decongestant. Take as directed on label.

- Cat's Claw can ease cold symptoms. Take according to label directions.
- Chamomile helps in loosening mucus and healing nasal and bronchial passages. Inhale steam for 15 minutes three times daily while symptoms are acute or take as tea.
- Chickweed tea relieves nasal congestion.
- Feverfew loosens mucus in bronchial passages. Take 80 to 100 mg daily of powdered whole leaf.
- Hyssop acts as an expectorant. Take as tea.
- Lemon Balm
- Lemon Grass acts as a tonic.
- Licorice fights viral and bacterial infection. Follow label directions.
- Olive Leaf extract fights viruses, bacteria, fungi, and parasites.
- St. John's Wort has antiviral properties.
- Chicken soup is effective in reducing the duration of a cold.
- Activated Charcoal may accelerate the recovery.
- Oregano Oil consumed orally.
- Red Clover helps clear toxins in the lymphatic system.
- Shark Liver Oil

☞ DANDRUFF

DANDRUFF is a condition in which the scalp is covered in flakes of dead skin. Every 24 days the skin on your head is slowly sloughed off. Dandruff occurs when this process is accelerated. Disorders often occur when the sloughed cells are not dead before they are shed.

What do dandruff and dry cracked heels have in common? If you answered essential fatty acids, you are correct. A person came to me recently and asked if we had a cream for her heels. "They are so nasty, I can't wear sandals," she said. In fact, they were so bad they would bleed at times. I suggested EFAs, and two weeks later her heels were well. Not only did her heels heal, she said her dandruff condition had cleared up, too. Almost without fail, when EFAs are added to the diet, dandruff subsides.

TOP NATURAL AIDS

- Alpha-Linolenic Acid (LNA) is an Omega-3 fatty acid. Two excellent sources are flaxseed oil and fish oil.
- Vitamin B-complex—100 mg twice daily
- Linoleic Acid (LA) is an Omega-6 fatty acid. It can be obtained in evening primrose oil, borage and blackcurrant oil.
- Selenium—100 mcg twice daily
- Vitamin B6—50 mg twice daily
- Vitamin E—400 IU daily
- Kelp—1,000 to 1,500 mg daily
- Flax Oil

IMPORTANT AIDS

- Zinc—30 to 50 mg daily
- Vitamin B12—1,000 to 2,000 mcg daily
- Vitamin A—15,000 to 20,000 IU daily with mixed carotenoids
- Almond Oil applied topically to the scalp.
- Collagen

OTHER POTENTIAL AIDS

- Biotin—7,000 to 15,000 mcg daily
- Vitamin B2—100 mg twice daily
- Vitamin C with bioflavonoids—3,000 to 6,000 mg daily in divided servings
- Lecithin capsules—1,200 mg three times daily before meals

THESE FOODS OR HERBS MAY HELP

- Burdock Root—1 to 2 grams of powdered dry root three times daily
- Olive Oil
- Tea Tree Oil (as a component of shampoo) is regarded as an effective remedy for dandruff.

☞ DEPRESSION

MY EXPERIENCE WOULD SUGGEST that in many cases depression is an indicator of something else, just as a headache or a fever is. While there are many causes, it's very important to get to the root of the ailment.

Recently, a forty-year-old man came to see me with his mother. He was angry and depressed. He did not want to see me, and he made it very clear. He had been quite ill for many years, to the point of leaving his work. He had been to see many doctors and was told he had a severe case of Candidiasis. He had been treated by traditional means with little or no relief. It had become so brutal that his liver was severely compromised as well as his lungs. After convincing him to try one more time, he started with a liver cleanse. He came back a few weeks later, and his countenance was so different I almost didn't recognize him. Within 60 days his doctor took him off his medication and he went back to work.

TOP NATURAL AIDS

- 5-Hydroxytryptophan (5-HTP)—300 to 600 mg daily
- Liver cleanse—see Appendix A under "coffee enema"
- Get at least eight hours of sleep a night.
- Have neurotransmitters checked (see Appendix A).
- S-Adenosylmethionine (SAMe)—start with 400 to 500 mg three times daily, maintain at 400 mg daily
- Eliminate sugar
- Taurine—2 grams three times daily
- DHEA—50 mg daily
- Tyrosine—7 to 30 grams daily. Don't take if using an MAO inhibitor.
- Zinc deficiency—50 mg daily, and don't exceed 100 mg daily from all sources
- Folic Acid—400 mg (15–38% of depression patients are found to have low folic acid)
- Vitamin B6—50 to 100 mg (if taking 100 mg, divide into two servings)

- Essential Fatty Acids, including black currant seed, borage, flaxseed, and evening primrose oil
- Vitamin B12—up to 1,000 mcg divided into two servings
- Ginkgo Biloba—80 mg twice daily of 50:1 extract standardized to contain 24% ginko-flavone glycosides
- St. John's Wort—900 to 1,050 mg daily standardized to contain 0.2–0.3% Hypericin + 2–3% Hyperforin. Do not take with prescription antidepressants.
- Kava Kava—150 mg twice daily. Do not take with prescription antidepressants.
- Ashwagandha—6,000 mg daily for at least two months

IMPORTANT AIDS

- L-Phenylalanine—500 mg daily, gradually increased to 3 to 4 grams daily
- DL-Phenylalanine—100 to 400 mg daily
- D-Phenylalanine—500 to 1,000 mg twice daily between meals with water or juice only
- Calcium—1,500 to 2,000 mg daily
- Chromium—300 mcg daily
- Magnesium—1,000 mg daily
- Inositol—5 to 12 grams daily
- Vitamin C—1,000 to 3,000 mg daily for at least three weeks
- NADH—5 to 50 mg daily
- Damiana—2 to 4 grams taken two to three times daily or as directed on label
- Valerian—200 to 300 mg before bedtime if experiencing sleeplessness. Don't use Valerian continuously.
- Flaxseed Oil—1 to 2 tablespoons daily

OTHER POTENTIAL AIDS

- Acetyl-L-Carnitine (ALC)—500 to 3,000 mg daily
- Glutamine—250 to 1,000 mg daily
- Proline is an amino acid that aids in the production of

collagen. Take as directed on label.
- Threonine—2,000 mg daily
- Melatonin is useful, 3 mg before bedtime. Note: some authorities warn against using it for depression.
- Pregnenolone—30 mg daily
- Natural Progesterone—20 mg daily in cream form
- Phosphatidylserine—300 to 400 mg daily for 30 to 60 days
- Prostaglandin E1 (PGE1) induces a sense of well-being.
- DHA, an essential acid found primarily in fish oil
- EPA
- Bromine
- Manganese—2.5 to 5 mg daily
- Potassium—100 to 500 mg daily
- Selenium—50 to 200 mcg daily
- Anacardic Acid possesses antidepressant properties.
- Biotin—30 to 100 mcg daily of extract standardized to contain 0.3% Hypericin
- Vitamin B3—15 to 50 mg three times daily
- Vitamin B1—50 to 100 mg daily
- Vitamin B2—5 to 10 mg daily
- Vitamin B5—250 mg twice daily
- Vitamin D—400 IU daily

FOODS *and* HERBS THAT MAY HELP

- Mango
- Camu-Camu
- Cat's Claw—take according to label directions
- Golden Root
- Gotu Kola—20 to 60 mg three times daily of extract standardized to contain 40% asiaticoside, 29–30% madecassic acid, and 1–2% madecassoside
- Korean Ginseng strengthens adrenal glands.
- Marapuama
- Noni—as juice, four ounces 30 minutes before breakfast; as

liquid concentrate, 2 tablespoons daily; as powdered extract, 500 to 1,000 mg daily
- Passionflower—use in tea by steeping 1 teaspoon for 10 to 15 minutes; for tinctures and powdered extracts follow label directions
- Schizandra
- Suma—500 mg twice daily

EXERCISE

- Regular exercise helps to prevent and relieve depression.
- Regular aerobic exercise reduces the severity of depression.
- Regular (three times per week) isotonic exercise (strength-building) reduces the severity of depression.

☞ DIABETES

DIABETES occurs when the pancreas is not capable of secreting enough insulin to keep up a normal blood sugar (glucose) level, leading to high blood sugar levels. A person is regarded as having diabetes if their blood sugar is more than 140 mg per deciliter after an overnight fast. Ninety percent of non-insulin dependent diabetes can be treated with careful attention to a proper diet and exercise. A high fiber diet, low in fat.

TOP NATURAL AIDS

- Alpha-lipoic Acid has a key role in turning glucose into energy. For complications of diabetes, a typical serving is 300 to 600 mg daily.
- Collagen liquid—1 tablespoon with 1,000 mg of vitamin C at bedtime
- Clustered Water for Type II.
- Prickly Pear for Type I.
- Garlic stabilizes blood sugar levels. Take as directed on label.
- Potassium—100 to 500 mg daily
- Vitamin D—200 to 400 IU daily
- Chromium—200 to 400 mcg twice daily
- Vitamin B-complex—50 mg of each major B vitamin twice daily
- Gamma-linolenic Acid helps with damaged nerve function. Take 480 mg daily.
- Chromium Picolinate—400 to 600 mcg daily
- Brewer's Yeast—9 grams daily
- Magnesium—750 mg daily
- Manganese—5 to 15 mg daily
- Raw Adrenal Glandular—take as directed on label
- Selenium—200 mcg daily
- Vanadium may reduce the need for insulin. Take 250 mcg two to three times daily.
- Zinc—50 to 80 mg daily

- Coenzyme Q10—100 mg daily
- Inositol—1,000 mg daily
- Bilberry tea promotes insulin production. Take 80 mg two to three times daily before meals.
- Siberian Ginseng may help stabilize blood sugar. Take according to label directions.
- Stevia is an herb that works as a natural sweetener that may help regulate blood sugar. Stevia has no calories and may be used according to taste.
- EDTA Chelation IV or at-home suppositories

IMPORTANT AIDS

- Beta-carotene—10,000 IU twice daily
- L-Carnitine—500 mg twice daily on an empty stomach
- Taurine—500 mg twice daily on an empty stomach
- Conjugated Linoleic Acid (CLA) may reduce blood sugar levels. Take 3 to 5 grams daily.
- Vitamin C with bioflavonoids—3,000 to 6,000 mg daily in divided servings
- Vitamin E—800 to 1200 IU and up daily
- Aloe Vera juice appears to improve blood sugar levels in Type II diabetics. Take 1 tablespoon twice daily.
- American Ginseng appears to improve blood sugar levels in diabetics. Take as directed on label.
- Blueberry Leaf tea may reduce the need for insulin. Drink 2 to 3 cups daily.
- Milk Thistle acts as a liver tonic. Take 200 to 300 mg twice daily for 1 to 2 months.

OTHER POTENTIAL AIDS

- L-Glutamine—500 mg twice daily on an empty stomach
- Arabinoxylans—10,000 mg daily
- Cellulose helps to lower blood sugar levels. It's found in several foods, including apples, beets, Brazil nuts, broccoli, carrots,

celery, green beans, lima beans, pears, peas, and whole grains.

- Glucomannans help to lower blood sugar. Take 3 to 5 grams daily in divided portions between meals.
- Guar Gum helps to normalize blood sugar. It binds with toxins and carries them out of the body. It should be taken as directed.
- DHEA lowers the requirement for exogenous insulin. A typical serving is 50 to 200 mg daily.
- Biotin—50 mg daily
- Calcium AEP reduces the requirement for exogenous insulin.
- Copper complex—take as directed on label
- Germanium—10 mg daily
- Glutathione is a potent antioxidant manufactured in the liver. The best way to supplement the body is to take N-acetyl-cysteine as directed on label.
- Silymarin—200 to 800 mg daily reduces blood sugar levels, insulin levels, glycosuria and glycosylated hemoglobin levels in diabetes
- Quercetin helps to prevent many of the complications that arise from diabetes. Take 100 mg three times daily.
- Methylsulfonylmethane (MSM)—2,000 mg daily
- Biotin lowers fasting blood sugar levels. Take 50 mg daily.
- Vitamin B6—50 to 100 mg daily
- Banana Leaf
- Blue Cohosh
- Caterpillar Fungus
- Cat's Claw stimulates the immune system. Take as directed on label.
- Dandelion tea regulates blood sugar levels.
- Goldenseal promotes tissue healing.
- Korean Ginseng tea is believed to lower blood sugar levels.
- Neem Leaf extract consumed orally
- Olive Leaf fights all kinds of bacteria, fungi, viruses, and parasites. Take as directed.

- Schizandra
- Legumes, Kidney Beans, Lentils boiled and taken as a "bean tea" will detoxify the pancreas.
- Evening Primrose Oil—4,800 mg daily
- Flaxseed Oil—1 to 2 tbsp. daily
- Fenugreek Seeds help reduce blood sugar levels. Take 500 mg two to three times daily in capsule form or a cup of fenugreek tea daily.
- Asparagus juice
- Cedar Berries are superior nourishment for the pancreas.
- Celery juice
- Garlic may help regulate blood sugar. Take 1,000 mg of dried extract or one fresh clove daily.
- Jerusalem Artichoke is important for fat digestion.
- Oat Bran is very useful for maintaining steady blood sugar levels.
- Onions
- Spinach
- Spirulina helps stabilize blood sugar levels.

Exercise is crucial for burning calories and normalizing metabolism and also heightens the body's sensitivity to insulin. Read Chapter 17.

☞ DIGESTIVE DISORDERS— CONSTIPATION

CONSTIPATION is a malady that involves a decrease in the regularity of bowel movements.

Acid indigestion refers to the body's failure to digest food properly due to insufficient stomach acids and can lead to a multitude of problems—bad breath, Crohn's disease, diarrhea, diverticulitis, gas, food allergies, reflux, irritable bowel syndrome, peptic ulcers, and more.

Personally, I believe that most of America is constipated. The typical American diet does not lead to a healthy GI (gastrointestinal) tract. While I accept that most GI issues are from diet, some may be caused from prescribed medications as well as physical maladies such as Hirschsprung's disease, which affects 1 out of 1,000 babies. Many babies go undiagnosed and are simply labeled as chronic constipation.

Probiotics are essential to the health of the digestive system. Today's high antibiotic use kills off all bacteria, so we must supplement with good flora on a regular basis. A Candida cleanse as well as a parasite cleanse will usually get people off to the right start. Identifying the source of the problem will help you the rest of your life.

Remember: if the food you eat is not eliminated in 18 hours, you are most likely constipated. Many practitioners agree that disease starts in the colon! Beware and act!

Follow these tips: Stop eating foods you may be allergic to. Follow the One Perfect Diet. Antibiotic overuse may contribute to this problem. Use probiotics often. Use a parasite cleanse twice a year. Chew your food thoroughly. Limit the amount of liquids you drink with any meal. Don't eat when you're stressed. Limit red meats. Don't eat anything for two hours prior to bedtime.

TOP NATURAL AIDS

- Digestive enzymes
- Parasite Cleanse (ParaCease)
- Probiotic Ultra Pro
- Bromelain—500 to 2,000 mg daily in divided servings

- Papain—100 mg daily
- Fructooligosaccharides (FOS)—1 to 2 capsules or 1 tsp. powder three times daily
- Hemicelluloses is an indigestible carbohydrate that absorbs water. It helps relieve constipation and is found in many common foods, including apples, bananas, beans, beets, cabbage, corn, green leafy vegetables, pears, and whole grain cereals.
- Lignans are great natural aids. The richest source of lignans is flaxseed, which can be eaten raw or added to cereal—5 to 35 grams daily or 2 to 3 teaspoons of ground flaxseed meal consumed with water.
- Lactobacillus acidophilus—a daily serving should contain 3 to 5 billion live organisms
- Vitamin B-complex—50 mg three times a day
- Vitamin B12—1,000 to 2,000 mcg daily
- Aloe Vera juice—1 cup two to three times daily
- Psyllium Seeds—take as directed on label
- Garlic—900 mg daily of garlic powder extract standardized to contain 1.3% alliin

IMPORTANT AIDS

- Methylsulfonylmethane (MSM)—500 to 2,000 mg daily
- Cellulose is an indigestible carbohydrate located in the outer layer of many vegetables and fruits. It relieves constipation. Cellulose is found in apples, beets, broccoli, carrots, celery, green beans, lima beans, pears, peas, and whole grains.
- Lemon juice
- Cascara Sagrada acts as a colon cleanser.
- Dandelion—250 mg three to four times daily of a 5:1 extract
- Fenugreek—5 to 30 grams of defatted fenugreek three times daily with meals
- Senna
- Milk Thistle—200 mg two to three times daily of an extract standardized to contain 70% silymarin
- Apple Pectin—500 mg daily (take separately from other supplements)

OTHER POTENTIAL AIDS

- Arginine—2 to 3 grams daily
- Chitosan—3 to 6 grams daily, taken with food
- Glucomannan—3,000 to 4,000 mg daily
- Psyllium is a grain widely used for its fiber content. It cleans the intestines and also works as a stool softener. Follow directions for use.
- Propionic Acid
- Calcium—1,500 to 2,000 mg daily
- Magnesium Sulfate (Epsom Salts) is a fine laxative.
- Potassium—100 to 500 mg daily
- Acetylcholine is produced in the intestines where its function is to enhance the process of peristalsis, thereby helping to prevent constipation.
- Folic Acid—high servings of up to 60 mg daily
- Inositol—50 to 200 mg daily
- Para-aminobenzoic Acid (PABA)—up to 50 mg daily
- Vitamin B1—50 mg three times daily
- Vitamin B5—50 mg three times daily
- Vitamin C with bioflavonoids—5,000 to 20,000 mg daily in divided servings
- Vitamin E—600 IU daily, take before meals

FOODS *and* HERBS THAT MAY HELP

- Apricot juice
- Banana
- Figs
- Grapefruit juice
- Prunes
- Tamarind
- Barley
- Bran
- Fo-Ti
- Nettle—4 to 6 grams daily of the whole root or concentrated extract as directed on label

- Noni juice—4 ounces 30 minutes before morning meal; 2 tablespoons of liquid concentrate, or 500 to 1,000 mg of powdered extract daily
- Raspberry Leaf—take as tea or use in capsule or extract form according to label directions
- Green Tea—as tea, 3 cups daily; as extract, 100 to 150 mg three times daily of green tea extract standardized to contain 80% total polyphenols and 50% epigallocatechin gallate
- Yellow Dock improves colon and liver function. Take 2 to 4 grams of dried root, 2 to 4 ml of liquid extract, or 1 to 2 ml of tincture
- Oils (dietary oils)
- Castor Oil
- Olive Oil
- Molasses
- Artichoke Leaf—6 grams of dried herb divided into 3 servings
- Avocado
- Beetroot juice
- Cabbage juice
- Carrots
- Green Peas
- Kelp—take as directed on label
- Potato juice
- Rhubarb
- Rutabaga
- Spinach
- Turnips

Exercise
Colon Therapy

☞ DRUG ADDICTION

DRUG DEPENDENCE is a vague term that arises from a sustained use of drugs that produce a craving, abuse, and misuse of any drug.

A total body cleanse will help remove the toxins that cause the body's craving for the drug. Neurotransmitters should be tested as there may be an essential natural element missing or depletion that the drugs are attempting to mimic (see Appendix A). Also consider the One Perfect Diet to reverse problems that nutritionally void foods may have caused. It's difficult for the abuser to think rationally when the food he/she is eating is empty of the nutrients they need.

TOP NATURAL AIDS

- Dandelion Root for liver detoxification—250 mg three times daily for six weeks
- Milk Thistle for liver detoxification—200 to 300 mg daily
- HsiaoYaoWan—500 mg three times daily
- Vitamin B-complex food based
- Vitamin B12—1,000 mg daily
- Vitamin B5—500 mg three times daily
- Vitamin B3—500 mg three times daily
- Probiotics and Enzymes are essential
- Coffee enema—see Appendix A

IMPORTANT AIDS

- Tyrosine may be helpful regarding alcohol, amphetamines, cocaine, and tobacco
- Vitamin C—1,000 mg three times daily
- Calcium—1,500 mg daily
- Magnesium—1,000 mg daily
- Kudzu breaks addictive behavior.
- Clustered Water to correct damage

OTHER POTENTIAL AIDS

- Acetyl-L-Carnitine—concerning alcohol, 500 to 1,000 mg three times daily

- S-Adenosylmethionine (SAM)—400 mg three to four times daily with meals for 2 to 4 weeks
- Melatonin—3 mg before bedtime
- AL 721 reduces or completely eliminates the withdrawal symptoms.
- Charcoal may reduce the craving for recreational drugs such as alcohol, amphetamines, and cocaine.
- Vitamin B3—50 to 100 mg daily

☞ EAR INFECTION

THE MOST COMMON FORM OF EARACHE is caused by an infection of the middle ear and is what most young children suffer from. It is associated with irritation, itching, discharge, pain, and temporary, mild loss of hearing. Anyone with symptoms of an acute infection should seek the help of a physician.

TOP NATURAL AIDS

- A Candida cleanse along with enzymes, garlic oil, and probiotics has proven time and time again to be helpful.
- Vitamin A—5,000 to 50,000 IU for two days
- Thymus extract—500 mg
- Manganese—3 to 10 mg daily
- Evening Primrose Oil—500 mg three times daily
- Vitamin C with bioflavonoids—1,000 to 3,000 mg daily divided servings
- Zinc—15 mg with 3 mg copper
- Carotenoid complex with beta-carotene—5,000 to 25,000 IU daily
- Garlic Oil Drops in the ear

IMPORTANT AIDS

- Vitamin B-complex—50 mg twice daily
- Vitamin E—200 to 400 mg daily

OTHER POTENTIAL AIDS

- Clupanodonic Acid
- Fish Oils contain the important Omega-3 fatty acids Eicosapentaenoic Acid (EPA) and Docosahexaenoic Acid (DHA). Therapeutic servings include 1,800 mg of EPA and 900 mg of DHA daily.
- Chickweed juice—use for eardrops
- Hops (for earache)—take as directed on label
- Echinacea and Goldenseal combination every two hours while symptoms are acute but limited to four servings.

☞ ECZEMA

ECZEMA is a skin ailment involving superficial inflammation of the skin. Itching, small blisters, and a red rash are also present. Detoxing the eliminative organs and supplementing with probiotics is important. When there is an imbalance in the digestive tract, the warning signs will show up somewhere, and the skin is your largest organ.

Eliminate milk, eggs, and peanut products from your diet. Detect any food allergies you may have and say away from them. Often foods that make you feel tired and sluggish are the ones to avoid.

One recent study by a Chinese doctor showed microscopic skin parasites. Tea Tree Oil topically as well as cleansing internally is effective.

TOP NATURAL AIDS

- Vitamin A—25,000 to 200,000 IU daily for 30 days, but not when pregnant
- Green Tea
- Beta-carotene—10,000 to 30,000 IU daily
- Quercetin—150 to 300 mg daily
- Vitamin B-complex—50 mg of each major B vitamin three times daily
- Alpha-Linolenic Acid (LNA) is an Omega-3 essential fatty acid. It promotes healthy skin. Flaxseed oil is the best dietary source for LNA—1 to 2 tbsp. daily.
- Probiotics
- Eicosapentaenoic Acid applied topically or consumed orally.
- Gamma-Linolenic Acid (GLA)—550 mg daily
- Linoleic Acid (LA) is an Omega-6 essential fatty acid. Flaxseed oil is an excellent dietary source for LA—1 to 2 tbsp. daily.
- Sulfur (MSM)
- Zinc—30 mg with 3 mg copper daily
- Biotin—300 mg daily
- Vitamin B3—100 mg three times daily
- Vitamin B6—50 mg three times daily
- Vitamin B12—1 mg daily

- Vitamin C with bioflavonoids—1,000 mg three to five times daily
- Burdock—500 mg in capsule form or 1 cup of tea two to three times daily.
- Borage Seed Oil—as directed on label
- Evening Primrose Oil—1,000 to 3,000 mg daily
- Fish Oils—3,000 to 4,000 mg daily consumed orally or applied topically

IMPORTANT AIDS

- Selenium—100 mcg daily (in the form of either selenomethionine or selenium yeast)
- Vitamin D3—400 to 1,000 IU daily
- Vitamin E—at least 400 IU daily
- Chamomile oil applied topically reduces inflammation.
- Red Clover purifies the blood and benefits the skin. Take 500 mg or 1 cup of tea two to three times daily.
- Licorice consumed orally or applied topically fights inflammation and infection. Take 250 mg of deglycyrrhizinated licorice (DGL) twice daily.
- Betaine HCL—take as directed
- Magnesium—100 mg daily
- Olive Oil

OTHER POTENTIAL AIDS

- Alpha-Hydroxy Acids (solutions containing at least 12% AHAs)
- Delta-6 Desaturase (the enzyme that converts linoleic acid to gamma-linolenic acid and which converts alpha-linolenic acid to stearidonic acid)
- Glutathione Peroxidase
- Forskolin
- Glycyrrhetinic Acid applied topically.
- Lactobacillus Acidophilus—two capsules with meals
- Calcium

- Potassium
- Silicon
- Nitrogenous Compounds
- Inositol
- Para-aminobenzoic Acid (PABA)
- Vitamin B2
- Thymus Extract
- Yogurt applied topically.
- Calendula (Marigold)
- Chaparral tea is beneficial for skin disorders.
- Goldenseal—dissolve 2 to 3 tbsp. in a quart of hot water and bathe skin or take 100 to 200 mg orally two to three times daily.
- Kelp—1,000 mg daily
- Pau D'arco
- Sarsaparilla tea
- Sassafras oil applied topically.
- Witch Hazel applied topically.
- Yellowdock
- Topical Oils
- Emu Oil applied topically or consumed orally.
- Lavender oil added to bath water.
- Neem Oil applied topically.
- Oregano Oil applied topically.
- Tea Tree Oil applied topically.
- Potato applied topically.
- Rhubarb juice

☞ EDEMA

EDEMA indicates that the soft tissues of the body have an unusually high fluid content between the cells. There are many forms of edema that effect different areas of the body. It can occur in the face, arms, neck, legs, ankles, and 5% of pregnant women have a form of it called preeclampsia.

One man's edema was so bad he would be hospitalized every couple of weeks for relief. After using Dr. Lorenzen Clustered Water for only a short time, all his edema was gone.

One employee in our business broke down and cried when Dr. Lorenzen visited our office, telling how she had come off the Lasix (a drug used to reduce the amount of free water in the body years before) after using the Clustered Water for only two days.

In previous pregnancies I would gain water weight, but with baby number eight and in my forties, I drank Clustered Water and didn't experience any unhealthy water gain or edema.

Edema can be caused by *Candida Albicans* proliferation. Read the Candida section.

Reduce salt, elevate your feet when possible, and adopt the One Perfect Diet.

TOP NATURAL AIDS

- Food-based Multivitamin
- Collodial Minerals—one to two ounces daily
- Clustered Water
- Vitamin B-complex—50 mg daily of each B vitamins
- Vitamin C with bioflavonoids—5,000 mg daily
- Bromelain—400 mg three times daily
- Vitamin B6—50 mg three times daily
- Grape Seed extract—100 mg three times daily
- Turmeric—500 mg four times daily only while condition is acute
- Chymotrypsin
- Papain alleviates the edema associated with the inflammation caused by sports injuries or surgery.

- Magnesium alleviates the edema that often occurs as a side effect of pre-menstrual syndrome (PMS), and edema can occur as a result of magnesium deficiency.
- Uva Ursi—25 to 40 drops

IMPORTANT AIDS

- Free-form Amino Acid complex—take as directed on label
- Alfalfa—2,000 to 3,000 mg daily in divided servings
- Vitamin E—400 to 800 IU daily (limit to 400 if one has high blood pressure)
- Magnesium—1,000 mg daily
- Butcher's Broom draws water from the leg and ankle. A daily serving should supply 50 to 100 mg of ruscogenins daily.
- Echinacea—300 to 500 mg three times daily (take with either bromelain or turmeric). Use in cycles of one week on, two weeks off.
- Juniper Berries stimulate kidney activity, increasing elimination of water. Take as a tea or chew approximately 5 berries daily.
- Common Melilot stimulates lymph circulation. Apply topically as salve.

OTHER POTENTIAL AIDS

- Calcium—1,200 mg daily
- Vitamin A—10,000 IU daily
- Candida Cleanse
- Taurine—100 to 500 mg daily
- Proteases as used in enzymes therapy
- Chymotrypsin
- Papain
- Copper—2 to 3 mg daily
- Potassium—100 to 500 mg daily
- Sulfur (MSM)—take as directed on label
- Oxygen, Body Oxygen, Hyperbaric Oxygen

FOODS *and* HERBS THAT IMPROVE EDEMA

- Pineapple
- Watermelon
- Bilberry—288 to 576 mg daily of standardized 25% anthocyanosides
- Calendula reduces inflammation. Take as directed.
- Cornsilk acts as a diuretic.
- Dandelion Leaves produce a mild diuretic effect.
- Ginkgo Biloba—40 to 80 mg three times daily of a 50:1 extract standardized to contain 24% ginkgo-flavone glycosides
- Horse Chestnut helps eliminate excess fluid in the tissues. Take 500 mg daily.
- Shepherd's Purse is traditionally used as a topical application. Don't use if pregnant, as Shepherd's Purse can stimulate uterine contractions.
- Flaxseed—1 to 2 tbsp. daily
- Celery acts as a diuretic.

Exercise is very important. Remember that the body is 70% water. A good portion of that water is in the lymph system. But the lymph system does not move unless you do. Read the Exercise chapter.

☞ EMOTIONAL SWINGS

MOOD is the state of mind or state of feeling or emotion at a particular moment. It's been said that taking care of your emotional health and well-being can make you up to sixteen years younger on the inside. We can all use this!

In China, doctors check those experiencing emotional upheavals first for liver disorders. I have also seen this to be true. We start with a liver cleanse as well as the herbs to cause the liver to flush and function better. See "Coffee Enema" in Appendix A.

Neurotransmitters should also be evaluated (see Appendix A). The right foods and nutrients are vital to stable emotions. We must give the brain the right fuel if we expect it to function as it should! Remember: the wrong foods will usually equal the wrong emotional response.

A lack of B-vitamins plays a key to emotions and should be used to bring balance as well.

Check your environment also! Chemical poisoning and dust can cause a negative emotional response. Check adrenal function and supplement accordingly.

TOP NATURAL AIDS

- Magnesium—500 mg daily
- Vitamin B-complex—50 mg three times daily
- Chromium—200 mg daily
- Calcium—1,500 mg daily. Use of more than 1,500 mg daily of calcium suppresses the activity of the neurons associated with mood and emotion.
- Supplemental Vitamin B1—50 mg daily
- Vitamin B1—10 to 300 mg daily
- Vitamin B12—50 to 300 mcg daily
- 5-HTP—100 to 200 mg three times daily
- Melatonin—1 to 3 mg before bed

IMPORTANT AIDS

- Dehydroepiandrosterone (DHEA)—50 to 200 mg daily

- An overactive or underactive thyroid condition can cause emotional swings. An overactive (hyperthyroid) condition can create nervousness and tremors, while an underactive (hypothyroid) condition can result in fatigue and loss of memory. A blood test for thyroid conditions can help determine whether your thyroid is functioning normally.
- Phosphatidylserine—300 mg daily for at least 60 days
- Methylsulfonylmethane (MSM)—3,000 to 9,000 mg daily improves mood

OTHER POTENTIAL AIDS

- Caffeine can significantly bolster mood.
- Acetyl-L-Carnitine (ALC)—100 to 500 mg daily
- Phenylalanine—2,000 mg daily or more
- Tyrosine—500 mg daily
- Androstenedione—100 mg twice daily with food
- Cortisol is involved in the maintenance of positive moods. However, excessive cortisol production or release interferes with mood.
- Human Growth Hormone (hGH)—take under doctor's supervision
- Supplemental Pregnenolone—50 to 100 mg daily
- Prostaglandin E1
- Bromine induces subjective effects of happiness and well-being, thereby improving mood.
- Copper—1 to 3 mg daily
- Selenium—100 mcg daily
- Neurotransmitters—dopamine, norepinephrine, and serotonin can improve moods. See Neurotransmitter section in Appendix A.

HERBS

- Chamomile—take as tea or use tinctures and pills according to label directions
- Ginkgo Biloba—80 mg twice daily of a 50:1 extract

standardized to contain 24% ginkgo-flavored glycosides
- Korean Ginseng—200 to 300 mg of standardized extract. Note: ginseng should be taken in cycles of three weeks on, two weeks off.
- Passionflower—use in tea or take tinctures and powdered extracts according to label directions

Exercise: Exercise improves mood (high-intensity exercise improves mood to a greater extent than low-intensity exercise).

✍ ENERGY

EVERYONE WANTS MORE ENERGY! There are many reasons we lack energy, but there are common denominators. It comes down to the amount of energy your body makes minus the amount of energy you expend. There are only a couple of ways the body makes energy— eating great foods, digesting it efficiently, exercising, and breathing deep copious quantities of oxygen. If you do feel tired, rundown, and depressed, change your diet and make sure you are eating organic super foods and supplements. Eat uncooked, fresh fruits and vegetables, nuts, seeds, sprouts, and grains. Then mix in some lightly cooked or steamed vegetables, grains, beans, and meats. Energy is the capacity to engage in vigorous behavior. Endogenous, cellular energy is produced within the mitochondria of cells as part of the Krebs Cycle. So, support your metabolism, feed it the B vitamins, liquid minerals, amino acids, and fatty acids it craves.

FOUR STEPS *to* MORE ENERGY THIS WEEK!

1. Reread the Four Foundations and apply them to your life.
2. Start the food suggestions above with a short fast, reread Chapter 18.
3. Begin taking your top natural supplemental aids.
4. Exercise. It's easy. Reread Chapter 17.

Dr. Andrew Weil offers this thought: Changes in weather, stress, sleeping patterns, and even the amount of daylight you're exposed to can all affect energy levels. Regular exercise is one of the best ways I know to stay energized throughout the day. A brisk walk in the morning or a short stroll in the afternoon can offset the "lows" that are part of the daily energy cycle. Exercise can also improve both the quality and quantity of sleep, which can do wonders for maintaining activity during the day. While maintaining optimum health—through exercise, diet, and sleep—is undoubtedly the best way to boost energy, those with chronic energy problems may also want to try the following supplements:

- Ashwaganda, an Ayurvedic herb prized for its ability to help the body deal with stress, especially for men.

- American Ginseng, which contains active ingredients that often enhance mental activity and physical endurance.
- Cordyceps, a traditional Chinese medicinal mushroom that may help fight fatigue and boost energy levels.

TOP NATURAL AIDS

- Food-based Multivitamin
- Liquid Minerals
- Food-based vitamin B-complex
- Coenzyme Q10—150 mg daily
- Biotin
- Folic Acid
- Lipoic Acid
- A Candida Cleanse is very beneficial for energy.
- Clustered Water. Lack of energy can be caused by dehydration. Optimal intake of water helps to preserve energy levels. Read Chapter 9 for how much.
- Many people (aged over forty) who use Thyroid Extract (containing 1 grain of a combination of all four thyroid hormones) report an increase in subjective feelings of energy.
- Carnitine facilitates the production of energy within the body by carrying fatty acids into the mitochondria and stimulating their oxidation into energy.
- Body Oxygen
- Creatine
- SOD
- Octacosanol

IMPORTANT AIDS

- Arginine and Ornithine (when consumed simultaneously) enhance the release of Human Growth Hormone (hGH).
- Asparagine is a source of energy in the brain.
- Aspartic Acid is a source of energy in the brain.
- Tyrosine—1,000 to 6,000 mg daily increases energy production
- Supplemental Dehydroepiandrosterone (DHEA)

- Leucine can be utilized within the body in the production of energy.
- Phenylalanine—1,500 mg daily
- Dimethyl Glycine (DMG)
- All dietary carbohydrates are converted within the body to glucose, which is then used in the Krebs Cycle (via Adenosine Triphosphate) as a source of energy within the body.
- NADH
- Inosine
- Citric Acid—3,000 to 6,000 mg daily
- Fumaric Acid—3,000 to 6,000 mg daily
- Hydroxycitric Acid (HCA)
- Malic Acid—3,000 to 6,000 mg daily
- Pyruvic Acid—6,000 mg daily
- Manganese
- Alpha-Linolenic Acid (LNA)
- All dietary fats can be used by the body for energy production.

OTHER POTENTIAL AIDS

- Betaine
- Caffeine
- Alanine
- Acetyl-L-Carnitine (ALC)
- Glucogenic Amino Acids
- Glutamic Acid
- Human Growth Hormone (hGH)
- Pregnenolone
- Progesterone
- Forskolin
- Linoleic Acid (LA)
- Chromium
- Iodine
- Magnesium
- Phosphorus
- Succinic Acid—3,000 to 6,000 mg daily
- Bananas
- Oats
- Ashwagandha
- Astragalus
- Ginger
- Golden Root
- Korean Ginseng
- Maca
- Sarsaparilla
- Schizandra
- Flaxseed Oil

☞ EYES

TOP NATURAL AIDS

- Bilberries improve both day and night visual acuity—160 mg and up daily
- Lutein has proven effective in maintaining or restoring eyesight—5 mg three times daily
- Vitamin A fights against free-radical damage—25,000 IU daily with 50,000 IU daily of beta-carotene
- Evening Primrose Oil—1,000 mg three times daily
- Vitamin E—400 IU daily
- Vitamin B-complex—100 mg twice daily
- Vitamin C with bioflavonoids—2,000 mg three times daily
- Vitamin B2—100 mg daily

IMPORTANT AIDS

- Zinc—40 to 80 mg with 3 mg copper daily
- Ginkgo Biloba may help inhibit macular degeneration. Take 40 to 60 mg two to three times daily of a formula containing at least 24% gingko heterosides.

OTHER POTENTIAL AIDS

- Eyebright—500 mg twice daily
- Chromium—50 to 200 mcg daily
- Blurred vision may be associated with a sodium deficiency.
- Carnosine (N-Acetyl-Carnosine) eye drops applied topically.
- Flaxseed Oil—take 1 to 2 tbsp. daily
- Fennel can be used as an eyewash. Follow label directions.

☞ FIBROCYSTIC BREASTS

FIBROCYSTIC BREAST DISEASE occurs in 24 percent of premenopausal women and produces numerous levels of pain and is a benign tumor of fibrous connective tissues of the breasts. Also known as Benign Breast Disease; Breast Engorgement; Breast Tenderness; Chronic Mastitis; Cystic Hyperplasia; Cystic Hyperplasia of the Breast; Cystic Mastitis; Cystic Mastopathy; Fibrocystic Disease of the Breast; Fibrocystic Mastopathy; Mammary Intraduct Epithelial Hyperplasia; MIEH.

I have a friend who is fine as long as she stays away from coffee. When she starts drinking coffee, the breast issues reoccur. My advice: stay off coffee. Coffee depletes vital nutrients from the body, and the caffeine is known as methylxanthines, which elevates the levels of compounds that promote overpopulation linked to this ailment.

However, most of the fibrocystic breasts are linked to estrogen dominance. When you cleanse the liver, estrogen is metabolized in the liver. You need to bring nutrients back into proper range as well as perform a saliva hormone test to see what is actually needed. Stay away from plastics as they have Xenoestrogens. Do not eat any animal product that is not hormone free. The same hormones given to animals mimic those in the human body.

Women who have fewer than three bowel movements a week have a 4.5 times greater rate of FBD than those with regular bowel movements. Keep your liver in good working order and supplement with iodine.

TOP NATURAL AIDS

- Probiotic Ultra Pro daily
- Multivitamin daily
- Collodial Minerals—1 to 2 ounces daily
- Vitamin C with bioflavonoids—2,000 to 4,000 mg daily in divided portions
- Iodine—500 mcg daily
- Coenzyme Q10—30 to 100 mg daily
- Evening Primrose Oil may reduce the size of the lumps. Take 3,000 mg daily for at least six months.

- Vitamin E protects the breast tissue. Take 600 IU daily of the d-alpha-tocopherol form.
- Quercetin helps reduce the discomfort of fibrocystic breasts. Take 300 mg three times daily, 30 minutes before eating.
- Kelp is an excellent source of iodine. A deficiency of iodine is often linked to fibrocystic breasts. Take 1,500 to 2,000 mg of kelp daily in divided servings.
- Milk Thistle helps rid the body of toxins. Take 100 to 200 mg twice daily for seven days before menstruation.

IMPORTANT AIDS

- Vitamin A—15,000 IU daily
- Beta-carotene—30,000 IU daily in divided portions
- Vitamin B-complex—100 mg daily of each of the major B vitamins
- Zinc—50 mg daily
- Vitamin B6—50 mg three times daily
- Chaste Tree Berry helps regulate hormones. Take 125 mg twice daily of a standardized extract ten days before your menstrual period.

OTHER POTENTIAL AIDS

- Serrapeptase
- Exogenous Progesterone applied topically to the breasts.
- Polyunsaturated Fatty Acids
- Selenium—at least 100 to 200 mcg daily
- Vitamin A—150,000 IU daily, which is a high serving
- Gotu Kola—take as directed
- Red Clover benefits fibrocystic breasts.
- Turmeric has anti-inflammatory and anticancer properties.
- Pau d'arco fights tumors.
- Pine Bark and Grape Seed extracts both contain potent anti-inflammatory properties. Take 50 mg two to three times daily of either one.

Exercise to move your lymph system.

☞ FIBROMYALGIA

A SOFT TISSUE MUSCULOSKELETAL SYNDROME that is similar to chronic fatigue syndrome in that it involves chronic achy muscular pain without an obvious physical cause. Approximately 85% of fibromyalgia patients are young women, and 90% of fibromyalgia patients are women.

The word *fibromylagia* means muscle tissue pain. Of course, that is no surprise to anyone who has it. A dear friend, Penny Lorenzen, was attacked by this dreaded disease when no one had ever heard of it. The best medical care in the world was available to her. Her father was the attorney general to Ronald Reagan, and her husband, Dr. Lee Lorenzen, worked at the University of Irvine, creating pharmaceuticals. With all the knowledge and all the medicine available, they could not do anything to help Penny. One night as they were on their way to the hospital in the ambulance, Dr. Lorenzen had a great idea. He decided to pray. Right after that, God supernaturally led him to research water. That is how the Clustered Water product was birthed, and how Penny was healed. Dr. Lorenzen no longer makes pharmaceuticals but has dedicated his life to alternative research. We have had innumerable testimonials over the years of this incredible product doing the same and much more for others.

TOP NATURAL AIDS
- Clustered Water—begin with 4 ounces and gradually increase. Read Chapter 9.
- 5-HTP (5-Hydroxytryptophan)—50 to 300 mg daily
- St. John's Wort—300 mg three times daily of a standardized extract containing 0.3% hypericin to control stress
- Malic Acid—2,400 mg daily combined with 600 mg of magnesium
- Coenzyme Q10—60 mg twice daily between meals
- Vitamin B-complex—50 mg of each of the major B vitamins three times daily
- Vitamin C with bioflavonoids—5,000 to 10,000 mg daily in divided portions

- NADH—10 to 15 mg upon awakening, on empty stomach
- Proteolytic Enzymes—take as directed
- Garlic—5,000 mcg of standardized allicin three times daily
- Turmeric (curcumin)—400 to 500 mg three times daily with food

IMPORTANT AIDS

- Acidophilus Probiotics—as directed on label
- Flaxseed Oil—1 to 2 tbsp. daily
- Capsaicin applied topically seems to inhibit the release of neurotransmitters that transmit pain. Mix 1 part cayenne (capsaicin) powder with 3 parts Wintergreen oil and apply to skin.
- Supplemental S-Adenosylmethionine (SAMe)—800 mg daily or more
- DHEA (Dehydroepiandrosterone)
- Methylsulfonylmethane (MSM) helps relieve pain. Take orally or use topically as cream as directed on label.
- Calcium—1,500 mg daily, 750 mg at night before bed
- Vitamin B12—200 to 400 mcg daily
- Chlorella
- Evening Primrose Oil—1,000 mg three times daily
- Grape Seed extract—300 to 500 mg daily
- Fish Oils contain the important Omega-3 fatty acids Eicosapentaenoic Acid (EPA) and Docosahexaenoic Acid (DHA). Therapeutic servings include 1,800 mg of EPA and 900 mg of DHA daily.

OTHER POTENTIAL AIDS

- Bromelain—400 mg three times daily between meals
- Creatine Monohydrate—as directed on label
- Phenylalanine (DL-Phenylalanine form)—500 mg daily, every other week
- Lipoic Acid—100 mg three times daily

- Hyaluronic Acid consumed orally.
- Gamma-amino-butyric acid (GABA)—as directed on label
- Human Growth Hormone (hGH) should be used under doctor's supervision.
- Chromium—200 to 400 mcg daily
- Melatonin—take as directed, 1 to 2 hours before bedtime
- Progesterone
- Relaxin
- L-tyrosine helps relax muscles. Take 500 to 1,000 mg daily at bedtime.
- Magnesium (Malate form)—300 to 600 mg daily
- Neurotransmitters—see Appendix A
- Insufficient production of Serotonin has been speculated to be a cause of fibromyalgia.
- Aloe Vera consumed orally stimulates cell regeneration.
- Olive Leaf fights bacteria, viruses, fungi, and parasites.
- Siberian Ginseng helps provide energy. Start with 100 mg twice daily and gradually increase amount, if needed. Use a standardized extract containing 0.5% eleutheroside E and take in cycles of six weeks on, one week off.
- Astragalus enhances immune function.
- Dandelion tea helps reduce pain. Take twice daily.
- Kelp helps support the thyroid.

☞ GALLBLADDER

THE GALLBLADDER is a pear-shaped sac lying underneath the right lobe of the liver in which bile is stored.

TOP NATURAL AIDS

- Vitamin C—1,000 to 3,000 mg daily
- Artichoke Leaf—250 to 500 mg two to three times daily
- Dandelion increases the flow of bile to the gallbladder and also stimulates the release of stored bile.
- Vitamin E—600 IU daily
- Lecithin—1,200 mg three times daily before meals
- Gallbladder Flush—This flush involves a three-day fast on olive oil mixed with lemon juice and a potassium broth made from carrots, spinach, celery, parsley, and water. Cook the vegetables in three quarts of water to make the potassium broth by bringing to a boil, then cover it and let it sit without heat for an hour. Then drain and refrigerate, using only the liquid. Mix 8 ounces of the broth with 3 tablespoons of olive oil mixed with the juice of 3 lemons. All these liquids should be taken four to five times a day. After completing the flush, read the Acid/Alkaline section and follow the alkaline diet with sea vegetables and green drinks.

IMPORTANT AIDS

- Choline—50 to 200 mg daily
- Ginger stimulates the secretion of bile.

OTHER POTENTIAL AIDS

- Glutamine
- Lipases
- Cholecystokinin (CCK)
- Secretin
- Cynarin
- Coffee
- Burdock root
- Calendula
- Greater Celandine
- Globe Artichoke

☞ GOUT

GOUT is a form of arthritis and is regarded as a form of rheumatism. Excess uric acid forms in the blood, tissue, and urine. Swelling, inflammation, and pain are common as the accumulation of crystals of uric acid surround the joints. Ninety-five percent of those afflicted with gout are men ages 30 and over. Gout was once called "the rich man's disease" because of high consumption of red meat, wine, cheese and too many night shade vegetables—green peppers, eggplant, turnip greens, mustard greens, collard greens, and tomatoes.

My husband experienced relief from this ailment by drinking black cherry juice. Avoid alcohol, high fats, and refined carbohydrates. Drink plenty of good water (see Chapter 9), and if you are overweight follow the suggestions made herein. As always check with your doctor.

TOP NATURAL AIDS

- Black Cherry juice—8 ounce concentrate, no sugar added
- Clustered Water
- Quercetin—450 to 750 mg daily between meals
- Vitamin E with mixed tocopherols—400 IU daily taken with meals
- Flaxseed Oil—500 to 1,000 mg or 1 to 2 tablespoons daily
- Vitamin C with bioflavonoids—up to 1,000 mg daily
- Vitamin B-complex—50 mg of each B vitamin except vitamin B12 (those with gout should not take B12), one to three times daily with meals
- Turmeric—250 to 500 mg three times daily
- Bilberry—80 mg three times daily of extract standardized to contain 25% anthocyanosides
- Stinging Nettle Root—250 mg three times daily
- Bromelain—500 mg every three hours during an acute gout attack or 1,000 mg daily for preventative purposes

IMPORTANT AIDS

- Glucosamine Sulfate—300 mg twice daily

- Methylsulfonylmethane (MSM)—take as directed on label
- Folic Acid—10 to 40 mg daily
- Juniper Berry—350 to 500 mg twice daily
- Celery juice helps flush out uric acid from tissues to ease painful joints.

OTHER POTENTIAL AIDS

- Proteolylic enzymes—2 capsules with meals and 2 capsules between meals
- Glycine—up to 30 grams daily
- Orotic Acid—4,000 mg daily for six days
- Cherry (or Cherry juice)—12 ounce concentrate daily for 3 to 6 days
- Burdock—1 to 2 grams of powdered dry root three times daily
- Butcher's Broom—1 serving should supply 50 to 100 mg of ruscogenins daily
- Horseradish stimulates elimination of wastes and toxins from the system. Use pulp topically as a poultice, drink horsetail tea three times daily, or drink 1 cup of horsetail juice made of grated horseradish root boiled in water daily on an empty stomach for 10 days.
- Lavender baths
- Paprika
- Rosemary stimulates blood flow and calms the nerves. Take extract as directed on label.
- Sarsaparilla acts as a diuretic.
- Skullcap—1 to 2 grams three times daily
- Yucca—2 to 4 tablets daily of concentrated yucca saponins
- Rye
- Beetroot
- Lettuce
- Potato (raw juice)

HAIR LOSS

HAIR LOSS can be from several different factors:

- Stress
- Genetics
- Hormone imbalance
- Nutritional deficiency
- Clogged hair follicles
- Demodex Follicularum (mites). These mites are present in virtually everyone by the time a person reaches middle age. In most cases they cause no harm. Studies say that the hair loss in some may be the response that each individual has to the presence of these mites. If the body initiates the inflammatory response as it tries to reject the mites, it may close down the follicles, thus killing the mites but also killing the hair.
- Poor circulation
- Thyroid disease
- Fungal infections
- Toxic liver
- Miscellaneous medications

TOP NATURAL AIDS

- Folic Acid—800 mcg daily
- Essential Fatty Acids
- Raw Thymus
- Vitamin B-complex—aids in fighting stress
- Vitamin C—3,000 to 10,000 mg daily
- Zinc stimulates hair growth by enhancing immune function.
- All oxygen enhancing products for circulation—Body Oxygen, Clustered Water, Coenzyme Q10
- Copper—3 mg daily works with zinc to aid in hair growth
- Lots of garlic in diet and supplement to get rid of mites
- Tea Tree Oil kills bacteria and mites. Use 10 drops into the scalp and massage in, then shampoo.
- If caused from hypothyroid, work on increasing thyroid

function (if this is the case, contact me—we are having success with natural thyroid stimulation).

- Let hair dry naturally and use a pick to comb out.
- Avoid crash diets that cause nutritional imbalances.
- Do not wear tight ponytail holders or other devices that would cause problems in circulation to scalp.
- Biotin—300 mcg daily
- Saw Palmetto may help with male pattern baldness—160 mg twice daily of an extract standardized to contain 90% essential fatty acids and sterols

✍ HEADACHE

HEADACHES are a widespread problem. If you watch television at all, you know that ache felt deep within the skull. Excessive proliferation of *Candida Albicans* (when it enters the bloodstream) can cause headaches. Headaches may be an early symptom of lead poisoning as well as many other problems. It is important to get to the root of the problem. While it could be something serious, it may also be something as simple as blood sugar levels being too low and the need to eat. Poor eyesight, stress, and too much caffeine are just a few of the potential root causes. Hormone imbalance and low minerals, such as magnesium, can also play a role. Many people simply do not get proper rest! A lack of B-vitamins can also be a root cause. Or as the kid said in Arnold Schwarzenegger's *Kindergarten Cop*, "Maybe it's a brain tumor." Pain relievers may give temporary relief, but you may be able to go beyond that naturally.

TOP NATURAL AIDS

- Coenzyme Q10—200 mg twice a day
- Riboflavin (Vitamin B2)—200 to 400 mg daily
- 5-HTP—100 to 200 mg three times daily
- Calcium—500 mg three times daily
- Magnesium—250 mg three times daily
- Vitamin B-complex—50 mg three times a day
- Candida Cleanse
- Valerian—2 to 3 grams of dried herb, 270 to 450 mg of an aqueous valerian extract, or 600 mg of an ethanol extract, taken before bedtime

IMPORTANT AIDS

- Vitamin B6—50 mg three times a day
- Vitamin E—starting with 400 IU daily and gradually increasing to 1,200 IU daily
- Quercetin—500 mg twice daily
- Feverfew—150 mg of extract or 200 to 400 mg of herb two to

three times daily. Do not use if pregnant.

- Lavender relieves stress.
- Peppermint Tea relieves headache located in front of head.
- Ginger Tea
- Skullcap Tea
- Evening Primrose Oil—500 mg three to four times daily

OTHER POTENTIAL AIDS

- Supplemental Melatonin—10 mg daily
- Iron—10 to 30 mg daily, if you are deficient

OTHER VITAMINS

- Biotin—400 to 800 mcg daily
- PABA—10 to 50 mg daily
- Vitamin B1—1,000 to 4,000 mg daily
- Vitamin B5—50 to 100 mg daily

THESE FOODS and HERBS MAY BE HELPFUL

- Basil
- Blue Vervain
- Camu-Camu
- Chamomile—take as tea or as directed in tincture and pill form
- Damiana—2 to 4 grams taken two to three times daily or take as directed
- Equisetum (also known as Horsetail)—1 gram in capsule form or take as tea up to three times daily. Note: avoid Marsh Horsetail, which is highly toxic.
- Hops—0.5 grams one to three times daily
- Marjoram
- Passionflower tea relaxes the nervous system.
- Rosemary stimulates circulation and fights inflammation.
- Schizandra
- White Willow Bark—for relief, take extract supplying 80 to 120 mg of salicin. Note: do not use if allergic to aspirin.

- Wood Betony relaxes muscles.
- Fish Oils—approximately 4,500 mg daily containing 800 mg of EPA and 500 mg of DHA helps to prevent and treat headaches
- Lettuce juice

Exercise will help.

✍ HEART

THE HEART is the powerfully built pumping organ of the cardiovascular system. Love conquers all, even heart attacks. Reread "Foundations for the Gospel of Health."

A Swedish study proved that frequent social interaction among men—friendships, golf outings, poker nights, etc.—correlated into a more than 50% reduction in heart disease among test subjects. That's a far greater reduction in risk than any prescription drug I know about. Another new European study, this one from the U.K., shows that having loving, close relationships with spouses, relatives or close friends helped to measurably lower heart attack victims' risk of suffering a second cardiovascular event.

According to an article on HealthDay online, heart attack survivors without some type of intimate relationship to lean on for emotional support or social interaction were twice as likely to suffer major heart problems within one calendar year of their initial cardiac event. Highlighting more than 1,000 heart attack patients, the article did not specify the sex of the study's subjects. If this study had been specifically structured to measure the phenomenon in one sex, I assume the article's author would have mentioned it. Regardless of whether it's equally applicable to both sexes or not, this is the second study I've run across in recent months supporting the notion that close relationships of one type or another can cut the risk of heart trouble in half.

TOP NATURAL AIDS

- Vitamin C—1,000 to 3,000 mg daily
- Vitamin E (d-alpha-tocopherol)—400 to 600 IU daily
- Vitamin B-12—250 to 300 mg 3 times daily
- Folic Acid—400 mcg daily
- Acetyl-L-Carnitine (ALC) helps prevent fatty buildup in the heart. Take 500 to 2,500 mg daily in divided amounts.
- Alpha-Linolenic Acid (LNA)
- Linoleic Acid (LA)
- Magnesium—750 to 1,000 mg daily

- Selenium—100 to 200 mcg daily
- Coenzyme Q10—30 to 100 mg daily
- Hawthorn Berry dilates coronary blood vessels and restores heart muscle.
- Fish Oils contain the important Omega-3 fatty acids Eicosapentaenoic Acid (EPA) and Docosahexaenoic Acid (DHA). Therapeutic servings include 1,800 mg of EPA and 900 mg of DHA daily.
- Garlic provides protection from heart disease by preventing blood clots and helps lower high blood pressure. Do not use if taking blood thinners.
- Potassium—100 mg daily
- Turmeric
- Body Oxygen
- Vitamin A—5,000 to 10,000 IU daily
- Grape Seed extract—150 to 300 mg daily
- Lecithin—take as directed
- Polycosanol—take as directed

IMPORTANT AIDS

- Capsaicin—apply topically in cream form or take 1 to 2 standard capsules one to three times daily.
- Chelation Suppositories with Ethylene-Diamine-Tetra-Acetate (EDTA)
- Beta-carotene—5,000 to 25,000 IU daily
- Dehydroepiandrosterone (DHEA)—take as directed on label
- Calcium—1,500 to 2,000 mg daily
- Zinc—30 to 50 mg daily
- Choline helps metabolize cholesterol. A typical serving is 50 to 200 mg daily.
- Ginkgo Biloba improves circulation.

OTHER POTENTIAL AIDS

- Taurine—100 to 500 mg daily

- Chondroitin Sulfate—take as directed on label
- Lycopene—take as directed on label
- Regular sunlight exposure causes the heart to become stronger and to pump more blood by an average of 39% in 90% of cases.
- Octacosanol helps lower cholesterol levels. Take 5 to 10 mg twice daily.
- Manganese—3 to 10 mg daily
- Phosphorus is necessary for proper heart rhythm. Take as directed on label.
- Pangamic Acid
- Pyruvic Acid
- Quercetin—70 to 140 mg daily
- Vitamin B1—50 to 100 mg daily
- Vitamin K—100 to 500 mcg daily
- Wheat Grass
- Blessed Thistle—take as directed on label
- Cocoa
- Ginger—as tea or as directed on label.
- Korean Ginseng—take as directed on label
- Golden Root
- Goldenseal cleanses the body. Take as directed and don't use for prolonged periods.
- Gotu Kola
- Motherwort acts as a tonic for the heart. Take 4.5 grams of dried herb daily or its equivalent.
- Olive Leaf appears to lower high blood pressure.
- Siberian Ginseng—take as directed on label

Exercise

☞ HEARTBURN

OFTEN APPEARS TO RISE from the abdomen toward or into the throat. Heartburn is distress or pain felt behind the breastbone in the upper chest. Symptoms may appear an hour or so after a meal.

TOP NATURAL AIDS

- Apple Cider Vinegar before each meal—1 tablespoon in 4 ounces of water, may add lemon and honey to taste.
- Ginger—one or two 500 mg capsules as needed
- Pancreatin—500 to 1,000 mg daily taken after two largest meals
- Protease—300 IU daily taken after two largest meals
- Bromelain—take as directed on label
- Glutamine—500 mg of L-glutamine two to three times daily for up to 4 weeks
- Amylase—2,500 IU after two largest meals
- Cellulose
- Lipases—5,000 IU after two largest meals
- Proteolytic Enzymes help digest the protein in food. They come in various forms, so follow label directions.
- Vitamin E—400 IU one to two times daily (avoid dl-alpha tocopherol form)
- Aloe Vera—as juice, 1 tbsp. twice daily

IMPORTANT AIDS

- Betaine Hydrochloride (Betaine HCl)—2 ml diluted in 200 ml water and sipped through a straw (to avoid contact with the teeth) alleviates many cases of heartburn by increasing the level of hydrochloric acid in the stomach.
- Papaya Tablets—take as directed on label
- Vitamin B-complex—50 mg of each major B vitamin three times daily
- Extra Vitamin B12—1,000 to 2,000 mcg daily
- Calcium—600 mg of the liquid or tablet form of the calcium

carbonate form of calcium taken every two to three hours
- Magnesium (tablets chewed)—150 to 200 mg twice daily
- Zinc—15 mg with 3 mg copper
- Bifidobacteria bulgaricus powder or liquid formulas are best. If taking capsules, it is preferable to pour contents on tongue rather than swallowing them whole.
- Methylsufonylmethane (MSM)—3,000 mg daily
- Vitamin A—5,000 to 10,000 IU daily

OTHER POTENTIAL AIDS

- Vitamin B5 (Pantethine form)—600 to 900 mg
- Kiwi
- Barberry—take as directed on label
- Cinnamon—2 to 4 grams daily of bark or 0.05 to 0.2 grams daily of essential oil
- Dill Seeds
- Goldenseal—1 tsp. of fluid extract or tincture
- Neem Leaf extract consumed internally alleviates heartburn. Follow label directions.
- Slippery Elm—9 to 30 grams
- Cabbage juice extract
- Potato juice diluted
- Antacid commercials confuse what heartburn really is in many cases. They are used to nullify the stomach's hydrochloric acid, thinking that excessive hydrochloric acid (hyperchlorhydria) is the underlying cause of heartburn. In fact, inadequate production of hydrochloric acid (hypochlorhydria) is a far more frequent. So the problem may only be worsened by use of antacids.

☞ HEMORRHOIDS

HEMORRHOIDS are varicose veins of the anus that may be tender, painful swellings in and around the anus. Getting to the root is very important. Typically, this is diet-related or may stem from constipation and straining caused from medications or diet. It is extremely important to eat a high-fiber diet. I suggest All Bran in the evenings. A warm sitz bath is helpful and topical OTC ointments may provide temporary relief.

TOP NATURAL AIDS

- Vitamin B6—50 mg three times daily
- Troxerutin—500 to 4,000 mg daily
- Vitamin C—3,000 to 5,000 mg daily
- Vitamin E with mixed tocopherols—600 IU daily
- Butcher's Broom—300 to 500 mg three times daily
- Comfrey ointment applied topically.
- Goldenseal applied topically or ingested orally.
- Collagen liquid with vitamin C taken at night is beneficial to the veins in the anus wall.
- Probiotic

IMPORTANT AIDS

- Pycnogenol—200 to 400 mg daily
- Vitamin B-complex—50 to 100 mg of each major B vitamin three times daily
- Vitamin B12—1,000 mcg twice daily
- Flaxseed Oil or Olive Oil—1 tbsp. daily
- Calcium—1,500 mg daily; combined with magnesium, 750 mg daily
- Inositol—50 mg twice daily
- Psyllium—use as directed on label
- Vitamin A cream applied topically.
- Bilberry—80 mg three times daily of extract standardized to contain 25% anthocyanosides

- Butcher's Broom—100 mg 3 times daily
- Chamomile reduces inflammation.
- Gotu Kola normally takes at least 4 weeks to work.
- Horse Chestnut—300 mg twice daily of standardized form to contain 50 mg escin per serving, for a total daily amount of 100 mg escin

OTHER POTENTIAL AIDS

- Bromelain—500 mg two to three times daily
- Choline—50 mcg twice daily
- Cellulose is an indigestible carbohydrate located in the outer layer of many vegetables and fruits. It relieves constipation. Cellulose is found in apples, beets, broccoli, carrots, celery, green beans, lima beans, pears, peas, and whole grains.
- Vitamin E cream applied topically.
- Kelp—150 mcg daily
- Gotu Kola—20 to 60 mg three times daily of an extract standardized to contain 40% asiaticoside, 29–30% asiatic acid, 29–30% madecassic acid, and 1–2% madecassoside
- White Oak Bark ointment applied topically.
- Witch Hazel ointment applied topically.
- Yellow Dock—2 to 4 ml of liquid extract, 1 to 2 ml of tincture, or 2 to 4 grams of dried root
- Grape Seed extract—take as directed on label

☞ HEPATITIS C

HEPATITIS C is a form of viral hepatitis that is caused by an RNA virus (the hepatitis C virus). It accounts for approximately 20% of the cases of acute viral hepatitis, 65% of the cases of chronic hepatitis. Most patients do not discover that they have Hep-C for 10 to 30 years after contracted. Curiously, many patients acquire hepatitis C without any known exposure to blood or drug use.

While there are many different protocols, the one that really worked for my husband was taken from Isaiah 58—by fasting your health will spring forth speedily. He fasted, prayed, and did the do's. He used the herbal protocol for hepatitis C as well as megadoses of Clustered Water. He literally drank up to a gallon and a half a day. Clustered Water may have a very positive affect on DNA damage as well as increases absorption of nutrients up to 600 times, plus cleans the lymphatic system. I know it seems impossible to believe, but Jim is living proof. He is in complete remission and back to the man I married twenty-four years ago.

This is a serious ailment that should be evaluated by a physician. See the list of doctors in Appendix C.

TOP NATURAL AIDS

- Clustered Water Advanced formula. Begin with 2 to 4 ounces a day and gradually increase until consuming 100 to 126 ounces daily.
- Thymus Extracts
- Liver Extracts—500 to 1,000 mg crude polypeptides per day
- Coenzyme Q10—25 mg two to three times daily
- Choline Citrate—250 mg twice daily
- Vitamin C with bioflavonoids—1,000 mg five to ten times daily
- Free-form Amino Acid Complex—take as directed on label
- Vitamin B-Complex—at last 100 mg of each major B two to three times daily
- S-Adenosylmethionine (SAMe)—400 mg three to four times daily
- Artichoke Extract

- Chlorella
- Thymic Formula—6 capsules daily
- Phosphatidylcholine—3,000 mg daily
- Green Tea—as tea, 3 cups daily; as extract, 100 to 150 mg three times daily of green tea extract standardized to contain 80% total polyphenols and 50% epigallocatechin gallate
- Super Milk Thistle—containing 160 to 320 mg of silymarin daily
- Dandelion Root—500 mg daily for up to one month
- Lipoic Acid—600 mg daily

IMPORTANT AIDS

- Grape Seed extract—50 mg twice daily
- Chlorophyll—500 mg two to three times daily
- L-cysteine—500 mg twice daily on empty stomach
- L-methionine—500 mg twice daily on empty stomach
- Selenium—400 mcg daily
- L-Arginine—2 to 3 grams daily
- Vitamin E—800 to 1,200 IU daily
- Astragalus—take as directed on label. Do not use if fever is present.

OTHER POTENTIAL AIDS

- Karawatake Mushrooms
- Glycyrrhizin
- Curcumin—400 to 600 mg three times daily
- Lactoferrin—1,000 to 1,400 mg daily
- Thymic Protein A
- Whey Protein—30 to 60 grams daily
- Vitamin B12—100 mcg taken in sublingual (under the tongue) form
- Ginger—500 mg twice daily with meals

Exercise and **weight control** combined with **periodic fasting**.

☞ HIGH BLOOD PRESSURE

IT'S CALLED THE SILENT KILLER because so many people are not aware they have it. It must be diagnosed by measuring the blood pressure. Hypertension involves the elevation of the blood pressure above the normal range expected in a particular age group.

Pulse pressure is the difference between peak systolic blood pressure and diastolic blood pressure. A person with a blood pressure reading of 120/80 has a pulse pressure of 40. If your pulse pressure is 60 or over you may be at increased risk of atherosclerosis. In patients aged 60 years and older, pulse pressure is the best predictor of coronary heart disease, with systolic blood pressure also playing a positive predictive role.

Regular exercise often permits persons afflicted with severe hypertension to reduce their servings of anti-hypertensive pharmaceutical drugs. In one study, hypertension patients riding a stationary bike for 15 minutes daily for eight months were able to reduce their prescribed servings of anti-hypertensive medication by an average of 40%, while their blood pressure fell to pre-exercise levels. This regime also reversed enlargement of the heart in hypertension patients. Aerobic exercise lowers blood pressure by an average of 9.9/5.9 mm Hg in hypertension patients.

A couple of years ago I was taping a television show in California. Afterward the producer said he had something private to ask. He told me he had recently been diagnosed with high blood pressure. He was in his forties and in good health and average weight. He asked if there was anything natural he could try. I told him that Seven Flowers, a combination product of herbal flowers, has been effective with high blood pressure that was stress-related. He began using the product, his blood pressure normalized, and his doctor withdrew the prescription. A year later it was still normal.

TOP NATURAL AIDS

- Calcium—1,500 to 3,000 mg twice daily; taken with magnesium, 750 to 1,000 mg

- Evening Primrose Oil—500 mg three times daily
- Selenium—200 mcg daily
- Carnitine—500 mg one to two times daily
- Coenzyme Q10—200 to 300 mg daily
- Garlic—500 mg three times daily
- Parsley—500 mg twice daily for one week out of each month
- Hawthorn Berry—100 to 200 mg three times daily (use standardized extract containing 1.8% vitexin-2 rhamnosides)
- Blackcurrant Seed Oil—500 to 1,000 mg two to three times daily
- Borage Seed—500 to 1,000 mg two to three times daily
- Fish Oils contain the important Omega-3 fatty acids EPA and DHA. Therapeutic servings include 1,800 mg of EPA and 900 mg of DHA daily.
- Flaxseed Oil—1 to 2 tbsp. daily
- Chelation with EDTA

IMPORTANT AIDS

- Lecithin—1,200 mg two to three times daily with meals
- Vitamin A—5,000 IU daily
- Beta-carotene—25,000 IU daily
- Vitamin C with bioflavonoids—3,000 to 6,000 mg daily with divided servings
- Vitamin E—400 IU daily (if taking a blood thinner, consult your physician)
- Kelp—1,000 to 1,500 mg daily
- Siberian Ginseng is especially helpful for anyone suffering from high blood pressure and fatigue. Take 100 mg in the morning of a standardized extract containing 0.5% eleutheroside E. Persons with high blood pressure should not take Chinese (Korean) or American Ginseng.
- Valerian—600 mg of ethanol extract or 2 to 3 grams of dried herb taken shortly before bedtime
- Maitake Mushrooms—3 to 7 grams daily of dried maitake in capsule or tablet form

OTHER POTENTIAL AIDS

- Zinc—30 mg with 3 mg copper daily
- Choline—1,000 mg daily
- Lipoic Acid—300 to 600 mg daily
- Vitamin B3 (as niacinamide)—50 to 100 mg daily
- Vitamin B6—50 to 100 mg daily

FOODS *and* HERBS THAT HELP

- Algae are a rich source of nutrients. Take as directed.
- Chlorella is the richest source for chlorophyll. It detoxifies the body and renews tissue.
- Kombu
- Shark
- Velvet Deer
- Cod, Herring, Mackerel, Salmon, Tuna
- Bananas
- Cumquats
- Watermelon
- Oats
- Rice
- Wheat
- Allspice
- Barberry—take as directed on label
- Bilberry—80 mg three times daily of extract standardized to contain 25% anthocyanosides
- Black Cohosh—1 to 2 tablets twice daily of a standardized extract containing 1 mg of 27-deoxyacteine per tablet
- Black Cumin
- Brahmi
- Cat's Claw—take according to label directions
- Cornsilk
- Devil's Claw—400 mg three times daily for 4 to 6 weeks
- Dong Quai—10 to 40 drops of tincture one to three times daily or 1 standard capsule three times daily

- Fo-Ti—500 to 1,000 mg one to two times daily
- Golden Root
- Goldenseal—250 to 500 mg three times daily
- Gotu Kola—20 to 60 mg three times daily of an extract standardized to contain 40% asiaticoside, 29–30% Asiatic acid, 29–30% madecassic acid, and 1–2% madecassoside. Gotu Kola normally takes at least 4 weeks to work.
- Holy Basil
- Olive Leaf
- Red Clover—choose extract providing 40 to 160 mg of isoflavones daily
- Skullcap—1 to 2 grams three times daily
- Stevia is an herb that works as a natural sweetener that works especially well in liquids. Use the powder form according to taste.
- Green Tea—as tea, 3 cups daily; as extract, 100 to 150 mg three times daily of green tea extract standardized to contain 80% total polyphenols and 50% epigallocatechin gallate
- Reishi—2 to 6 grams daily of raw fungus or an equivalent serving in concentrated extract form
- Shiitake Mushrooms along with Maitake and Reishi help to reduce high blood pressure. Take as directed.
- Grape Seed extract—take according to label directions
- Sesame Seeds
- Onions (cooked)
- Spinach

Exercise—start today!

☞ HIGH CHOLESTEROL

HIGH BLOOD CHOLESTEROL has no symptoms, but is considered to be the underlying cause of atherosclerosis and cardiovascular diseases, such as heart attacks and stroke. A high blood cholesterol level (above 190 to 200 mg/dL) is a contributor to plaque buildup in the arteries and impeded blood flow.

A slightly overweight friend in his mid forties was telling me about his recent checkup where he was told he had high tryglicerides and possible artery blockage that showed up in a body scan. He asked me what I would do in his situation. I said, "I would take daily nutrients, do an organ cleanse, and take the natural things that will drop the bad cholesterol and raise the good and help get the tryglicerides in range." Three weeks later, he said the doctor called him in, and he was actually concerned he was going to be told to go to the hospital. To his surprise, the doctor asked what he'd been taking. The doctor said he had never seen anyone's levels come down that quickly and all signs of trouble disappear. He asked for details on what he had done. The friend said he had gone on natural supplements. The doctor told him to keep doing whatever I said! He was taking daily supplements to get him up to par nutritionally—a food-based daily multivitamin, liquid minerals, collagen for muscle tone, weight loss, and sleep, vitamin C, polycosanol, and Coenzyme Q10. He felt so good he had started exercising.

TOP NATURAL AIDS

- Food-based Multivitamin daily
- Collodial Minerals—1 or 2 ounces a day
- Liquid Collagen—1 tablespoon with 1,000 mg vitamin C at bedtime
- Polycosanol should be taken in conjunction with Coenzyme Q10.
- Niacin—100 mg daily. I have seen this and polycosanol with Coenzyme Q10 work miracles on people.
- Vitamin C with bioflavonoids—3,000 to 8,000 mg daily in divided servings

- Chelation therapy by IV or suppository is extremely effective in some cases.
- Chrominum Picolinate—1,000 mcg daily
- Capsaicin, a form of Cayenne—1 to 2 standard capsules one to three times daily
- L-Carnitine—1,500 mg daily
- Lecithin in granule form—1 tbsp. three times daily before meals; in capsule form, 1,200 mg three times daily before meals
- Garlic—900 mg daily of an extract standardized to contain 1.3% alliin, or about 12,000 mcg of alliin daily
- Vitamin A with mixed carotenoids—5,000 IU daily
- Vitamin B-complex with extra thiamine—don't exceed 300 mg daily
- Vitamin E with mixed tocopherols—800 IU daily
- Beta-carotene—25,000 IU daily
- Glucomannan—1,000 mg taken approximately one hour prior to each meal
- Curcumin—400 to 600 mg three times daily
- Coenzyme Q10—100 mg daily
- Oats
- Ginger
- Hawthorn berries prevent hardening of the arteries. Take 40 drops of tincture three times daily or 100 to 200 mg three times daily (use standardized extract containing 1.8% vitexin-2 rhamnosides).
- Red Yeast Rice lowers both triglycerides and LDL cholesterol, while raising HDL (good) cholesterol. Take 600 mg one to four times daily, if not sensitive to yeast.
- Olive Oil
- Almonds

IMPORTANT AIDS

- Calcium—1,500 to 2,000 mg daily
- Zinc—15 mg with 3 mg copper

- Choline—500 mg daily
- Selenium—100 mcg daily
- Evening Primrose Oil—3,000 mg three times daily
- Chondroitin Sulfate (CSA)—3,000 mg daily
- Apple Pectin—2,000 to 3,000 mg daily
- Grapefruit Pectin—take as directed on label
- Guggulsterones—100 mg daily
- Lactobacillus Acidophilus—a daily serving should supply 3 to 5 billion live organisms, take 30 minutes before eating
- Vitamin B5 (pantethine form)—900 mg daily
- Vitamin B6—50 to 100 mg three times daily
- Shiitake Mushrooms
- Artichoke Leaf—250 to 300 mg two to three times daily
- Ginsengs
- Green Tea—as tea, 3 cups daily; as extract, 100 to 150 mg three times daily of green tea extract standardized to contain 80% total polyphenols and 50% epigallocatechin gallate
- Gugulipid has two active components that reduce both cholesterol and triglyceride levels.
- Fish Oils reduce the absorption of dietary cholesterol and reduce the synthesis of cholesterol within the liver. They contain the important Omega-3 fatty acids EPA and DHA. Therapeutic servings include 1,800 mg of EPA and 900 mg of DHA daily.
- Flaxseed Oil—1 to 2 tbsp. daily or 500 to 750 mg twice daily

OTHER POTENTIAL AIDS

- Arginine—2 to 3 grams daily
- Creatine Monohydrate—2 to 5 grams daily
- Ethylene-Diamine-Tetra-Acetate (EDTA), the synthetic amino acid used in chelation therapy, best in the suppository form.
- Hydroxy Methylbutyrate (HMB)—3,000 mg daily
- Taurine—100 to 500 mg daily
- Dimethyl Glycine (DMG)—take as directed on label

- Pangamic
- Chitin
- Sunlight and Ultraviolet Radiation lower total serum cholesterol levels
- Progesterone
- Alpha-Linolenic Acid—12 grams daily
- Capric Acid
- Caproic Acid
- Caprylic Acid
- Conjugated Linoleic Acid (CLA)—3 to 5 grams daily
- Policosanol
- Saponins
- Squalene
- Stearic
- Germanium—100 to 300 mg daily
- Magnesium—400 to 800 mg daily
- Cynarin
- Epigallo-Catechin-Gallate (EGCG)
- Hesperidin—50 to 100 mg daily
- Naringin
- Quercetin—70 to 140 mg daily
- Silymarin bound to phosphatidylcholine should be taken in amounts of 100 to 200 mg twice daily.
- Soy Protein is known to reduce cholesterol. Typical servings range from 20 to 40 grams daily.
- Tocotrienols
- Royal Jelly—50 to 100 mg daily
- Yogurt
- Apples
- Bananas, especially unripened
- Grapefruit
- Oranges
- Pears
- Strawberries

- Barley
- Barley Grass
- Siberian Ginseng—100 to 200 mg twice daily for 4 to 6 weeks
- Arjun
- Black Cohosh—1 to 2 tablets twice daily of a standardized extract containing 1 mg of 27-deoxyacteine per tablet
- Carob
- Chillis
- Holy Basil
- Milk Thistle—200 mg twice daily of extract containing 80% flavonoids
- Skullcap—1 to 2 grams three times daily
- Turmeric—take in a form which provides 400 to 600 mg of curcumin three times daily
- One tablespoon (8 grams) of powdered, activated Charcoal taken after every meal.
- Pecan Nuts
- Coconut Oil
- Rice Bran Oil
- Salmon Oil—4 grams daily
- Lecithin—10,500 mg daily
- Fenugreek Seeds (recommended in capsule form)—5 to 30 grams of defatted fenugreek three times daily with meals
- Psyllium Seed Husks
- Avocado
- Cabbage
- Carrots
- Celery
- Globe Artichoke—6 grams of dried herb or its equivalent daily divided into 3 portions
- Onions
- Rutabaga
- Sweet Potatoes
- Turnips

✒ HYPERTHYROIDISM AND THYROID

HYPERTHYROIDISM is an ailment characterized by over-activity of the thyroid gland, which is located in the front of the neck and has two lobes—one on either side of the larynx.

TOP NATURAL AIDS

- Multivitamin and mineral complex—use super high potency formula and take according to label directions
- Magnesium—200 to 300 mg three times daily
- Evening Primrose Oil—500 mg three times daily
- Guggul as directed
- Broccoli
- Brussels Sprouts
- Cabbage
- Cauliflower

IMPORTANT AIDS

- Vitamin C with bioflavonoids—3,000 to 5,000 mg daily
- Vitamin E—400 IU daily (don't exceed this amount)
- Calcium—400 mg three times daily

OTHER POTENTIAL AIDS

- Fluoride inhibits thyroid function and may therefore be useful for hyperthyroidism patients.
- Carnitine—500 to 1,000 mg three times daily
- Vitamin A—5,000 to 10,000 IU daily

GOOD FOODS *for* HYPERTHYROIDISM

- Kale
- Mustard Greens
- Peaches
- Pears
- Rutabagas

- Soybeans
- Spinach
- Turnips
- Onions
- Whole Grains

CHECKING *for* HYPOTHYROIDISM (LOW THYROID)

Use your basal body temperature to determine if natural supplementation is helping. See Appendix A for how to take this test.

TOP NATURAL AIDS

- Iodine—150 mcg daily
- Selenium—200 mcg
- Zinc—30 mg daily
- Bovine Thyroid—take according to label directions
- L-Tyrosine—200 mg daily
- Carotenoid-complex containing beta-carotene—5,000 to 25,000 IU daily
- Iodine Kelp is an excellent source of iodine. Take 100 to 225 mcg daily.
- Zinc—30 to 50 mg daily
- Collagen
- Eat lots of fish

IMPORTANT AIDS

- Vitamin A—25,000 IU daily
- Gugulipid extract—a daily serving should supply 100 mg of guggulsterones

OTHER POTENTIAL AIDS

- Aspartic Acid
- Cysteine—500 to 1,500 mg daily
- Lycopene—6.5 mg daily

- Boron—3 to 6 mg daily
- Manganese—3 to 10 mg daily
- Vitamin B2—15 to 50 mg daily
- Dandelion Root—500 mg twice daily for 6 weeks
- Gamma-aminobutyric acid (GABA)—500 mg two to three times daily (take every other week)
- If you're taking a thyroid medication, ask your doctor about Armor Thyroid.

Exercise

☞ HYPOGLYCEMIA

HYPOGLYCEMIA is a "Catch-22" disease where insulin over-counteracts high blood sugar levels, leading to low blood sugar (blood glucose), which leads to a craving for more sugar.

Some studies suggest that Candida is responsible for some hypoglycemia. I personally had a bout with this many years ago, and a Candida Cleanse accompanied by Body Oxygen helped me. This course of action goes together with enzymes and probiotics. Keep some good protein snacks around, such as almonds, boiled eggs, walnuts, yogurt, and cottage cheese as well as carrot sticks, herbal teas, etc.

TOP NATURAL AIDS

- Candida Cleanse
- Adrenal Glandular—50 to 100 mg twice daily
- Vitamin C—1 gram with 250 mg of Pantothenic Acid
- N-acetyl-cysteine—500 mg daily
- Proteolytic enzymes—follow label directions, take between meals
- Vitamin B-complex—50 to 100 mg of each major B vitamin daily
- Pantothenic Acid—500 mg one to two times daily
- Zinc—15 mg twice daily
- Pancreatin—take as directed on label
- Chromium Picolinate—300 to 600 mcg one to two times daily
- Vitamin B3 (niacinamide form)—take as directed on label
- Milk Thistle—100 mg twice daily for three months
- Dandelion Root—500 mg twice daily for 6 weeks, then stop for 4 weeks, then repeat cycle.
- Licorice Root—300 to 500 mg two to three times daily for 5 days, stop for 2 weeks, repeat. Avoid licorice completely if you have high blood pressure.
- N-Sulin Health—an herbal product from Silver Creek Labs is excellent for hypoglycemia.

IMPORTANT AIDS

- Calcium—500 mg twice daily
- L-Carnitine—500 to 1,000 mg daily
- Vitamin C with bioflavonoids—3,000 to 8,000 mg in divided servings
- L-Glutamine and Glutamic Acid—500 mg three times daily on empty stomach. Don't take with milk.
- Magnesium—340 mg daily
- Spirulina—1 tbsp. or 3 capsules daily
- Bilberry—80 mg three times daily of extract standardized to contain 25% anthocyanosides
- Ginseng—200 to 400 mg of extract daily or 15 to 20 drops of ginseng tincture in liquid three times daily after meals

OTHER POTENTIAL AIDS

- Quercetin—70 to 140 mg daily
- Alanine—300 to 600 mg daily
- Glycine
- Leucine deficiency can cause hypoglycemia in infants.
- Tyrosine—500 mg daily
- Medium-Chain Triglycerides (MCTs)
- Potassium—100 to 500 mg daily
- Blueberries
- Golden Root
- Garlic

☞ IMMUNE SYSTEM

THE IMMUNE SYSTEM covers all structures and processes that are involved in defeating the attempts of environmental forces to overrun, destroy, or gain control of any part of the body.

Your mind and emotions affect your immune system. Reread the "Foundations to the Gospel of Health." Eliminate sugar, stress, excess weight, alcohol, and a sedentary lifestyle. Get plenty of rest, ideally waking naturally and when you're ready (this may mean going to bed earlier). Drink a lot of water and juiced vegetables.

I am a perfect example of the value of a healthy immune system. I have birthed eight children with my wonderful husband, Jim, who was told he most likely had hepatitis C in his body for 30 years. I have never had a hepatitis vaccine, and even if I did, they don't work on hepatitis C. Yet I don't have the virus.

My secret is no secret. Take care of the body, the Temple, and it will take care of you. Cleanse often, eat right, and drink half your body in ounces of water as well as supplement with the right things for you. And never underestimate the value of forgiveness.

TOP NATURAL AIDS

- Multivitamin
- Collodial Minerals—1 to 2 ounces daily
- Thymic Formula—as directed
- Vitamin C with bioflavonoids—5,000 to 20,000 mg daily in divided portions
- Vitamin B-complex—100 mg one to three times daily
- Evening Primrose Oil 500 mg three times daily
- Vitamin A—10,000 IU daily
- Beta-carotene—25,000 IU daily
- Beneficial Bacteria such as lactobacillus acidophilus enhance the function of the immune system.
- Selenium—200 mcg daily
- Zinc (chelate form)—50 to 80 mg daily
- Coenzymes Q10 can double the immune system's ability to clear invading organisms from the blood. Take 100 mg daily.

- Vitamin E—400 IU daily
- Clustered Water
- Pyconogenol
- Astragalus generates anticancer cells in the body.
- Citrus Seed extract is a superior germ fighter.
- Echinacea enhances lymphatic function. Take 1 capsule three times daily or 15 to 30 drops of extract in liquid three times daily for 2 to 5 days.
- Garlic has superior antibacterial, antiviral and antifungal properties.
- Spleen extract if a bacterial infection is present.
- Liver Cleanse—see Appendix A

IMPORTANT AIDS

- Dimethyl Glycine (DMG) improves the immune system's responses by 400 to 1,000%. Take as directed on label.
- Lecithin—1,200 mg three times daily with meals
- Germanium
- Kelp—2,000 to 3,000 mg daily
- Spirulina cleanses, heals, and protects the immune system.
- Barley Grass juice contains chlorophyll that helps build tissues and detoxify the system.
- Maitake, Reishi, and Shiitake Mushrooms all build immunity and fight viral infections and cancer. Take as directed on label.

OTHER POTENTIAL AIDS

- Berberine
- Acetyl-L-Carnitine (ALC)
- Alanine (Beta-Alanine form)
- Arginine in non-excessive quantities
- Glutamine
- Supplemental Dehydroepiandrosterone (DHEA)
- Human Growth Hormone (hGH) is a naturally occurring hormone that strengthens the immune system. It requires a doctor's supervision.
- Melatonin

- Bromelain
- Copper—excess copper decreases immunity. Take a probiotic supplement as directed on label.
- Curcumin
- Lactoferrin
- Whey Protein
- Lipoic Acid
- Vitamin B1
- Vitamin B6—50 mg three times daily
- Vitamin B12—1,000 to 2,000 mcg daily
- Vitamin D
- Manganese—2 mg daily
- Chlorella
- Thymus Extract—take as directed on label
- Quercetin
- Yogurt adds beneficial bacteria to the system. Choose yogurt with live cultures.
- Eggs
- Ashwagandha—1 tsp. of powder twice daily boiled in milk or water.
- Barberry stimulates intestinal movement.
- Boneset acts as an anti-inflammatory and reduces fever.
- Burdock Root may help prevent cancer.
- Cat's Claw stimulates the immune system.
- Devil's Claw reduces pain and inflammation.
- Goldenseal strengthens immune system.
- American Ginseng, Korean Ginseng, Sanchi Ginseng, and Siberian Ginseng all contain germanium, a trace element that boosts the immune system and has anticancer properties. Take according to label directions.
- Ligustrum
- Enoki Mushrooms
- Flaxseed Oil—1 to 2 tbsp. daily
- Shark Liver Oil—take as directed on label
- Cabbage
- Brewer's Yeast

☛ INDIGESTION

INDIGESTION involves unpleasant symptoms in the abdomen and pain centered in the upper abdomen, rumbling noises, and a sense of fullness or bloating. Although promoted to aid indigestion, antacids actually inhibit digestion, creating gas, bloating, and constipation. Antacids suppress or neutralize gastric acid, an action that provides no therapeutic benefit.

TOP NATURAL AIDS

- Protease—300 IU after two largest meals
- Pancreatin—500 to 1,000 mg after two largest meals (use only eight weeks)
- Probiotics
- Parasite and Candida Cleanse
- Lactobacillus Acidophilus—a daily serving should supply 3 to 5 billion live organisms, take 30 minutes before eating
- Betaine HCL—3 capsules daily after meals
- Digestive Enzymes
- Proteolytic Enzymes—take as directed on label
- Aloe Vera juice—1/4 cup on empty stomach twice a day
- Chamomile as tea, tincture, or pill—take as directed on label
- Gentian Root—500 mg twice daily with meals
- Dandelion—chewing 2 to 3 fresh sprigs will stimulate bile flow, resulting in almost immediate relief

IMPORTANT AIDS

- Bromelain or Papain—1,000 mg three times daily
- Lecithin—1 to 3 tbsp. three times daily
- Amylase—2,500 IU after two largest meals
- Lipases—5,000 IU after two largest meals
- Alfalfa—take in liquid or tablet form as directed
- Lemon Balm—tea consumed with meals or 9 to 15 ml of Balm fluid extract/tincture daily
- Calamus

- Ginger—500 mg one to two times daily
- Peppermint—6 to 15 ml of fluid extract/tincture daily
- Garlic—2 capsules three times daily with meals

OTHER POTENTIAL AIDS

- Vitamin B-complex—100 mg of each major B vitamin three times daily with meals
- Zinc—20 to 50 mg daily
- Copper—2 to 3 mg daily
- Manganese—3 to 10 mg daily
- Selenium—100 to 300 mcg daily
- Threonine is an essential amino acid that helps the body maintain a proper protein balance.
- Supplemental Pancreatic Enzymes—take as directed on label
- Artichoke Leaf extract—2 grams of dried herb or its equivalent three times daily
- Asafetida
- Cassia Bark
- Feverfew—80 to 100 mg of powdered leaf daily
- Apple Cider Vinegar
- Mastic—1,000 to 2,000 mg daily
- Neem Leaf extract consumed internally—take according to label directions
- Parsley in liquid extract form—take 2 ml three times daily. Excessive parsley should be avoided during pregnancy.
- Turmeric—2,000 mg daily
- Caraway Seeds
- Coriander Seeds

☞ INFERTILITY—FEMALE AND MALE

FEMALE INFERTILITY is the helplessness of females to bring on conception after repeated attempts over a 12-month period.

Having eight children of my own, most people say that if they could only drink my water they would get pregnant. I have seen female infertility turn around and a baby in 9 months by just cleansing and making sure the body is being supplemented with what is needed to conceive. I recall woman named Janet who had a child but was unable to conceive for several years. There was no success! She pursued alternative help. Within 6 months she was pregnant and went on to have two more children. She was simply put on a regimen of healthy foods and supplements. Her body knew what to do from there.

TOP NATURAL AIDS

- Vitamin B12—2,000 mg daily
- Vitamin C with bioflavonoids—2,000 to 6,000 mg daily in divided portions
- Vitamin B6 helps balance progesterone levels. Take 100 to 800 mg daily.
- Collodial Silver
- Zinc—80 mg daily
- Selenium—200 to 400 mcg daily (if you become pregnant, reduce amount to 40 mcg daily)
- Probiotic Supplement—as directed on label
- Phosphatidyl Choline—1,000 mg daily
- Octacosanol—take as directed on label
- Folic Acid—as directed on label
- Vitamin E—200 IU daily gradually increased to 1,000 IU daily
- Dong Quai is believed to promote fertility. Take 4 capsules daily 10 days before menstruation.

IMPORTANT AIDS

- Essential Fatty Acids found in flaxseed oil, evening primrose oil, borage oil, and black currant seed oil. Take 500 to 1,000 mg of any of these oils two to three times daily.

- DHEA (Dehydroepiandrosterone)—80 mg daily
- PABA—400 mg daily for at least three months
- Red Clover blossom tea helps balance hormonal functions and improve fertility. Strain and drink throughout the day.

OTHER POTENTIAL AIDS

- Coenzyme Q10—200 mcg daily
- Progesterone cream applied topically—use according to label directions.
- Potassium Chloride
- Inositol
- Vitamin D
- Velvet Deer Antler
- Caterpillar Fungus
- Chaste Berry (Vitex)
- False Unicorn
- Ginsengs
- Maca

MALE INFERTILITY is the inability in a male to induce conception. The body must be healthy with proper supplementation. That takes detoxing along with diet change and supplements. We have also seen a lot of help from Chelation Therapy.

TOP NATURAL AIDS

- Arginine—8,000 mg daily
- Selenium—100 mcg daily
- Zinc—50 to 100 mg daily
- Phosphatidylcholine—1,000 mg daily
- Vitamin C—5 grams daily
- Vitamin E—start with 200 IU daily and gradually increase to 1,000 IU daily

IMPORTANT AIDS

- Carnitine—400 to 3,000 mg daily
- Alpha-Linolenic Acid (LNA)—500 to 1,000 mg daily
- Docosahexaenoic Acid (DHA)
- Gamma-Linoleic Acid (GLA)—500 to 1,000 mg daily
- Linoleic Acid—500 to 1,000 mg daily
- Chromium Orotate—10 to 20 mg daily
- Coenzyme Q10—200 mg daily
- Folic Acid—400 mcg daily
- Vitamin B12—1,000 to 6,000 mcg daily
- Astragalus
- Grape Seed extract
- Korean Ginseng increases testosterone levels. Take 100 mg twice daily for 2 to 3 weeks of a standardized extract containing 7% ginsenosides. Take Korean Ginseng in cycles of 3 weeks on, two weeks off.
- Royal Jelly—20 mg daily
- Flaxseed Oil—1 to 2 tbsp. daily

OTHER POTENTIAL AIDS

- Selenium—200 mcg daily
- Digestive Enzymes (full-spectrum supplement)—as directed on label
- Taurine
- Lycopene—at least 4 mg daily
- Melatonin
- Inositol
- Vitamin A—15,000 IU daily
- Ashwagandha
- Caterpillar Fungus
- Maca
- Siberian Ginseng

☞ INSOMNIA

INSOMNIA is the inability to fall asleep or remain asleep. It may vary in intensity from restlessness or bothered sleep to the reduction of the regular length of sleep or to total wakefulness. Roughly 50% of adults experience significant insomnia at some stage(s) of their lives.

The first thing I suggest for someone who has trouble sleeping is a cleanse. If you go right to sleep but wake around 2:30 to 3:30 a.m., a liver cleanse with an herbal liver product and coffee enema may help (see Appendix A). If that does not make a significant difference, I suggest checking neurotransmitters with a simple urine test (see Appendix A). It will tell you where your serotonin levels are, among other things, and what to supplement to get them corrected.

My publisher, John Peterson, just had too much on his mind and too much energy. He is also the author of *Pushing Yourself to Power*. He is always looking to improve his health and workouts. I sent him some Collagen Crush along with vitamin C. While it is typically used to improve muscle mass and decrease fat, it also makes you sleep like you were twenty. John suggested we sell it as a sleep aid. I have heard that comment from virtually everyone who has used it. You sleep deep and hard. It works for me, and I like the other benefits of collagen, also!

TOP NATURAL AIDS

- Collagen—1 tablespoon liquid with 1,000 mg vitamin C on empty stomach.
- Vitamin B-complex—take as directed on label
- 5-Hydroxytryptophan (5-HTP)—take as directed on label
- Calcium Magnesium liquid with 500 mg of calcium and 250 to 500 mg of magnesium
- Melatonin—suggested that people prone to insomnia start by using 1 mg of melatonin two hours prior to retiring. If no progress occurs, increase serving to 2 or 3 mg.
- Inositol—1,000 to 10,000 mg per night

- Vitamin B6—50 to 100 mg daily
- Lemon Balm tea
- Kava Kava—200 to 300 mg per night
- Passionflower has a gentle sedative effect.
- Valerian Root—200 to 300 mg 30 minutes before bedtime of a standardized extract containing 0.5% isovalerenic acids

IMPORTANT AIDS

- Vitamin B12—200 to 400 mcg daily
- Chamomile as tea, tincture, or pill—take according to label directions

OTHER POTENTIAL AIDS

- Vitamin C with bioflavonoids—500 mg daily
- Zinc—15 mg daily
- Taurine—100 to 500 mg daily
- Iron—5 to 10 mg
- Potassium—100 to 500 mg daily
- Gamma Aminobutyric Acid (GABA)—1 to 3 grams administered sublingually at night
- Choline—take according to label directions
- Vitamin B1—50 to 100 mg daily
- Apple juice or Grapefruit juice consumed when retiring at night.
- Reishi Mushrooms—2 to 6 grams daily of raw fungus or an equivalent amount of concentrated extract
- Black Cohosh—1 to 2 tablets twice daily of a standardized extract containing 1 mg of 27-deoxyacteine per tablet
- Catnip can be taken as tea or a liquid extract. Follow label directions and consume up to three times daily.
- Fo-Ti—take according to label directions
- Gotu Kola—20 to 60 mg three times daily of an extract standardized to contain 40% asiaticoside, 29–30% asiatic acid, 29–30% madecassic acid, and 1–2% madecassoside. Gotu Kola normally takes at least 4 weeks to work.

- Hops—0.5 grams one to three times daily
- Marjoram
- St. John's Wort—300 mg three times daily of an extract standardized to contain 0.3% hypericin.
- Schizandra
- Zizyphus

HELPFUL FOODS

- Bananas
- Tuna
- Turkey
- Yogurt
- Whole Grain Crackers
- Grapefruit
- Nut Butter
- Dates
- Dill Seeds
- Lettuce

Fallacy—Milk does not induce sleep (as the tryptophan in milk is suppressed by the other amino acids in milk).

☞ KIDNEYS

THE KIDNEYS are a pair of organs situated at the back of the abdomen, below the diaphragm on each side of the spine, responsible for the disposal of waste materials from the blood. The kidneys monitor the quality of blood so that the body is not poisoned by the end products of its own metabolism and the proper volume and composition of its body fluids is maintained. Approximately 25% of the blood pumped by the heart each minute is filtered by the kidneys, and toxins are excreted from the body via this filtration mechanism (via urine).

TOP NATURAL AIDS

- Magnesium—750 to 1,000 mg daily
- Vitamin C with bioflavoniods—1,000 mg twice daily
- Vitamin B6—50 mg twice daily
- Coenzyme A—use as directed
- Potassium (citrate form)—100 to 500 mg daily
- Chlorophyll
- Clustered Water
- Organ GI Cleanse

IMPORTANT AIDS

- Calcium—1,500 to 2,000 mg daily
- Zinc—50 to 80 mg daily with 3 mg copper
- Digestive Enzymes help with nutrient assimilation.
- Dandelion leaves, coffee, and tea reduce uric acid levels and improve kidney function.
- Parsley juice helps kidney function.

OTHER POTENTIAL AIDS

- Arginine increases the activity of the thymus gland. Take as directed on label.
- Glutamine assists in maintaining a proper acid/alkaline balance in the body. Take as directed on label.

- Taurine is vital for the proper utilization of several minerals. A typical serving ranges from 100 to 500 mg daily.
- Beta-carotene—5,000 to 25,000 IU daily
- Lycopene is a powerful antioxidant. Take as directed on label.
- Melatonin is a natural hormone that acts as an antioxidant. Take as directed on label.
- Alpha Linolenic Acid (LNA)
- Linoleic Acid (LA)
- Charcoal assists people with failing kidneys to excrete waste products that their kidneys would otherwise have difficulty handling, but high servings around 20 to 50 grams daily must be used to obtain this benefit.
- Phosphorus is essential for kidney function. Take as directed on label.
- Optimal Sodium levels are required for the correct function of the kidneys.
- Cynarin
- Silymarin stimulates the regeneration of the kidneys.
- Coenzyme Q10—30 to 100 mg daily
- Biotin—400 to 800 mcg daily
- Choline is necessary for kidney function. A typical serving is 50 to 200 mg daily.
- Lipoic Acid helps provide energy to the body's cells. Take as directed on label.
- Vitamin B1—50 to 100 mg daily
- Watermelon
- Caterpillar Fungus
- Oyster Mushrooms
- Wheat Grass juice
- Borage acts as an adrenal tonic.
- Chaparral fights free radicals and protects against heavy metals.
- Cocoa
- Cornsilk aids the kidneys by acting as a diuretic.
- Ginkgo Biloba benefits kidney disorders.

- Green Tea acts as an antioxidant.
- Lemon Grass tea acts as a body tonic.
- Milk Thistle stimulates the regeneration of the kidneys.
- Rosehips tea—good for bladder infections
- Sarsaparilla stimulates excretion of fluids.
- Artichoke
- Beetroot juice
- Fennel
- Lettuce
- Rhubarb, especially Rheum palmatum

People with Kidney Ailments Should Avoid These Herbs—Juniper, Licorice, Valerian, and Yohimbe.

☞ KIDNEY STONES

KIDNEY STONES form in the tissues of the kidneys or the draining structures of the urinary tract.

TOP NATURAL AIDS

- Vitamin B-complex—50 mg daily serving of the major B vitamins
- Magnesium—400 to 600 mg daily combined with 100 mg vitamin B6 daily
- Inositol Hexaphosphate (Phytic Acid)—take according to label directions
- Vitamin B6—10 to 100 mg daily
- Vitamin C mineral ascorbate—2,000 to 4,000 mg daily
- Clustered Water
- Cat's Claw
- Choline and Inositol reduce inflammation.
- Potassium Citrate—2,500 mg daily
- Kidney Rescue™

IMPORTANT AIDS

- Vitamin A—25,000 IU daily
- Zinc—50 to 80 mg daily
- L-Methionine—500 mg daily on an empty stomach
- Lipase—5,000 IU three times daily with meals
- Amylase—2,500 IU three times daily with meals
- Protease—300 IU three times daily with meals
- Pancreatin—500 to 1,000 mg three times daily with meals. Don't use pancreatin longer than two months continuously.
- Potassium—100 mg daily
- Uva Ursi helps cleanse the urinary tract. Take 500 mg twice daily.
- Dandelion Root—500 mg twice daily taken in cycles of 6 weeks on, 4 weeks off
- Horsetail stimulates excretion of kidney stones. Take as tea.

- Parsley juice diluted in water along with dandelion, alfalfa, dill, and fennel contain substances that help prevent kidney stones. Take 1 tbsp. of juice daily or 500 mg twice daily.

OTHER POTENTIAL AIDS

- Glutamine—300 mg daily
- Folic Acid—25 to 50 mg daily
- Glutamic Acid
- Chelation Suppositories, Ethylene-Diamine-Tetra-Acetate (EDTA)
- L-Arginine—500 mg daily
- Lysine—50 to 100 mg daily
- The N-Acetyl-Cysteine (NAC)—take according to label directions
- Chondroitin Sulfate—400 mg three times daily
- Glucosamine Sulfate—500 mg three times daily
- Calcium—1,500 to 2,000 mg daily
- Manganese—3 to 10 mg daily
- Citric Acid
- Water, when consumed in quantities sufficient to produce 2 to 3 quarts of urine daily, prevents the formation of kidney stones.
- Lemon juice
- Rice, especially rice bran
- Blue Vervain reduces tension and stress.
- Buchu acts as a diuretic and helps with bladder infections.
- Burdock—1 to 2 grams of powdered dry root three times daily
- Collinsonia (Stoneroot)—take according to label directions
- Cornsilk acts as a diuretic.
- Horsetail bath
- Juniper Berries help cleanse the urinary tract. Juniper Berry can be taken as tea (1 tbsp. of berries to a cup of boiling water). It is particularly effective when combined with other herbs such as uva ursi and parsley.
- Pumpkin Seeds

- Parsnip
- Radish
- Watermelon
- Celery
- Asparagus
- Watercress

Fallacies—Kidney stones do not develop as a result of consuming calcium supplements (except when a person suffers from hypercalciuria). And kidney stones do not develop as a result of consuming vitamin C supplements.

✍ LIVER

THE LIVER is the second largest organ in the body and stores and filters the blood to remove infectious organisms. It processes approximately three pints of blood every minute. It is the most important organ for the cleansing of toxic chemicals that enter the body.

TOP NATURAL AIDS

- Milk Thistle protects the liver from toxins and stimulates the production of new liver cells.
- Supplemental S-Adenosylmethionine (SAM) enhances the health of, regenerates and normalizes the function of the liver. A typical serving is 200 mg twice daily.
- Artichoke Extract protects cell walls from damage.
- Clustered Water
- Vitamin B-complex—50 mg twice daily
- Vitamin B12—1,000 to 2,000 mcg daily
- Probiotic—as directed
- Choline is vital for the normal function of the liver and prevents dietary fats from accumulating in the liver—50 to 200 mg daily.
- Coffee Enema—see Appendix A
- Garlic allows the liver to detoxify cancer-causing chemicals.
- Betaine detoxifies and stimulates the liver. Take according to label directions.
- Arginine assists the detoxification. Take according to label directions.
- Enzymes
- Carnitine
- Cystine
- Taurine—100 to 500 mg daily
- Glutathione Peroxidase protects the cells of the liver.
- Phosphatidylcholine is essential for the detoxification functions.
- Folic Acid—200 mcg daily

- Evening Primrose Oil—500 mg twice daily with meals
- Glutathione can repair liver damage.
- Silymarin protects the liver.
- Chlorophyll clears toxins from the liver.
- Inositol facilitates the removal of fats from the liver—50 to 200 mg daily.
- Wheat Grass juice
- Alfalfa detoxifies the liver.
- Dandelion (coffee, leaves, and root) is an outstanding liver tonic—250 mg three times daily for 6 weeks. Repeat cycle.
- Stay away from wine and acetomenaphin. They can damage the liver.

IMPORTANT AIDS

- Glycyrrhizin
- Lipoic Acid is used therapeutically to treat liver ailments—50 mg twice daily along with grape seed extract or pine bark extract.
- Zinc—30 to 50 mg daily
- Vitamin A—5,000 to 10,000 IU daily
- Vitamin B5 (especially the pantethine form)—50 to 100 mg daily
- Vitamin B6—50 to 100 mg daily
- Vitamin C—1,000 to 3,000 mg daily
- Vitamin E—400 IU daily
- Grape Seed extract—50 mg three times a day along with lipoic acid.

OTHER POTENTIAL AIDS

- Aspartic Acid (in non-excessive quantities)
- Branched Chain Amino Acids
- Carnosine
- Glutamine
- Leucine
- Ornithine
- Thioproline
- Threonine

- Pangamic Acid
- Fructooligosaccharides (FOS)
- Sunlight
- Superoxide Dismutase (SOD)
- Melatonin
- Alpha Linolenic Acid (LNA)
- Beta-Ecdysterone
- Ecdysteroids
- Gamma-Linolenic Acid (GLA)
- Linoleic Acid (LA)
- Gomisan A
- Wuweizisu C
- NADH
- Molybdenum—30 to 100 mcg daily
- Vanadium—200 mcg to 1 mg of vanadyl sulfate
- Catechins
- Curcumin
- Cyanidin
- Cynarin
- Pyrroloquinoline Quinone (PQQ)
- Biotin—400 to 800 mcg daily
- Spirulina
- Liver Extract
- Bee Pollen
- Bee Propolis
- Black Cherry juice
- Grape juice
- Lemon juice drunk upon awakening in the morning
- Pear juice
- Reishi Mushrooms
- Andrographis
- Artichoke Leaf
- Ashwagandha
- Astragalus
- Barberry
- Black Cumin seeds
- Blessed Thistle
- Burdock root
- Chaparral
- Devil's Claw
- Dong Quai
- Gentian
- Ginsengs
- Goldenseal
- Gotu Kola
- Green Tea
- Licorice
- Picrorrhiza
- Sage
- Tea, especially Green Tea
- Turmeric
- Yellow Dock
- Flaxseed Oil
- Beetroot
- Brussels Sprouts
- Fennel
- Globe Artichoke
- Tomato

🖝 LYME DISEASE

LYME DISEASE is an inflammatory ailment caused by Borrelia burgdorferi (a species of detrimental bacteria transmitted by a specific type of tick, Ixodes dammini, that is carried by deer and mice). It has also been suggested that Lyme disease can also be transmitted by other insects, including fleas, mosquitoes, and mites; and via human to human contact.

My husband, Jim, had Lyme disease, and I thank God he was healed through prayer and the good Lord leading us to natural treatment that worked quickly and effectively. Jim had Lyme disease for three years. The first two and a half years were spent using allopathic medicine, antibiotics, as well as other medications for pain, nerves, etc. There was little or no improvement. Jim was so ill some days he could barely walk from the bed to the couch or the couch to the bed.

God led Jim to read a book written by an M.D. on oxygen therapies. After reading the book, he felt confident that this could help him. Remember: bad bacteria cannot live in the presence of oxygen. We found a doctor in our area who performed Oxygen IVs. I will never forget after Jim's first IV he came to our office and said he felt life being pumped back into his body. After only 14 treatments in a seven-week period, Jim was totally healed.

TOP NATURAL AIDS
- Green Drinks such as Creation's Bounty
- Body Oxygen, oxygen therapy, and IV oxygen drip performed by an M.D.
- Probiotics and Enzymes are essential.
- Multivitamin and minerals—take as directed daily
- Essential Fatty Acids—take as directed on label
- Evening Primrose Oil—1,000 mg two to three times daily
- Kelp—1,000 to 1,500 mg daily
- Bromelain—500 to 1,000 mg two to three times daily on an empty stomach

- Vitamin C—5,000 to 10,000 mg three times daily in divided servings for 2 months
- Goldenseal—250 mg three times daily
- Oxygen Baths—add 1 cup of H_2O_2 to a warm bath and soak for 1 hour daily
- Garlic—500 mg twice daily for two months

IMPORTANT AIDS

- Pancreatin
- Selenium—200 mcg daily
- Oregano—75 mg three times daily. Use standardized extract with 5% total alkaloids and don't use longer than one week at a time.
- Milk Thistle strengthens the immune system.
- Red Clover fights infection and purifies the blood.

OTHER POTENTIAL AIDS

- Cat's Claw—500 mg three times daily until improvement
- Olive Leaf assists with nearly any infectious disease.

☞ MEMORY PROBLEMS

MEMORY is the range of processes involved in the storage and retrieval of information within the central nervous system. The structures of the limbic system are involved in memory. I have seen overwhelming increase in memory by those who cut out the bad fats and increase the good fats as well as by checking neurotransmitters and supplementing accordingly (see Appendix A). Vitamin B12 along with a B-complex is also extremely beneficial. However, so many times there is just too much stress and not enough sleep. You must sleep for the brain to do what the brain is supposed to do correctly.

In a study by Dr. Michael Smidt with the elderly, by supplementing with essential fatty acids for 12 weeks the elderly reversed memory loss by 12 years!

TOP NATURAL AIDS

- Hyperzine-A—50 mcg twice daily
- Ginkgo Biloba—40 to 60 mg two to three times daily of a product containing 24% ginkgoheterosides
- Evening Primrose Oil—1,000 mg three times daily
- Vitamin B6—at least 20 mg daily
- Vitamin B12—500 mcg daily or injections as necessary
- Chelation Suppositories with Ethylene-Diamine-Tetra-Acetate (EDTA), the synthetic amino acid used in chelation therapy.
- Vitamin B-complex
- Essential Fatty Acids
- Choline enhances the production of acetylcholine, a key neurotransmitter. Take 200 to 350 mg two to three times daily.
- DMAE—100 mg daily
- Lecithin—1,200 mg two to three times daily with meals
- Carotenoid Complex with beta-carotene—25,000 IU daily
- L-Tyrosine—500 mg first thing in the morning for 1 to 2 months
- Vitamin B3—141 mg daily
- American Ginseng has been found to help memory. Take as directed.

- Gotu Kola can help improve mental clarity and function. Take 200 mg two to three times daily for up to 6 weeks. Choose a standardized extract containing 16% triterpenes.
- Korean Ginseng—200 mg of extract standardized to contain 4 to 7% ginsenosides.
- Siberian Ginseng—100 mg twice daily

IMPORTANT AIDS

- Vitamin A—15,000 IU daily
- Acetyl-L-Carnitine (ALC)—500 mg twice daily
- Glutamine—take as directed on label
- Phenylalanine—take as directed on label
- DHEA—5 mg daily, then gradually increase according to label directions
- 7-Keto DHEA appears to be more effective than regular DHEA in improving memory. Unlike regular DHEA, it doesn't convert to estrogen or testosterone in the body.
- Boron—3 to 6 mg daily
- Manganese—3 to 10 mg daily
- Vitamin E—400 IU daily, gradually increase to 1,200 daily
- Brahmi increases circulation in the brain and improves short- and long-term memory. Take as directed.
- Aged Garlic Extract
- Melatonin—2 to 3 mg daily taken before bedtime

OTHER POTENTIAL AIDS

- Glutamic Acid is used by the brain as fuel. Take as directed on label.
- N-Acetyl-Cysteine (NAC)
- Taurine—100 to 500 mg daily
- hGH (human growth hormone) improves brain function. Take under the supervision of a physician.
- Pregnenolone—take as directed on label
- Magnesium—750 to 1,000 mg daily

- Potassium—100 mg daily
- Norepinephrine
- Oxygen Therapy or Inhalation of Pure Oxygen (Hyperbaric Oxygen)
- Choline—200 to 350 mg two to three times daily
- Cytidine Diphosphate Choline (CDP-Choline)
- Folic Acid—800 mcg daily
- Lipoic Acid—300 to 600 mg daily
- Vitamin B1—50 to 100 mg daily
- Ashwagandha—1 tsp. daily of powder, boiled in milk or water
- Astragalus—take as directed
- Golden Root
- Rosemary tea ingested orally or Rosemary oil massaged topically onto the temples.
- Sage tea
- Schizandra
- Lecithin—15 grams daily

✍ MENOPAUSE

MENOPAUSE is the point in time in a woman's life when the ovaries stop producing an egg cell every four weeks, and therefore menstruation ends and the woman is no longer able to become pregnant. The woman undergoes a number of hormonal changes, including a reduction in estrogen production, an increase in pituitary hormone, and higher amounts of male hormones (androgen). Female menopause usually occurs between the ages of 45 and 55. In Western nations, the average age of menopause onset is 51.

Since hormones are metabolized in the liver, my first thought is to clean the liver, whether it is PMS or hot flashes with menopause. I realize for some this is all it takes, but if you have waited until menopause to do something natural, a liver cleanse may not go far enough.

The midwife who delivered our fifth child said she had to get to the health food store before it closed or she would have hot flashes. She took 1,500 mg of Evening Primrose Oil and 400 IU of vitamin E with food in the morning and repeated in the evening, making a total of 3000 EPO and 800 IU of vitamin E. As long as she did that the dreaded menopause was a breeze. Without it she said she would become symptomatic.

TOP NATURAL AIDS

- Boron—1 to 2 mg daily
- Vitamin C—at least 1,200 mg daily taken in divided servings
- Calcium—1,000 mg twice daily with 500 mg magnesium (avoid Dolomite form)
- 1,500 mg of Evening Primrose Oil and 400 IU Vitamin E with food twice daily
- Pantothenic Acid relieves hot flashes. Take 250 mg twice daily for up to one week at a time.
- Soy Protein—60 grams daily
- Vitamin E—at least 800 IU daily for at least three months
- Black Cohosh—20 to 40 mg twice daily

- Dong Quai—200 mg of a standardized extract 3 times daily
- Flaxseed Oil—1 tbsp. or 500 to 1,000 mg twice daily
- Vitamin B-complex—100 mg three times daily
- Vitamin B6—50 mg three times daily
- Chaste Tree Berry—200 mg two to three times daily two weeks before period; or 400 mg daily if you are no longer having periods
- Ginkgo Biloba—40 to 60 mg two to three times daily of a product containing 24% ginkgoheterosides

IMPORTANT AIDS

- Chromium—100 to 200 mcg one to two times daily
- Natural Progesterone Cream—apply topically as directed on label
- The ideal proportions of estrogens (preferably natural estrogens) for post-menopausal women in estrogen replacement therapy is 80% Estriol, 10% Estradiol, and 10% Estrone.
- Hypothalamus Protomorphogen—100 mg twice daily before first two meals of the day
- Siberian Ginseng—300 to 400 mg daily. Ginseng should be taken in cycles for approximately two weeks on, two weeks off.
- Royal Jelly—take as directed on label until symptoms subside

OTHER POTENTIAL AIDS

- DHEA enhances memory and sex drive and reduces stress. Take as directed on label. It's converted to testosterone and estrogens in the body and should be used with caution by women taking hormone replacement therapy. Take as directed.
- 7-keto DHEA is a form of DHEA that isn't converted into sex hormones. Take as directed.
- Aniseed tea
- Ginseng for two weeks, then repeat cycle. Don't use Dong Quai if you experience heavy menstrual bleeding.

- False Unicorn Root stimulates ovarian hormones. Drink tea brewed from root several times daily.
- Kava Kava—300 mg of Kava Kava standardized to contain 30% Kava Lactones daily. Excess amounts of Kava Kava can cause drowsiness.
- Passionflower—take as tea or use tinctures or powdered extracts as directed on label
- Red Clover—use a daily amount that provides 40 to 160 mg of isoflavones
- Sarsaparilla helps regulate hormones.
- Suma—500 mg twice daily
- Tribulus terrestris helps with low libido. Take 85 to 250 mg three times daily with meals.
- Oat Straw—500 mg twice daily

Exercise reduces the symptoms associated with menopause.

☞ MIGRAINE HEADACHES

MIGRAINE is a type of recurrent, throbbing, vascular headache. They are characterized by changes (contraction followed by dilation) in cerebral blood vessels. Chocolate is estimated to be responsible for an estimated 60% of migraines (anyone craving chocolate usually lacks magnesium). Some researchers have proposed (chronic) dehydration as an underlying cause of migraines. So we've made Clustered Water our first suggestion.

I will never forget a dear lady who came to me for counseling many years ago. She had horrific migraines and had tried every medication her doctor would prescribe. I suggested a complement of herbs with feverfew as the key ingredient. She came in a few days later to report that the headaches were gone, and she needed more so that she could go on vacation. She had relief with no side effects.

Feverfew is so effective I actually used it when a migraine came on during a stressful delivery.

In counseling those who suffer with migraines, I suggest an organ cleanse as well as Clustered Water.

TOP NATURAL AIDS

- Clustered Water
- Evening Primrose Oil—1,000 mg three times daily
- Pantothenic Acid (Vitamin B5)—100 mg twice daily
- Collagen
- Superunsaturated Fatty Acids (Omega-3 Fatty Acids)
- 5-Hydroxytryptophan (5-HTP)—take as directed on label
- Alpha-Linolenic Acid reduces the severity, frequency, and duration of migraine attacks by 86%.
- Calcium, especially when consumed in conjunction with Vitamin D—500 mg twice daily
- Magnesium—600 mg daily
- Insufficient production of Serotonin can be the underlying cause of migraines.
- Vitamin B-complex—50 mg three times a day

- Vitamin B2—up to 400 mg daily
- Vitamin B3—500 to 1,000 mg
- Vitamin B6—take as directed on label
- Vitamin C with bioflavonoids—3,000 to 6,000 mg daily
- Feverfew helps dilate cerebral blood vessels, which eases migraines. Take 50 to 80 mg daily. Liquid tincture is best.
- Ginger tea helps a tension or migraine headache located at the front of the head.
- Ginkgo Biloba—2 to 3 capsules daily
- Fish Oils—15 to 20 grams daily

IMPORTANT AIDS

- Coenzyme Q10—60 mg daily
- Quercetin—500 mg daily before meals
- Rutin—200 mg daily
- Chamomile tea

OTHER POTENTIAL AIDS

- Supplemental S-Adenosylmethionine (SAM)
- Glucosamine—500 mg three times daily
- Progesterone cream applied topically—follow label directions
- Vitamin D, especially when consumed in conjunction with calcium.
- Thymus Extract—take as directed on label
- Butterbur (root)—50 mg twice daily of an extract that has been processed to remove potentially toxic substances called pyrrolizidine alkaloids.

Acupuncture, see reference in Appendix B.

☞ NAIL PROBLEMS

NAILS are made of Keratin that protect the end of each finger and toe.

TOP NATURAL AIDS

- Lactobacillus Acidophilus—take as directed on label
- Silica—1,000 mg daily
- Calcium—1,000 mg daily
- Total Liquid Mineral Supplement
- Magnesium—750 to 1,000 mg daily
- Zinc—80 mg daily taken with 3 grams of copper
- Vitamin A—25,000 IU daily, plus carotenoid complex, take as directed on label
- Horsetail will make nails stronger and appear more attractive. Take 2 tbsp. of horsetail juice daily or combine with 1 tbsp. of beet, celery, parsley, or kale juice for better effect.
- Collagen liquid—1 tablespoon at bedtime with 1,000 mg vitamin C

IMPORTANT AIDS

- Vitamin C with bioflavonoids—1,000 to 3,000 mg daily
- Alpha-Linolenic Acid (LNA)
- Digestive enzymes—take as directed with meals
- Linoleic Acid (LA)
- MSM—500 mg three to four times daily with meals
- Vitamin B-complex—take as directed
- Gotu Kola—20 to 60 mg three times daily of an extract standardized to contain 40% asiaticoside, 29–30% asiatic acid, 29–30 % madecassic acid, and 1–2% madecassoside.
- Flaxseed Oil—1 to 2 tbsp. daily
- Fish Oils contain the important Omega-3 fatty acids EPA and DHA. Therapeutic servings include 1,800 mg of EPA and 900 mg of DHA daily.

OTHER POTENTIAL AIDS

- Glucosamine—500 mg three times daily
- Hydrochloric Acid (Hypochlorhydria)
- L-glutamine—500 mg daily
- Vitamin D3—400 IU daily
- Iodine—100 to 225 mcg daily
- Iron—take as directed on label if you have an iron deficiency
- Biotin—300 mg three times daily
- Folic Acid—400 mcg three times daily
- Gotu Kola—normally takes at least 4 weeks to work
- Tea Tree Oil applied topically.
- Apple Cider Vinegar—take some with each meal
- Cucumber
- Onion
- Parsnip juice
- Whole grains
- Almonds

☞ NERVOUS SYSTEM

THE NERVOUS SYSTEM is the network of cells specialized to carry information in the form of nerve impulses to and from all parts of the body in order to initiate bodily activity and mental function. One major problem we see concerns neurotransmitters.

The body must have the right nutrients to support the nervous system. In counseling, many people who seem stressed and are experiencing mental and physical signs of nervous disorders can be helped significantly by just supplementing with B-complex vitamins. B-complex is very important on a daily basis, and in stressful times intake should increase significantly.

Sugars also stress the body as well as sugar additives and some studies show Canola oil aggravates the central nervous system. Canola oil comes from rape seed and is a neurotoxin. Rape seed is also found in almost all peanut butter.

TOP NATURAL AIDS

- Multivitamin and mineral complex providing 25,000 IU of natural beta-carotene, 100 mg of potassium, and 200 mcg of selenium daily
- Vitamin B-complex—100 mg of each major B vitamin daily
- Vitamin E protects the fatty acids in the nervous system from oxidation. Take 400 to 600 IU daily with meals.
- 2,000 mg of calcium and 1,000 mg of magnesium daily
- Check Neurotransmitters—see Appendix A
- Check Thyroid—see Appendix A

IMPORTANT AIDS

- Vitamin C with bioflavonoids—3,000 to 10,000 mg daily
- Coenzyme Q10—30 to 300 mg daily, divided into two or three servings

OTHER POTENTIAL AIDS

- Vitamin B3 aids the function of the nerves.
- Minerals—excessive copper can over-excite the nerves.

☞ OBESITY

OBESITY is applied to persons who are more than 20% above their recommended body weight as measured by Body Mass Index (BMI). A high-glycemic index diet increases the risk of obesity by increasing insulin levels, which in turn suppresses the "burning" of body fat for the production of energy and redirects glucose to be stored as body fat.

While I was going into church recently, a man stopped me to report he had lost over 40 pounds in the last 6 months on my program. First, he did a cleanse, which changed his body chemistry. Then he started eating right, following the One Perfect Diet plan. He feels great and looks fantastic.

You will also want to read "Quick Weight Loss for Anyone Who Wants to Take Charge of Their Health" in Chapter 18 of this book.

I am living proof that the One Perfect Diet works. After having birthed 8 children, I still weigh the same 118 pounds I did in high school.

TOP NATURAL AIDS

- Increasing Dietary Protein ingestion to an amount that equals 25% of total calorie intake facilitates weight loss.
- Lecithin—1,200 mg three times daily before meals
- Green Drinks such as Creation's Bounty
- Carnitine—1,000 to 2,000 mg daily
- Vitamin B-complex—at least 50 mg of each major B vitamin three times daily
- Collagen liquid—1 tablespoon at bedtime with 1,000 mg vitamin C
- Psyllium—1 tablespoon in water before each meal
- Gamma-Linolenic Acid (GLA) from evening primrose oil, borage oil, and black currant oil
- Linoleic Acid (LA)
- Alpha-Linolenic Acid (LNA)
- Docosahexaenoic Acid (DHA)
- Chromium Picolinate reduces sugar cravings. Take 200 to 600 mcg daily.

- Iodine—100 to 225 mcg daily. Kelp is a good source of iodine—1,000 to 1,500 mg daily
- Spirulina—8,400 mg daily
- Green Tea—300 mg of standardized extract containing 50% catechin and 90% total polyphenols 30 minutes before the first two meals of the day
- Flaxseed—1 to 2 tbsp. daily
- Natural Sunlight at least one hour a day.

IMPORTANT AIDS

- DMAE—take as directed on label
- L-Arginine—500 mg before bedtime. Take with water or juice, not milk. Lysine enhances Arginine's role in facilitating weight loss.
- L-Tyrosine—500 mg each morning for 3 weeks
- Branched-Chain Amino Acids (BCAAs)
- Cysteine
- Glucomannans—3,000 mg daily taken with a large glass of water before bed
- Conjugated Linoleic Acid (CLA)—3,300 mg daily
- Pyruvic Acid—6,000 mg daily
- Coenzyme Q10—30 to 100 mg daily
- Bladderwrack—150 mg twice daily with meals for two months
- Choline—50 to 200 mg daily
- Dandelion—500 mg three times daily with meals for two months
- Guggulipid—500 mg three times daily
- Siberian Ginseng helps reduce sweet cravings. Take 100 mg daily for two weeks each month. Choose a standardized extract containing 0.5% eleutheroside E.

OTHER POTENTIAL AIDS

- Calcium—1,000 mg daily
- Capsaicin
- Alanine
- Beta 1,6 Glucan

- Chitosan is a form of fiber derived from crustacean shells. It is not well digested by the human body, and as it passes through the digestive tract, it appears to bond with ingested fat and carry it out of the body—3 to 6 grams daily, taken with food.
- Chondroitin Sulfate—400 mg three times daily
- Guar Gum
- Hemicelluloses
- Carnitine Palmitoyltransferase
- Pancreatic Enzymes
- 7-Keto DHEA
- DHEA—take as directed on label
- hGH
- Pregnenolone—take as directed on label
- Optimal levels of Thyroid Hormones
- Magnesium
- Manganese
- Phosphorus
- Vanadium
- Norepinephrine (NE)—see Appendix A on "Neurotransmitters"
- Hydroxycitric Acid—250 to 1,000 mg three times daily
- Vitamin B5
- Vitamin C with bioflavonoids—3,000 to 6,000 mg daily
- Vitamin D
- Grapefruit juice
- Chickweed tea helps metabolize fat.
- Ginger cleanses the colon and stimulates circulation.
- Korean Ginseng
- Yohimbe
- Maitake Mushrooms—take extract as directed on label
- Fish Oils—6,000 mg daily
- Garlic helps stabilize blood sugar levels.
- Red Clover—500 mg daily one week per month

ANY Exercise Is Essential!
Fallacy—Cider vinegar does not alleviate obesity.

☞ OILY SKIN

SEBORRHEA is an ailment involving the excessive production and secretion of sebum by the sebaceous glands. With every skin disorder, first investigate the colon and digestive tract. Cleanse and then supplement according to the individual needs. A proper balance of essential fatty acids is required as well as a good balance of good bacteria. Many people are depleted of good bacteria from the use of prescription drugs and antibiotics. A good skin care line is also required, preferably chemical free.

Karen is in her early twenties and has been working in my office for several years now. During that time her complexion has improved dramatically. She cleansed and began to supplement for general health. When she first started, her skin actually got worse—all those toxins were pouring out. But she kept at it, and now she is absolutely beautiful, and so is her skin.

TOP NATURAL AIDS

- Evening Primrose Oil—1,000 mg three times daily with Probiotics such as Acidophilus and/or Bifidus (take as directed on label)
- Liquid Collagen before bedtime
- Vitamin B-complex—50 mg of each major B vitamin taken three times daily
- Vitamin E with mixed tocopherols—400 to 800 IU daily
- Biotin—300 to 400 mcg three times daily
- Vitamin B6—50 mg three times daily
- Aloe Vera ointment helps with the itching and scaliness associated with seborrhea.
- Flaxseed Oil—1 tbsp. daily
- Essential Fatty Acids

IMPORTANT AIDS

- Vitamin C—up to 5,000 mg
- Vitamin B12—100 mcg daily of sublingual form
- Liquid Collagen before bedtime

- Zinc—50 mg daily
- Digestive Enzymes—5,000 IU of lipase, 2,500 IU of amylase, and 300 IU of protease taken twice daily with two largest meals
- Methylsulfonylmethane (MSM)—take as directed on label
- Vitamin A—25,000 IU daily
- Coenzyme Q10—60 mg twice daily for one month, then reduce to 30 mg one to two times daily
- Selenium lotion applied topically or taken orally—100 mcg daily for two months
- Emu Oil applied topically.
- Oat Straw used in a bath may help relieve itching and inflammation.

OTHER POTENTIAL AIDS

- Pancreatin—500 to 1,000 mg twice daily taken with two largest meals of the day. Don't take pancreatin longer than 2 months.
- Lentinan cream applied topically.
- Progesterone cream applied topically.
- Potassium—100 to 500 mg daily
- Pycnogenol—take as directed on label
- Alpha-Hydroxy Acids (AHAs) applied topically.
- Kelp—1,000 to 1,500 mg daily
- Lecithin—1,200 mg three times daily with meals
- Aniseed Tea
- Horseradish juice diluted by 50% and applied topically.
- Lavender Oil applied topically.
- Potato applied topically.
- Dandelion—250 mg three to four times daily of a 5:1 extract or 5 to 10 ml three times daily of a 1:5 tincture in 45% alcohol
- Red Clover—40 to 160 mg of isoflavones daily
- Eating Yogurt helps supply good bacteria to the body.

☞ OSTEOPOROSIS

OSTEOPOROSIS is a condition where bones become porous, brittle, and less dense as a result of a loss of bone mass. Twenty-five to 30% of white and oriental women and 20% of black women develop osteoporosis. Men have 25% the rate of osteoporosis as females.

A liquid calcium supplement is very important regarding osteoporosis, because calcium is so hard to absorb. It is vital to take vitamin D along with the calcium.

Sunshine is very important because it takes cholesterol in the body and converts it to vitamin D so calcium would naturally be better absorbed and utilized.

Most people are not calcium deficient but have misplaced calcium in the body. Chelation treatments, whether by IV or suppository, are quite effective for pulling calcium from areas where it should not be, such as plaque, gall stones, etc., and putting it back in the bones and teeth.

TOP NATURAL AIDS

- High Potency Multivitamin
- Collodial Mineral—1 to 2 ounces daily
- Glucosamine—500 mg three times daily
- Chondroitin
- Copper—3 mg daily
- Vitamin B-complex—50 mg of each major B vitamin
- Vitamin B6—200 mg daily
- Vitamin B12—1,000 to 2,000 mcg daily
- Chelation
- Calcium liquid—as directed
- Zinc—50 mg daily
- Boron—3 to 5 mg daily
- Calcium—250 mg daily of each of the four following supplements—Calcium Citrate, Calcium Carbonate, Calcium Aspartate, and Calcium Chelate
- Manganese may help prevent osteoporosis. Take 5 mg daily.

- Magnesium—200 mgs daily of each of the following three supplements—Magnesium Oxide, Magnesium Citrate, and Magnesium Chelate
- Phosphorus—take as directed
- Silicon—50 mg daily of the orthosilicic acid form of silicon
- Vitamin D3—400 IU daily

IMPORTANT AIDS

- Methylsulfonylmethane (MSM) helps build healthy new cells. Take as directed on label.
- Vitamin A with mixed carotenoids—25,000 IU daily
- Vitamin D—400 IU daily
- Supplemental, exogenous, natural progesterone helps post-menopausal women regain some bone density.
- Superunsaturated Fatty Acids
- DHEA—5 to 50 mg daily
- Chromium Picolinate—400 to 600 mcg daily
- Soy Isoflavones help maintain bone density. Take 1,000 mg one to two times daily.
- Vitamin C with bioflavonoids—3,000 mg and up daily
- Vitamin E
- Vitamin K—100 mcg daily
- Fish Oils contain the important Omega-3 fatty acids EPA and DHA. Therapeutic servings include 1,800 mg of EPA and 900 mg of DHA daily.
- Flaxseeds

OTHER POTENTIAL AIDS

- Collagen
- Arginine
- Creatine Monohydrate—5,000 mg daily combined with isotonic exercise
- Chelation Suppositories with EDTA, the synthetic amino acid used in chelation therapy, increases bone mineral density in

osteoporosis patients (it is believed to "work" by "pulsing" parathyroid hormone which enhances calcium metabolism).

- Aromatase
- Superoxide Dismutase (SOD)
- Human Growth Hormone (hGH) builds bone mass, and the decline in hGH production that occurs in tandem with the progression of the aging process has been implicated by some researchers as a principal underlying cause of osteoporosis.
- Melatonin
- Bicarbonate in the form of Sodium Bicarbonate
- Germanium
- Potassium, especially the Potassium Bicarbonate form
- Nitric Oxide. See Appendix A on "Neurotransmitter."
- Ipriflavone—600 mg daily
- Kelp—2,000 to 3,000 mg daily
- Whey Protein
- Milk and other dairy products such as yogurt are good sources of natural calcium.
- Green Tea
- Horsetail and Oat Straw help the body absorb calcium. Take 500 mg twice daily of either one.
- Soybeans
- Ginseng—tea form, 3 cups daily; or tincture, 20 drops in water daily
- Garlic improves circulation.
- Onions
- Apple Cider Vinegar

FOODS THAT ARE BENEFICIAL

- Figs
- Broccoli
- Dark green leafy vegetables
- Flounder
- Hazelnuts
- Kale
- Kelp
- Molasses
- Oats
- Salmon

- Sardines
- Soybeans
- Turnip Greens
- Watercress
- Wheat Germ

AVOID THESE FOODS *and* BEVERAGES

- Yeast products
- Carbonated soft drinks
- Alcohol
- Sugar
- Anything with high amounts of caffeine

☞ OXYGEN

OXYGEN is essential to human life. The human body dies from oxygen deficiency more rapidly than when deprived of any other nutrient. Oxygen is an odorless, colorless gas that comprises 20% of the atmosphere. For instance, although the brain comprises only 2% of the body's weight, it consumes 20% of the body's oxygen intake. Inhalation of pure oxygen improves the memory.

SUBSTANCES THAT MAY IMPROVE OXYGEN LEVELS

- Betaine is also known as Trimethylglycine (TMG). Suggested servings range from 375 to 1,000 mg daily.
- Dimethyl Glycine (DMG) is popular among many athletes as a performance enhancer. Follow label directions.
- Pangamic Acid
- Various forms of modified oxygen (e.g. hydrogen peroxide) are often utilized as therapeutic agents in oxygen therapy, which increases the delivery of oxygen to cells and therefore promotes cellular respiration.
- Thyroid Hormones
- Alpha-Linolenic Acid (LNA)
- Fish Oils contain the important Omega-3 fatty acids Eicosapentaenoic Acid (EPA) and Docosahexaenoic Acid (DHA). Therapeutic servings include 1,800 mg of EPA and 900 mg of DHA daily.
- Germanium
- Magnesium—750 to 1,000 mg daily
- Calcium Phosphate
- Potassium Phosphate
- Sodium Phosphate
- Vitamin B2 works with two enzymes critical for providing energy to the body. Suggested servings range from 15 to 50 mg daily.
- Korean Ginseng

- Maral Root
- Siberian Ginseng
- Suma boosts the immune system and relieves fatigue. Take as directed on label.
- Body Oxygen

☞ PANCREAS

THE PANCREAS is a big gland just under the stomach and partially into the curve of the duodenum of the small intestine. The pancreas is a part of the digestive system.

TOP NATURAL AIDS

- Probiotic—as directed
- Vitamin C with bioflavonoids—1,000 mg four times daily
- Chromium Picolinate—150 to 400 mcg daily
- Calcium—1,500 mg daily
- Magnesium—1,000 mg daily
- Pancretin—1 to 2 capsules three times daily
- Licorice in DGL form is very helpful with chronic conditions—300 mg three times daily
- Niacin—15 to 50 mg daily
- Vitamin B5—100 mg daily
- Vitamin B-complex—50 mg twice daily
- Garlic—take as directed
- Digestive Enzyme—take as directed
- Goldenseal increases the effectiveness of insulin.

IMPORTANT AIDS

- Phosphatidylcholine
- Zinc—30 to 50 mg daily
- Dandelion Root improves fat digestion—1 cup of tea twice daily
- Coenzyme Q10—30 to 100 mg daily

OTHER POTENTIAL AIDS

- Cystine facilitates the supply of insulin
- Beta-carotene
- Lycopene
- Secretin

- Manganese—3 to 10 mg daily
- Selenium—100 to 200 mcg daily
- Sulfur
- Glutathione
- Silymarin
- Biotin—400 to 800 mcg daily
- Vitamin K—100 to 500 mcg daily
- Cascara sagrada acts as a colon cleanser and helps eliminate parasites.

☞ PMS

PREMENSTRUAL SYNDROME is a group of symptoms, such as nervous tension, irritability, tenderness of the breasts, and headache, experienced by some women in the days preceding menstruation and caused by hormonal changes.

While I am keeping my advice regarding PMS short here, look to the Menopause section for more expansive advice for PMS sufferers. However, women and men both love the specific advice given here. Women love it because they suffer from it, and men because they have to deal with it. But it can be helped, and in a big way. I truly thank God that I haven't had to deal with PMS for the majority of my adult life because I've been very cautious to not put harmful chemicals into my body that greatly affect the hormone balances in the body (such as birth control pills or milk filled with bovine hormones).

TOP NATURAL AID

- Take 1,200 to 1,500 mg of Evening Primrose Oil and 200 to 400 IUs of Vitamin E twice a day. Increase the Vitamin E up to 1,000 IUs daily until night sweats and symptoms decrease. This is so easy. It also gives you essential fatty acids, aids your brain functions, helps your skin and joints, and much more.

This simple combination works so well that my own teenage daughters have been known on occasion to have their teachers call me to get this little remedy. The teachers love it and pass it on to their colleagues, and my daughters score a few extra points with the teachers. I use this advice myself! I really like the way it affects me in a number of ways, especially my curly hair.

Give it a try for 30 to 60 days, and you'll love it! It's simple, inexpensive, and has only good side effects. Add a good food-based B complex to it, and you soon will be another one of my great testimonials.

☞ PROSTATE CANCER

PROSTATE CANCER is a form of cancer involving the growth/formation of malignant tumors in the prostate. Seventy-five percent of all cases of prostate cancer are diagnosed in men over the age of 65. Prostate cancer is the most commonly-occurring cancer in men.

Recently a chemist was telling me that he had a prostate problem since he was a young man. What totally reversed his condition was chelation suppositories.

Men should stay away from dairy that is not hormone free. Studies show that all American men will have prostate problems.

TOP NATURAL AIDS

- Chelation
- Lycopene—3 mg twice daily
- Selenium—daily consumption of 200 mcg of selenium is associated with an average reduction in the risk of prostate cancer of 63%. If you have prostate cancer, take 300 mg of selenium daily.
- Zinc (picolinate or oxide form)—15 to 60 mg daily taken with food and add 4 mg copper to increase benefits
- Vitamin C with bioflavonoids—5,000 to 20,000 mg daily in divided servings
- Vitamin E with mixed tocopherols—400 IU twice daily
- Vitamin B6—100 mg daily
- Green Tea contains a powerful substance that kills prostate cancer cells. Take as tea, 3 cups daily; or as extract, 100 to 150 mg three times daily of green tea extract standardized to contain 80% total polyphenols and 50% epigallocatechin gallate
- Saw Palmetto—150 to 250 mg twice daily of extract containing 85–95% essential fatty acids
- Tomato Sauce Tomatoes, especially cooked, contain lycopene, a powerful antioxidant.

IMPORTANT AIDS

- Modified Citrus Pectin appears to be particularly effective in combating prostate cancer. Take 50 to 100 mg daily.
- Vitamin A—50,000 to 100,000 IU daily for 10 days
- Vitamin D3—3,000 to 4,000 IU daily
- Magnesium—750 to 1,000 mg daily
- Shark Cartilage—1 gram for every 2 pounds of body weight, divided into 3 servings; for prevention, 2,000 to 4,500 mg three times daily
- Nettle Root—100 to 300 mcg of extract two to three times daily
- Maitake Mushrooms—can be consumed as food (3 to 7 grams daily), taken as tea, or taken in equivalent amounts in capsule or tablet form (3,000 to 7,000 mg).
- Grape Seed extract—take according to label directions
- Garlic extract inhibits the proliferation of prostate cancer cells. A typical serving is 900 mg daily of a garlic powder extract standardized to contain 1.3% alliin.
- DHEA (Dehydroepiandrosterone) helps prevent prostate cancer and inhibits the further progression of existing prostate cancer—50 to 200 mg daily

OTHER POTENTIAL AIDS

- Researchers have established links between low consumption of complex carbohydrates, such as those found in fresh fruits and vegetables, and prostate cancer.
- Lutein—5 to 30 mg daily
- D-Glucaric Acid appears to assist in eliminating carcinogenic substances from the body. It can be found in apples, sprouts, and grapefruit.
- Beta-carotene—50 mg daily
- Melatonin—take as directed on label
- Progesterone
- Conjugated Linoleic Acid (CLA)—3 to 5 grams daily
- Docosahexaenoic Acid (DHA)—900 mg daily

- Eicosapentaenoic Acid (EPA)—1,800 mg daily
- Myristoleic
- Boron—3 mg daily
- Inositol Hexaphosphate (Phytic Acid) appears to aid in the prevention and treatment of cancer. It's found naturally in nuts, lentils, whole grains, citrus fruit, and veal.
- Quercetin—70 to 140 mg
- Silymarin—100 to 200 mg twice a day (look for a form bound to phosphatidylcholine)
- Soy Protein
- Coenzyme Q10—100 mg daily
- Vitamin B1—100 mg daily
- Vitamin B2—100 mg daily
- Vitamin D—400 IU daily
- Potassium—100 mg daily
- Calcium—1,500 mg daily
- Vitamin B12—2,000 mcg daily

THESE FOODS AND HERBS MAY HELP

- Miso
- Pumpkin Seeds daily
- Tempeh
- Rice
- Rye Bran
- Milk Thistle—200 mg twice daily of extract containing 80% flavonoids
- Pygeum—50 mg twice daily of an extract standardized to contain 14% triterpenes and 0.5% n-docosanol
- Skullcap—1 to 2 grams three times daily (usually not taken long term)
- Soybeans
- Fish Oils contain the important Omega-3 fatty acids EPA and DHA. Therapeutic servings include 1,800 mg of EPA and 900 mg of DHA daily.

- Kelp—1,000 to 1,500 mg daily
- High consumption of Oily Fish helps to prevent prostate cancer. Beneficial fish include herring, mackerel, salmon, and sardines.
- Flaxseeds—30 grams daily
- Beetroot
- Cabbage Family Vegetables—broccoli, Brussels sprouts, cabbage, and cauliflower at least three servings per week
- Goldenseal, Buchu, Echinacea, Pau d'arco, and Suma herbs all contain cancer-fighting substances. They should be taken as tea, using two at a time and alternating between them.

Exercise: Regular exercise helps to lower the risk of prostate cancer

☞ PSORIASIS

PSORIASIS is a type of chronic skin disease in which itchy, scaly red patches form on the elbows, forearms, knees, legs, or scalp. The underlying cause of psoriasis is uncontrolled cell growth. Thymic formula has been proven to be very effective as a remedy for psoriasis. It is very important to deal with this at an early stage as it is said to be a precursor for autoimmune disorders.

TOP NATURAL AIDS

- Fish Oils—10 to 12 grams daily, providing 1,800 mg of Eicosapentaenoic Acid (EPA) and 1,200 mg of Docosahexaenoic Acid (DHA)
- Flaxseed Oil—500 mg three times daily
- Milk Thistle—200 to 300 mg daily of extract standardized to contain 80% flavonoids
- Selenium—200 mcg daily
- Vitamin B-complex—50 mg of each of the major B vitamins three times daily
- Thymic Formula—6 tablets daily
- Evening Primrose Oil—1,000 mg twice daily
- Alpha-Linolenic Acid (LNA)
- Docosahexaenoic Acid (DHA)—to 1,200 mg daily
- EPA applied topically.
- Clustered Water to correct DNA damage—6 to 8 glasses daily.
- Linoleic Acid (LA)
- Silymarin (from Milk Thistle) helps keep the blood clean. Take 300 mg three times daily.
- Vitamin A—30,000 to 50,000 IU daily ingested orally or applied topically
- Vitamin C with bioflavonoids—2,000 to 10,000 mg daily
- Red Clover is very beneficial for skin problems. Apply topically in a cream or ointment or drink 3 cups of tea daily.

IMPORTANT AIDS

- Vitamin D3—400 IU daily
- Kelp—1,000 to 1,500 mg daily
- Probiotic supplement—take as directed on label. For best results, alternate between acidophilus and bifidobacteria.
- Digestive Enzyme—take as directed
- Calcium—1,500 mg daily
- Magnesium—750 mg daily
- Glutathione—500 mg twice daily on empty stomach
- Lecithin—1,200 mg three times daily with meals
- Zinc—50 to 100 mg daily with 3 mg copper daily. Don't take more than 100 mg of zinc daily.
- Methylsulfonylmethane (MSM)
- Folic Acid—400 mcg daily
- Vitamin B12—3,000 mg daily in 3 x 1,000 mg servings administered orally or by a physician via injections has totally cured many cases of psoriasis.
- Vitamin E applied topically or consumed orally—start with 400 IU daily and gradually increase amount to 1,200 IU daily over 3 to 4 weeks
- Shark Cartilage—1 gram per 15 pounds of body weight daily, divided into 3 servings
- Comfrey ointment applied topically.
- Gotu Kola accelerates healing. Take 200 mg two to three times daily for one month of standardized extract containing 16% triterpenes.
- Yellow Dock helps detoxify skin. Applying a yellow dock poultice can help psoriasis.

OTHER POTENTIAL AIDS

- Collagen
- Allantoin ointment applied topically.
- Berbamine
- Capsaicin—0.025% cream applied topically

- Cysteine
- Pregnenolon—50 to 600 mg daily
- Progesterone cream applied topically.
- Alkylglycerols—400 mg daily
- Sarsaparilla works as a detoxifying agent.
- Iron Phosphate
- Potassium Sulfate
- Silicon
- Sulfur
- Zinc Pyrithione applied topically.
- Alpha-Hydroxy Acids (AHAs) applied topically.
- Curcumin applied topically to the skin.
- Coenzyme Q10
- Vitamin D applied topically or administered orally.
- Bovine Cartilage—take as directed on label
- High consumption of fresh Fruit
- Increase the consumption of Rice
- Aloe Vera—0.5% extract applied topically via a suitable skin-penetrating carrier vehicle such as ointment, cream, or shampoo
- Barberry ointment applied topically or capsules/extract consumed orally.
- Chamomile ointment applied topically.
- Neem Seed oil applied topically and leaf extract consumed orally.
- Olive Leaf extract
- Oregon Grape apply topically three times daily using an ointment or cream containing 10% Mahonia extract
- Shark Liver Oil—2,000 mg daily
- Apricot Kernel Oil applied topically.
- Jojoba Oil applied topically.
- Lavender Oil applied topically to affected areas or used as a shampoo on the scalp.
- Oregano Oil

- Dandelion juice helps rejuvenate the liver. Take 1 tbsp. of oil daily.
- Sesame Seed Oil applied topically.
- Tamanu Oil applied topically.
- Tea Tree Oil as an ingredient in shampoo
- Wheat Germ Oil applied topically.
- Cider Vinegar applied topically or in a bath temporarily alleviates psoriasis.
- Carrots
- Garlic
- Onion
- Rhubarb juice
- Tomato
- Bathing in Sea Water provides temporary relief of the symptoms of psoriasis.
- Sunlight
- Fasting improves the condition of psoriasis patients (probably by decreasing levels of gastrointestinal tract toxins and by decreasing levels of polyamines substances implicated in psoriasis).

☞ RESPIRATORY SYSTEM

THE RESPIRATORY SYSTEM is the combination of organs and tissues associated with respiration—the process of obtaining oxygen and releasing waste carbon dioxide.

A man's X-rays showed something in his lungs. He had had a real bout with Candida Albicans accompanied by a dry non-productive cough. He underwent a cleanse, and in 30 days he was like new.

A young woman said her mom had a serious lung condition and that she was on an oxygen tank. She started using a couple ounces of Body Oxygen each day, and within a few weeks was no longer in need of the oxygen to do simple tasks, such as to walk across a room.

In Seattle, Washington, a woman I met told me she had a long drive home that night, so I gave her a Body Oxygen sublingual spray to promote energy and help her stay awake. She called a few days later and said she had experienced a beneficial side effect, "Going from using an inhaler every couple of hours to every couple of days."

While all these stories are different, there maybe a common link—fungus in the body.

TOP NATURAL AIDS

- Eliminative organ cleanse, such as the Creation's Cleanse, once a year
- Oxygen-enhancing products such as Body Oxygen
- Chelation IV or Suppositories
- Vitamin C—10,000 mg
- Coenzyme Q10
- Goldenseal—250 to 500 mg three times daily (don't take for longer than 2 weeks). Goldenseal should not be taken by pregnant women.
- Apples
- Probiotics
- Horseradish

- Peppermint slightly numbs mucous membranes. It can be taken as tea.

IMPORTANT AIDS

- Cysteine, particularly the N-Acetyl-Cysteine form—500 to 1,500 mg daily
- Copper—1 to 3 mg daily
- Thymus Extract—follow label directions
- Echinacea and Goldenseal combinations are great for upper respiratory infections.

OTHER POTENTIAL AIDS

- Fenugreek
- Thyme—best taken in combination with Fenugreek
- Carrots

☞ RINGING IN EARS

TINNITUS is a sensation of sound in one ear, both ears, or the head—ringing, buzzing, roaring, hissing, whistling, throbbing, or booming. May be a single sound or different sounds and can materialize gradually or all of a sudden. An iron deficiency may be to blame.

TOP NATURAL AIDS

- Candida Cleanse
- Ginkgo Biloba helps improve hearing loss due to reduced blood flow. Take 40 to 60 mg three times daily of a standardized extract containing 24% ginkgo heterosides.
- Vitamin B-complex—at least 50 mg of each major B vitamin twice daily
- Vitamin A—50,000 IU daily
- Vitamin B12—1 mg daily
- Vitamin E—600 IU daily
- Vitamin D (especially when used in conjunction with calcium) improves hearing
- Enzymes with cellulase
- Magnesium—400 to 800 mg daily
- Manganese—10 mg daily
- Potassium—100 mg daily
- Zinc (sulfate form)—600 mg daily

IMPORTANT AIDS

- Coenzyme Q10—30 mg daily
- N-acetylcysteine—500 mg two to three times daily
- Folic Acid—400 mcg daily
- Vitamin C with bioflavonoids—3,000 to 6,000 mg daily in divided portions
- Kelp—150 mg twice daily for one month. If it helps, cut back gradually to lowest amount that maintains good hearing.

OTHER POTENTIAL AIDS

- Melatonin can help provide restful sleep.

- Calcium—800 to 1,200 mg daily
- Methylsulfonylmethane (MSM) instilled into the ears via MSM eardrops.
- Choline
- Vitamin B3—high servings of either form
- Vitamin B5
- Vitamin B6
- Body Oxygen
- Black Cohosh
- Fresh Plantain extract is excellent for the ears. Drink 2 tbsp. of juice three times daily for six weeks.
- Fenugreek Seeds
- Horsetail in vegetal silica form, an aqueous extract derived from the herb, has been used to treat tinnitus. Take 3 to 4 capsules daily.

OXYGEN THERAPIES

- Hyperbaric Oxygen is highly effective for the treatment of noise-induced tinnitus.
- Ozone Therapy administered by a physician has successfully treated some cases of tinnitus.

✐ SCHIZOPHRENIA

SCHIZOPHRENIA is a severe mental disorder characterized by a disintegration of the process of thinking, loss of contact with reality, and loss of emotional responsiveness. Schizophrenia patients usually feel that their thoughts, sensations, and actions are controlled by or shared with others. Great benefit has come from checking the neurotransmitters (see Appendix A).

I recall a wonderful man who came to see me. He been diagnosed with schizophrenia years before and was fine as long as he was on prescription medication. However, while he was on the medication he suffered a variety of side effects that interfered with his daily life. He was so sleepy and groggy he could hardly work or function, and by the time he came to me he was absolutely distraught.

The first thing we did was a urine test for neurotransmitters (see Appendix A). His were totally out of balance. We did not attempt to take him off any medication, but we added the supplements he needed to allow his body to become regulated again. Within two weeks he began to feel better and have more energy.

There was a study Dr. Airola quoted in the Hunger Cure. It was conducted in a mental hospital for schizophrenics in Russia. Patients were not given any food and made to drink raw fruit and vegetable juices only. 60–70% of the patients went home well. What do I think did it? Well, our bodies need the right kind of fuel. These people were most likely extremely toxic and needed to get the toxins out as well as put the right nutrients in. When put in the right environment, the body knows how to heal itself!

TOP NATURAL AIDS

- Vitamin B-complex—50 mg three times daily
- 5-Hydroxytryptophan (5-HTP)—take as directed on label
- Evening Primrose Oil—1,000 mg three times daily with 200 IU vitamin E
- Glutamic Acid

- Manganese—3 to 10 mg daily
- Zinc—15 mg daily with 3 mg copper
- Folic Acid—2,000 mcg daily
- Vitamin B3—3,000 mg daily
- Vitamin B12—1,000 mcg twice daily
- Vitamin C with bioflavonoids—10 to 20 grams daily
- Fish Oils contain the important Omega-3 fatty acids Eicosapentaenoic Acid (EPA) and Docosahexaenoic Acid (DHA). Therapeutic servings include 1,800 mg of EPA and 900 mg of DHA daily.
- Flaxseed Oil supplies essential fatty acids the brain needs for proper function.
- Ginkgo Biloba improves brain function and circulation.
- Oxygen and Oxygen Therapy

IMPORTANT AIDS

- Garlic
- Cysteine—take as directed on label
- Methionine—take as directed on label
- Glycine—15 to 60 grams daily. Note: if you are taking some of the newer anti-psychotic medications, such as clozapine, don't use glycine.
- L-Aspargine helps balance the central nervous system. An average serving is 2 to 3 grams daily.
- Magnesium—500 mg daily
- Lecithin—1,200 mg three times daily
- Selenium—100 mcg daily
- L-Glutamine—1,000 to 4,000 mg daily taken on an empty stomach
- Vitamin B6—50 to 100 mg daily
- Vitamin E with mixed tocopherols—800 IU daily
- Kelp—1,000 to 5,000 mg daily
- Chelation Suppository or IV to remove heavy metals

OTHER POTENTIAL AIDS

- Gamma-aminobutyric acid (GABA) aids in proper brain function.
- Collagen
- Glutathione Peroxidase—take as directed on label
- Vitamin D during pregnancy increases the risk of schizophrenia in children.
- Raw Thyroid Glandular—take as directed on label
- Neurotransmitter test kit—see Appendix A

☞ SEXUAL DRIVE

TWENTY-TWO PERCENT OF WOMEN REPORT LOW SEXUAL DESIRE, and there is no available data relating to men.

I still remember a call I received in 1984. A lady confided that she thought she loved her husband, but could not figure out why she did not want to have sex with him. He was a good man. They had two wonderful children together, but since her last child she could not be intimate. She had been to church counselors and to a psychiatrist. She thought she had some deep-seeded emotional things going on. She came in, and we worked on her thyroid with some natural products that are listed here. Two weeks later she came back to tell me her husband was the happiest man on the face of the earth. Amazing what the right fuel in the tank can do!

TOP NATURAL AIDS

- Vitamin B-complex—50 mg of each of the major B vitamins three times daily
- Vitamin E—400 to 800 IU daily
- Zinc deficiency can cause lowered sexual desire—80 mg daily.
- Yohimbine increases sexual desire in males.
- Damiana improves sexual desire in males—250 to 500 mg twice daily for up to one month.
- Ginkgo Biloba increases sexual desire—40 mg three times daily of a product standardized to contain 24% ginkgo-flavone glycosides. To attain results, herb must be taken for at least six months.
- Horny Goat Weed
- Kelp—2,000 to 2,500 mg daily
- Chelation Suppository or IV to remove heavy metals

IMPORTANT AIDS

- Arginine enhances (male and female) sexual desire—250 mg daily
- Bee Pollen—1 tsp. in morning
- Vitamin A—25,000 IU daily, but not if pregnant
- PABA—100 mg daily

- Lecithin—2,400 mg three times daily with meals
- Tyrosine—2,000 to 4,000 mg daily
- Progesterone increases sexual desire in females—apply 1/2 tsp. of progesterone cream topically every day from day 14 to 28 of the menstrual cycle.

OTHER POTENTIAL AIDS

- L-Dopa
- Supplemental Androstenedione—approximately 30 to 60 minutes prior to intended sexual activity take 100 mg with food.
- Dehydroepiandrosterone (DHEA)—25 mg daily for women, 50 mg daily for men
- Estradiol increases female sexual desire. Estradiol is a form of estrogen produced by the ovaries. It is usually combined with estrone in estrogen tablets normally prescribed for menopausal symptoms.
- Human Growth Hormone (hGH)—take under a doctor's supervision
- Boron—1 to 2 mg daily
- Neurotransmitters—see Appendix A
- Choline—50 to 200 mg daily
- Vitamin C with bioflavonoids—1,000 mg daily
- Oats
- American Ginseng (men)
- Ashwagandha—1 tsp. of powder twice daily, boiled in milk or water.
- Korean Ginseng—1,800 mg daily for males
- Nettle—1 cup of nettle seed tonic 2 hours before having sex
- Maca
- Marapuama—1,750 mg daily
- Tribulus terrestris—85 to 250 mg three times daily with meals. If possible, try to use product standardized to provide 40% furostanol saponins.
- Velvet Beans—due to the L-Dopa content
- Oat Straw—500 mg two to three times daily

☞ SICKLE-CELL ANEMIA

SICKLE-CELL ANEMIA is an hereditary form of anemia that results from faulty hemoglobin molecules (known as sickle-cell hemoglobin or Hbs) causing the body's red blood cells to have an abnormal "sickle" figure.

A young girl came to me suffering from sickle-cell anemia. In a short period of time she gained great benefit from Body Oxygen and Clustered Water. While it did not get rid of the disease, it did bring relief.

TOP NATURAL AIDS

- Body Oxygen
- Clustered Water
- Folic Acid—5 mg or more daily
- Oxygen Therapy, Hyperbaric Oxygen and Ozone
- Zinc (sulfate form)

IMPORTANT AIDS

- Vitamin B2—10 mg daily
- Vitamin C when used in conjunction with aged garlic extract, vitamin E, and folic acid reduces painful episodes.
- Vitamin E alleviates many cases of sickle-cell anemia.

OTHER POTENTIAL AIDS

- Suma helps the body adapt to stress. It is typically taken in amounts of 500 mg twice daily.

☞ SINUSITIS

SINUSITIS is an inflammation of one or more of the paranasal sinuses. According to the Mayo Clinic Ear Nose and Throat Department in 2003, 96% of all sinus-related infections are from fungus.

I have seen amazing results with sinus-related issues from initiating a Candida Cleanse with additional probiotics and enzymes. Colloidal Silver works wonders for many sufferers.

TOP NATURAL AIDS

- Colloidal Silver—take as directed on label
- Candida Cleanse
- Probiotics—take as directed on label
- Quercetin—300 to 1,200 mg daily
- Vitamin C with bioflavonoids—3,000 to 10,000 mg daily in divided portions
- Goldenseal—take as tea or use some of the tea to rinse nasal passages three times daily. Don't use goldenseal internally for more than 7 days at a time.
- Enzymes high in cellulase
- Bromelain reduces the inflammation associated with sinusitis. Take 500 mg three times daily between meals. Bromelain is even more effective used in conjunction with goldenseal.
- Vitamin A with mixed carotenoids—10,000 IU daily and natural beta-carotene—15,000 IU daily
- Vitamin B-complex—75 to 100 mg of each major B vitamin three times daily with meals
- Vitamin B5—100 mg three times daily with meals
- Vitamin B6—50 mg three times daily with meals
- Vitamin B12—1,000 mcg three times daily with meals
- Echinacea boosts the immune system. Take 250 to 500 mg every two hours with acute symptoms—no more than 12 hours.
- Garlic has antibacterial properties. Take 500 mg four times daily, up to ten days.

IMPORTANT AIDS

- Flaxseed Oil—1 to 2 tbsp. daily
- Bee Pollen speeds up the healing process. Start with 1 tsp. daily and gradually increase until taking 1 tbsp. daily with juice.

OTHER POTENTIAL AIDS

- Acidophilus—take as directed on label
- Serrapeptase—30 mg daily for at least three days
- Raw Thymus Glandular—500 mg twice daily
- Vitamin E (d-alpha-tocopherol form)—400 to 1,000 IU daily
- Coenzyme Q10—60 mg daily
- Zinc—15 to 25 mg twice daily (don't exceed 100 mg in one day)
- Propolis lozenges
- Alfalfa acts as an anti-inflammatory. Take as directed on label.
- Andrographis—400 mg three times daily (standardized to contain 4–6% andrographolide)
- Black Cohosh—1 to 2 tablets twice daily of standardized extract containing 1 mg of 27-deoxyacteine per tablet
- Chillis
- Eyebright tea combats hay fever.
- Golden Rod tea
- Horseradish—inhaling fresh horseradish very effectively clears the sinuses
- Lavender tea
- Nettle helps with allergies and respiratory problems—400 to 800 mg every four hours
- Olive Leaf has antibacterial and anti-inflammatory properties.
- Peppermint—use in tea form or boil a few drops of Japanese peppermint oil, thyme, tea tree oil, and chamomile and inhale the steam.
- Ribwort
- Chicken (hot soup) promotes healing and helps mucus to flow.
- Eucalyptus Oil vapors inhaled
- Tea Tree Oil vapors inhaled

- Grapefruit Seed extract diluted in water and inserted into the nostrils via an eyedropper or consumed orally in the amount of 100 mg two to three times daily.
- Red Clover helps to clear congestion.
- Tomato juice
- Oregano helps fight infection. Take 75 mg of a standardized extract three times daily.
- Sea Salt Water can be used in conjunction with a Neti Pot (designed for nasal irrigation and available at many health food stores) or inhale the steam for 5 to 10 minutes from a boiling pot (stay at least 6 inches from pot to avoid scalding).

☞ SORE THROAT

SORE THROAT is characterized by the inflammation of the pharynx (throat). As with any ailment or disorder, look for the root problem. Have you been talking too much, or is there a bacterium, fungus, or a virus?

Licorice Root tea helps many singers and speakers who have strained their vocal cords. It seems to reduce inflammation in the throat. If the throat is enlarged and sore from the lymph being swollen, Clustered Water may help as it clears the lymph.

TOP NATURAL AIDS

- Licorice soothes the throat. Take as tea or in lozenge form. Don't use licorice for more than seven days in a row, and not at all if you have high blood pressure.
- Zinc tablets sucked in the mouth—take as directed on label and don't exceed 100 mg of zinc in one day
- Vitamin C with bioflavonoids—5,000 to 20,000 mg daily. Take in divided servings or as tablets sucked in the mouth.
- Silver (especially the Mild Silver Protein form of Silver consumed orally)—take as directed on label
- Vitamin A—25,000 IU daily for one week, then reduce to 10,000 IU daily. Take in conjunction with carotenoid complex with beta-carotene as directed on label.
- Bee Propolis consumed internally or gargled protects mucous membranes and helps soothe the throat. Take as directed on label.
- Garlic—500 mg three times daily until recovered
- Echinacea—350 to 500 mg every two hours during acute phase. More effective when combined with goldenseal.
- Goldenseal—250 to 500 mg every two hours during acute phase. More effective when combined with echinacea.
- Olive Leaf is a powerful antibacterial agent. Take 250 mg four times daily of standardized extract at first symptoms.
- Grapefruit Seed—drink 3 to 5 drops of extract in a cup of

water three times daily or use 5 to 10 drops of extract in a glass of water for a gargle.

IMPORTANT AIDS

- Vitamin E—600 IU daily
- Marshmallow Root tea soothes the throat.
- Sage tea detoxifies the blood.
- Slippery Elm soothes inflamed mucous membranes.

OTHER POTENTIAL AIDS

- Bromelain
- Iodine, especially 1 ml of the povidine iodine form diluted in 20 ml of water and used as a gargle in the mouth every three to four hours.
- Blackberry juice soothes and/or heals the throat.
- Grapefruit juice
- Andrographis
- Bayberry prepared as a gargle
- Black Walnut
- Blackberry Root
- Gotu Kola—20 to 60 mg three times daily of an extract standardized to contain 40% asiaticoside, 29–30% asiatic acid, 29–30% madecassic acid, and 1–2% madecassoside
- Hawthorn assists with absorption of vitamin C.
- Myrrh fluid extract used as a gargle
- Thyme eliminates mucus and has strong antiseptic properties.
- Usnea
- White Oak works as an antiseptic.
- Wild Indigo
- Oregano Oil consumed orally or used as a gargle.
- Tea Tree Oil used as a gargle in warm water.
- Cider Vinegar used as a gargle.
- Fenugreek Seeds can reduce sore throat pain. Use 20 drops of extract in a cup of water and gargle three times daily.

- Rye Sprouts—concentrated extracts of rye sprouts such as Oralmat sprayed into the throat every four hours
- Onion poultice wrapped around the neck.
- Water
- Sea Salt Water—1 tsp. of sea salt in a glass of warm water and use as a gargle

☞ STRESS

STRESS is any issue that threatens the well-being of the body, such as injury, disease, or worry. Sixty percent of the population of the United States believe that they are under a great deal of stress at least once per week. Stress is linked to 80% of all major illnesses.

TOP NATURAL AIDS

- Vitamin C with bioflavonoids—2,500 to 5,000 mg daily
- Collagen
- Vitamin B6
- Vitamin B12—500 mcg twice daily for one month
- Vitamin B-complex—three times daily
- Gamma Aminobutyric Acid (GABA)—750 mg twice daily
- Inositol—50 mg twice daily
- Vitamin B3 (niacinamide form)—500 mg twice daily
- Vitamin B5—250 mg twice daily
- Valerian helps with sleep and can also ease stress-related headaches. Take 250 to 500 mg 30 minutes before bed of a standardized extract containing at least 0.5% valerenic acids.
- St. John's Wort—200 to 300 mg two to three times daily of a standardized extract containing 0.3% hypericin

IMPORTANT AIDS

- L-Glutamine—1,000 to 2,000 mg two to three times daily for 3 months
- Calcium—2,000 mg daily
- Magnesium—1,000 mg daily
- Zinc—30 mg daily
- Royal Jelly—3 tsp. daily
- L-Tyrosine—500 mg twice daily on an empty stomach with water or juice
- S-Adenosylmethionine (SAMe)—take as directed on label
- Siberian Ginseng prevents stress damage to the thymus gland.

Take 100 mg 30 minutes before bedtime of a standardized extract containing 0.5% eleutheroside E.

- Taurine—take as directed on label
- Adrenal Glandular Extract—150 to 200 mg twice daily for 3 weeks
- Melatonin—start with 1.5 mg daily at bedtime and gradually increase up to 5 mg daily if lower amounts are not effective
- Raw Thymus Glandular—take as directed on label
- Coenzyme Q10—30 to 100 mg daily
- Probiotic supplements with acidophilus, bifidobacteria, or both. Take as directed on label.
- Ashwagandha acts as a sedative.
- Kava Kava relaxes the mind and the body. Take 200 mg twice daily of standardized extract containing 30% kavalactones.
- Skullcap tea helps with nervous disorders.
- Korean Ginseng—100 mg twice daily of standardized extract containing 7% ginsenosides. Take in cycles of 2 to 3 weeks on, two weeks off.

OTHER POTENTIAL AIDS

- Acetyl-L-Carnitine (ALC)
- Chromium—150 to 400 mcg daily
- Potassium—100 mg daily
- Vitamin B1—100 to 500 mg daily
- Threonine
- Dehydroepiandrosterone (DHEA)—50 to 200 mg daily
- Human Growth Hormone (hGH)
- Pregnenolone—50 to 100 mg daily
- Cholesterol indirectly counteracts excessive stress.
- Phosphatidylserine—100 mg two to three times daily
- Superunsaturated Fatty Acids
- Lecithin—2,400 mg three times daily with meals
- Iron—18 to 30 mg daily, if deficient in iron
- Phosphorus

- Neurotransmitters—see Appendix A
- Panaxic Acid
- Para-aminobenzoic Acid (PABA)—300 to 400 mg daily
- Vitamin E—start with 200 IU daily, gradually increase to 400 IU daily (use supplement with mixed tocopherols)
- Reishi, Maitake, and Shiitaki Extracts all help the body handle stress. Take as directed on label.
- American Ginseng—200 mg daily of an extract standardized to contain 4–7% ginsenosides
- Astragalus—250 mg three times daily
- Catnip causes drowsiness. Take as directed on label.
- Chamomile oil used in aromatherapy aids sleep.
- Golden Root
- Gotu Kola—20 to 60 mg three times daily of an extract standardized to contain 40% asiaticoside, 29–30% asiatic acid, 29–30% madecassic acid, and 1–2% madecassoside
- Holy Basil
- Hops eases nervousness. Take 0.5 grams one to three times daily.
- Lavender oil applied topically as a massage or use 5 drops of oil in bath water.
- Licorice Root
- Maca improves the body's ability to handle stress.
- Sarsaparilla increases energy and regulates hormones.
- Schizandra

☞ SUNBURN

SUNBURN is an inflammation of the skin and is caused primarily by the UV-B rays from the sun.

TOP NATURAL AIDS

- Vitamin C with bioflavonoids—10,000 mg daily and up divided into several portions for two weeks following a sunburn. For added protection, take 2,000 mg daily consumed orally in conjunction with 1,000 IU Vitamin E for eight days prior to sunlight exposure.
- Vitamin E oil or ointment applied topically three to four times daily or, for added protection, 1,000 IU consumed orally in conjunction with 2,000 mg of vitamin C for eight days prior to sunlight exposure.
- Beta-carotene helps heal the skin. Take 25,000 IU twice daily for 3 days following a sunburn, then reduce to 10,000 IU twice daily for two weeks, then reduce to 2,500 to 5,000 IU daily.
- Aloe Vera is very effective for burns. For best results, use gel directly from the aloe vera leaf and apply to skin. If you use a commercial product, aloe should not be combined with mineral oil, paraffin waxes, alcohol, or coloring.
- Selenium lotion applied topically helps to prevent sunburn. Additionally, take 200 mcg orally daily.
- Vitamin A—25,000 IU daily for 2 weeks
- Potassium—100 mg daily
- St. John's Wort oil applied as a salve acts as a painkiller and promotes healing.
- Tea Tree Oil applied topically—use cream containing at least 5% tea tree oil.

IMPORTANT AIDS

- Zinc aids in healing. Take 15 to 30 mg twice daily with food for two weeks following a sunburn.

- L-Cysteine—500 mg daily on an empty stomach. Take with water or juice, not milk.
- Para-aminobenzoic Acid (PABA)—25 mg daily with meals
- Vitamin B6—50 mg three times daily
- Pycnogenol may reduce the risks associated with skin damage. Take as directed on label.

OTHER POTENTIAL AIDS

- Alpha-Hydroxy Acids
- Glycolic Acid applied topically to sunburned skin alleviates the pain.
- Coenzyme Q10—60 mg daily
- Colloidal Silver apply topically as directed on label.
- Lycopene is a powerful antioxidant. Take 6.5 mg daily.
- Glucose Tyrosinate added to standard sunscreens and applied topically further enhances the ability of sunscreens to protect against sunburn.
- Melatonin cream applied topically prior to sun exposure prevents sunburn.
- Methylsulfonylmethane (MSM)—500 to 2,000 mg daily consumed orally or lotion applied topically
- Vitamin B2
- Vitamin B3
- Vitamin B5 applied topically as an ingredient in skin creams.
- Green Tea helps to prevent sunburn.
- Korean Ginseng lotion applied topically.
- Gotu Kola accelerates healing. Take 200 mg twice daily of standardized extract containing 16% triterpenes.
- Fish Oils—10 grams daily administered orally
- Potato—boiled peel applied topically as a dressing accelerates the healing of sunburn
- Tomato, especially tomato paste

☞ TEETH

TEETH, used for cutting and chewing food, are embedded in a socket in the jawbone. The exposed part of the tooth (crown) is covered with enamel, and the part within the bone (root) is coated with cementum. The bulk of the tooth consists of dentine enclosing the pulp. Brush teeth with hydrogen peroxide and toothpaste to kill off fungus and bacteria.

Many years ago my husband had an abscessed tooth. The dentist said he needed a root canal immediately. The oral surgeon was out of town for a few days so they sent us home with pain meds and antibiotics. In the meantime I recalled an old recipe for this very thing, which came from Chief Two Tree in the North Carolina mountains. In three days the abscess was gone! He still needed the tooth filled, but we saved $1,200.

Chief Two Tree said to take activated charcoal to draw out the poison. Activated charcoal absorbs 15,000 times its weight; Black Walnut Hull pulls out poisons; Alfalfa is for the mineral content, and White Willow is for pain. During the first hour, make a poultice with 2 capsules of charcoal and 2 tablespoons of cooked oatmeal. Put some of the mixture in cheesecloth and keep on the tooth for 30 minutes. At the same time, take two capsules internally. Next, combine 2 of each of the other herbs with enough oatmeal to keep it together. Apply the same way and take two of each capsules internally. Repeat during all waking hours for two to three days until infection is gone.

TOP NATURAL AIDS

- Probiotic Supplement
- Calcium—1,500 mg daily. Calcium supplements that are liquid are much easier to absorb.
- Coenzyme Q10—30 to 100 mg daily
- Vitamin K—100 to 500 mcg daily
- Vitamin E—600 IU daily
- L-tyrosine—500 mg daily

- Magnesium—750 mg daily
- Vitamin C with bioflavonoids helps to maintain the health of the teeth. Take 3,000 mg daily in divided portions. Don't use chewable vitamin C as it could erode tooth enamel.

IMPORTANT AIDS

- Silica—1,000 mg daily
- Zinc—30 mg daily with 3 mg copper
- Vitamin D3—400 mg daily

OTHER POTENTIAL AIDS

- Charcoal (fine powder rubbed topically onto the teeth) whitens teeth.
- Iodine—100 to 225 mcg daily
- Phosphorus
- Collagen
- Vitamin D—400 IU daily
- Strawberries (mashed and used topically as a toothpaste) whiten the teeth.
- Flaxseeds strengthen the teeth.
- Carrot juice
- Cucumber juice
- Horsetail contains silica, which hardens tooth enamel. Mix a liquid capsule with your regular toothpaste when you brush.
- Thyme reduces the level of bacteria in the mouth.

☞ URINARY TRACT INFECTIONS

URINARY TRACT INFECTIONS are infections typically produced by detrimental bacteria of the urinary tract. They can involve the kidney, the renal pelvis, the ureter, the bladder, the urethra, or amalgamation of any of these organs. Often the entire urinary tract is affected. UTIs affect 35–40% of the population each year. The occurrence of UTIs is said to increase with age in both men and women.

Many benefits have been received by simply doing a parasite cleanse. There are parasites that live in the bladder. We have seen men and women helped by cleansing and supplementing with essential fatty acids.

TOP NATURAL AIDS

- Vitamin A—25,000 IU daily
- Vitamin C with bioflavonoids—4,000 to 5,000 mg daily in divided portions
- Body Oxygen
- Probiotics help to prevent and treat urinary tract infections. Take a probiotic supplement as directed on label.
- Essential Fatty Acids
- Zinc—50 mg with 3 mg copper daily
- Cranberries help to prevent and control urinary tract infections in 73% of patients. Drink 1 quart of pure, unsweetened cranberry juice over the course of a day, along with several glasses of quality water (preferably purer than tap water). Or take 500 mg of cranberry extract two to three times daily with large glasses of pure water until the infection clears.
- Garlic
- Grapefruit Seed extract effectively fights bacteria. Take 100 to 200 mg three times daily for ten days.
- Goldenseal helps if there is bleeding with the infection. Take 250 mg four times daily of an extract standardized to contain at least 5% total alkaloids.

IMPORTANT AIDS

- Colloidal Silver—take as directed on label.
- Potassium—100 mg daily
- Calcium—1,500 mg daily
- Magnesium—750 to 1,000 mg daily
- Vitamin E—600 IU daily
- N-Acetylcysteine—500 mg twice daily on an empty stomach
- Buchu helps with the burning sensation that sometimes accompanies an infection.
- Dandelion tea helps relieve bladder discomfort and acts as a diuretic.
- Uva Ursi (also known as Bearberry) is known for relieving urinary disorders. Take 100 mg twice daily for 3 to 4 days. Use a standardized extract and try to combine it with a soothing herb such as cornsilk, or substitute Pipsissewa for Uva Ursi.

OTHER POTENTIAL AIDS

- Berberine
- Vitamin B-complex—50 mg of each major B vitamin twice daily
- Mannose—2,500 to 5,000 mg every four to six hours or more
- Blueberries are excellent antioxidants. They may be as effective as cranberries in helping with urinary tract infections.
- Barberry
- Horseradish
- Neem
- Olive Leaf
- Oregano helps fight infection. Take 75 mg three times daily of a standardized extract.
- Oregon Grape

☞ VAGINITIS

VAGINITIS is inflammation of the vagina. It is usually caused by a chemical imbalance of the vagina or from infection. I've seen it over and over! This is related to yeast and fungus in the body. A Candida cleanse, probiotic, and enzymes that contain cellulase will be of benefit. Dietetic change is required, eliminating processed foods and white deadly things—flour, sugar, salt—and addictive coffee and sodas.

TOP NATURAL AIDS

- Candida Cleanse
- Probiotic supplement—take as directed on label
- Vitamin B-complex—50 mg of each major B vitamin twice daily
- Vitamin C with bioflavonoids—2,000 to 5,000 mg daily divided into several servings
- Biotin—300 mcg three times daily
- Aged Garlic Extract—500 mg three times daily for 10 days
- Aloe Vera helps with healing and fighting infection. It can be taken internally as juice, used in a douche, or used topically in gel form to relieve itching.
- Tea Tree Oil provides relief from herpes blisters, fungal infections, warts, and other infections. It may be used as a douche, a topical cream, or in suppository form.
- Echinacea—as directed
- Digestive Enzyme high in cellulase to break down yeast
- Pau d'arco tea several times daily—hot or cold, no sugar.
- Douche with Probiotics or Colloidal Silver

IMPORTANT AIDS

- Vitamin A can effectively take care of (senile) vaginitis. 25,000 IU daily for two weeks.
- Beta-carotene—10,000 IU twice daily
- Vitamin D3—1,000 mg daily
- Vitamin E—400 IU daily

- Calcium—1,500 mg daily
- Magnesium—1,000 mg daily
- Calendula helps heal and soothe irritated tissues. It can be used as a vaginal suppository or applied locally to the vagina.

OTHER POTENTIAL AIDS

- Insufficient production of estrogens may cause vaginitis.
- Supplemental, natural, exogenous progesterone cream applied topically to the vagina alleviates vaginitis.
- Yogurt can be taken internally or applied directly to the vagina. Use plain yogurt that contains live yogurt cultures.
- Olive Leaf—250 mg of standardized extract four times daily for one week
- Apple Cider Vinegar—add 3 cups to bath water to treat vaginitis
- Cinnamon and dandelion both inhibit the growth of Candida. They can be used in a douche or taken orally.
- Overgrowth of Candida may cause vaginitis. Please see Candida.

☞ VARICOSE VEINS

VARICOSE VEINS are a disorder in which the veins (usually in the legs) become swollen, extended, and twisted. The fundamental cause of varicose veins is a deficiency of tone in the tissues supporting the vein and later the breakdown in the valves further up (typically) the leg. I have had much success with those who will exercise and lose weight. Clustered Water and Horsetail have been beneficial for many with circulation problems.

TOP NATURAL AIDS

- Coenzyme Q10—100 mg daily
- Essential Fatty Acids—take 500 to 1,000 mg twice daily of black currant seed, borage, or evening primrose oil daily
- Flaxseed Oil—1 to 2 tbsp. daily
- Vitamin C—1,000 mg; with mixed bioflavonoids, 100 mg—three times daily
- Vitamin B-complex—50 mg twice daily with meals
- Vitamin E—200 IU twice daily, gradually increased to 400 IU three times daily. After 3 weeks at highest level, go back to 200 IU twice daily.
- Troxerutin—500 to 4,000 mg daily
- Bilberry strengthens the walls of the veins. Take 20 to 20 mg three times daily of a product containing 25% anthocyanidins. Don't take bilberry if you are already taking pine bark or grape seed extract.
- Gingko Biloba—three times daily
- Horse Chestnut—10 drops of tincture in liquid three times daily, or 500 mg of Horse Chestnut seed extract standardized to contain 20% escin daily or use as a topical salve
- Grape Seed extract—50 mg two to three times daily

IMPORTANT AIDS

- Glutathione
- Vitamin A—10,000 IU daily

- Vitamin B6—50 mg daily
- Vitamin B12—300 to 1,000 mcg daily
- Vitamin D3—1,000 mg daily; with calcium, 1,500 mg daily; with magnesium, 750 mg daily, all at bedtime
- Lecithin—1,200 mg three times daily with meals
- Zinc—80 mg plus 3 mg copper daily
- Butcher's Broom—300 to 500 mg three times daily
- Witch Hazel ointment applied topically two to three times daily for at least two weeks.

OTHER POTENTIAL AIDS

- Chelation Suppositories with Ethylene-Diamine-Tetra-Acetate (EDTA), the synthetic amino acid used in chelation therapy, alleviates varicose veins.
- Proteases as used in enzyme therapy.
- Bayberry tea applied topically to the legs.
- Calendula applied topically.
- Dandelion Root helps reduce pain. Take as juice or tea twice daily for 4 to 6 weeks.
- Gotu Kola—200 mg twice daily of standardized extract containing 16% triterpenes.
- Hawthorn—100 to 200 mg three times daily of an extract standardized to contain 1.8% vitexin-2 rhamnosides
- Noni consumed orally—4 ounces of juice 30 minutes before breakfast or 2 tbsp. daily of liquid concentrate
- Apple Cider Vinegar can help reduce pain and improve circulation. Saturate a cloth with it and apply compress for 15 to 20 minutes twice daily.

☞ WRINKLES

WRINKLES are visible furrowing on the surface of the skin. I said previously that we do not get toxic because we get old, we age because we are toxic. We must cleanse the harmful toxins from the body and supplement with the right nutrients. Personally, I have seen liquid Collagen do wonders for my appearance along with vitamin C and water, water, water.

TOP NATURAL AIDS

- Methylsulfonylmethane (MSM)—take as directed on label
- Evening Primrose Oil—1,000 mg three times daily
- Vitamin A—25,000 IU daily for three months, then reduce to 15,000 IU daily
- Vitamin B-complex—50 mg of each major B vitamin
- Vitamin B12—1,000 to 2,000 mcg daily
- Collagen liquid—1 tbsp. with 1,000 mg vitamin C before bed.
- Clustered Water—8 ounces or more daily

IMPORTANT AIDS

- Kelp—1,000 to 1,500 mg daily
- Selenium—200 mcg daily
- Alpha-Hydroxy Acids (especially Glycolic Acid and Lactic Acid)
- Vitamin C with bioflavonoids—3,000 to 5,000 mg daily in divided portions
- Vitamin E administered orally or applied topically—start with 400 IU daily and gradually increase to 800 IU daily. Take with evening primrose oil.
- Zinc—50 mg with 3 mg copper daily
- Grape Seed extract applied topically or consumed orally.

OTHER POTENTIAL AIDS

- Chelation Suppositories with Ethylene-Diamine-Tetra-Acetate (EDTA)
- Beta-Glucans applied topically.

- Hyaluronic Acid applied topically or consumed orally or by injection (called Restilin and given by a dermatologist to hydrate the skin).
- Papain applied topically or ingested orally.
- Superoxide Dismutase (SOD) cream applied topically.
- Dehydroepiandrosterone (DHEA) administered either orally or applied topically as DHEA skin cream.
- Post-menopausal women using (natural) Progesterone cream applied topically.
- Pregnenolone cream applied topically.
- Progesterone cream applied topically helps to remove fine wrinkles.
- Premature wrinkles can occur as a result of silicon deficiency.
- Stretch marks can occur after pregnancy as a result of silicon deficiency.
- Coenzyme Q10 applied topically.
- Lipoic Acid (1% cream/lotion) applied topically.
- Para-aminobenzoic Acid (PABA)
- Vitamin A applied topically.
- Vitamin B5
- Vitamin D3—400 IU daily
- Vitamin K applied topically.
- Glucosamine Sulfate—take as directed on label
- Calcium—1,500 mg daily
- Magnesium—750 mg daily
- Bee Pollen
- Bovine Colostrum applied topically.
- Flaxseed Oil capsules—1,000 mg daily or 1 tsp. liquid
- Royal Jelly cream applied topically.
- Grape juice applied topically.
- Chamomile, especially German chamomile, applied topically.
- Emu Oil applied topically.
- Alfalfa
- Burdock root
- Red Raspberry
- Thyme

APPENDIX A
BENEFICIAL AT-HOME HEALTH TESTS *and* FORMULAS

NEUROTRANSMITTERS

IN 1921 AN AUSTRIAN SCIENTIST NAMED OTTO LOEWI DISCOVERED neurotransmitters—chemicals that act as electrical switches and transmit nerve impulses from one nerve cell to another in the brain. Neurotransmitters are basically responsible for transmitting data. If you are deficient of neurotransmitters, you basically have a power failure and there are blips in the brain. For example, if you are telling someone a story and suddenly a specific piece of information is missing, you just had a short circuit.

Major neurotransmitters are acetylcholine, dopamine, gamma-aminobutyricacid (GABA), norepinephrine, and serotonin. These neurotransmitters are responsible for major bodily functions. Once again, we emphasize the importance of the diet to supply the body with vital nutrients.

Serotonin, for example, is considered essential for relaxation, sleep, and concentration. A lack of serotonin can influence behaviors such as depression, suicide, impulse aggression, alcoholism, sexual deviance, and explosive rage. An overabundance of serotonin is linked to masked aggression, obsessive compulsion, fearfulness, lack of self-confidence, and shyness. Women only produce two-thirds as much serotonin as men. This is believed to be the reason women are more susceptible to serotonin-related disorders such as depression and obesity.

Norepinephrine is the neurotransmitter also known as adrenaline, which is key to the fight or flight response. It also affects the heart and blood vessels as well as the ability to focus your attention. A deficiency of dopamine is directly related to Parkinson's disease. Acetylcholine is possibly the most widely used neurotransmitter in the body, essential for sustaining the memory and the ability to learn.

If you notice any of the symptoms listed above, it is vital to be tested for your neurotransmitters. Home kits are available with consultation from Silver Creek Labs. Contact our office for this vital tool.

CANDIDA

It is estimated that over 90% of the U. S. population has some degree of Candida overgrowth. What is *Candida Albicans*? It is a yeast organism that normally lives in the mouth, on your skin, and in your intestinal tract. If you are a female, it can also live in the vagina.

In a normal healthy body, the immune system and the "friendly bacteria" that inhabit the intestinal tract keep Candida overgrowth under control. However, in today's polluted and stressful environment and with less than perfect dietary habits, most of us do not live at our maximum health potential. When our immune system is weak, or we have taken a series of antibiotics, the natural balance of our body is disturbed. Antibiotics are prescribed to eliminate unhealthy bacteria in the body. However, they also eliminate healthy or "good" bacteria, enabling the Candida organism to multiply unchecked.

Candida is a living organism which excretes toxic waste. This can lead to a variety of problems including: poor digestion, fatigue, bloating, gas, poor elimination, mood swings, sugar and carbohydrate cravings, head pain, brain fog, female issues, skin rashes, lowered immunity, cold hands or feet, and much more. Not only does a diet of excessive sugar and carbohydrates contribute toward increased susceptibility, but oral contraceptives and chemicals found in today's food and drinks play a major role as well. People who have been battling chronic symptoms such as fatigue and low immunity without relief should explore that possibility of Candida overgrowth and take the necessary steps to alleviate this condition.

The following self-analysis is provided for educational purposes only. It is not intended to diagnose, treat, cure, or prevent disease. Diagnosis and treatment of specific health conditions should be completed by a health-care practitioner.

1. During your lifetime, have you taken any antibiotics or tetracyclines (symycin, Panmycin,
   Vibramycin, Monicin, etc.) for acne or other
   conditions for more than one month?   25 pts.
2. Have you taken a broad-spectrum antibiotic for
   more than 2 months or 4 or more times in a
   1-year period? These could include any antibiotics taken for respiratory, urinary, or other
   infections.   20 pts.
3. Have you taken a broad-spectrum antibiotic
   even for a single course? These antibiotics
   include ampicillin, amoxicillin, Keflex, etc.   6 pts.
4. Have you ever had problems with persistent
   Prostatitis, vaginitis, or other problems with
   your reproductive organs?   25 pts.
5. Women   Have you been pregnant?
   2 or more times?   5 pts.
   1 time?   3 pts.
6. Women—Have you taken birth control pills?
   More than 2 years?   15 pts.
   More than 6 months?   8 pts.
7. If you were NOT breast-fed as an infant.   9 pts.
8. Have you taken any cortisone-type drugs
   (Prednisone, Decadron, etc.)?   15 pts.

9. Are you sensitive to and bothered by exposure
to perfumes, insecticides, or other chemical
odors . . .   20 pts.
Do you have moderate to severe symptoms?   20 pts.
Mild symptoms?   5 pts.
10. Does tobacco smoke bother you?   10 pts.
11. Are your symptoms worse on damp, muggy
days or in moldy places?   20 pts.
12. If you have had chronic fungus infections of
the skin or nails (including athlete's foot, ring-
worm, jock itch), have the infections been . . .
Severe or persistent?   20 pts.
Mild to moderate?   10 pts.
13. Do you crave sugar (chocolate, ice cream,
candy, cookies, etc.)?   10 pts.
14. Do you crave carbohydrates (bread, bread,
and more bread)?   10 pts.
15. Do you crave alcoholic beverages?   10 pts.
16. Have you drunk or do you drink chlorinated
water (city or tap)?   20 pts.
TOTAL   _____

SCORE YOUR SYMPTOMS

For each of your symptoms, enter the corresponding number in
the point score column.

No symptoms .0
Occasional or mild 3
Frequent or moderately severe 6
Severe and/or disabling 9

SYMPTOMS   **POINTS**
1. Constipation   _____
2. Diarrhea   _____
3. Bloating   _____
4. Fatigue or lethargy   _____

5. Feeling drained   _____

6. Poor memory   _____

7. Difficulty focusing/brain fog   _____

8. Feeling moody or despaired   _____

9. Numbness, burning, or tingling   _____

10. Muscle aches   _____

11. Nasal congestion or discharge   _____

12. Pain and/or swelling in the joints   _____

13. Abdominal pain   _____

14. Spots in front of the eyes   _____

15. Erratic vision   _____

16. Cold hands and/or feet   _____

17. Women—endometriosis   _____

18. Women—menstrual irregularities   _____

19. Women—premenstrual tension   _____

20. Women—vaginal discharge   _____

21. Women—persistent vaginal
    burning or itching   _____

22. Men—prostatitis   _____

23. Men—impotence   _____

24. Loss of sexual desire   _____

25. Low blood sugar   _____

26. Anger or frustration   _____

27. Dry patchy skin   _____

TOTAL   _____

CANDIDA SELF-TEST

For each of your symptoms, enter the appropriate figure in the point score column.

No symptoms .0

Occasional or mild 3

Frequent or moderately severe 6

Severe and/or disabling 9

1. Heartburn   _____
2. Indigestion   _____
3. Belching and intestinal gas   _____
4. Drowsiness   _____
5. Itching   _____
6. Rashes   _____
7. Irritability or jitters   _____
8. Uncoordinated   _____
9. Inability to concentrate   _____
10. Frequent mood swings   _____
11. Postnasal drip   _____
12. Nasal itching   _____
13. Failing vision   _____
14. Burning or tearing of the eyes   _____
15. Recurrent infections or fluid in the ears   _____
16. Ear pain or deafness   _____
17. Headaches   _____
18. Dizziness/loss of balance   _____
19. Pressure above the ears—your head feels as though it is swelling   _____
20. Mucus in the stools   _____
21. Hemorrhoids   _____
22. Dry mouth   _____
23. Rash or blisters in the mouth   _____
24. Bad breath   _____
25. Sore or dry throat   _____
26. Cough   _____
27. Pain or tightness in the chest   _____
28. Wheezing or shortness of breath   _____
29. Urinary urgency or frequency   _____
30. Burning during urination   _____

TOTAL   _____

CANDIDA SELF-ANALYSIS RESULTS

Total Score from Section 1   _____

Total Score from Section 2   _____

Total Score from Section 3   _____

TOTAL SCORE   _____

If your score is at least:	Your symptoms are:
180 Women / 140 Men	Almost certainly yeast connected
120 Women / 90 Men	Probably yeast connected
60 Women / 40 Men	Possibly yeast connected

If your score is less than:	
60 Women / 40 Men	Probably not yeast connected

If you scored below 60 for women or 40 for men, WAY TO GO! You are probably not plagued with the symptoms of *Candida Albicans*. You are obviously following a very healthy lifestyle, and you deserve a huge pat on the back! However, if your score was above 60 for women or 40 for men, you may want to consider looking into a means to get the *Candida* overgrowth under control.

THYROID— THE BASAL TEMPERATURE TEST

Since the thyroid gland controls your metabolism, one simple measure of your metabolic rate is your body temperature, which can be observed by both you and your physician. This temperature test should be done immediately upon awakening in the morning and before you get out of bed. Here are the specific steps that should be taken:

1. If you are male or a non-menstruating female, take an oral mercury thermometer that has been shaken down below 95 degrees and placed at the bedside the previous evening. When you wake up, place the thermometer under your arm with the bulb in the armpit and no clothing between it and the armpit for 10 minutes. This reading

taken in the armpit is somewhat lower and somewhat more accurate than by mouth. Repeat the test five days in a row. This is known as your Early AM Basal Temperature. Normal temperature ranges from 97.8 degrees to 98.2 degrees. If your temperature is low, your thyroid gland is probably underactive.

2. If you are a female who menstruates, do the above test on the second and third day of your period in the same manner.

3. If you have a very young child and are unable to take his/her armpit temperature, you can take the rectal temperature for two minutes. Normal would be 1 degree higher than the above—that is 98.8 degrees to 99.2 degrees.

4. Record your results below and bring this record to your physician.

RESULTS   **TEMPERATURE**
Date:_____   Day 1: _____
Date:_____   Day 2: _____
Date:_____   Day 3: _____
Date:_____   Day 4: _____
Date:_____   Day 5: _____

If your Barnes Basal Temperature Test reveals a consistently below-normal temperature, ask your physician for more than the usual thyroid panel of tests. Ask for the TSH (thyroid stimulating hormone) test, which is a more accurate index of thyroid functions. If your blood tests are normal, but you haven't been tested for thyroid antibodies, insist on this as a next step.

COFFEE ENEMA

Utilizing a standard enema bag, the coffee is absorbed directly through the colon wall and goes via the portal vein directly to the liver. It stimulates the liver to produce bile and could cause nausea. If it is too great, reduce the amount of coffee used or use the enema on a full stomach. The coffee should be stronger than for drinking. Do not dilute the coffee.

This enema is most often used in metabolic cancer therapy and is extremely valuable in many successful detoxification programs. Coffee enemas alkalinize the first part of the intestines, enhance enzyme function, and stimulate the production and release of bile. Enemas, however, do tend to delete the potassium level; therefore, care must be taken for proper supplementation.

The type of coffee to be used is ground (drip coffee), not instant or decaffeinated. Mix 2 tbsp. coffee to 1 qt. steam distilled water at body temperature—2 cups, twice daily.

Take this enema preferably on your knees or lie down on your back, legs drawn close to abdomen, and breathe deeply while enema is given slowly. Retain fluid 10 to 15 minutes.

Coffee enemas are given for stimulation and detoxification of the liver, not for the function of cleansing the intestines.

To detoxify in serious conditions, take two coffee enemas per day. Follow this routine for two weeks, then coffee enemas should be reduced to only one per week for one month. Your body may have a build-up of toxins or poisons from time to time. Symptoms indicating toxicity are a decrease in appetite, headaches, increase in tiredness, and a general lack of well-being. When these occur, increase coffee enemas once again to one per day until symptoms subside, or for a maximum of three to four days. Then return to a routine.

When doing enemas, be sure to supplement with blackstrap molasses to replace deleted potassium. 1 tablespoon with 4 ounces of organic milk or rice or almond milk gives 435 mgs of potassium. Take with every enema.

STANLEY BURROUGHS' MASTER CLEANSE

Another favorite juice preparation is Stanley Burroughs' "Master Cleanser." In a gallon of steam-distilled water, mix the juice of five fresh lemons and a half cup of grade B maple syrup. Add one or more tablespoons of hot cayenne pepper (at least 90,000 heat units) to your taste tolerance. This is especially good for alkalinizing the body and raising body temperature to help resolve infection and flu-type illnesses.

APPENDIX B
SUGGESTED PROFESSIONAL SERVICES

Acupuncture. This professionally provided service may help some specific diseases, alleviating pain and promoting overall well-being. Tiny needles are inserted along the body's meridians, allowing energy to flow and hopefully healing occurs.

Applied Kinesiology. The idea here is that muscles correspond to specific bodily organs, and that a weak muscle may be an indication of a weak organ. This diagnostic procedure may be done by a practitioner or the patient and involves testing for muscle strength. This test is also useful in determining what health products may be beneficial to the patient. One form of this procedure requires the patient to hold the supplement in their hand while another person applies pressure to the other arm that is horizontally extended. If the patient's resistance is enhanced, the supplement is deemed of value. Conversely, if the arm is weakened, the material in question may be deemed unhelpful.

Chelation Therapy. It is estimated that up to 25% of the American population suffers from heavy metal poisoning to some extent. The primary form of chelation is administered by a medical doctor through an intravenous drip. However, an alternative is also available in suppository form and gives the individual the opportunity to administer this valuable resource to themselves at home. Usually 30 to 40 treatments are recommended in either protocol. The primary substance used is EDTA, which has been found to remove heavy metals, excess calcium, plaque, and improve blood circulation. Many health-care professionals now consider chelation as a viable alternative to coronary bypass surgery and angioplasty. This procedure has also proven valuable in anti-aging and arthritic conditions. Many individuals experience improved motor skills and enhanced mental functions. Many of the doctors listed in Appendix C provide this service.

Chiropractic. Promotes self-healing through the manipulation of the body by a licensed chiropractor. There are over 20 different chiropractic techniques, which all originated with the founder, Chiropractic B. J. Palmer. Dr. Palmer said the Master Maker of the human body did not create you and then run off and leave you masterless. He stayed on the job as the fellow within, as nerve transmissions, controlling every function of life. Chiropractic has and is helping millions of people naturally, and chiropractors may now be found in almost every locale.

Colonic Irrigation. A healthy colon provides the foundation for a truly healthy body. Colon Therapy provides a safe and gentle method of treatment and form of healing procedure in which very large quantities of liquids are infused into the colon via the rectum, a few pints at a time, to wash away and remove its contents. CI differs from an enema, which involves using a smaller amount of liquid into the rectum only. A "high colonic" may involve the use of twenty or more gallons pumped by a machine or transmitted with an apparatus that relies upon gravity to achieve its purpose.

Stress, travel, and improper nutrition may cause constipation or sluggish bowel movements. It is possible for the walls of the intestines to accumulate feces and mucous from months or years of intestinal cramming. This prevents the colon from proper absorption and elimination, and foods may remain undigested. Wastes from the blood arrive at the inner wall of the colon and cannot pass through this area packed with hardened feces and mucous, so they may be reabsorbed into the body. Add to this the toxins resulting from the fermentation and putrefaction of undigested food, and it's easy to imagine the need for colon therapy.

During this thirty-minute to one-hour procedure, it is common to see mucous, whole food, rubbery-like substance, parasites, Candida, and other undesirable waste pass through the viewing tube.

Enzyme Therapy. Positive research regarding this therapy is growing, but even now enzyme therapy shows undeniable links to anti-aging and the following maladies—circulatory problems, HIV, herpes, cancer, skin disorders, arthritis, bursitis, cancer, digestive disorders, back pain, multiple sclerosis, immune deficiencies, and viruses. Enzymes are obtained naturally from fruit, vegetables, and other living foods; they are also available in supplemental form via capsules and tablets. We recommend Collodial minerals derived from plant enzymes and other ancient sources in a liquid that is quickly absorbed and utilized by the body.

Massage. A list of massage techniques includes Swedish, Rolfing, Hellerwork, reflexology, shiatsu, deep-tissue massage, Trager, Feldenkrais, and craniosacral. Rolfing and Hellerwork are the most intense forms but may provide the best possible results, such as enhanced breathing, corrected posture, tolerance to stress, and heightened energy levels. These do come with a price in that sessions are intense and painful at times, but carry a bevy of rewards that may even include emotional well-being. Other forms of massage are more gentle and soothing. They promote relaxation, improved circulation, lymph movement, and other benefits. Massage is practiced more outside of the United States, but with each passing year this ancient treasure is adopted by more health conscious Americans.

Oxygen Therapy. Anaerobic or bad bacteria cannot live in an oxygen-rich environment, thus promoting life and energy to cells throughout the body. There are several kinds of Oxygen Therapy: Intravenous, Hyperbaric, and Ozone. Also enhancing oxygen baths and liquid supplements are available at most health food stores. Some ailments that have been helped with these therapies are carbon monoxide poisoning, gangrene, wounds that do not heal, strokes, lead poisoning, viral problems, flesh-eating bacteria, Lyme disease, hepatitus B, hepatitus C, HIV, herpes, arthritis, respiratory conditions, multiple sclerosis, STDs, parasites, AIDS, sickle-cell anemia, and cancer. Ask one of the physicians listed in Appendix C for more information and availability.

Reflexology. This technique is based on the premise that every organ, muscle, nerve, and gland has a corresponding reflex point located in the hands and feet. Manipulation of any one of these reflex points causes blood to flow and increase circulation to and in the point of interest. Through this manipulation the nerve endings are stimulated and begin to communicate with the desired organ, muscle, nerve, or gland, thus promoting natural healing mechanisms to

APPENDIX C

AMERICA'S LEADING COMPLEMENTARY ALTERNATIVE MEDICAL DOCTORS

THE ACAM (AMERICAN COLLEGE FOR ADVANCEMENT IN MEDICINE) is a medical society devoted to the education of medical professionals. The following list of more than 775 of America's leading complimentary alternative medical doctors is information provided on its Web site (www.acam.org) and is for educational purposes only. ACAM does not provide medical advice to the public. Please check with a physician if you suspect you are ill or are in need of specific medical advice. ACAM does offer the public two excellent resources: (**1**) A doctor search, and (**2**) ACAM book catalog.

A—allergy
AA—anti-aging
AN—anesthesiology
AC—acupuncture
AR—arthritis
AU—auriculotherapy
BA—bariatrics
CD—cardiovascular disease
CT—chelation therapy
CS—chest disease
DD—degenerative disease
DIA—diabetes
END—endocrinology
FP—family practice
GD—general dentistry
GE—gastroenterology
GP—general practice
GER—geriatrics
GYN—gynecology
HGL—hypoglycemia
HO—hyperbaric oxygen
HOM—homeopathy
HYP—hypnosis
IM—internal medicine
LM—legal medicine
MM—metabolic medicine

NT—nutrition
OBS—obstetrics
OD—orthodontia
OME—orthomolecular
  medicine
ON—oncology
OPH—ophthalmology
OSM—osteopathic
  manipulation
PD—pediatrics
PM—preventive medicine
PMR—physical medicine
  & rehabilitation
P—psychiatry
PO—psychiatry
  (orthomolecular)
PH—public health
P/S—prolotherapy/
  sclerotherapy
PUD—pulmonary diseases
R—radiology
RHU—rheumatology
RHI—rhinology
S—surgery
WR—weight reduction
YS—yeast syndrome

ALABAMA

BIRMINGHAM

Lymon Fritz, MD
3401 Independence Dr., #241
Birmingham, AL 35209
(205) 877-8585
AA,HRT,CT,WR,BA,NT

Michael S. Vaughn, MD
One Lakeshore Dr., #100
Birmingham, AL 35209
(205) 930-2950
DIA,FP,IM,NT,PM,YS,AA

Glen Wilcoxson, MD
5501 Hwy. 280 East
Birmingham, AL 35242
(205) 995-5020
BA,CT,NT,PM,RHU,YS

DAPHNE

Glen P. Wilcoxson, MD
P.O. Box 1347
Daphne, AL 36526
(251) 447-0333/888-4
FAX (251) 447-0009
BA,CT,NT,PM,RHU,YS

FAIRHOPE

Edward D. Hubbard, MD
761-A Middle Avenue
Fairhope, AL 36532
(251) 990-0662
CT,DD,GP,HYP,P/S

Charles Runels Jr., MD
82 Plantation Pointe
Fairhope, AL 36532
(334) 625-2612
FAX (334) 625-2615
BA,CT,DIA,PMR,IM,CD

GULF SHORES

Gregory S. Funk, DO, BPCT
2103 W. 1st Street
Gulf Shores, AL 36547
(251) 968-2441
FAX (251) 968-5555
FP,GP,OS

HEFLIN

Gus J. Prosch Jr., MD
P.O. Box 427
Helflin, AL 36264
(205) 222-0960
FAX (256) 748-3126
A,AR,CT,GP,NT,OME

MONTGOMERY

Teresa D. Allen, DO, APCT
7047 Halcyon Park Drive
Montgomery, AL 36117
(334) 273-0904
FAX (334) 273-0905
CT,IM,NT,YS,PM,P/S

Scott Bell, MD
7020 Sydney Curve
Montgomery, AL 36117
(334) 277-5363
FAX (334) 277-5362
PM,IM,CT,AA

OXFORD

Jose Oblena, MD
1720 Hwy. 78 East, #11
Oxford, AL 36203
(256) 835-2366
FAX (256) 835-2017
IM

ALASKA

ANCHORAGE

Sandra Denton, MD, APCT
Alaska Alternative Medicine Clinic,
LLC
333 Denali Street, #100
Anchorage, AK 99503
(907) 563-6200
FAX (907) 561-4933
A,AC,AR,HO,CD,CT,DD,DIA,END,
FP,NT,HRT

KODIAK

Ronald Brockman, DO
P.O. Box 95
Kodiak, AK 99615
(907) 563-9166
FAX (907) 563-9466
AR,OSM,S

SOLDOTNA

Robert Thompson, MD, BPCT

161 N. Binkley St., #201
Soldotna, AK 99669
(907) 260-6914
FAX (907) 260-6924
OB-GYN

ARIZONA

AJO

Patrick Mulcahy, DO
410 N. Malacate
Ajo, AR 85321
(520) 387-5706
FAX (520) 387-6036
NT,FP,OSM,PM,WR,YS

CAVE CREEK

Frank W. George, DO, MD (H),
BPCT
6748 E. Lone Mountain Rd.
Cave Creek, AZ 85331
(480) 595-5508
FAX (480) 575-1570
CT,DD,GP,MM,NT,OS

FLAGSTAFF

Marnie Vail, MD, BPCT
702 North Beaver Street
Flagstaff, AZ 86001
(928) 214-9774
FAX (928) 214-9772
FP,HOM,CT

GLENDALE

Lloyd D. Armold, DO, MD (H), APCT
7200 W. Bell Rd., #G-103
Glendale, AZ 85308
(623) 939-8916
FAX (623) 486-8973
AR,CT,FP,HPT,PM,OSM

MESA

Thomas J. Grade, MD
6309 E. Baywood Ave.
Mesa, AZ 85206
(480) 325-3801
FAX (480) 325-3805
AC,AN,AU,CT,IM,PUD

William W. Halcomb, DO, MD, MD (H)
4323 E. Broadway, #109
Mesa, AZ 85206
(602) 832-3014
FAX (602) 832-5216
A,CT,GP,HO,OSM,PM

Charles D. Schwengel, DO, MD (H)
1215 E. Brown Road, #12
Mesa, AZ 85203
(480) 668-1448
FAX (480) 668-1448
CT,HOM,P/S,AC,OSM,HPT

PARKER

Jeff A. Baird, DO, BPCT
1413 – 16th Street
Parker, AZ 85344
(928) 669-9229
AC,CT,FP,OS,AA,HPT,HRT,P/S,UV

PAYSON

Garry F. Gordon, MD, DO, MD (H), APCT
708 E. Hwy., 260, Bldg. C-1, #F
Payson, AZ 85541
(928) 472-4263
FAX (928) 474-3819
CD,CT,ON,IM,MM,NT,AA,PM,LM,DD

PHOENIX

Edward C. Kondrot, MD, BPCT
2001 W. Camelback Rd., #150
Phoenix, AZ 85015
(602) 347-7950
CT,NT,HOM

Stanley R. Olsztyn, MD (H)
4350 E. Camelback Rd., #B-220
Phoenix, AZ 85018
(602) 840-8424
FAX (602) 840-8545
A,CT,PM,DD,AR,HPT,HOM,NT,WR,YS

Geoffrey Radoff, MD (H)
2525 W. Greenway Rd., #210
Phoenix, AZ 85018
(602) 993-0200
FAX (602) 993-0207
FP

Bruce H. Shelton, MD (H), BPCT
14231 N. 7th Street, #A2
Phoenix, AZ 85022
(602) 504-1000
FAX (602) 504-1008
A,AA,DD,FP,HOM,HPT,UV,PT,CT,HRT,OME,YS

Linda C. Wright, MD, MD (H), BPCT
Alliance Health & Rehabilitation
Phoenix, AZ 85032
(602) 485-8000
FAX (602) 485-8010
A,CT,HGL,NT,PM,YS,PMR

SCOTTSDALE

Gordon H. Josephs, DO, MD (H), APCT
7315 E. Evans Road
Scottsdale, AZ 85260
(480) 998-9232
FAX (480) 998-1528
CT,CD,DIA,NT,OME,YS,UV,HPT,AC,PT

Alan K. Ketover, MD, MD (H)
10595 N. Tatum Blvd., #E-146
Scottsdale, AZ 85253
(602) 381-0800
FAX (602) 381-0054
A,CT,HOM,NT,PM,YS,Env. Med.

Warren M. Levin, MD
11659 E. Bloomfield Drive
Scottsdale, AZ 85259
(480) 209-1844
FAX (480) 209-1846
A,AC,CT,NT,OME,PM

SEDONA

Lester Adler, MD
40 Soldiers Pass Rd., #12
Sedona, AZ 86336
(520) 282-2520
CT,GP,IM,MM,NT,P/S,PM

Mark E. Laursen, MD
150 Thunderbird Drive
Sedona, AZ 86336
(520) 204-0023
FAX (520) 204-1571
GP,Emerg. Med.

Annemarie S. Welch, MD
2301 West Hwy. 89A, #104
Sedona, AZ 86336
(520) 282-0609
FAX (928) 282-9401
IM,CT,NT,YS,DD,PM

SHOW LOW

William W. Halcomb, DO, MD, MD (H),
2000 N. 16th Avenue
Show Low, AZ 85901
(602) 832-3014
FAX (602) 832-5216
A,CT,GP,HO,OSM,PM

TUCSON

Alexander P. Cadoux, MD (H),
APCT
6884 E. Sunrise Dr., #160
Tucson, AZ 85750
(520) 529-9665
FAX (520) 529-9669
A,CT,FP,MM,NT,PM

ARKANSAS

LITTLE ROCK

Norbert J. Becquet, MD, FACAM,
APCT
613 Main Street
Little Rock, AR 72201
(501) 375-4419
FAX (501) 375-4067
AR,CT,OPH,PM,RHU,Pain Control

SPRINGDALE

Jeffrey R. Baker, MD
900 Dorman St., #E
Springdale, AR 72762
(479) 756-3251
CT,FP,NT,PM,YS,GP

CALIFORNIA

ATASCADERO

Carmelo A. Plateroti, DO, BPCT
8548 El Camino Real
Atascadero, CA 93422
(805) 462-2262
FAX (805) 462-2264
CT,NT,PM,HPT,YS,AA

AZUSA

William C. Bryce, MD, DO, PhD
400 N. San Gabriel Ave.
Az, CA 91702
(626) 334-1407
FAX (626) 334-1116
AA,END,CT,NT,PM,WR

BAKERSFIELD

Shivinder S. Deol, MD
4000 Stockdale Hwy. Ste.D
Bakersfield, CA 93309
(661) 325-7452
FAX (661) 325-7456
P/S,WR,NT,PM,HGL,DD,AA,AR,BA,
DIA,FP,HRT

BEVERLY HILLS

Cathie-Ann Lippman, MD
291 S. La Cienega Bl., Suite 207
Beverly Hills, CA 90211
(310) 289-8430
A,AC,PM,YS,EV,HOM

BURBANK

Maxwell Cotter, MD
500 E. Olive Ave., #102
Burbank, CA 91501
(818) 843-2415
FAX (818) 843-6253
GP,HOM,PM,FP,IM,P

David J. Edwards, MD
2202 W. Magnolia
Burbank, CA 91506
(818) 842-4184 (800)
A,AR,CD,CT,NT,OME,RHU,WR,YS

Douglas Hunt, MD
3808 Riverside Dr., #510
Burbank, CA 91505
(818) 566-9889
FAX (818) 566-9879
A,BA,CT,HGL,MM,NT,PM,AA,YS,WR,
DIA

Nancy T. Mullan, MD
2829 West Burbank Blvd., #202
Burbank, CA 91505
(818) 954-9267
FAX (818) 954-0620
A,HRT,NT,PO,YS,WR

BURNEY

Charles K. Dahlgren, MD
37491 Enterprise Dr., #C
Burney, CA 96013
(530) 335-3833
A,NT,RHI,S

CARMEL

Denise Mark, MD, APCT
Monterey Bay Wellness
Carmel, CA 93923
(831) 642-9266
FAX (831) 642-9276
DIA,DD,IM,PM,Natural Horm.

Jerry Wyker, MD
25530 Rio Vista Drive
Carmel, CA 93923
(831) 625-0911
FAX (831) 625-0467
CT,AA,NT,PM,HOM

CARMEL VALLEY

Howard Press, MD
13748 Center St., #B
Carmel Valley, CA 93924
(831) 659-5373
FAX (831) 659-5290
CT,DD,FP,NT,PM,YS

CARMICHAEL

Bernard McGinity, MD
6945 Fair Oaks Blvd.
Carmichael, CA 95608
(916) 485-4556
FAX (916) 485-1491
GP,AC,HYP,NT,YS,HPT,PT

Philip J. Reilly, MD
4800 Manzanita Ave., #17
Carmichael, CA 95608
(916) 488-9524
AU,FP,P/S,AA,HPT,NT,OSM,P/S,PT

CLOVIS

John Nelson, MD
684 Medical Center Dr. E., #106
Clovis, CA 93611
(559) 299-0224
FAX (559) 299-4201
CD,CT,DIA,NT,AA,END

CONCORD

John Toth, MD, APCT
2299 Bacon St., #10
Concord, CA 94520
(925) 687-9447
FAX (925) 687-9483
A,CD,CT,GP,HGL,NT

COVINA

James Privitera, MD
256 W. San Bernadino Ave.
Covina, CA 91723
(626) 966-1618
FAX (626) 966-7226
A,CT,MM,NT

DIAMOND BAR

Hitendra Shah, MD
23341 Golden Springs Dr., #208
Diamond Bar, CA 91765
(909) 860-2610
FAX (909) 860-1192
AA,CT,DIA,FP,HGL,P/S,YS

EL CAJON

Neil W. Hirschenbein,
MD,PhD,CCN,CNS,AHMA
1685 E. Main St., #301
El Cajon, CA 92021
(619) 579-8681
FAX (619) 579-0759
IM,AA,CD,HRT,NT,PM

David A. Howe, MD, BPCT
505 N. Mollison Ave., #103
El Cajon, CA 92021
(619) 440-3838
FAX (760) 489-2238
CT,GP,NT,PM,PMR,P/S

ENCINITAS

Mark Drucker, MD
4403 Manchester Ave., #107
Encinitas, CA 92024
(760) 632-9042
FAX (760) 632-0574
BA,CT,NT,PM,WR

ENCINO

Ilona Abraham, MD, APCT
17815 Ventura Blvd., Stes. 111 & 113
Encino, CA 91316
(818) 345-8721
FAX (818) 345-7150
CD,CT,PO,HO,END,AA,P/S,Natural Horm.

ESCONDIDO

Aline Fournier, DO
307 S. Ivy
Escondido, CA 92025
(760) 746-1133
FAX (760) 746-9880
CT,FP,OS,PM,P/S,YS

Ratibor Pantovich, DO
560 E. Valley Pkwy.
Escondido, CA 92025
(760) 480-2880
FAX (760) 480-0102
BA,CT,OS

FOUNTAIN CITY

Allen Green, MD
18153 Brookhurst St.
Fountain Valley, CA 92708
(714) 378-5656
FAX (714) 378-5650
A,AA,CT,FP,NT,HRT

Rosemarie Melchor, MD
11190 Warner Ave., #111
Fountain Valley, CA 92708
(714) 751-5800
FAX (714) 751-5860
AA,CD,FP,HRT,IM,NT

FOSTER CITY

Bruce Wapen, MD
969-G Edgewater Blvd., #807
Foster City, CA 94404
(650) 577-8635
FAX (650-577-0191
EM

FRESNO

David J. Edwards, MD
360 S. Clovis Ave.
Fresno, CA 93727
(559) 251-5066
FAX (559) 251-5108
A,AR,CD,CT,NT,OME,RHU,WR,YS

Patrick A. Golden, MD, APCT
1187 E. Herndon, #101
Fresno, CA 93720
(559) 432-0716
FAX (559) 432-4545
CD,IM,CT,HRT

GLENDALE

Abraham Maissian, MD, BPCT
1737 W. Glenoaks Blvd.
Glendale, CA 91201
(818) 243-1186
FAX (818) 243-3868
A,CD,CT,DD,FP,IM,PD

HEMET

Hitendra Shah, MD
229 West 7th Street
Hemet, CA 92583
(909) 487-2550
FAX (909) 487-2552
AA,CT,DIA,FP,HGL,P/S,YS

HOLLYWOOD

James Julian, MD
1654 Cahuenga Blvd.
Hollywood, CA 90028
(323) 467-5555
FAX (323) 462-6377
AR,BA,CT,NT,PM

HUNTINGTON BEACH

Francis Foo, MD
10188 Adams Ave.
Huntington Beach, CA 92646
(714) 968-3266
FAX (714) 968-6408
FP,S,CT

INDIO

Robert Harmon, MD
41-800 Washington St., #110
Indio, CA 92201
(619) 345-2696
CT,DD,FP,GP,PM,YS

IRVINE

Allan E. Sosin, MD, APCT
16100 Sand Canyon Ave., #240
Irvine, CA 92618
(949) 753-8889
FAX (949) 753-0410
CT,CD,DIA,GER,IM,NT,P/S

Ronald Wempen, MD, BPCT
14795 Jeffrey Rd., Suite 101
Irvine, CA 92618
(949) 551-8751
FAX (949) 551-1272
A,AA,CT,EV,HRT,OME,YS

LAGUNA HILLS

Peter Muran, MD, BPCT
23521 Paseo de Valencia, #204
Laguna Hills, CA 92653
(949) 472-3717
FAX (714) 430-1443
BA,FP,GER,PM,YS

LA JOLLA

Charles Moss, MD, BPCT
8950 Villa La Jolla, #A217
La Jolla, CA 92037
(858) 457-1314
FAX (858) 457-3615
AC,CT,FP,HGL,MM,NT,YS,Env.Med.

LAKE FOREST

Michael Grossman, MD, BPCT
24432 Muirlands Blvd., #111
Lake Forest, CA 92630
(949) 770-7301
FAX (949) 770-0634
AC,DD,FP,NT,PM,YS

LONG BEACH

H. Richard Casdorph, MD, PhD,
FACAM, APCT
1703 Termino Ave., Suite 201
Long Beach, CA 90804
(562) 597-8716
FAX (562) 597-4616
AA,CD,CT,DIA,IM,WR

LOS ALTOS

Robert F. Cathcart III, MD
127 Second St., Suite 4
Los Altos, CA 94022
(650) 949-2822
FAX (650) 949-5083
A,AR,CT,EV,OME,YS

F. T. Guilford, MD
5050 El Camino Real, #110
Los Altos, CA 94022
(650) 964-6700
FAX (650) 433-0947
A,CT,NT,PM

Raj Patel, MD
5050 El Camino Real, #110
Los Altos, CA 94022
(650) 964-6700
FAX (650) 964-3495
A,AA,CD,CT,NT,OME

D. Graeme Shaw, MD
5050 El Camino Real, #110
Los Altos, CA 94022
(650) 964-6700
FAX (650) 964-3495
A,CT,IM,NT,PM,YS,HRT

LOS ANGELES

Michael Galitzer, MD
12381 Wilshire Blvd., #102
Los Angeles, CA 90025
(310) 820-6042
FAX (310) 207-3342
AC,CT,FP,HOM, NT,OME

Hans D. Gruenn, MD, BPCT
2211 Corinth Ave., #204
Los Angeles, CA 90064
(310) 966-9194
FAX (310) 966-9196
AC,CT,GP,NT,PM,PMR,YS

Karima Hirani, MD
12732-B W. Washington Blvd.
Los Angeles, CA 90066
(310) 577-0753
FAX (310) 577-0728
FP

Murray Susser, MD, APCT
2211 Corinth Ave., #204
Los Angeles, CA 90064
(310) 966-9194
FAX (310) 966-9196
A,CT,NT,OME,HGL,YS,HPT,HRT,FP,AR

MALIBU

William Rader, MD
22619 Pacific Coast Highway, #125
Malibu, CA 90265
(310) 455-5300
FAX (310) 455-5318

MISSION HILLS

Sion Nobel, MD
10306 N. Sepulveda Blvd.
Mission Hills, CA 91345
(818) 361-0115
FAX (818) 361-9497
AA,CT,PM,PMR,HRT,ON(Prostate)

MODESTO

Christine G. Tazewell, MD
1524 McHenry Ave., #310
Modesto, CA 95350
(209) 575-4700
FAX (209) 577-6699
IM,CD,DIA,HGL,NT,PM

MONROVIA

Ayad Alanizi, MD, FRCS
513 E. Lime, #201
Monrovia, CA 91016
(626) 294-0979
FAX (626) 256-4899
GP,FP,S,P/S

NAPA

Eleanor Hynote, MD
935 Trancas Street, Ste. 1A
Napa, CA 94558
(707) 255-4172
FAX (707) 255-2605
HRT,CD,CT,IM,NT,WR,GYN,MM,PM,YS

NEWPORT BEACH

Julian Whitaker, MD, APCT
4321 Birch St., Suite 100
Newport Beach, CA 92660
(949) 851-1550
FAX (949) 955-3005
CD,CT,DIA,DD,NT,PM,AA,AR,AC,HO,
HRT,OME,P/S

NORTH HOLLYWOOD

Christine Daniel, MD
12650 Sherman Way, #4
N. Hollywood, CA 91605
(818) 982-8062
FAX (818) 982-8794
CT,DD,GP,HO,PM,PMR

ORANGE

Gary Peralta Ruelas, DO
1509 East Chapman Ave.
Orange, CA 92866
(714) 771-2880
FP

PALM DESERT

Robert Neal Rouzier, MD
77564B Country Club Dr., #320
Palm Desert, CA 92211
(760) 772-8883
CT,HRT,FP,IM,NT,PM

PALM SPRINGS

Robert Neal Rouzier, MD
2825 Tahquitz Canyon, Suite 200
Palm Springs, CA 92262
(760) 320-4292
FAX (760) 322-9475
CT,HRT,FP,IM,NT,PM,HO

Priscilla A. Slagle, MD
946 Avenida Palos Verdes
Palm Springs, CA 92262
(760) 323-4259
FAX (760) 323-4259
A,HYP,NT,PM,PO,YS

PASADENA

Maria Sulindro, MD, BPCT
1017 S. Fair Oaks Ave.
Pasadena, CA 91105
(626) 403-9000
FAX (626) 403-2580
PMR,PM,NT,DD,WR

PLEASANTON

Lynne Mielke, MD
4463 Stoneridge Dr., #A
Pleasanton, CA 94566
(925) 846-6300
FAX (925) 846-6323
P

REDLANDS

Felix Prakasam, MD
2048 Orange Tree Lane
Redlands, CA 92374
(909) 798-1614
AN,CT,DD,HO,NT,OSM

SACRAMENTO

Michael Kwiker, DO
3301 Alta Arden, Suite 3
Sacramento, CA 95825
(916) 489-4400
FAX (916) 489-1710
AA,AC,CD,CT,DIA,GP,HRT,NT,YS

SAN DIEGO

Neil W. Hirschenbein,
MD,PhD,CCN,CNS, AHMA
9339 Genesee Ave., #150
San Diego, CA 92122
(858) 713-9401
IM,AA,CD,HRT,NT,PM

James Novak, MD
4440 Lamont Street
San Diego, CA 92109
(858) 272-0022
FAX (858) 272-7460
CT,GP,MM,NT,OME

SAN FRANCISCO

Joel F. Lopez, MD
345 W. Portal Ave.
San Francisco, CA 94127
(415) 566-1000
FAX (415) 665-6732
CT,GP,AA,HRT,IM,NT,PM

Paul Lynn, MD, APCT
345 W. Portal Ave., 2nd Floor
San Francisco, CA 94127
(415) 566-1000
FAX (415) 665-6732
A,AR,CT,DIA,DD,NT,PM,HRT

Wai-Man Ma, MD, BPCT
728 Pacific Ave., #611
San Francisco, CA 94133
(415) 397-3888
FP

Gary Ross, MD
500 Sutter, #300
San Francisco, CA 94102
(415) 398-0555
FAX (415) 398-6228
A,AC,CT,DD,FP,NT,PM,HRT

SAN RAMON

Richard Gracer, MD
5401 Norris Canyon Rd., #102
San Ramon, CA 94583
(925) 277-1100
FAX (925) 283-2009
FP,DD,OME,PM,P/S,CT,OSM,WR

SANTA ANA

Catherine Arvantely, MD
1820 E. Garry, #116
Santa Ana, CA 92705
(949) 660-1399
FAX (949) 251-1209
FP,NT,PM,OME,HRT,YS,GYN

SANTA BARBARA

Kenneth J. Frank, MD
831 State St., #280
Santa Barbara, CA 93101
(805) 730-7420
FAX (805) 435-1909
NT

James L. Kwako, MD
1805-D East Cabrillo Blvd.
Santa Barbara, CA 93018
(805) 565-3959
FAX (805) 565-3989
AC,CT,FP,NT,PM,AA,HRT

Bob Young, MD, BPCT
119 North Milpas
Santa Barbara, CA 93103
(805) 963-1824
FAX (805) 963-1826
CT,CD,DIA,DD,NT,PM,RHU

SANTA MONICA

Joseph Sciabbarrasi, MD
1821 Wilshire Blvd., #400
Santa Monica, CA 90403
(310) 828-4175
FAX (310) 828-4324
AC,CT,CD,HOM,NT,YS,HRT

SEBASTOPOL

Norman Zucker, MD
2405 Burnside Rd.
Sebastopol, CA 95472
(707) 823-6116
A,CT,EV,NT,MM,YS

STUDIO CITY

Charles Law Jr., MD
3959 Laurel Canyon Blvd., Ste. I
Studio City, CA 91604
(818) 761-1661
FAX (818) 761-0482
AC,BA,CT,GP,NT,PM

TEMPLETON

Carmelo A. Plateroti, DO, BPCT
1111 Las Tablas Rd.,#M
Templeton, CA 93465
(805) 434-2821
FAX (805) 434-2526
CT,NT,PM,HPT,YS,AA

TUSTIN

Leigh Erin Connealy, MD
14642 Newport Ave., #200
Tustin, CA 92780
(714) 669-4446
FAX (714) 669-4448
AC,BA,FP,END,MM,NT,PM

Allan Harvey Lane, MD, BPCT
12581 Newport Avenue, Ste. B
Tustin, CA 92780
(714) 544-9544
FAX (714) 544-9611
CD,CT,HRT,IM,NT,OME

Stephanie Mason, MD
14642 Newport Ave., #200
Tustin, CA 92780
(714) 669-4446
FAX (714) 669-4448
AA,CT,FP,MM,NT,PM

UKIAH

Lawrence G. Foster, MD
230 Hospital Drive, #B
Ukiah, CA 95482
(707) 463-3502
S

UPLAND

Bryan P. Chan, MD, BPCT
1148 San Bernardino Rd., #E-102
Upland, CA 91786
(909) 920-3578
FAX (909) 949-1238
FP

VISTA

Les Breitman, MD, BPCT
Institute for Anti-Aging Medicine
Vista, CA 92083
(760) 414-9955
CT,AA,HPT,HRT,LM,ON,PT,UV

WEST TOLUCA LAKE

Salvacion Lee, MD
11336 Camarillo St., #305
West Toluca Lake, CA 91602
(818) 505-1574
FAX (818) 505-1574
BA,CT,GP,HGL,NT,PM,HPT,WR

COLORADO

ASPEN

Rob Krakovitz, MD
430 W. Main Street
Aspen, CO 81611
(970) 927-4394
A,OME,HGL,NT,PM,YS

AURORA

Terry Grossman, MD, MD(H), NMD, APCT
3150 S. Peoria St., Unit H
Aurora, CO 80014
(303) 338-1323
FAX (303) 338-1324
CT,FP,NT,MM

BOULDER

Michael A. Zeligs, MD, BPCT
1000 Alpine, #211
Boulder, CO 80304
(303) 442-5492
FAX (303) 447-3610
AN

BROOMFIELD

Ron Rosedale, MD, APCT
P O Box 6278
Broomfield, CO 80030
(303) 530-5555
FAX (303) 530-5522
CT,CD,DIA,MN,NT

COLORADO SPRINGS

George Juetersonke, DO, APCT
3525 American Drive
Colorado Springs, CO 80917
(719) 597-6075
CT

Joel Klein, MD
5455 N. Union Blvd.,#201
Colorado Springs, CO 80918
(719) 457-0330
FAX (719) 457-0860
FP,OME,YS,NT

DENVER

Terry Grossman, MD, MD(H), NMD, APCT
2801 Youngfield St., #117
Denver, CO 80401
(303) 233-4247
FAX (303) 233-4249
CT,FP,NT,MM

DURANGO

Ronald E. Wheeler, MD
2901 Main Avenue
Durango, CO 81301
(970) 259-4081
FAX (970) 247-3074
S,Oncology

FORT COLLINS

Roger Billica, MD
1020 Luke Street, #A
Fort Collins, CO 80524
(970) 495-0999
FAX (970) 495-1016
GP,FP,CT,EV,HRT,NT,PM,WR

GRAND JUNCTION

Joseph M. Wezensky, MD
2650 North Ave., Suite 101
Grand Junction, CO 81501
(970) 263-4660
FAX (970) 248-9519
CT,P/S,HYP,EV,AA,WR

GREENWOOD VILLAGE

Snna S. Choi, MD
8200 E. Belleview Ave., #240E
Greenwood Village, CO 80111
(303) 721-1670
FAX (303) 721-8117
GYN,OBS

PUEBLO

David Walters, DO
2403 Santa Fe Dr., #7
Pueblo, CO 81006
(719) 543-7894
FAX (719) 546-2833
FP

CONNETICUT

BRIDGEPORT

Tadeusz A. Skowron, MD
50 Ridgefield Ave., #317
Bridgeport, CT 06610
(203) 368-1450
GP,IM

HAMDEN

Robert Lang, MD, PC
60 Washington Ave., #105
Hamden, CT 06518
(203) 248-4362
FAX (203) 248-6933
DIA,END,HGL,MM,NT

MADISON

Robert Lang, MD, PC
11 Woodland Road
Madison, CT 06443
(203) 318-5200
FAX (203) 318-5203
DIA,END,HGL,MM,NT,HRT,MM

RIDGEFIELD

Marcie Wolinsky-Friedland, MD
Americas Medical Center
Ridgefield, CT 06877
(203) 431-6165
FAX (203) 431-6167
CT,END,IM,HRT,NT,P/S,RHU

STAMFORD

Alan R. Cohen, MD, BPCT
80 Mill River St., #2200
Stamford, CT 06902
(203) 363-1547
CT,FP,NT,PD,PM,YS

Warren M. Levin, MD, APCT
111 High Ridge Rd.
Stamford, CT 06905
(203) 834-1174
FAX (203) 834-1175
A,AC,CT,NT,OME,PM

Henry C. Sobo, MD
111 High Ridge Rd.
Stamford, CT 06905
(203) 348-8805
FAX (203) 348-6398
A,AA,BA,CD,CT,DD,DIA,HOM,IM,NT,
PM,HGL,WR,YS,HRT

TORRINGTON

Jerrold N. Finnie, MD, APCT
333 Kennedy Dr., #204
Torrington, CT 06790
(860) 489-8977
A,CT,CS,NT,RHI,YS

DELAWARE

NEWARK

Gerald Lemole, MD
4745 Ogletown-Stanton Rd., #205
Newark, DE 19713
(302) 738-0448
FAX (302) 738-0328
CD

NEW CASTLE

Jeffrey K. Kerner, DO, BPCT
200 Bussett Ave.
New Castle, DE 19720
(302) 328-0669
FAX (302) 328-8937
CT,FP,NT,OS,PM,HRT

DISTRICT OF COLUMBIA

WASHINGTON

George H. Mitchell, MD
2639 Connecticut Ave. NW,
Suite C-100
Washington, DC 20008
(202) 265-4111
A,NT,AA,DD,EV,HRT,PM,YS

Bruce Rind, MD
5225 Wisconsin Ave., NW
Washington, DC 20015
(202) 237-7000

Aldo M. Rosemblat, MD, APCT
5225 Wisconsin Ave. N.W., #401
Washington, DC 20015
(202) 237-7000
FAX (202) 237-0017
AC,S

FLORIDA

APOPKA

Allan Zubkin, MD
424 N. Park Ave.
Apopka, FL 32712
(407) 886-0611
FAX (407) 886-2817
GP,WR,MM,CT

BOCA RATON

Leonard Haimes, MD, BPCT
7300 N. Federal Hwy.,# 100
Boca Raton, FL 33487
(561) 995-8484
FAX (561) 995-7773
A,BA,CT,IM,NT,PM,HRT

Dean R. Silver, MD
24 SE 6th Street
Boca Raton, FL 33432
(561) 391-1884
FAX (561) 391-1456
ON,AA,CT,HO,HPT,HRT

BONITA SPRINGS

Dean R. Silver, MD
Chart Medical
Bonita Springs, FL 34135
(239) 949-0101
FAX (239)949-4334
ON,AA,CT,HO,HPT,HRT

BOYNTON BEACH

Kenneth Lee, MD
1501 Corporate Dr., #240
Boynton Beach, FL 33426
(561) 736-8806
CD,GER,IM,NT,GP

Sherri W. Pinsley, DO
1325 S. Longress, #207
Boynton Beach, FL 33426
(561) 752-5776
CT,DD,GP,NT,OS,PMR

BRADENTON

Eteri Melnikov, MD, APCT
4216 Cortez Road, W.
Bradenton, FL 34210
(941) 739-2225
FAX (941) 753-6821
CT,CD,HPT,UV,YS,GP,PT

BRANDON

Erika Bradshaw, MD
1209 Lakeside Drive
Brandon, FL 33510
(813) 661-3662
FAX (813) 661-0515
IM

CLEARWATER

Colin Chan, MD
2685 Ulmerton Rd., #101
Clearwater, FL 33762
(727) 571-1688
FAX (727) 217-4131
FP

David Minkoff, MD
301 Turner Street
Clearwater, FL 33756
(727) 442-5612
CT,NT,PM,CD,PMR

David M. Wall, MD
3023 Eastland Blvd., Suite H113
Clearwater, FL 33761
(727) 791-3830
FAX (727) 791-3629
AN,AC,DD,NT,PM

CORAL SPRINGS

Jerald H. Ratner, MD
9750 N.W. 33rd St., #211
Coral Springs, FL 33065
(954) 752-9450
FAX (954) 752-9888
P

Anthony J. Sancetta, DO, BPCT
8217 W. Atlantic Blvd.
Coral Springs, FL 33071
(954) 757-1211
FAX (954) 757-1255
CT,GP,NT,OS,PM,PMR

DADE CITY

Edward Harshman, MD
38047 Pasco Ave.
Dade City, FL 33525
(352) 518-0725
FAX (352-518-0726
PMR,CT,GP

DAYTONA BEACH

John Ortolani, MD
1430 Mason Ave.
Daytona Beach, FL 32117
(386) 274-3601
FAX (386) 274-2009
FP,GP

FORT LAUDERDALE

Cristino C. Enriquez, MD, BPCT
767 S. State Road 7
Fort Lauderdale, FL 33317
(954) 583-3335
FAX (954) 463-8006
CD,CT,IM,PM,PUD,HPT

FORT MYERS

Robert A. Didonato, MD
3443 Hancock Bridge Pkwy., #301
Ft. Myers, FL 33903
(239) 997-8800
FAX (239) 997-7706
CT,NT,GP,AA

Gary L. Pynckel, DO, APCT
3840 Colonial Blvd., #1
Fort Myers, FL 33912
(941) 278-3377
FAX (941) 278-3702
CT,FP,GP,OSM,PM

Dean Silver, MD
4650 South Cleveland Ave., #3-A
Fort Myers, FL 33907
(239) 939-4700
FAX (239) 939-4704
ON,AA,CT,HO,HPT,HRT

GAINESVILLE

Robert Erickson, MD
905 NW 56th Terrace, Ste. B
Gainesville, FL 32605
(352) 331-5138
FAX (352) 331-9399
CT, PM,HPT,HRT,NT

Hanoch Talmor, MD
4421 NW 39th Ave., Bldg. 2-1
Gainesville, FL 32606
(352) 377-0015
FAX (352) 378-1895
CT,FP,UV,PD,PM,HOM

HIALEAH

Francisco Mora, MD
1490 West 48th Place, #398
Hialeah, FL 33012
(305) 820-6211
FAX (305) 822-0116
AU,HOM,HYP,NT,P/S,PM

HOLLYWOOD

Michelle Morrow, DO
5821 Hollywood Blvd.
Hollywood, FL 33021
(954) 436-6363
FAX (954) 436-6731
BA,FP,NT,OS,PM

HOMOSASSA SPRINGS

Carlos F. Gonzalez, MD, APCT
7989 So. Suncoast Blvd.
Homosassa Springs, FL 32646
(352) 382-2900
FAX (352) 382-1633
A,CD,CS,END,PMR,RHU

INDIALANTIC

Glen Wagner, MD, BPCT
121 - 6th Ave.
Indialantic, FL 32903
(407) 723-5915
A,AC,CT,GP,NT,YS

INDIAN HARBOUR BEACH

Daniel B. Hammond, MD
1413 South Patrick Drive
Indian Harbour Beach, FL 32937
(321) 777-9923
FAX (321) 777-4707
DIA,FP,GP,HGL,NT,PM

JACKSONVILLE

Norman S. Cohen, MD, APCT
4237 Salisbury Road, #110
Jacksonville, FL 32216
(904) 296-1116
FAX (904) 296-1467
CT,OBS-GYN,Altern.Med

Stephen Grable, MD
7563 Philips Hwy., #206, Bldg. 100
Jacksonville, FL 32256
(904) 296-9355
FAX (904)296-1472
IM,PM,YS,DD,CT,NT

KEY BISCAYNE

Sam Baxas, MD
30 West Mashta Drive, Ste. 200
Key Biscayne, FL 33149
(305) 361-9249(or 36
FAX (305) 361-2179
CT,GP,FP,CD,DIA,PM

KISSIMMEE

Carmelita Bamba-Dagani, MD
500 North John Young Pkwy.
Kissimmee, FL 34741
(407) 935-1060
FAX (407) 931-2056
AN,AC,AU,CT,Pain Mngt.

LAKELAND

Harold Robinson, MD
4406 S. Florida Ave., Suite 27
Lakeland, FL 33803
(941) 646-5088
CT,UV,AR,HGL,NT,PM

S. Todd Robinson, MD, APCT
4406 S. Florida Ave., Suite 30
Lakeland, FL 33803
(941) 646-5088
CT,FP,GP,HGL,NT,PM

LAKE MARY

Diab Ashrap, MD
P.O. Box 951957
Lake Mary, FL 32795
(407) 805-9222
FAX (407) 444-5299
IM

Jeffrey Mueller, MD, BPCT
635 Primera Blvd., #111
Lake Mary, FL 32746
(407) 833-3881
FAX (407) 833-3883
AN,GP,PM,Cancer Co-management

LAUDERHILL

Herbert R. Slavin, MD, APCT
7200 W. Commercial Blvd., Suite #210
Lauderhill, FL 33319
(954) 748-4991
FAX (954) 748-5022
CT,DIA,HRT,AA,IM,NT

LECANTO

Azael P. Borromeo, MD, APCT
2653 N. Lecanto Hwy.
Lecanto, FL 34461
(352) 527-9555
FAX (352) 527-2609
BA, GP, PATHOLOGY, S

MARCO ISLAND

Richard Saitta, MD
1010 N. Barfield Dr.
Marco Island, FL 34145
(941) 642-8488
AC,CT,HO,IM,NT,PM

MELBOURNE

Neil Ahner, MD, APCT
1270 N. Wickham Road
Melbourne, FL 32935
(321) 253-2009
FAX (321) 253-5561
CT,NT,HRT,MM,AA,CD

Rajiv Chandra, MD, BPCT
Alpha Medical / TruMed
Melbourne, FL 32901
(321) 951-7404
FAX (312) 951-0575
CD,CS,GP,IM,NT,PM

MERRITT ISLAND

Glenn R. Johnston, MD
585 N. Courtney Parkway
Merritt Island, FL 32953
(321) 454-4428
FAX (321) 454-4033
AA,CT,HRT,MM,PS,WR

MIAMI

Joseph G. Godorov, DO
9055 S.W. 87th Ave., Suite 307
Miami, FL 33176
(305) 595-0671
A,AR,CD,CT,DIA,END,HRT,HGL,IM,NT,
PM, P/S,YSDE

Angelique Hart, MD
1 South Drive
Miami, FL 33166
(305) 882-1442
FAX (305) 889-1040
AN,CT,GP,NT,PM,OME,WR

Ivonne F. Torre-Coya, MD
2580 SW 107th Avenue
Miami, FL 33165
(305) 223-0132
FAX (305) 553-6488
BA,CT,FP,HGL,YS

MILTON

William Watson, MD
5536 Stewart Street
Milton, FL 32570
(850) 623-3836
FAX (850) 623-2201
BA,GP,S,CT,PM,WR

MOUNT DORA

Jack E. Young, MD, PhD, APCT, MD(H)
2260 W. Old US Hwy. 441
Mount Dora(Orlando area), FL 32757
(352) 385-4400
FAX (352) 385-4402
AA,CT,HPT,HRT,NT,PT

NAPLES

David Perlmutter, MD
800 Goodlette Rd. N., #270
Naples, FL 34102
(239) 649-7400
FAX (239) 649-6370
DD,END,HO,FP,NT,PM,Neurology

NEW SMYRNA BEACH

William Campbell Douglass, MD, MS, APCT
2111 Ocean Drive
New Smyrna Beach, FL 32169
(386) 426-8803
FAX (509) 421-8604
AA,CD,CT,DIA,HOM,HRT,PT,UV,YS

NORTH MIAMI BEACH

Stefano DiMauro, MD
16695 N.E. 10th Avenue
N. Miami Beach, FL 33162
(305) 940-6474
FAX (305) 944-8601
A,CT,DIA,FP,NT,PMR

Wynne A. Steinsnyder, DO
17291 N.E. 19th Avenue
N. Miami Beach, FL 33162
(305) 947-0618
FAX (305) 940-1345
OS,GP,PMR,S,Urology

OCALA (FORT MCCOY)

George Graves, DO
11512 County Road 316
Ocala (Ft. McCoy), FL 32134
(352) 236-2525
FAX (352) 236-8610
A,AR,BA,CT,GP,OS

ORANGE CITY

Travis L. Herring, MD
106 West Fern Dr.
Orange City, FL 32763
(386) 775-0525
FAX (386) 775-3911
CT,FP,HOM,IM,BA,WR,PM

ORLANDO

Kirti Kalidas, MD
6651 Vineland Road, #150
Orlando, FL 32819
(407) 355-9246
FAX (407) 370-4774
IM,CT,EV,HPT,HOM,HRT

Robert J. Rogers, MD
2170 West State Road 434, #190
Orlando, FL 32779
(407) 682-5222
FAX (407) 682-5274
AA,CT,DIA,HRT,PM,PT,WR,YS

ORMOND BEACH

Hana Chaim, DO
595 W. Granada Blvd., #D
Ormond Beach, FL 32174
(386) 672-9000
A,CT,Env. Med.,FP,Sclerotherapy

PALM BEACH GARDENS

Neil Ahner, MD, APCT
10333 N. Military Trail, Ste. A
Palm Beach Gardens, FL 33410
(561) 630-3696
FAX (561) 630-1991
CT,NT,HRT,MM,AA,CD

PALM HARBOR

Carlos M. Garcia, MD, APCT
36555 U.S. Hwy. 19 North
Palm Harbor, FL 34684
(727) 771-9669
FAX (727) 771-8071
AN,CD,CT,IM,PM,Pain Mgmt.

PANAMA CITY

Naima Abdel-Ghany, MD, PhD, APCT
2424 B Frankford Avenue
Panama City, FL 32405
(850) 872-8122
FAX (850) 872-9925
A,CD,CT,IM,PUD,PH,PM,Anti-Aging
Med.

James W. De Ruiter, MD
2202 State Ave., #311
Panama City, FL 32405
(850) 747-4963
FAX (850) 747-0074
OBS-GYN

Samir M.A. Yassin, MD
516 S. Tyndall Pkwy., #202
Panama City, FL 32404
(850) 763-0464
FAX (850) 763-2064
CT,DIA,GP,HPT,PM,UV

PENSACOLA

R. W. Lucey, MD
710 Underwood Ave.
Pensacola, FL 32504
(850) 477-3453
FAX (850) 474-9420
FP

PLANTATION

Adam Frent, DO
1741 N. University Drive
Plantation, FL 33322
(954) 474-1617
FAX (954) 472-1631
CT,DIA,DD,AA,WR,PM,HPT,HRT,MM

Alvin Stein, MD
4101 NW 4 St., #S-401
Plantation, FL 33317
(954) 581-8585
FAX (954) 581-5580
CT,PMR,P/S

PUNTA GORDA

James Coy, MD, BPCT
310 Nesbit St., P.O. Box 511315
Punta Gorda, FL 33951
(941) 575-8080
FAX (941) 575-8108
A,CT,GP

ST. PETERSBURG

John P. Lenhart, MD, BPCT
6110 - 9th Street N.
St. Petersburg, FL 33703
(727) 526-0600
FAX (727) 345-0928
AC,BA,NT,PM,PMR,P/S

Ray C. Wunderlich Jr., MD, PhD, APCT
8821 MLKing St., North
St. Petersburg, FL 33702
(727) 822-3612
FAX (727) 578-1370
CT,NT,YS,MM,PM

SARASOTA

W. Frederic Harvey, MD
3982 Bee Ridge Rd., Bldg.H, #J
Sarasota, FL 34239
(941) 929-9355
GER,IM,MM,NT,PM

Rebecca Roberts, DO
1521 Dolphin St., #101
Sarasota, FL 34236
(941) 365-6273
FAX (941) 365-4269
CT,FP,NT,OS,PM,YS

Alan Sault, MD
2000 So. Tamiami Trail
Sarasota, FL 34239
(941) 955-5579
FP,PM,NT,AA,DD,HRT,YS

Ronald E. Wheeler, MD
The Sarasota City Center
Sarasota, FL 34236
(941) 957-0007
S,Oncology

SEBASTIAN

Peter Holyk, MD, CNS, BPCT
Contemporary Health Innovations,
Inc.
Sebastian, FL 32958
(772) 338-5554
FAX (772) 388-2410
A,CT,DIA,DD,NT,PM,AA,EV,HO,HPT,
HRT,PT,UV

SPRING HILL

Nabil Habib, MD, BPCT
3300 Josef Avenue
Spring Hill, FL 34609
(352) 683-1166
FAX (352) 683-2902
S

Calin V. Pop, MD
4215 Rachel Boulevard
Spring Hill, FL 34607
(352) 597-2240
FAX (352) 597-2990
MM,CT,GP,IM,NT,OME,HRT

STUART

Neil Ahner, MD, APCT
705 North Federal Hwy.
Stuart, FL 34994
(772) 692-9200
FAX (772) 692-9888
CT,NT,HRT,MM,AA,CD

Sherri W. Pinsley, DO
7000 SE Federal Hwy., #302
Stuart, FL 34997
(561) 220-1697
FAX (561) 220-7332
CT,DD,GP,NT,OS,PMR

TAMARAC

George A. Lustig, MD
7401 N. University Dr., #101
Tamarac, FL 33321
(954) 724-0099
FAX (954) 724-0070
CD,IM,NT

TAMPA

Robert J. Casanas, MD
4810 Bay Heron Place, #1012
Tampa, FL 33661
(813) 390-3037
CT,PM,AC,IM

Carlos M. Garcia, MD, APCT
4710 Havana Ave., #107
Tampa, FL 33616
(813) 350-0140
FAX (813) 350-0713
AN,CD,CT,IM,PM,Pain Mgmt.

Edward Harshman, MD
1710 West M.L. King Blvd.
Tampa, FL 33607
(352) 518-0725
FAX (352-518-0726
PMR,CT,GP

Eugene H. Lee, MD
1804 W. Kennedy Blvd. #A
Tampa, FL 33606
(813) 251-3089
FAX (813) 251-5668
AC,CT,NT,PM,GP,HGL

TEQUESTA

R. J. Oenbrink, DO
396 Tequesta Drive
Tequesta, FL 33469
(561) 746-4333
FAX (561) 746-4449
FP,NT,GP

UMATILLA

Louis Radnothy, DO
390 S. Central, P.O. Drawer 2325
Umatilla, FL 32784
(352) 669-3175
FAX (352) 669-3640
FP

VENICE

Matthew Burks, MD
420 Nokomis Ave., So.
Venice, FL 34285
(941) 488-8112
FAX (941) 488-7444
AN,CT,NT,PMR,AR,DD,PM

Arlene Martone, MD
4140 Woodmere Park Blvd., #2
Venice, FL 34293
(941) 408-9838
FAX (941) 408-9588
GYN,AA,CT,EV,HRT,NT,WR

THE VILLAGES

Nelson Kraucak, MD, FAAFP-ABFT, APCT
1501 us Hwy. 441 North, #1702
The Villages, FL 32159
(352) 750-4333
FAX (352) 750-2023
FP,AC,AA,CT,P/S,PT

WEST PALM BEACH

Daniel N. Tucker, MD
1411 N. Flagler Dr., #6700
West Palm Beach, FL 33401
(561) 835-0055
FAX (561) 835-1742
A,CS,PUD,RHI

WINTER PARK

Joya Lynn Schoen, MD, BPCT
1850 Lee Road, Ste. 240
Winter Park, FL 32789
(407) 644-2729
FAX (407) 644-1205
UV,CT,HPT,HOM,MM,NT

GEORGIA

ATLANTA

M. Truett Bridges, Jr, MD, BPCT
4920 Roswell Rd., #35
Atlanta, GA 30342
(404) 843-8880
FAX (404) 843-8687
AN,AC,AU,CT,PM,NT

Stephen B. Edelson, MD, APCT
3833 Roswell Rd., #110
Atlanta, GA 30342
(404) 841-0088
FAX (404) 841-6416
CT,NT,YS,EV,PM,RHU,ON,CD,GYN, HRT

Milton Fried, MD, APCT
4426 Tilly Mill Road
Atlanta, GA 30360
(770) 451-4857
FAX (770) 451-8492
A,CT,IM,NT,PM,PO

Sn E. Kolb, MD
4370 Georgetown Square
Atlanta, GA 30338
(770) 390-0012
FAX (770) 457-4428
S,HO,CT

William Richardson, MD, APCT
3280 Howell Mill Rd., #205
Atlanta, GA 30327
(404) 350-9607
FAX (404) 350-9481
AA,CT,FP,NT,WR,YS

BRUNSWICK

Ralph G. Ellis Jr, MD, APCT
158 Scranton Connector
Brunswick, GA 31525
(912) 280-0304
FAX (912) 280-0601
CT,DD,NT,PM,CD,Oxidative Therapy

CANTON

William Early, MD, BPCT
320 Hospital Rd.
Canton, GA 30114
(770) 479-5535
FAX (770) 720-3294
IM,GE

CARTERSVILLE

Claude R. Poliak, MD, APCT
17 Bowens Court SE
Cartersville, GA 30120
(770) 607-0220
FAX (770) 607-0208
OPH,CT,NT,A,EV,AA

COLUMBUS

Jan McBarron, MD
2904 Macon Rd.
Columbus, GA 31906
(706) 322-4073
FAX (706) 323-4786
BA,NT,PM

FORT OGLETHORPE

Charles C. Adams, MD, BPCT
100 Thomas Rd.
Fort Oglethorpe, GA 30742
(706) 861-7377
FAX (706) 861-7922
IM,CT,NT,A,Anti-Aging Med.

GAINESVILLE

John L. Givogre, MD, BPCT
530 Springs Street
Gainesville, GA 30501
(770) 503-7222
FAX (770) 718-0009
AN,CT,PMR,AC,P/S

Kathryn Herndon, MD
530 Spring St.
Gainesville, GA 30503
(770) 503-7222
AC,AU,CT,NT,OS,PMR

MACON

James T. Alley, MD
2518 Riverside Dr.
Macon, GA 31204
(478) 745-3727 or (8
CT,NT,HRT, Rehab.

MARIETTA

Ralph Lee, MD
110 Lewis Dr., Ste. B
Marietta, GA 30060
(770) 423-0064
FAX (770) 423-9827
CT,GP,NT,PM,YS

ROSWELL

Marcia V. Byrd, MD
11050 Crabapple Rd., #105-B
Roswell, GA 30075
(770) 587-1711
FAX (770) 518-8810
A,CT,GP,NT,PM,YS,AA,HPT

SMYRNA

Donald Ruesink, MD
1004 Lincoln Trace Cir. SE
Smyrna, GA 30080
(770) 818-9908
CT,NT

STOCKBRIDGE

Michael Rowland, MD
130 Eagle Springs Court, Ste. A
Stockbridge, GA 30281
(770) 507-2930
FAX (770) 507-0837
CT,FP,DIA,NT,DD,CD

T.R. Shantha, MD, PhD
115 Eagle Spring Dr.
Stockbridge, GA 30281
(770) 474-4029
FAX (770) 474-2038
nesthisiology

TIFTON

Lora Efaw, MD
1807 Old Ocilla Rd.
Tifton, GA 31794
(229) 388-9393
FAX (229) 388-9855
FP

HAWAII

HONOLULU

Frederick Lam, MD, APCT
1270 Queen Emma St., #501
Honolulu, HI 96813
(808) 537-3311
A,AC,CT,FP,HGL

Pritam Tapryal, MD
1270 Queen Emma St. #501
Honolulu, HI 96813
(808) 537-3311
FAX (808) 536-6361
GP

KAPAA, KAUAI

Thomas R. Yarema, MD, BPCT
4504 Kukui St., #13
Kapaa, Kauai, HI 96741
(808) 823-0994
FAX (808) 823-0995
AA,AC,CT,FP,HPT,NT

KAPAAU

Alan D. Thal, MD
P.O. Box 879
Kapaau, HI 96755
(808) 889-0770
FAX (808) 889-0797
A,AA,AR,CT,HRT,CD,WR

KEALAKEHUA

Clif Arrington, MD
P.O. Box 649
Kealakekua, HI 96750
(808) 322-9400
BA,CT,FP,NT,PM

IDAHO

NAMPA

Stephen Thornburgh, DO, APCT
824 - 17th Ave. So.
Nampa, ID 83651
(208) 466-3517
AC,CT,HOM,OSM,HPT,HRT,FP

ILLINOIS

ARLINGTON HEIGHTS

William J. Mauer, DO, MD (H),
FACAM, APCT
3401 N. Kennicott Avenue
Arlington Heights, IL 60004
(847) 255-8988/(800)
FAX (847) 255-7700
CT,DIA,GP,NT,OSM,PM

BELVIDERE

Oscar I. Ordonez, MD
6413 Logan Ave., #104
Belvidere, IL 61008
(815) 547-8187
FAX (815) 544-3114
A,CT,IM,NT,PM

BRAIDWOOD

Bernard G. Milton, MD
233 E. Reed St.
Braidwood, IL 60408
(815) 458-6700
AC,AU,CT,FP,HGL,YS

CHICAGO

Alan F. Bain, DO
111 N. Wabash Ave. Ste. 1005
Chicago, IL 60602
(312) 236-7010
FAX (312) 236-7190
AC,CT,IM,NT,OS

David Edelberg, MD
2522 N. Lincoln Avenue
Chicago, IL 60614
(773) 296-6700
FAX (773) 296-1131
AC,DD,CT,IM,NT,YS

Razvan Rentea, MD
3525 W. Peterson, Suite 611
Chicago, IL 60659
(773) 583-7793
FAX (773) 583-7796
NT,PD,HOM,CT,P,HRT

ELK GROVE VILLAGE

Zofia Szymanska, MD
850 Biesterfield Rd., #4006
Elk Grove Village, IL 60007
(847) 437-4418
FAX (847) 437-9431
GYN,OBS,YS,PM,END,NT

GENEVA

Richard E. Hrdlicka, MD
302 Randall Rd., #206
Geneva, IL 60134
(630) 232-1900
A,BA,FP,NT,PM,YS

HAZEL CREST

Prakash G. Sane, MD, BPCT
17680 South Kedzie Ave.
Hazel Crest, IL 60429
(708) 799-2499
FAX (708) 799-4093
FP

HOFFMAN ESTATES

Sn Busse, MD
Governor's Place Medical Bldg.
Hoffman Estates, IL 60195
(847) 781-7500
FAX (847) 781-7502
A,CT,DD,END,NT,PM,FP

METAMORA

Robert E. Thompson, MD
205 S. Englewood Drive
Metamora, IL 61548
(309) 367-2321
FAX (309) 367-2324
OB/GYN,FP,CT

MOLINE

Terry W. Love, DO, APCT
2610 - 41st Street
Moline, IL 61252
(309) 764-2900
AR,CT,GP,OSM,RHU,PM

OAK PARK

Paul J. Dunn, MD
1140 Westgate
Oak Park, IL 60301
(708) 358-0111
FAX (708) 358-1485
CT,HGL,NT,OSM,PM,YS

Ross A. Hauser, MD
715 Lake Street, Suite 600
Oak Park, IL 60301
(708) 848-7789
FAX (708) 848-7763
AN,CT,DD,NT,PMR,RHU,P/S

Carlos M. Reynes, MD
1140 Westgate
Oak Park, IL 60301
(708) 358-0111
IM,NT,PM,WR,DIA,YS

OTTAWA

Terry W. Love, DO, APCT
645 W. Main Street
Ottawa, IL 61350
(815) 434-1977
AR,CT,GP,OSM,RHU,PM

QUINCY

Walter Barnes, MD
3701 East Lake Centre Dr, #1
Quincy, IL 62301
(217) 224-3757
FAX (217) 224-5941
PM,CT

WHEATON

Fred J. Schultz, MD
2150 Manchester Rd.
Wheaton, IL 60187
(630) 933-9722
FAX (630) 933-9724
A,END,FP,NT,PM,YS,CD,DD,DIA,IM,
OME

INDIANA

CLARKSVILLE

George Wolverton, MD, APCT
647 Eastern Blvd.
Clarksville, IN 47129
(812) 282-4309
CD,CT,FP,GYN,PM,PD

GOSHEN

Douglas W. Elliott, MD, BPCT
21764 Omega Court
Goshen, IN 46528
(574) 875-4227
FAX (574) 875-7828
FP,NT

HUNTINGTON

Thomas J. Ringenberg, DO, BPCT
941 Etna Avenue
Huntington, IN 46750
(260) 356-9400
FAX (260) 356-4254
FP,OSM,AA,NT,PM

INDIANAPOLIS

David Darbro, MD
8202 Clearvista Pkwy., Bldg. 7, #A
Indianapolis, IN 46256
(317) 913-3000
FAX (317) 913-1000
A,AR,CT,DD,FP,AA,END,HGL,HRT,OME,
YS

David R. Decatur, MD
8925 N. Meridian, #150
Indianapolis, IN 46260
(317) 818-8925
AC,CD,CT,HYP,NT,PM

L. Dale Guyer, MD
836 East 86th Street
Indianapolis, IN 46240
(317) 580-9355
FAX (317) 580-9342
AA,CT,P/S,CD,NT,FP

Samia Mercho, MD
11216 Fall Creek Rd.
Indianapolis, IN 46256
(317) 595-8823
FAX (317) 535-4697
IM

JEFFERSONVILLE

H. Wayne Mayhue, MD
207 Sparks Ave., #301
Jeffersonville, IN 47130
(812) 288-7169
FAX (812) 288-2861
OB-GYN

LAFAYETTE

Charles Turner, MD, BPCT
2433 S. 9th Street
Lafayette, IN 47909
(765) 471-1100
FAX (765) 471-1009
FP,A,CT,P/S,NT,HO,AA,HPT,HRT,OSM,
PT

LYNN

David Chopra, MD
P. O. Box 636
Lynn, IN 47355
(317) 874-2411
AC,BA,CT,DD,GER,IM

MOORESVILLE

Richard N. Halstead, DO
17 Moore Street
Mooresville, IN 46158
(317) 831-0853
FAX (317) 831-0864
A,AA,CT,OSM,PM,P/S

NORTH MANCHESTER

Marvin D. Dziabis, MD
Health Restoration Clinic
No. Manchester, IN 46962
(260) 982-1400
FAX (260) 982-1700
CD,CT,HPT,ON,PT,YS

PARKER CITY

Oscar I. Ordonez, MD
218 S. Main Street
Parker City, IN 47368
(765) 468-6337
A,CT,IM,NT,PM

SOUTH BEND

Keim T. Houser, MD
515 N. Lafayette Blvd.
South Bend, IN 46601
(219) 232-2037
GYN,OBS

WASHINGTON

Anne L. Kempf, DO
RR 3, Box 357 Bedford Road
Washington, IN 47501
(812) 254-5868
AU,CT,GP,OS,FP,HRT,YS

VALPARAISO

Myrna D. Trowbridge, DO
850-C Marsh St.
Valparaiso, IN 46385
(219) 462-3377
FAX (219) 464-4530
AC,AR,CT,FP,NT,OSM

KANSAS

GARDEN CITY

Terry Hunsberger, DO
603 N. 5th. Street
Garden City, KS 67846
(316) 275-3760
FAX (316) 275-3704
BA,CT,FP,NT,OSM,PM

HAYS

Roy N. Neil, MD
105 West 13th
Hays, KS 67601
(913) 628-8341
BA,CD,CT,DD,NT,PM

KANSAS CITY

Jeanne A. Drisko, MD, BPCT
3901 Rainbow Blvd.
Kansas City, KS 66160
(913) 588-6208
FAX (913) 588-6271
GP,NT,PM,R

LIBERAL

Bob Sager, MD
2330 N. Kansas Ave.
Liberal, KS 67901
(620) 626-7080
FAX (620) 626-6633
AC,CT,FP,NT,YS,WR

TOPEKA

John Toth, MD, APCT
2115 S.W. 10th
Topeka, KS 66604
(785) 232-3330
FAX (785) 232-1874
FP,NT,PM,P/S

KENTUCKY

BEREA

Edward K. Atkinson, MD
P.O. Box 57
Berea, KY 40403
(859) 925-2252
FAX (859) 925-2252
AN,CT

SOMERSET

Stephen S. Kiteck, MD
600 Bogle St.
Somerset, KY 42503
(606) 677-0459
FP,IM,PD,PM

LOUISIANA

ALEXANDRIA

James W. Welch, MD
4300 Parliament Dr.
Alexandria, LA 71303
(318) 448-0221
S

BATON ROUGE

Stephanie F. Cave, MD, BPCT
10562 S. Glenstone Place
Baton Rouge, LA 70810
(225) 767-7433
FAX (225) 767-4641
FP,A,NT,PM,YS,DD

Mark Cotter, MD
5207 Essen Lane
Baton Rouge, LA 70809
(225) 766-3171
FAX (225) 766-3271
AR,DIA,MM,NT,OM,WR

BELLE CHASSE

Lawrence A. Giambelluca, MD
8200 Highway 23
Belle Chasse, LA 70037
(504) 398-1100
FAX (504) 398-1030
CT,FP

CHALMETTE

Saroj T. Tampira, MD
9000 Patricia St., Ste. 118
Chalmette, LA 70043
(504) 277-8991
FAX (504) 277-8997
CD,DD,DIA,IM

HARAHAN

Kashmir K. Rai, MD, BPCT
For Better Health, LLC
Harahan, LA 70123
(504) 818-2525
FAX (504) 818-0492
A,CT,FP,HGL,NT,PM,GP

LAFAYETTE

Sydney Crackower, MD
701 Robley Dr., #100
Lafayette, LA 70503
(337) 988-4116
CT,FP,GER

Norman Dykes, MD
501 W. SaintMary Blvd., #308
Lafayette, LA 70506
(337) 234-1119
FAX (337) 234-1477
IM

Sangeeta Shah, MD
211 E. Kaliste Saloom
Lafayette, LA 70508
(337) 235-1166
FAX (337) 235-1168
BA,DIA,HGL,NT,PM,CT

METAIRIE

Janet Perez-Chiesa, MD, FACP, BPCT
4532 W. Napoleon Ave., #210
Metairie, LA 70001
(504) 456-7539
FAX (504) 456-7542
CT,GP,IM,PM,Neurology

NEW ORLEANS

James P. Carter, MD, APCT
2134 Napoleon Ave.
New Orleans, LA 70115
(504) 779-6363
FAX (504) 779-9963
GP,NT,PM

SLIDELL

James Fambro, MD
303 Leeds Drive
Slidell, LA 70461
(985) 781-8248
FAX (985) 781-8248
Emergency Med, Sport Med.

MAINE

GRAY

Raymond Psonak, DO
51 West Gray Rd., Ste.1A
Gray, ME 04039
(207) 657-4325
FAX (207) 657-4325
A,CT,DD,NT,Immune D/O,Env.Med.

PORTLAND

Alan N. Weiner, DO
4 Milk Street
Portland, ME 04101
(207) 828-8080
FAX (207) 828-6816
CT,NT,AC,OS,AA,EV

WATERVILLE

Arthur Weisser, DO,APCT
81 Grove Street
Waterville, ME 04901
(207) 873-7721
FAX (207) 873-7724
CT,FP,GP,NT,OS,PM

MARYLAND

ANNAPOLIS

Jacob E. Teitelbaum, MD
466 Forelands Road
Annapolis, MD 21401
(410) 573-5389
FAX (410) 266-6104
IM,CFS,Fibromyalgia

BALTIMORE

Binyamin Rothstein, DO, APCT
2835 Smith Ave., #203
Baltimore, MD 21209
(410) 484-2121
AA,FP,HRT,OSM,P/S,RHU

BELCAMP

Philip W. Halstead, MD
1200 Brass Mill Road
Belcamp, MD 21017
(410) 272-7751
FAX (410) 273-0476
IM,DIA,NT,PM

GREENBELT

Frank Melograna, MD
7755 Belle Point Drive
Greenbelt, MD 20770
(301) 474-3636
FAX (301-513-5087
Urology

LAUREL

Paul V. Beals, MD, BPCT
9101 Cherry Lane Park, Suite 205
Laurel, MD 20708
(301) 490-9911
FAX (202) 986-3255
CT,FP,NT,AR,CD,HPT

LUTHERVILLE

Elisabeth Lucas, MD
1205 York Road, Ste. 30A
Lutherville, MD 21093
(410) 823-3101
FAX (410) 823-1021
IM,AA,HGL,WR,HOM,NT,YS,DIA,HRT

Kenneth B. Singleton, MD
2328 W. Joppa Rd., #310
Lutherville, MD 21093
(410) 296-3737
FAX (410) 296-0650
IM,NT,AC

ROCKVILLE

Norton Fishman, MD, CNS
Optimal Health Physicians
Rockville, MD 20850
(301) 330-9430
FAX (301) 330-6515
CT,GER,IM,PM,CD,HRT,NT

STEVENSVILLE

Paul V. Beals, MD, BPCT
133 Log Canoe Circle
Stevensville, MD 21666
(410) 604-6344
CT,FP,NT,AR,CD,HPT

MASSACHUSETTS

ARLINGTON

Michael Janson, MD, FACAM, APCT
180 Massachusetts Ave., Ste. 303
Arlington, MA 02474
(617) 547-0295
FAX (617) 588-0624
A,CD,CT,NT,OME,YS

Glenn Rothfeld, MD
WholeHealth New England
Arlington, MA 02474
(781) 641-1901
FAX (781) 641-3963
GP,AC,CT,NT,PM,YS

BOSTON

Ruben Oganesov, MD, APCT
39 Brighton Ave.
Boston, MA 02134
(617) 783-5783
FAX (617) 783-1519
AC,CT,GP,NT,PMR

Earl Robert Parson, MD
495 Summer Street (MEPS)
Boston, MA 02210
(617) 753-3113
CT,AR,DD,GP,PM,WR

BREWSTER

Lorraine Hurley, MD
210 Griffith's Pond Rd.
Brewster, MA 02631
(508) 896-1142
FAX (508) 896-1143
FP,NT,GP

CAMBRIDGE

Guy Pugh, MD, BPCT
2500 Massachusetts Ave
Cambridge, MA 02140
(617) 661-6225
FAX (617) 492-2002
A,AC,CT,GP,NT,IM

FRAMINGHAM

Carol Englender, MD, BPCT
160 Speen Street, #203
Framingham, MA 01701
(508) 875-0875
FAX (508) 875-0005
A,FP,NT,PM,EV

MALDEN

George Milowe, MD, APCT
11 Bickford Road
Malden, MA 02148
(781) 397-7408
FAX (781) 324-2610
AC,CT,NT,PM,PO,Herbs

NORTHAMPTON

Barry D. Elson, MD
395 Pleasant Street
Northampton, MA 01060
(413) 584-7787
FAX (413) 584-7778
A,CT,NT,HPT,HRT,PMR

WEST BOYLSTON

N. Thomas La Cava, MD
360 West Boylston St., Suite 107
West Boylston, MA 01583
(508) 854-1380
FAX (508) 854-0446
EV,PD,OMF,CT,A,HOM,HRT

MICHIGAN

BAY CITY

Parveen A. Malik, MD
808 N. Euclid Ave.
Bay City, MI 48706
(989) 686-3760
FAX (989) 686-5615
CT,FP,GP,NT,P/S

CLARKSTON

Nedra Downing, DO, BPCT
5639 Sashabaw Road
Clarkston, MI 48346
(248) 625-6677
FAX (248) 625-5633
A,GP,NT,OS,PM,YS

FARMINGTON HILLS

Helen Lee, MD
30275 W. 13 Mile Rd.
Farmington Hills, MI 48334
(248) 626-7544
FAX (248) 626-9698
A,AC,CT,GP,NT,PM

FLINT

William M. Bernard, DO, BPCT
1044 Gilbert Street
Flint, MI 48532
(810) 733-3140
FAX (810) 733-5623
A,CT,FP,GER,OSM,PM

Kenneth Ganapini, DO, BPCT
1044 Gilbert Street
Flint, MI 48532
(810) 733-3140
FAX (810) 733-5623
CT,FP,GP,OSM,PM,YS

Janice Shimoda, DO, BPCT
1044 Gilbert Street
Flint, MI 48532
(810) 733-3140
FAX (810) 733-5623
CT,FP,NT,PM

GRAND RAPIDS

Tammy Born, DO, APCT
3700 - 52nd Street S.E.
Grand Rapids, MI 49512
(616) 656-3700
FAX (616) 656-3701
CT,FP,PM,YS,P/S,PT

Robert A. DeJonge, DO, BPCT
2251 East Paris
Grand Rapids, MI 49546
(616) 956-6090
FAX (616) 956-6099
FP,AA,NT

GROSSE POINTE

Cynthia Browne, MD, PhD
Van Eslander Cancer Center
Grosse Pointe, MI 48236
(313) 647-3100
FAX (313) 647-3131
ON,NT

R.B. Fahim, MD, BPCT
20825 Mack Ave
Grosse Pointe, MI 48236
(313) 640-9730
FAX (313) 640-9740
CT,MM

LAPEER

Paul D. Lepor, DO, BPCT
1254 North Main St.
Lapeer, MI 48446
(810) 664-4531
A,PD,PM

MADISON HEIGHTS

Rodney Moret, MD
1400 East 12 Mile Road
Madison Heights, MI 48071
(248) 547-2223
FAX (248) 547-2226
GP

NORWAY

F. Michael Saigh, MD
411 Murray Rd. West U.S. 2
Norway, MI 49870
(906) 563-9600
FAX (906) 563-7110
FP

PARCHMENT

Eric Born, DO, APCT
2350 East G Avenue
Parchment, MI 49004
(616) 344-6183
FAX (616) 349-3046
DIA,FP,NT,OS,PM,YS

PONTIAC

Vahagn Agbabian, DO
28 No. Saginaw St., Suite 1105
Pontiac, MI 48342
(248) 334-2424
FAX (248) 334-2924
CT,HPT,DIA,CD,IM,OME,NT,UVT,HRT

ROMEO

James Ziobron, DO
71441 Van Dyke
Romeo, MI 48065
(810) 336-3700
FAX (810) 336-9443
A,CT,DD,YS,HPT,NT,P/S

SALINE

John G. Ghuneim, MD, BPCT
Innovations in Health, Inc.
Saline, MI 48176
(734) 429-2581
FAX (734) 429-3410
AC,AU,CT,IM,NT,PM, P/S

SOUTHFIELD

Mark Hertzberg, MD
25865 W. 12 Mile Road, #104
Southfield, MI 48034
(248) 357-3220
FAX (248) 357-3639
IM,AA,PM

TAWAS CITY

Michael D. Papenfuse, DO
200 Hemlock Rd.
Tawas City, MI 48764
(517) 362-9229
FAX (517) 362-9228
AN,OS,P/S,YS

WEST BLOOMFIELD

David Brownstein, MD
5821 W. Maple Rd., #192
West Bloomfield, MI 48322
(248) 851-1600
FAX (248) 851-0421
FP,AC,A

Jeffrey Nusbaum, MD
5821 West Maple Road, #192
West Bloomfield, MI 48322
(248) 851-1600
FAX (248) 851-0421
A,AA,AR,DD,OME,NT,FP

MINNESOTA

BLOOMINGTON

George Kramer, MD
10564 France Ave., South
Bloomington, MN 55431
(612) 706-1418
FAX (952) 881-5871
P/S,PMR,AC,AU

Kevin T. Wand, DO
Midwest Wellness Center
Bloomington, MN 55431
(952) 942-9303
FAX (952) 881-6871
A,CT,FP,GER,NT,PD,YS

MINNETONKA

Jean R. Eckerly, MD, APCT
13911 Ridgedale Dr., #350
Minnetonka, MN 55441
(952) 593-9458
FAX (952) 593-0097
CT,IM,NT,OME,PM

SAINT LOUIS PARK

Michael A. Dole, MD, APCT
3408 Dakota Ave.S
St. Louis Park, MN 55416
(952) 924-1053
FAX (952) 924-0254
CT,HRT,PM,YS,OME,A

SORTELL

Tom Sult, MD, BPCT
100 2nd Street S.
Sortell, MN 56377
(320) 251-2600
GP

MISSISSIPPI

COLDWATER

Pravin P. Patel, MD
P. O. Box 1060
Coldwater, MS 38618
(601) 622-7011
FAX (662) 622-0257
CT,FP

COLUMBUS

Jacob Skiwski, MD, BPCT
3491 Bluecutt Rd.
Columbus, MS 39701
(601) 329-2955 or 32
A,CT,NT,GP,PD

OCEAN SPRINGS

James H. Waddell, MD
1520 Government Street
Ocean Springs, MS 39564
(228) 875-5505
FAX (228) 872-8207
AC,AN,AU,CT

PICAYUNE

Thomas Purser, III, MD
1911 Read Rd.
Picayune, MS 39466
(601) 798-0535
FAX (601) 798-0377
Orthopedics

MISSOURI

COLUMBIA

Bonnie Friehling, MD
5108 Buckeye Drive
Columbia, MO 65203
(573) 256-4665
GP,FP,CT,HRT,NT

KANSAS CITY

Edward McDonagh, DO, FACAM, APCT
2800-A Kendallwood Pkwy.
Kansas City, MO 64119
(816) 453-5940
FAX (816) 453-1140
CD,CT,DD,FP,HO,PM

Charles Rudolph, DO, PhD, FACAM, APCT
2800-A Kendallwood Pkwy.
Kansas City, MO 64119
(816) 453-5940
FAX (816) 453-1140
CD,CT,DD,FP,HO,P/S

SAINT LOUIS

Lena R. Capapas, MD, BPCT
522 N. New Ballas Rd., #334
St. Louis, MO 63141
(314) 995-9713
FAX (314) 995-1404
IM,CD

Octavio R. Chirino, MD
9701 Landmark Pkwy. Dr., #207
St. Louis, MO 63127
(314) 842-4802
OBS,GYN,NT,Hormone Repl.

Varsha Rathod, MD
1977 Schuetz Rd.
St. Louis, MO 63146
(314) 997-5403
FAX (314) 997-6837
IM,CT,HRT,AR,NT,HGL,YS

Simon M. Yu, MD, APCT
11710 Old Ballas Rd., #205
St. Louis, MO 63141
(314) 432-7802
FAX (314) 432-1971
CD,CT,DIA,IM,NT,PM

SPRINGFIELD

Neil Nathan, MD
2828 N. National, #D
Springfield, MO 65803
(417) 869-7583
FAX (417) 869-7592
AC,CT,FP,NT,OSM,P/S

William Sunderwirth, DO
2828 N. National
Springfield, MO 65803
(417) 837-4158
CT,DIA,GP,OS,PM,S

MONTANA

BELGRADE

Curt Kurtz, MD
8707 N. Jackrabbit, Ste. C
Belgrade, MT 59714
(406) 587-5561
FAX (406) 585-8536
FP,HYP,YS

BILLINGS

David C. Healow, MD
2501 - 4th Avenue North, #C
Billings, MT 59101
(406) 252-6674
AC,AN

NEBRASKA

HARTINGTON

Steve Vlach, MD
405 W. Darlene St., P.O. Box 937
Hartington, NE 68739
(402) 254-3935
FAX (402) 254-2393
CD,CT,DIA,FP,NT,WR,YS,Em Med

NORTH PLATTE

Loretta Baca, MD
302 S. Jeffers St.
North Platte, NE 69101
(308) 534-6687
FAX (308) 534-1874
IM,RHU,AC,AA,CT,DIA

OMAHA

James Murphy, Jr., DO
8031 W. Center Road, #221
Omaha, NE 68124
(402) 343-7963
FAX (402) 343-1330
OSM,CT,FP,HOM,NT

Eugene C. Oliveto, MD
10804 Prairie Hills Dr.
Omaha, NE 68144
(402) 392-0233
CT,NT,PM,P,PO

Jeffrey Passer, MD
9300 Underwood Ave., Suite 520
Omaha, NE 68114
(402) 398-1200
FAX (402) 398-9119
BA,END,IM,PM,HRT,AA,DIA

NEVADA

CARSON CITY

Frank Shallenberger, MD, HMD
Anti Aging Medicine
Carson City, NV 89703
(775) 884-3990
FAX (775) 884-2202
CT,GP,HOM,NEURL THER,OXID
MED,AA

HENDERSON

Dan F. Royal, DO
2501 N. Green Valley Pkwy.
#D-132
Henderson, NV 89014
(702) 433-8800
FAX (702) 433-8823
A,CT,HYP,NT,OS,PM

LAS VEGAS

Steven G. Holper, MD
3233 W. Charleston, #202
Las Vegas, NV 89102
(702) 878-3510
FAX (702) 878-1405
Phys. Rehab.

Robert D. Milne, MD
2110 Pinto Lane
Las Vegas, NV 89106
(702) 385-1393
FAX (702) 385-4170
FP,HPT,HOM,HRT,CT,P/S,PT,UV,AC,A

Adelaida Resuello, MD
1300 S. Maryland Pkwy.
Las Vegas, NV 89104
(702) 385-2691,Cell
FAX (702) 385-4457
IM,PD,BA,FP,GP

F. Fuller Royal, MD
3663 Pecos McLeod
Las Vegas, NV 89121
(702) 732-1400
FAX (702) 732-9661
A,AC,CT,GP,HYP,HOM

RENO

W. Douglas Brodie, MD, HMD
6110 Plumas St., #B
Reno, NV 89509
(775) 829-1009
FAX (775) 829-9330
CT,DD,FP,GP,HOM,IM,NT,PM

David A. Edwards, MD, APCT
615 Sierra Rose Drive, #3
Reno, NV 89511
(775) 828-4055
FAX (775)828-4255
AA,CD,CT,HPT,HOM,UV

Michael L. Gerber, MD, APCT
3670 Grant Dr., #101
Reno, NV 89509
(775) 826-1900
AA,CT,HOM,HRT,YS,NT,OME,AC,HPT

Corazon Ibarra, MD, MD(H), APCT
6490 S. McCarran Blvd., #D-41
Reno, NV 89509
(775) 827-6696
FAX (775) 827-8220
CT,PM,Biol. Med,Integrative Med.

NEW HAMPSHIRE

AMHERST

Michael Janson, MD, FACAM,
APCT
Center for Preventive Med.
Amherst, NH 03031
(603) 673-7910
A,CD,CT,NT,OME,YS

NEW JERSEY

BLOOMFIELD

Richard L. Podkul, MD
1064 Broad Street
Bloomfield, NJ 07003
(973) 893-0282
FAX (973) 893-0612
CT,A,IM,NT,DIA

BRIGANTINE

Michael J. Dunn, MD
1311 East Shove Drive
Brigantine, NJ 08203
(609) 266-0400
FAX (609) 266-2597
IM,CT,P/S

CEDAR GROVE

Robert Steinfeld, MD
912 Pompton Ave., Ste. 9B1
Cedar Grove, NJ 07009
(973) 571-0572
FAX (973) 835-8312
AA,CD,CT,HRT,NT,PM

CHERRY HILL

Scott R. Greenberg, MD, BPCT
1907 Greentree Rd.
Cherry Hill, NJ 08003
(856) 424-8222
FAX (856) 424-2599
CT,P/S,FP,PM,MM,NT,AA,WR,
MESOTHERAPY

Allan Magaziner, DO, FACAM,
APCT,CNS
1907 Greentree Road
Cherry Hill, NJ 08003
(856) 424-8222
FAX (856) 424-2599
A,CT,DD,NT,OME,OSM,PM

DENVILLE

Majid Ali, MD
95 E. Main Street, #101
Denville, NJ 07834
(973) 586-4111
FAX (973) 586-8466
A,PM,Pathology,Integrative Med.

EAST BRUNSWICK

James Lynch, Jr., MD
150 Tices Lane
East Brunswick, NJ 08816
(732) 254-5553
FP,IM

EDISON

Richard B. Menashe, DO
15 South Main St.
Edison, NJ 08837
(732) 906-8866
FAX (732) 906-0124
A,CD,CT,DD,OSM,NT,YS

ELIZABETH

Gennaro Locurcio, MD, BPCT
610 Third Avenue
Elizabeth, NJ 07202
(908) 351-1333
FAX (908) 351-3740
A,AC,CT,NT,P/S,PO

ENGLEWOOD

Gary Klingsberg, DO, APCT
Center for Nutrition & Preventive
Med.
Englewood, NJ 07631
(201) 503-0007
FAX (201) 503-0008
A,CT,Env.Med.,PM,YS

FAIR LAWN

Anthony M. Giliberti, DO
14-01 Broadway
Fair Lawn, NJ 07410
(201) 797-8534
GP,A,CD,DD,NT,PM

FRANKLIN LAKES

Stuart Weg, MD, BPCT
498 Island Way
Franklin Lakes, NJ 07417
(201) 447-5558
FAX (201) 447-9011
AN,CT,DD,Pain Mngt.

HACKENSACK

Robin Leder, MD, APCT
235 Prospect Ave.
Hackensack, NJ 07601
(201) 525-1155
FAX (201) 525-0915
A,CT,NT,PM

HADDONFIELD

Roberta Morgan, DO, BPCT
124 Kings Highway West
Haddonfield, NJ 08033
(856) 216-9001
FAX (856) 616-9837
CT,GP,GYN,PM,NT,OSM

LAKEWOOD

Gloria Freundlich, DO
122 Hope Chapel Road
Lakewood, NJ 08701
(732) 961-9217
CT,FP,NT,OSM,PM

LITTLE FALLS

Nancy Lentine, DO
96 E. Main Street
Little Falls, NJ 07424
(973) 237-0700
FAX (973) 237-0777
FP

MANAHAWKIN

Mark J. Bartiss, MD, BPCT
24 Nautilus Drive, #5
Manahawkin, NJ 08050
(609) 978-9002
FAX (609) 597-6186
BA,CT,DD,FP,NT,PM

MARLTON

Vivienne Matalon, MD
TLC Healthcare, Inc.
Marlton, NJ 08053
(856) 985-0590
FAX (856) 985-2866
IM,DIA,WR

MIDDLETOWN

David Dornfeld, DO
18 Leonardville Rd.
Middletown, NJ 07748
(732) 671-3730
FAX (732) 706-1078
CT,DIA,FP,NT,OSM,PM

Neil Rosen, DO
18 Leonardville Rd.
Middletown, NJ 07748
(732) 671-3730
FAX (732) 706-1078
AA,CD,FP,HPT,HRT,NT,OSM,PM,PMR,
YS

MILLBURN

Sharda Sharma, MD
131 Millburn Avenue
Millburn, NJ 07041
(973) 376-4500
FAX (973) 467-2285
FP,AC,NT,CT,HRT,WR,HGL,YS,DIA,NT

Daniel Zacharias, MD, BPCT
68 Essex Street
Millburn, NJ 07041
(973) 912-0006
FAX (973) 912-0007
GP,CT,Emergency Medicine

MILLVILLE

Charles Mintz, MD
10 E. Broad Street
Millville, NJ 08332
(609) 825-7372
FAX (609) 327-6588
GP,NT,PM

MORRISTOWN

Faina Munits, MD
4 Boxwood Drive
Morristown, NJ 07960
(973) 292-3222
FAX (973) 292-3443
A,CD,CT,DIA,DD,HGL,PM

Esra Onat, MD
26 Madison Ave.
Morristown, NJ 07960
(973) 889-0200
FAX (973) 889-3544
FP,PM,IM

NEWARK

Stephen Holt, MD, APCT, FACAM
105 Lock Street, Ste. 405
Newark, NJ 07103
(973) 824-8800
FAX (973) 824-8822
DD,GE,GP,IM,NT,PM

Herbert Smyczek, MD
132 Van Buren St.
Newark, NJ 07105
(973) 690-5513
FAX (973) 690-5514
CT,AA,HRT,MM,NT,PM

NORTHFIELD

Barry D. Glasser, MD
1907 New Road
Northfield, NJ 08225
(609) 646-9600
FAX (609) 484-8127
AC,FP,IM,R,Pain Mngt.

NORTH WILDWOOD

John G. Costino, DO
404 Surf Avenue
North Wildwood, NJ 08260
(609) 522-8358
FAX (609) 729-8662
GP,RHU,PMR,Sports Med.

ORANGE

Shashi Agarwal, MD
290 Central Ave.
Orange, NJ 07050
(973) 676-1234
FAX (973) 676-5858
IM

PARAMUS

Thomas A. Cacciola, MD, BPCT
403 Farview Ave.
Paramus, NJ 07652
(201) 261-8386
FAX (201) 261-8827
CT,IM,NT,PM,AA,CD

RIDGEWOOD

Arie Rave, MD, BPCT
1250 E. Ridgewood Ave.
Ridgewood, NJ 07450
(201) 689-1900
FAX (201) 447-9011
CD,CT,FP,HGL,IM,NT,RHU

ROSELLE PARK

Yulius Poplyansky, MD, BPCT
236 E. Westfield Avenue
Roselle Park, NJ 07204
(908) 241-3800
FAX (908) 241-9668
AA,CD,CT,END,IM,NT,PM

SHREWSBURY

David Dornfeld, DO
555 Shrewsbury Ave.
Shrewsbury, NJ 07702
(732) 219-0894
FAX (732) 219-0896
CT,DIA,FP,NT,OSM,PM

Neil Rosen, DO
555 Shrewsbury Ave.
Shrewsbury, NJ 07702
(732) 219-0894
FAX (732) 219-0896
FP,NT,OS,PM,PMR,EECP

SOMERSET

Marc Condren, MD
7 Cedar Grove Lane, #20
Somerset, NJ 08873
(908) 469-2133
A,FP,MM,NT,AA,CT

STOCKTON

Stuart H. Freedenfeld, MD
56 So. Main St., #A
Stockton, NJ 08559
(609) 397-8585
FAX (609) 397-9335
A,ON,CT,END,FP,YS

TRENTON

Imtiaz Ahmad, MD
1760 Whitehorse Hamilton Sq. Rd.,
#5
Trenton, NJ 08690
(609) 890-2966
FAX (609) 890-3326
CD,Vascular Surgery

Robert J. Peterson, DO
2239 Whitehorse/Mercerville Rd.,
#4
Trenton, NJ 08619
(215) 579-0330
AR,CD,CT,DD,DIA,NT,PM,YS,HPT

UNION CITY

Simon Santos, MD
410 - 36th Street
Union City, NJ 07087
(201) 863-7744
FAX (201) 863-7608
GP,FP,S

WOODBRIDGE

David M. Strassberg, MD, APCT
1 Woodbridge Center, #245
Woodbridge, NJ 07095
(732) 855-7700
GE,IM,NT,CD,CT,DIA

NEW MEXICO

ALBUQUERQUE

Ralph J. Luciani, DO, APCT
10601 Lomas Blvd. NE, #103
Albuquerque, NM 87112
(505) 298-5995
FAX (505) 298-2940
AC,AA,CT,FP,OSM,PM,P/S,YS

LAS CRUCES

Burton M. Berkson, MD, PhD
1155-C Commerce Dr.
Las Cruces, NM 88011
(505) 524-3720
FAX (505) 521-1815
Integrative Medicine

Wolfgang Haese, MD, DTM, APCT
4105 N. Main Street
Las Cruces, NM 88012
(505) 373-8415
FAX (505) 373-8416
AA,AC,CT,FP,HPT,HRT,PT,UV,OME,
Integrative Med.

SANTA FE

Shirley B. Scott, MD
P. O. Box 2670
Santa Fe, NM 87504
(505) 986-9960
GE,MM,PM,YS,HRT,AA

W. A. Shrader, Jr., MD
141 Paseo de Peralta
Santa Fe, NM 87501
(505) 983-8890
FAX (505) 820-7315
A,CT,EV

NEW YORK

ALBANY

Kenneth A. Bock, MD, FACAM,
APCT
10 McKown RD
Albany, NY 12203
(518) 435-0082
FAX (518) 435-0086
A,CD,CT,FP,NT,PM

ALBERTSON

Steven Rachlin, MD
927 Willis Avenue
Albertson, L.I., NY 11507
(516) 873-7773
FAX (516) 877-7365
A,CT,IM,NT,PM

BREWSTER

Jeffrey C. Kopelson, MD
221 Clock Tower Commons
Brewster, NY 10509
(914) 278-6800
FAX (914) 278-6897
CT,FP,NT,PM

BRONX

Richard Izquierdo, MD, BPCT
1070 Southern Blvd., Lower Level
Bronx, NY 10459
(718) 589-4541
A,FP,GP,NT,PD,PM

BRONXVILLE

Joseph S. Wojcik, MD
525 Bronxville Rd.,1-G
Bronxville, NY 10708
(914) 793-6161
A,CT,PD,PM,NT,Env.Med

BROOKLYN

Gloria W. Freundlich, DO
575 Ocean Parkway
Brooklyn, NY 11218
(718) 437-4459
CT,FP,NT,OSM,PM

Igor Ostrovsky, MD
3120 Brighton 5th Street, # 1-C
Brooklyn, NY 11235
(718) 934-1920
FAX (718) 934-2078
AN,AC,CT,NT

Robert Weiner, MD
2352 Ralph Ave.
Brooklyn, NY 11234
(718) 251-0200
FAX (718) 209-5697
FP

Pavel Yutsis, MD, APCT
264 1st Street
Brooklyn, NY 11215
(718) 621-0900
FAX (718) 621-9165
A,CT,FP,NT,PD,PM,YS

BUFFALO

Kalpana Patel, MD, APCT
65 Wehrle Drive
Buffalo, NY 14225
(716) 833-2213
FAX (716) 833-2244
A,CT,NT,PD,PM,HGL,YS

CHAPPAQUA

Savely Yurkovsky, MD
37 King Street
Chappaqua, NY 10514
(914) 861-9161
A,CD,CS,CT,NT,PM

DERBY

Robert F. Barnes, BPCT
7008 Erie Rd.
Derby, NY 14047
(716) 679-3510
CT,NT,PM,HPT,YS

EAST MEADOW

Kathryn Calabria, BPCT
30 Merrick Ave., #111
East Meadow, NY 11554
(516) 542-9090
FAX (516) 542-9258
AC,FP,OSM

FREDONIA

Robert F. Barnes, BPCT
3489 E. Main Rd.
Fredonia, NY 14063
(716) 679-3510
FAX (716) 679-3512
CT,NT,PM,HPT,YS

GLENS FALLS

Andrew W. Garner, MD, APCT
8 Harrison Avenue
Glens Falls, NY 12801
(518) 798-9401
FAX (518) 798-9411
FP,CT,PM

HAMBURG

Ronald P. Santasiero, MD
5451 Southwestern Blvd.
Hamburg, NY 14075
(716) 646-6075
FAX (716) 646-5912
AC,CT,PM,AA

HOWARD BEACH

Christopher Cimmino, DO
157-05 Crossbay Blvd.
Howard Beach, NY 11414
(718) 845-5252
FAX (718) 845-6464
FP,MM,NT,OSM,CT,HRT,P/S,UV,WR

Delfino Crescenzo, MD
161-50 92nd Street
Howard Beach, NY 11414
(718) 848-0425
FAX (718) 848-5830
NT,ON

William Miller, DO
157-05 Crossbay Blvd.
Howard Beach, NY 11414
(718) 845-5252
FAX (718) 845-6464
AA,CT,HPT,HRT,LM,UV,NT

LAKE SUCCESS

Maurice Cohen, MD
2 ProHealth Plaza
Lake Success, NY 11042
(516) 608-2806
FAX (516) 608-2805
GYN

LAWRENCE

Mitchell Kurk, MD, APCT
310 Broadway
Lawrence, NY 11559
(516) 239-5540
FAX (516) 371-2919
CT,FP,GER,NT,OME,PM

MERRICK

Sn Groh, MD
2916 Frankel Blvd.
Merrick, NY 11566
(516) 867-5132
FAX (516) 867-5519
CT,FP,GER,AC

MIDDLETOWN

Levi H. Lehv, MD
825 Route 211 East
Middletown, NY 10941
(914) 692-8338
FAX (914) 692-6177
BA,CT,DIA,IM,PM,Homeopathy

MT. KISCO

Neil C. Raff, MD
213 Main Street
Mt. Kisco, NY 10549
(914) 241-7030
IM,GE

NEW CITY

Arthur Landau, MD, BPCT
10 Esquire Road
New City, NY 10956
(845) 638-4464
FAX (845) 638-4509
A,BA,CT,IM,PM

NEW YORK

Majid Ali, MD
140 West End Ave., Suite I-H
New York, NY 10023
(212) 873-2444
FAX (212) 873-2452
A,PM,Pathology,Integrative Med.

Richard N. Ash, MD
800-A Fifth Ave. 61st St.
New York, NY 10021
(212) 758-3200
FAX (212) 754-5800
A,CD,CT,HYP,NT,MM,IM,Rec.therapy

Robert C. Atkins, MD
152 E. 55th St.
New York, NY 10022
(212) 758-2110
FAX (212) 751-1863
CT,HGL,OME

Eric R. Braverman, MD, APCT
185 Madison Ave., 6th floor
New York, NY 10016
(212) 213-6155
FAX (212) 213-6188
CT,IM,MM,PM,PO,Neurology

Claudia M. Cooke, MD
133 East 73rd Street, #506
New York, NY 10021
(212) 861-9000
FAX (212) 585-4177
AC,IM,PM,NT

Patrick Fratellone, MD
24 West 57th Street, #701
New York, NY 10019
(212) 977-9870
FAX (212) 977-9816
CD

Ronald Hoffman, MD, FACAM,
APCT, CNS
40 E. 30th Street
New York, NY 10016
(212) 779-1744
FAX (212) 779-0891
CT,AA,CD,DD,DIA,WR,YS,OME,NT,
MM,A,HGL,YS

Alexander N. Kulick, MD
625 Madison Avenue, #10-A
New York, NY 10022
(212) 838-8265
FAX (212) 752-5140
IM,AC,CT,NT,PM,WR

Warren M. Levin, MD, APCT
31 East 28th Street, 6th Flr.
New York, NY 10016
(212) 679-9667
FAX (212) 679-9730
A,AC,CT,NT,OME,PM

Gennaro Locurcio, MD, BPCT
112 Lexington Avenue
New York, NY 10016
(212) 696-2680
FAX (212) 696-2694
A,AC,CT,NT,P/S,PO

Jeffrey A. Morrison, MD, BPCT
103 Fifth Ave., 6th Floor
New York, NY 10003
(212) 989-9828
FAX (212) 989-9827
A,CT,FP,NT,PM,YS,P/S,HRT,EV,DD,HGL

Sabina Barbara Ostolski, DO
43 West 24th Street, 3rd Floor
New York, NY 10010
(212) 255-2466
FAX (212) 255-2474
AA,CT,DIA,IM,OSM,WR,NT

Gary Ostrow, DO
625 Madison Ave., #10-A
New York, NY 10022
(212) 838-8265
FAX (212-752-5140
BA,CT,NT,OSM,FP,P/S

Fred Pescatore, MD, BPCT
274 Madison Avenue, #402
New York, NY 10016
(212) 779-2944
FAX (212) 779-2941
CT,DIA,END,GP,PM,PH,AA,BA,CD,HRT,
MM

John P. Salerno, DO
One Rockerfeller Plaza, #1401
New York, NY 10020
(212) 582-1700
FAX (212) 582-1737
AA,AR,BA,CT,FP,HGL,HRT,NT,YS

Lawrence Young, MD
19 Bowery Street, Rm. 1
New York, NY 10002
(212) 431-4343
FAX (212) 925-8637
A,AC,NT,IM

NIAGARA FALLS

Paul Cutler, MD, FACAM, APCT
652 Elmwood Ave.
Niagara Falls, NY 14301
(716) 284-5140
FAX (716) 284-5159
A,CT,NT

ORANGEBURG

Neil L. Block, MD
14 Prel Plaza
Orangeburg, NY 10962
(914) 359-3300
AA,BA,END,PO,NT,FP

PELHAM MANOR

Erika Krauss, DO
4662 Boston Post Rd.
Pelham Manor, NY 10803
(914) 738-7100
FAX (914) 738-9249
GP,IM,PM,OS,NT,CD,DIA,YS,WR

RHINEBECK

Kenneth A. Bock, MD, FACAM,
APCT
108 Montgomery St.
Rhinebeck, NY 12572
(845) 876-7082
FAX (845) 876-4615
A,CD,CT,FP,NT,PM

Steven Bock, MD
108 Montgomery Street
Rhinebeck, NY 12572
(845) 876-7082
FAX (845) 876-4615
NT,CT,AC,FP,AA,A

ROCHESTER

Paul Cutler, MD, FACAM, APCT
1081 Long Pond Rd.
Rochester, NY 14626
(716) 284-5140
FAX (716) 284-5159
A,CT,NT

SETAUKET

William Flader, MD
100 North Country Road
Setauket, NY 11733
(631) 941-3137
FP

Johnny Slade, MD
100 North Country Rd.
Setauket, NY 11733
(631) 941-3137
FP

SUFFERN

Michael B. Schachter, MD, CNS, FACAM, APCT
Two Executive Blvd., #202
Suffern, NY 10901
(845) 368-4700
FAX (845) 368-4727
A,CT,NT,PO,ON,OME,HRT,P,EV,HPT, PM,YS,A

UTICA

Richard O'Brien, DO
2305 Genesee Street
Utica, NY 13501
(315) 724-8888
FP,OSM,CT

Margarita Schilling, MD
2305 Genesee Street
Utica, NY 13501
(315) 797-3799
FAX (315) 734-1912
IM,END

WOODSIDE

Fira Nihamin, MD
39 - 65 52nd Street
Woodside, NY 11377
(718) 429-0039
FAX (718) 429-6965
CD,DIA,DD,GP,GER,IM

NORTH CAROLINA

ASHEVILLE

James Biddle, MD, APCT
832 Hendersonville Road
Asheville, NC 28803
(828) 252-5545
FAX (828) 281-3055
CT,CD,IM,NT,DIA,A

Salvatore D'Angio, MD
25 Orange Street
Asheville, NC 28801
(828) 253-3140
FAX (828) 253-4044
CT,CD,MM,AC,NT,END

Ronald Parks, MD
1070-1 Tunnel Rd., #252
Asheville, NC 28805
(828) 225-1812
FAX (828) 225-7387
P,PO,EV,CT,HRT,Integr.Med.

John L. Wilson Jr., MD, APCT
Great Smokies Med. Ctr. Of Asheville
Asheville, NC 28806
(828) 252-9833
FAX (828) 255-8118
A,CT,EV,NT,PM,HYP,YS

Eileen M. Wright, MD
Park Terrace Center, 1312 Patton Ave.
Asheville, NC 28806
(828) 252-9833
FAX (828) 255-8118
GP,PM,CT,DIA,A,HGL,HRT,HYP,MM, UV,YS

CAROLINA BEACH

Keith E. Johnson, MD
1009 N. Lake Park Blvd., Box 16, C-5
Carolina Beach, NC 28428
(910) 458-0606
CD,CT,DIA,NT,PM,RHU,WR

CHARLOTTE

Rashid Ali Buttar, DO, APCT, FACAM
20721 Torrence Chapel, #101-102
Charlotte, NC 28031
(704) 895-9355
FAX (704) 895-9357
A,CD,CT,DD,END,NT,PM,PUD,MM

Tyler Freeman, MD
3135 Springbank Lane, #100
Charlotte, NC 28226
(704) 716-7979
FAX (704) 716-7980
CT,NT,IM,PM,WR,DD,HPT,UV,YS,HO

Mark O'Neal Speight, MD, BPCT
2317 Randolph Rd.
Charlotte, NC 28207
(704) 334-8447
FAX (704) 334-0733
YS,CT,DD,RHU,NT,PO,MM

FLETCHER (ASHEVILLE)

Stephen Blievernicht, MD, BPCT
242 Old Concord Rd.
Fletcher (Asheville), NC 28732
(828) 684-4411
FAX (828) 684-7657
P/S AC,AR,OSM,CT,PM,HRT

HILLSBOROUGH (CHAPEL HILL)

Dennis W. Fera, MD, BPCT
1000 Corporate Dr., #209
Hillsborough (Chapel Hill), NC 27278
(919) 732-2287
FAX (919) 732-3176
CT,PM,NT,GP,OS,P/S

MOORESVILLE

Anthony J. Castiglia, MD, BPCT
570 Williamson Road, Ste. C
Mooresville, NC 28117
(704) 799-9740
FAX (704) 799-9742
FP,CT,AR,END,MM,NT,PM

MOREHEAD CITY

Donald Brooks Reece II, MD, BPCT
#2 Medical Park
Morehead City, NC 28557
(252) 247-5177
FAX (252) 247-0223
CT,FP,GER,P/S,PM,WR

MURPHY

Robert E. Moreland, MD
75 Medical Park Lane, #C
Murphy, NC 28906
(828) 837-7997
FP

RALEIGH

John C. Pittman, MD, APCT
4505 Fair Meadow Lane, #111
Raleigh, NC 27607
(919) 571-4391
FAX (919) 571-8968
CT,AA,DD,NT,PM,YS,HGL,HRT,MM,WR

Thomas Spruill, MD
3900 Browning Place, #201
Raleigh, NC 27609
(919) 787-7125
FAX (919) 787-9952
P,PO

ROANOKE RAPIDS

Bhaskar D. Power, MD
1201 E. Littleton Rd.
Roanoke Rapids, NC 27870
(252) 535-1412
A,AR,CT,DD,GP,HOM,NT,PM,PUD,S

ROCKY MOUNT

Lemuel Kornegay, MD
500 Shady Circle
Rocky Mount, NC 27803
(252) 442-7017
FAX (252) 442-5022
CT,HPT

SOUTHERN PINES

Keith E. Johnson, MD
1852 U.S. Hwy. 1 South
Southern Pines, NC 28387
(910) 695-0335
FAX (910) 695-3697
CD,CT,DIA,NT,HPT,WR

TRYON

Mack Stuart Bonner Jr, MD,
BPCT
590 South Trade Street
Tryon, NC 28782
(828) 859-0420
FAX (828) 859-0422
Emergency Medicine

Connie G. Ross, MD, BPCT
590 South Trade Street
Tryon, NC 28782
(828) 859-0420
FAX (828) 859-0422
CT,NT,PM,FP

WINSTON-SALEM

Walter Ward, MD
1411B Plaza West Road
Winston-Salem, NC 27103
(336) 760-0240
FAX (336) 760-4568
A,CT,EV,NT,RHI,YS

NORTH DAKOTA

GRAND FORKS

Richard H. Leigh, MD, APCT
2600 Demers Ave., #108
Grand Forks, ND 58201
(701) 772-7696
A,CT,PM,HRT

MINOT

Brian E. Briggs, MD
718 - 6th Street S.W.
Minot, ND 58701
(701) 838-6011
FAX (701) 838-5055
CT,FP,NT

OHIO

BLUFFTON

L. Terry Chappell, MD, FACAM,
APCT
122 Thurman St. - Box 248
Bluffton, OH 45817
(419) 358-4627
FAX (419) 358-1855
CT,FP,A,AA,G,HRT,P/S,YS

CENTERVILLE

John Boyles, Jr., MD
7076 Corporate Way
Centerville, OH 45459
(513) 434-0555
A,GP,YS,EV,HGL,HRT,NT,RHI,S

CINCINNATI

Kaushal K. Bhardwaj, MD
9019 Colerain Ave.
Cincinnati, OH 45251
(513) 385-8100
FAX (513) 385-8106
A,AC,CT,IM,Prolotherapy

Ted Cole, DO, MA
11974 Lebanon Rd., Ste. 228
Cincinnati, OH 45241
(513) 563-4321
A,CT,FP,NT,OSM,PD

Leonid Macheret, MD
375 Glensprings Dr., #400
Cincinnati, OH 45246
(513) 851-8790
FAX (513) 851-0434
CT,NT,PM,P/S,WR,YS,FP,DIA,HGL,AC

Maureen Pelletier, MD
5400 Kennedy Ave.
Cincinnati, OH 45213
(513) 924-5324
FAX (513) 351-3800
AC,CT,GYN,MM,NT,PM

CLEVELAND

Radha Baishnab, MD
5599 Pearl Rd.
Cleveland, OH 44129
(440) 781-5100
FAX (440) 845-9376
CD,CT,IM,NT,PM

John M. Baron, DO, APCT
4807 Rockside, Ste. 100
Cleveland, OH 44131
(216) 642-0082
FAX (216) 642-1415
CD,CT,MM,NT,PM,RHU

James P. Frackelton, MD,
FACAM, APCT
24700 Center Ridge Rd.
Cleveland, OH 44145
(440) 835-0104
FAX (440) 871-1404
CT,HO,NT,PM

Stan Gardner, MD
24700 Center Ridge Rd.
Cleveland, OH 44145
(440) 835-0104
FAX (440) 871-1404
PM,PD,CT

Derrick Lonsdale, MD, FACAM,
APCT
24700 Center Ridge Rd.
Cleveland, OH 44145
(440) 835-0104
FAX (440) 871-1404
NT,PM,PD

COLUMBUS

Larry S. Everhart, MD
730 Mt. Airyshire Blvd., Ste. A
Columbus, OH 43235
(614) 848-2600
FAX (614) 888-3938
CD,DIA,IM,CT,NT,HRT

Bruce A. Massau, DO
1492 E. Broad St., #1203
Columbus, OH 43205
(614) 252-1500
FAX (614) 252-1685
CT,Pain Mgmt.

LANCASTER

Rene V. Blaha, MD
3484 Cincinnati - Zanesville Rd.
Lancaster, OH 43130
(740) 653-0017
FAX (740) 653-8707
FP

Jacqueline S. Chan, DO
3484 Cincinnati Zanesville Rd.
Lancaster, OH 43130
(740) 653-0017
FAX (740) 653-8707
CT,FP,OS,YS,OSM,AC,DD,HRT,NT,WR,
HOM

PAULDING

Don K. Snyder, MD
1030 West Wayne Street
Paulding, OH 45879
(419) 399-2045
FAX (419) 399-4389
CT,FP,A,EV

POWELL

Richard R. Mason, DO, NMD
10034 Brewster Lane
Powell, OH 43065
(614) 761-0555
FAX (614) 761-8937
CT,ON,END,OME

William D. Mitchell, DO, APCT,
FACOI
10034 Brewster Ln.
Powell, OH 43065
(614) 761-0555
FAX (614) 761-8937
CD,CT,GP,IM,PM,OSM

SANDUSKY

Douglas Weeks, MD, APCT
3703 Columbus Avenue
Sandusky, OH 44870
(419) 625-8085
CT,HO,NT,PM,AC,PMR

TOLEDO

James C. Roberts Jr., MD
4607 Sylvania Ave., #200
Toledo, OH 43623
(419) 882-9620
FAX (419) 882-9628
CD,EECP

YOUNGSTOWN

James Ventresco Jr., DO
3848 Tippecanoe Rd.
Youngstown, OH 44511
(330) 792-2349
CT,FP,NT,OSM,RHU

OKLAHOMA

BROKEN ARROW

R. Jeff Wright, DO
5050 E. Kenosha
Broken Arrow, OK 74014
(918) 496-5444
FAX (918) 496-5445
CT,DD,HPT,HRT,NT,WR,YS

GROVE

George Cole, DO
240 East 3rd Street
Grove, OK 74344
(718) 786-8746
FP,OSM,CT,Orthopedics

JENKS

Gerald Wootan, DO, BPCT, M.Ed
715 West Main St., #S
Jenks, OK 74037
(918) 299-9447
FP,GER,OS,PD,A,GYN,HO,CT,HPT,HRT,
PM,UV

OKLAHOMA CITY

Adam Merchant, MD
3535 N.W. 58th Street
Oklahoma City, OK 73112
(405) 942-8346
FAX (405) 942-8347
P/S,NT,AU,CT,AC

Charles D. Taylor, MD, APCT
4409 Classen Blvd.
Oklahoma City, OK 73118
(405) 525-7751
FAX (405) 525-0303
GP,GYN,HPT,HRT,PM,PMR

VALLIANT

Ray E. Zimmer, DO
602 N. Dalton
Valliant, OK 74764
(580) 933-4235
FAX (580) 933-4563
A,CT,PM,RHU,DIA,OSM

OREGON

ASHLAND

Franklin H. Ross Jr, MD
565 A Street
Ashland, OR 97520
(541) 482-7007
FAX (541) 482-5123
CT,AA,HPT,UV,WR,PM

BEND

Chris Hatlestad, MD
2195 NE Professional Ct.
Bend, OR 97701
(541) 388-3804
FAX (541) 388-3856
FP,NT,CT,AC,HRT,P/S,YS

JUNCTION CITY

John Gambee, MD
93244 Hwy. 99 South
Junction City, OR 97448
(541) 998-0111
FAX (541) 998-0114
A,CT,NT,PM,P/S,HPT,HRT

KLAMATH FALLS

Robert P. Beaman, MD
1903 Austin St., #B
Klamath Falls, OR 97603
(541) 885-9989
FAX (541) 885-7998
FP,CD,DIA,IM,PD,P

LAKE OSWEGO

Naina Sachdev, MD
121 C Avenue
Lake Oswego, OR 97034
(503) 636-2550
FAX (503) 636-3544
IM,PM,AA

MEDFORD

Helen Trew, MD
2921 Doctor's Park Drive
Medford, OR 97504
(541) 770-1143
FAX (541) 772-9149
CT,FP,HPT,HRT,PM,AA

PORTLAND

Jay H. Mead, MD
4444 SW Corbett Avenue
Portland, OR 97239
(503) 224-4003
FAX (503) 224-4854
CD,CT,DIA,END,MM,NT,AA,HGL

David J. Ogle, MD
Center for Environmental Med.
Portland, OR 97220
(503) 261-0966
FAX (503) 252-2697
A,CD,CT,DD,FP,NT

Jeffrey Tyler, MD
10529 NE Halsey Street
Portland, OR 97220
(503) 255-4256
CT,IM,GER,PD,PM

SALEM

Terence H. Young, MD
1205 Wallace Rd. NW
Salem, OR 97304
(503) 371-1558
AC,CT,HO,HPT,OSM,PT

SPRINGFIELD

S. Kathleen Hirtz, MD
1800 Centennial Blvd., #6
Springfield, OR 97477
(541) 726-1865
FAX (541) 726-2179
BA,HRT,PM,AA,CT,WR

PENNSYLVANIA

BANGOR

Francis J. Cinelli, DO
153 N. 11th Street
Bangor, PA 18013
(610) 588-4502
FAX (610) 588-6928
CT,GP,HYP,OSM,FP,P/S

BETHLEHEM

Sally Ann Rex, DO
1343 Easton Ave.
Bethlehem, PA 18018
(610) 866-0900
FAX (610) 866-8333
CT,GP,OS,PM,Occupational Med.

DARBY

Lance Wright, MD
112 S. 4th Street
Darby, PA 19023
(610) 461-6225
FAX (610) 583-3356
DD,HYP,NT,PM,PO,Integr.Med.

DOYLESTOWN

Steven C. Halbert, MD, APCT
Medical Healing Arts Center
Doylestown, PA 18901
(215) 348-4002
FAX (215) 887-1921
A,CT,IM,NT,YS

FARRELL

Robert D. Multari, DO
2120 Likens Lane, #101
Farrell, PA 16121
(412) 981-3731
FAX (412) 981-3740
A,CD,DD,DIA,GE,OSM,P/S,CT,IM

FOUNTAINVILLE

Harold H. Byer, MD, PhD, APCT
5045 Swamp Rd., #A-101
Fountainville, PA 18923
(215) 348-0443
FAX (215) 348-9124
AR,CT,DIA,S,OPH

GLEN MILLS

Robert J. Peterson, DO
2 Woodland Drive
Glen Mills, PA 19342
(610) 558-8225
AR,CD,CT,DD,DIA,NT,PM,YS,HPT

GREENSBURG

Ralph A. Miranda, MD, FACAM, APCT
RD. #12 - Box 108
Greensburg, PA 15601
(724) 838-7632
FAX (724) 836-3655
CT,FP,NT,OME,PM,ECP

GREENVILLE

Roy Kerry, MD
17 Sixth Avenue
Greenville, PA 16125
(724) 588-2600
FAX (724) 588-6427
A,DD,EM,NT,OTO,YS

HAVERTOWN

Domenick Braccia, DO
2050 West Chester Pike, 3rd Flr.
Havertown, PA 19083
(610) 924-0600
FAX (610) 924-0627
AC,FP,OS

HAZELTON

Martin Mulders, MD
53 West Juniper Street
Hazelton, PA 18201
(570) 455-4704
FAX (570) 455-4706
CT,GP,IM,NT,PM,HO,PT,HPT

JEANNETTE

R. Christopher Monsour, MD
70 Lincoln Way East
Jeannette, PA 15644
(724) 527-1511
FAX (724) 238-9368
Addiction,GER,P

JEFFERSONVILLE

Anthony J. Bazzan, MD, BPCT
2505 Blvd. Of Generals
Jeffersonville, PA 19403
(610) 630-8600
FAX (610) 630-9599
A,CD,CT,DD,IM,YS

Martin Mulders, MD
2505 Blvd. of the Generals
Jeffersonville, PA 19403
(610) 630-8600
FAX (610) 630-9599
CT,GP,IM,NT,PM,HO,PT,HPT

LOWER BURRELL

Louis K. Hauber, MD, BPCT
2533 Leechburg Rd.
Lower Burrell, PA 15680
(724) 334-0966
FAX (724) 339-4223
CT,P,NT,Complimentary Medicine

MANHEIM

Kenneth F. Lovell, DO
76 Doe Run Road
Manheim, PA 17545
(717) 665-6400
FAX (717) 664-4793
FP,CT

MECHANICSBURG

John M. Sullivan, MD, APCT
1001 S. Market St., #B
Mechanicsburg, PA 17055
(717) 697-5050
FAX (717) 697-3156
A,CT,DIA,FP,PD,YS

MEDIA

Arthur K. Balin, MD, PhD, FACP
110 Chesley Drive
Media, PA 19063
(610) 565-3300
FAX (610) 565-9909
CT,DD,END,GER,IM

MT. PLEASANT

Mamduh El-Attrache, MD
20 E. Main St.
Mt. Pleasant, PA 15666
(412) 547-3576
BA,CT,DIA,GER,OBS,PO

NARBERTH

Andrew Lipton, DO, APCT
822 Montgomery Ave., #315
Narberth, PA 19072
(610) 667-4601
FAX (610) 667-6416
CT,FP,OSM, AC

NEWTOWN

Robert J. Peterson, DO
1614 Wrightstown Rd.
Newtown, PA 18940
(215) 579-0330
AR,CD,CT,DD,DIA,NT,PM,YS,HPT

NORTH WALES

Domenick Braccia, DO, BPCT
1146 Stump Road
North Wales, PA 19454
(215) 368-2160
AC,FP,OS

PALMYRA

Adrian J. Hohenwarter, MD
741 S. Grant Street
Palmyra, PA 17078
(717) 832-5993
CT,FP,GP,PM, Natural Horm. Repl.

PENNDEL

Eric R. Braverman, MD, APCT
142 Bellevue Ave.
Penndel, PA 19047
(215) 702-1344
FAX (215) 757-1707
CT,IM,MM,PM,PO,Neurology

PHILADELPHIA

John Bowden, DO
1738 W. Cheltenham
Philadelphia, PA 19138
(215) 548-3390
FAX (215) 549-8998
DIA,FP,IM,OS,PM,PMR

Sarah M. Fisher, MD, BPCT
530 South 2nd St., #108
Philadelphia, PA 19147
(215) 627-3001
FAX (215) 627-0362
GP,NT,YS,Homeopathy

Alan F. Kwon, MD
211 South Street, #345
Philadelphia, PA 19147
(215) 629-5633
FAX (215) 629-5633
AN,HYP,PM,P/S,S

Patrick J. Lariccia, MD
51 N. 39th Street
Philadelphia, PA 19104
(215) 662-8988
FAX (215) 662-8859
AC,HYP,PMR,YS

PITTSBURGH

Dominic A. Brandy, MD
2275 Swallow Hill Road, #2400
Pittsburgh, PA 15220
(412) 429-1151
FAX (412) 429-0211
BA,NT, Cosm. Surg.

David Goldstein, MD
9401 McKnight Rd., #301-B
Pittsburgh, PA 15237
(412) 366-6780
MM,NT,PM,PMR

Ralph Miranda, MD, FACAM, APCT
Rd. #12 - Box 108
Pittsburg, PA 15601
(724) 838-7632
FAX (724) 836-3655
CT,FP,NT,OME,PM,ECP

QUAKERTOWN

William G. Kracht, DO, BPCT
5724 Clymer Rd.
Quakertown, PA 18951
(215) 536-1890
FAX (215) 529-9034
A,CT,FP,NT,OS,YS

SCRANTON

Kyung Lee, MD, BPCT
1027 Pittston Ave.
Scranton, PA 18505
(570) 961-0200
S

SPRINGFIELD

Walter W. Schwartz, DO
471 Baltimore Pike
Springfield, PA 19064
(610) 604-4800
FAX (610) 604-4815
CD,CT,IM,HRT

TOPTON

Conrad Maulfair, Jr., DO FACAM, APCT
403 N. Main St., P.O.Box 98
Topton, PA 19562
(610) 682-2104
FAX (610) 682-9781
A,CT,HGL

TREVOSE

Robert J. Peterson, DO
4616 Street Road
Trevose, PA 19053
(215) 579-0330
AR,CD,CT,DD,DIA,NT,PM,YS,HPT

WEST MIDDLESEX

Robert D. Multari, DO
15 Elliott Rd.
West Middlesex, PA 16159
(412) 981-2246
A,CD,DD,DIA,GE,OSM,P/S,CT,IM

WILLIAMSPORT

Francis M. Powers, Jr., MD
1201 Grampian Blvd., #3-A
Williamsport, PA 17701
(570) 322-6450
FAX (570) 322-0648
CT,NT,OME,YS,Therapeutic Radiology

WYNCOTE

Steven C. Halbert, MD, APCT
1442 Ashbourne Rd.
Wyncote, PA 19095
(215) 886-7842
FAX (215) 887-1921
A,CT,IM,NT,YS

RHODE ISLAND

NEWPORT

Dariusz J. Nasiek, MD
17 Friendship Street
Newport, RI 02840
(401) 846-1230
AN,PM,CT

SOUTH CAROLINA
BEAUFORT

Kenneth Orbeck, DO
9A Rue Du Bois Rd.
Beaufort, SC 29902
(843) 322-8050
FAX (842) 322-8059
FP

MYRTLE BEACH

Donald Tice, DO
4301 Highway 544
Myrtle Beach, SC 29588
(803) 215-5000
FAX (803) 215-5005
FP,OS,PMR

NORTH CHARLESTON

Art M. LaBruce, MD
9231A Medical Plaza Dr.
N. Charleston, SC 29406
(843) 572-1771
FAX (843) 572-8962
A,CT,NT,HPT,HRT,YS

W. COLUMBIA

James M. Shortt, MD, BPCT
3901 Edmund Hwy., #A
W. Columbia, SC 29170
(803) 755-0114
FAX (803) 755-0116
CT,Neural
Therapy,P/S,AA,FP,HGL,HRT,NT,HPT

SOUTH DAKOTA
CUSTER

Dennis R. Wicks, MD
1 Holiday Trail, HCR 83, Box 21
Custer, SD 57730
(605) 673-2689
CT,GP,S

TENNESSEE
ATHENS

H. Joseph Holliday, MD, FACAM,
APCT
1005 W. Madison Ave.
Athens, TN 37303
(423) 744-7540
FAX (423) 745-4898
CT,CD,CS,S,NT,HPT,PM,A

CHATTANOOGA

Charles C. Adams, MD
600 W. Main Street
Chattanooga, TN 37402
(706) 861-7377
FAX (706) 861-7922
IM,CT,NT,A,Anti-Aging Med.

CLEVELAND

Charles C. Adams, MD
2600 Executive Park Dr. NW
Cleveland, TN 37311
(423) 473-7080
FAX (413)473 7780
IM,CT,NT,A,Anti-Aging Med.

JOHNSON CITY

Robert C. Allen, MD
1416 S. Roan Street
Johnson City, TN 37601
(423) 979-6257
FAX (423) 979-6285
IM,Preventive-Holistic Med.

KINGSPORT

Pickens Gantt, MD
#307 - 2204 Pavilion Dr.
Kingsport, TN 37660
(423) 392-6330
FAX (423) 392-6053
CT,NT,PM,END,GYN

David Livingston, MD, BPCT
1567 N. Eastman Rd., #4
Kingsport, TN 37604
(423) 245-6671
FAX (423) 245-0966
BA,CD,CT,FP,PM

KNOXVILLE

Joseph E. Rich, MD, MPH
9217 Parkwest Blvd., Suite E-1
Knoxville, TN 37923
(865) 694-9553
FAX (865) 694-7658
A,CT,EV,HPT,HRT,OME,YS

MANCHESTER

David Florence, DO
1912 McArthur Drive
Manchester, TN 37355
(931) 728-5522
FAX (931) 728-2247
AA,CT,FP,MM,PM,PMR

MEMPHIS

Charles R. Wallace, Jr., MD
1325 Eastmoreland Ave., #425
Memphis, TN 38104
(901) 272-3200
FAX (901) 278-3441
Urology, Integrative Med.

MORRISTOWN

Donald Thompson, MD
1121 W. First North St.
Morristown, TN 37816
(423) 581-6367
FAX (423) 581-0808
GP,NT,PM,P/S

NASHVILLE

Stephen L. Reisman, MD
2325 Crestmoor Rd., #P-150
Nashville, TN 37215
(615) 298-2820
FAX (615) 298-2770
A,AC,HPT,HRT,CT,GP,HGL,NT,PM,YS

OLD HICKORY

Russell Hunt, MD
1415 Robinson Road
Old Hickory, TN 37138
(615) 541-0400
FAX (615) 847-4142
CT,FP,PM,NT,WR,A

TEXAS

AMARILLO

George Cole, DO
2300 Bell Street, #20
Amarillo, TX 79106
(806) 379-7770
FAX (806) 352-6599
FP,OSM,CT,Orthopedics

Gerald Parker, DO
4714 S. Western
Amarillo, TX 79109
(806) 355-8263
FAX (806) 355-8796
A,AC,AR,CT,GP,HO

John T. Taylor, DO
4714 S. Western
Amarillo, TX 79109
(806) 355-8263
FAX (806) 355-8796
A,AC,AR,CT,GP,HO

ARLINGTON

R. E. Liverman, DO
801 W. Road to Six Flags, #147
Arlington, TX 76012
(817) 461-7774
FAX (817) 801-5600
A,CT,NT,OSM,OME,DD,PO

AUSTIN

Ted Edwards Jr, MD
4201 Bee Caves Rd., #B-112
Austin, TX 78746
(512) 327-4886
GE,IM,PM, Sports Med.,CT

Vladimir Rizov, MD, BPCT
911 W. Anderson Lane, #205
Austin, TX 78757
(512) 451-8149
FAX (512) 451-0895
BA,CD,GER,HGL,HPT,,HOM,MM,NT,
PO,PT,WR

CONROE

Frank O. McGehee Jr, MD, BPCT
900 West Davis
Conroe, TX 77301
(936) 756-3366
PM,NT

DALLAS

George Cole, DO
14900 Landmark, #140
Dallas, TX 75240
(972) 702-9977
FP,OSM,CT,Orthopedics

Manuel Griego, Jr., DO
2701 S. Hampton Rd., #201
Dallas, TX 75224
(214) 330-9221
FAX (214) 331-9176
FM

FORT WORTH

Barry L. Beaty, DO
4455 Camp Bowie, #211
Fort Worth, TX 76107
(817) 737-6464
FAX (817) 737-2858
CT,FP,PM,PMR

Karen Birdy, DO
Trinity Holistic Family Medicine, PA
Fort Worth, TX 76132
(817) 737-3331
FAX (817) 737-2333
OSM,YS,NT,A,HOM,CT,AC,FP

Gerald Harris, DO, BPCT
1550 W. Rosedale St., #714
Fort Worth, TX 76104
(817) 336-4810
FAX (817) 336-4802
CT, Pain Mgmt.,P/S,PT,HPT

Joseph F. McWherter, MD, BPCT
1307 - 8th Ave.,#207
Fort Worth, TX 76104
(817) 926-2511
FAX (817) 924-0167
GYN,CT,AA,END,S,NT,HRT

Ricardo Tan, MD
3220 North Freeway, #106
Fort Worth, TX 76111
(817) 626-1993
AC,AU,CT,FP,NT,PM

GRAPEVINE

Constantine A. Kotsanis, MD
1600 W. College St., #260
Grapevine, TX 76051
(817) 481-6342
FAX (817) 488-8903
A,AC,CT,DD,NT,PM

HARLINGEN

Robert R. Somerville, MD
720 N. 77 Sunshine Strip
Harlingen, TX 78550
(956) 428-0757
FAX (956) 428-8560
A,CD,CT,DD,DIA,EV,HGL,HRT,NT,RHI,
YS

HOUSTON

Robert Battle, MD, APCT
9910 Long Point
Houston, TX 77055
(713) 932-0552
FAX (713) 932-0551
A,AA,CD,CT,HRT,HGL,DD,END,HPT,
P/S,FP

Moe Kakvan, MD, APCT
2909 Hillcroft, Ste. 250B
Houston, TX 77057
(713) 780-7019
FAX (713) 780-9783
CT,PM

Gilbert Manso, MD
7211 Regency Square Blvd., #200
Houston, TX 77036
(713) 840-9355
FAX (713) 840-9468
CT,DD,GP,HRT,NT,AA,HGL,MM,YS

Marina M. Pearsall, MD, PhD
4126 Southwest Freeway, #1620
Houston, TX 77027
(713) 522-4037
FAX (713)623-8007
AA,BA,CD,DE,DIA,IM,WR

R.G. Tannerya, MD
9627 Pagewood Lane
Houston, TX 77063
(713) 278-2111
AR,BA,CD,DIA,NT,PMR

Stephen Joel Weiss, MD
7907 Oakington Drive
Houston, TX 77071
(713) 691-0737
FAX (713) 695-0105
Ortho Surg

HUNTSVILLE

Frank O. McGehee Jr, MD, BPCT
1909 - 22nd Street
Huntsville, TX 77340
(936) 291-3351
FAX (936) 291-3519
PM,NT

IRVING

Frances J. Rose, MD
1701 W. Walnut Hill, #200
Irving, TX 75038
(972) 594-1111
FAX (972) 518-1867
A,AC,CT,FP,HGL,NT,PD,PM

JEFFERSON

Donald Ray Whitaker, DO
210 E. Elizabeth St.
Jefferson, TX 75657
(903) 665-7781
FAX (903) 665-7887
PM,NT,CT,WR,YS

KIRBYVILLE

John L. Sessions, DO, APCT
1609 South Margaret
Kirbyville, TX 75956
(409) 423-2166
CT,IM,OSM

LEWISVILLE

Smart Idemudia, MD, PhD
560 W. Main Street, #205
Lewisville, TX 75057
(972) 420-6777
FAX (972-420-0656
IM,GP,CT,DIA,HPT

LUBBOCK

Jim Reed, MD
6400 Quaker Ave., Ste. B
Lubbock, TX 79413
(806) 792-8444
FAX (806) 792-3499
DE

MCALLEN

Michael R. Kilgore, MD, BPCT
3600 N. 23rd, #201
McAllen, TX 78501
(210) 687-6196
CT,FP,GP,IM,PMR

PARIS

Gaylen Hayes, DO
520 North Collegiate Drive
Paris, TX 75460
(903) 784-1608
FAX (903) 784-0846
BA

PEARLAND

Dorothy Merritt, MD
Chelation Ctr. of Texas-Pearland
Pearland, TX 77581
(800) 360-3382
FAX (281) 412-7934
CT,HPT

PLANO

Don Dunlap, DO
5115 Teakwood Lane, #250
Plano, TX 75075
(866) 244-7246
FAX (817) 424-1059
FP

PLEASANTON

Gerald Phillips, MD
218 W. Goodwin Street
Pleasanton, TX 78064
(210) 569-2118
FAX (210) 569-5958
CD,CT,FP,HGL,NT,PM

ROCKPORT

Dorothy Merritt, MD
Chelation Ctr. Of Texas-Sacred
Sanctuary
Rockport, TX 78382
(361) 463-1353
FAX (361) 790-7171
CT,HPT

ROWLETT

Robert J. Gilbard, MD, FACOG
5429 Lakeview Pkwy
Rowlett, TX 75088
(972) 463-1744
FAX (972) 463-8243
AA,CT,HPT,HRT,ON,PT

SAN ANGELO

Benjamin Thurman, MD
610 S. Abe Street, #A
San Angelo, TX 76903
(915) 481-0596
FAX (915) 481-0597
AC,CT,HOM,NT,P/S,DD,HPT,HRT,PT,UV

TEXAS CITY

Dorothy Merritt, MD
6807 EF Lowry Expwy., #103
Texas City, TX 77591
(409) 938-1770
FAX (409) 938-0701
IM,NT,CT,HPT,PM,AC

Dorothy Merritt, MD
6807 Emmitt Lowry, #103
Texas City, TX 77591
(800) 360-3382
FAX (409) 938-0701
CT,HPT

WICHITA FALLS

Thomas Roger Humphrey, MD
2400 Rushing
Wichita Falls, TX 76308
(940) 766-4329
FAX (940) 767-3227
GP,PM,WR,CT,HPT,HYP

UTAH

ALPINE

Dianne Farley-Jones, MD
70 E. Red Pine Drive
Alpine, UT 84004
(801) 756-9444
FAX (801) 763-1070
FP,HOM,HRT,NT

DRAPER

Dennis Harper, DO, BPCT
12226 S. 1000 East, #10
Draper, UT 84020
(801) 277-5000
FAX (801) 277-5200
A,CT,AA,YS,AR,GP,HRT,NT,WR

VERMONT

COLCHESTER

Charles Anderson, MD
Health & Longevity Institute, Creek
Farm Plaza
Colchester, VT 05446
(802) 879-6544
A,FP,NT,YS

VIRGINIA

ARLINGTON

Marie Schum-Brady, MD
3500 N. 14th Street
Arlington, VA 22201
(703) 527-5384
FAX (703) 527-5881
GP,HGL.MM,NT,PM

ALEXANDRIA

Manjit R. Bajwa, MD
6391 Little River Turnpike
Alexandria, VA 22312
(703) 941-3606
FAX (703) 658-6415
CT,DD,FND,GP,HO,MM, HB Chamber

CHESAPEAKE

Ernest Aubrey Murden Jr, MD,
BPCT
4020 Raintree Rd., #C
Chesapeake, VA 23321
(757) 488-2080
FAX (757) 405-3025
A,CT,NT,RHI,HPT,HOM,PT,UV

FALLS CHURCH

Aldo M. Rosemblat, MD, APCT
6316 Castle Place, #200
Falls Church, VA 22044
(703) 241-8989
FAX (703) 532-6247
AC,S

HINTON

Harold Huffman, MD, APCT
P. O. Box 197
Hinton, VA 22831
(540) 867-5254
FAX (540) 867-9381
CT,FP,PM

LOUISA

David G. Schwartz, MD
P. O. Box 532
Louisa, VA 23093
(540) 967-2050
CT,FP,NT,HPT,YS

NELLYSFORD

Mitchell A. Fleisher, MD
Rockfish Ctr.#1, State Rt.664
Nellysford, VA 22958
(434) 361-1896
FAX (434) 361-1928
CT,FP,MM,NT,PM,
HOM,AA,HPT,OME,PT

ROANOKE

Joan M. Resk, DO
5249 Clearbrook Lane
Roanoke, VA 24014
(540) 776-8331
FAX (540) 776-8303
CD,CT,DD,OSM,NT,PM

RICHMOND

Kevin Harrison, DO
2621 Promenade Parkway
Richmond, VA 23113
(804) 897-8566
FAX (804) 897-8569
IM,CT

TROUT DALE

Eduardo Castro, MD
799 Ripshin Road, P.O. Box 44
Trout Dale, VA 24378
(276) 677-3631
FAX (276) 677-3843
A,CD,CT,HO,NT,PM

Elmer M. Cranton, MD, FACAM, APCT
799 Ripshin Road, Box 44
Trout Dale, VA 24378
(540) 677-3631
FAX (540) 677-3843
A,CD,CT,FP,HO,NT

WINCHESTER

James B. Hutt, Jr., MD
423 W. Cork Street
Winchester, VA 22601
(540) 347-0474
CT,AA,CD,HPT,NT,WR

WASHINGTON

BELLEVUE

David Buscher, MD
1603 - 116th N.E., Ste. 112
Bellevue, WA 98004
(425) 453-0288
FAX (425) 455-0076
EV,GP,NT

BELLINGHAM

Andrew Pauli, MD
Elan Vital Longevity Institute
Bellingham, WA 98225
(360) 527-9785
FAX (360)671-0981
DD,END,NT,PM,PO,P

CONNELL

Jon R. Mundall, MD
111 North Columbia Ave.
Connell, WA 99326
(509) 234-7766
FAX (509) 234-4320
A,CT,GP,MM,NT,PM

ELK

Stanley B. Covert, MD, BPCT
42207 N. Sylvan Road
Elk, WA 99009
(509) 292-2748
CT,FP,GP,Emerg.

FEDERAL WAY

Patric J. Darby, MD, MS
Paracelsus Clinic
Federal Way, WA 98003
(253) 529-3050
FAX (253) 529-3104
PD,P,PO,CT,OME

Thomas A. Dorman, MD, APCT
2505 South 320th St., #100
Federal Way, WA 98003
(253) 529-3050
FAX (253) 529-3104
CD,CT,IM,P/S

George Koss, DO
1014 South 320th Street
Federal Way, WA 98003
(253) 839-4100
FAX (253) 941-6116
FP,PM,NT,HGL,CD,CT

KIRKLAND

Jonathan Collin, MD, FACAM, APCT
12911 120th Ave. NE, #A-50, POB 8099
Kirkland, WA 98034
(425) 820-0547
FAX (425) 820-0259
CT,NT,PM

PORT TOWNSEND

Jonathan Collin, MD, FACAM, APCT
911 Tyler Street
Port Townsend, WA 98368
(360) 385-4555
FAX (360) 385-0699
CT,NT,PM

J. Douwe Rienstra, MD, BPCT
242 Monroe Street
Port Townsend, WA 98368
(360) 385-5658
FAX (360) 385-5142
GP,MM,NT,PM,BA,CT,HRT

RENTON

Jonathan Wright, MD
801 SW 16th Street
Renton, WA 98055
(425) 264-0059
FAX (425) 264-0071
A,CT,FP,MM,NT,END,AA,AR,CD,DIA,HRT

RICHLAND

Geoffrey S. Ames, MD
750 Swift Blvd., #1
Richland, WA 99397
(509) 943-3934
CT,MM,NT,Env.Med,HOM,Dermatology

SEATTLE

Ralph Golan, MD
7522 - 20th Ave., NE
Seattle, WA 98115
(206) 524-8966
FAX (206) 524-8951
AA,AR,AU,CT,CD,END,GE,HRT,WR,YS

SPOKANE

William Corell, MD
3424 Grand Blvd. South
Spokane, WA 99203
(509) 838-5800
FAX (509) 838-4042
CT,HPT,NT,AA,HGL,YS,MM

Burton B. Hart, DO
12104 E. Main Street
Spokane, WA 99206
(509) 927-9922
FAX (509) 926-2011
CT,PM,OSM,P/S,UV

VANCOUVER

Steve Kennedy, MD, BPCT
615 S.E. Chkalov, #14
Vancouver, WA 98683
(360) 256-4566
FAX (360) 253-3060
CT,PM,Detox.,Plastic Surgery

WINLOCK

David Ellis, MD
P.O. Box 567
Winlock, WA 98596
(360) 785-0300
FAX (360) 785-3330
FP,CT,NT,P/S,YS,OME

YELM

Elmer M. Cranton, MD, FACAM, APCT
503 First St. South, Suite 1
Yelm, WA 98597
(360) 458-1061
FAX (360) 458-1661
AA,CD,CT,HO,NT,PM,YS

Stephen Olmstead, MD
503 First St. South, Suite 1
Yelm, WA 98597
(360) 458-1061
FAX (360) 458-1661
CD,CT,HO,IM,PM,YS,AA,HRT

WEST VIRGINIA

BECKLEY

Prudencio Corro, MD, BPCT
251 Stanaford Rd.
Beckley, WV 25801
(304) 252-0775
A,CT,RHI

CHARLESTON

Steve M. Zekan, MD
1208 Kanawha Blvd. E.
Charleston, WV 25301
(304) 343-7559
FAX (304) 343-1219
CT,NT,PM,S

HURRICANE

John P. MacCallum, MD
3855 Teays Valley Road
Hurricane, WV 25526
(304) 757-3368
FAX (304) 757-2402
CT,MM,P,PM

Dallas B. Martin, DO, BPCT
1401 Hospital Dr., #302
Hurricane, WV 25526
(304) 757-8090
FAX (304) 757-8079
FP,OS

WISCONSIN

DELAFIELD

Carol Uebelacker, MD
700 Milwaukee St.
Delafield, WI 53018
(262) 646-4600
FAX (262) 646-4215
A,CD,BA,CT,FP,GYN

GREEN BAY

Eleazar M. Kadile, MD, APCT
1538 Bellevue St.
Green Bay, WI 54311
(920) 468-9442
FAX (920) 468-9714
AA,BA,CD,CT,DIA,EV,HRTWR,YS

LA CROSSE

Patrick J. Scott, MD
3454 Losey Blvd. South.
La Crosse, WI 54601
(608) 785-0038
FAX (608) 782-5959
A,CT,GP,NT,PM,YS

MILWAUKEE

J. Allan Robertson Jr., DO, APCT
1011 N. Mayfair Rd., #301
Milwaukee, WI 53226
(414) 302-1011
FAX (414) 302-1010
CT,HPT,GP,NT,OSM,YS

WAUWATOSA

Jerry N. Yee, DO
11803 W. North Avenue
Wauwatosa, WI 53226
(414) 258-6282
BA,CT,GP,OSM

WISCONSIN DELLS

Robert S. Waters, MD, APCT
Race & Vine Streets, Box 357
Wisconsin Dells, WI 53965
(608) 254-7178, (800
FAX (608) 253-7139
CT,PM,OME

WYOMING

CASPER

Dennis Wicks, MD
802 South Durbin St.
Casper, WY 82601
(307) 237-4444
CT,GP,Sa

Rebecca Painter, MD, APCT
201 West Lakeway, Suite 300
Gillette, WY 82718
(307) 682-0330
FAX (307) 686-8118
CD,CT,DIA,IM,PUD,RHU,A,HRT,YS

COLLAGEN CRUSH

A natural protein and amino acid. Drink Collagen Crush to burn fat and lose inches while it promotes restful sleep. Collagen Crush may help build lean muscle, maintain proper bowel and joint function, maintain cartilage, and promote healthy skin, hair and nails. A must with Ester-C® with Rose Hips!

16 fl oz. / 32 servings

BODY OXYGEN

Body Oxygen is a pleasant tasting nutritional supplement that is meticulously manufactured with cold pressed Aloe Vera. The Aloe is used as a stabilized carrier for numerous nutritional constituents including Magnesium Oxide, Hawthorn Berry, Ginkgo Biloba, Ginseng and St. John's Wort extracts. Body Oxygen can help naturally fight infections, inflammation and degeneration, presenting oxygen at the cellular level. It also commonly helps in colon cleansing, regular elimination, and provides a feeling of increased energy and mental alertness.

32 fl oz.

CALCIUM MAGNESIUM

The USDA reports that 78 percent of all adult women and 56 percent of adult men don't get enough calcium from their diets. The majority of teenagers are also lacking this vital nutrient. This calcium product is a delicious and refreshing drink that comes in a unique 100 percent ionized form—just the right ratio for optimum benefits. This product is essential for the support of healthy bones and teeth.

12 fl oz.

COLLODIAL MINERALS

Without minerals, the body cannot utilize any vitamins. These minerals are a concentrated liquid extracted from a very rare, ancient deposit of plant origin. Our special low temperature processing makes these minerals available in colloidal state with pure water. No synthetics, coloring or preservatives are added. Mined from the richest source in the United States for over 70 years, we guarantee the content of over seventy colloidal minerals in each serving. Provides benefits such as more energy within 24 hours to "no more forgetfulness."

32 fl oz.

CAT'S CLAW CLUSTERED WATER®

This product includes the Peruvian wonder herb, Cat's Claw. Cat's Claw has been used in Peru for thousands of years. This 4 oz. bottle produces 4 gallons of beverage. At 16 ounces a day this is a one month supply. Supports cellular hydration, weight management, reverses aging, energizes cells, removes toxins and acidic wastes, and restores pH balance and healing.

ADVANCED CLUSTERED WATER®

Water as God intended. Advanced Formula is for the immune-compromised and overweight people. Clustered Water increases vital nutrient absorption up to 600%. Delays and to some extent, reverses aging. Replenishes the most vital support of all cellular DNA, and the 4,000 plus enzymes that are involved in every metabolic process in your body. This 4 oz bottle produces 4 gallons of beverage.

CANDIDA CLEANSE

Constant fatigue, foggy thinking, bloated abdomen, dragging all the time, have itchy rashes. These symptoms, and many others, may be signs of yeast overgrowth, more specifically known as Candida Albicans, which may infect more than 80% of Americans. Here's the solution.

120 capsules

PARACEASE™

Parasite & Candida Cleanse
As we know, the state of our digestive tract may have a powerful influence on our health. This cleansing system, made up of 18 unique, specialized ingredients, is designed to gently, safely, and easily cleanse the body and colon. The following are some of the symptoms of parasites: Sugar cravings, constipation, bloating, dark circles under the eyes, joint pain, feeling sedated, recurring headaches, hemorrhoids, poor digestion, grinding teeth, stomach aches, rectal itching, insomnia. If you have any of these symptoms, consider a parasite cleanse. The ideal cleanse takes three months to complete.

120 capsules

WHEREVER SHE GOES, VALERIE SAXION constantly hears this complaint: "I can't remember when I last felt good. I'm exhausted and rundown. How can I start to feel good again?" This book is Saxion's response to that question, but it goes far beyond just feeling good. "So why don't you feel *great* all the time?" she asks. "Why are you willing to settle for less than 100 percent?" She then lays out a *Lifelong Plan for Unlimited Energy and Radiant Good Health* to help readers give their bodies the opportunity to start feeling great in four basic steps.

Specifically, Saxion guides her readers into an understanding of how their bodies work, how to stop eating junk food, and the importance of body oxygen, exercise, and water. *Candida*, detoxification, fasting, low thyroid, and weight loss are all covered as well as establishing a perfect diet that is filled with foods that supercharge the mind and body. Nature's prescriptions of vitamins, minerals, and herbs supplement all that she teaches.

Includes a state-by-state list of more than 800 of America's leading complementary alternative medical doctors.

OVER SEVEN WEEKS OF SIMPLE, INEXPENSIVE, HEALTHY MEALS
and smoothies to boost your kids' brainpower and energy levels as
well as promote growth!

You want the best of health and well-being for your children,
which begins with the nutritional quality of the food you provide
them. You hold the keys to the energy that will fuel their brains
and bodies as well as strongly influence their emotions. Getting it
right need not be complicated or expensive, and I promise you'll
spend a minimal amount of time in the kitchen. It starts with the
simple choices you make today, and your whole family will love
the results!

My delicious, balanced meals and smoothies will introduce your kids
to a lifetime of vibrant health and provide you with 7 weeks' worth of
great meals to replace the empty calories routinely served in school

cafeterias. I also instruct
you on the key nutrients
that provide your children
the vital mental building
blocks they need to suc-
ceed in life.

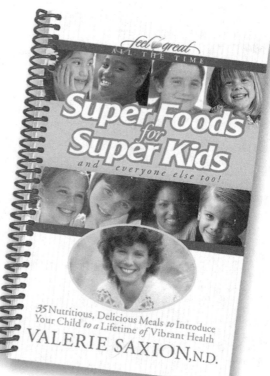

DO YOU HAVE A CHRONIC HEALTH PROBLEM that you just can shake off? Perhaps you have intestinal problems that come and go? Recurring bouts with diarrhea? Or you're tired all the time and feel depressed? Have you consulted with your doctor but not found an answer? It is very possible that the cause of what you are experiencing is directly due to parasites.

Don't cling to the notion that parasites are limited to the Third World. Parasitic experts estimate that there are between 100 and 130 common parasites being hosted in the American populace today, and a recent health report stated that 85 percent of Americans are infected with parasites. The trick is that the symptoms caused by parasites are subtle because they are experienced commonly by people without parasites, and the vast majority of health-care professionals have little training in diagnosing these masters of disguise and concealment.

If you're alive, you're at risk of this hidden crisis that is damaging millions of people needlessly today. It is a lot easier to become a parasitic host than you think!

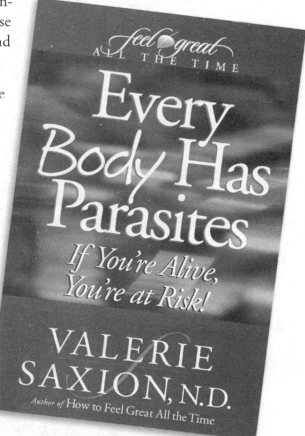

NEW *from* WENDIE PETT

CREATE THE BODY OF YOUR DREAMS, transform your health to vibrancy, and extend your youthfulness without the requirement of a gym or expensive exercise equipment or fad diets, and do it anytime and anyplace.

TRANSFORMETRICS™
THE ULTIMATE TRAINING SYSTEM

No matter what your present size or shape, *Every Woman's Guide to Personal Power* will guide you step by step through the most effective exercise system ever taught. Whether your goal is to drop a few pounds, shed several dress sizes, or to sculpt the body of your dreams, you will find everything you need to help your body achieve its natural, God-given strength and fitness potential. And it can be done in the privacy of your own home!

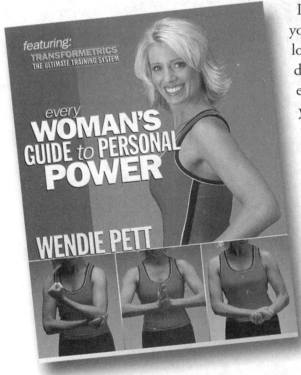

If you've never exercised in your life, or if you're an athlete looking to maximize your daily workout, here are the exact strategies and methods you need. Precisely illustrated with 100s of detailed photos showing every facet of every exercise, you'll never have to guess if you're doing it right. Feel what it's like to have twice as much energy as you've had in years and in less time than it requires to drive to the gym and change into exercise clothes.

IF YOU'VE BEEN LOOKING FOR AN EXERCISE SYSTEM that will give you the results you've always dreamed of having, does not require either a gym or expensive exercise equipment, can be done anytime and anyplace without requiring an outrageous commitment of time, you're holding it in your hands.

Based solidly upon the most effective exercise systems as taught by Earle E. Liederman and Charles Atlas during the 1920s, *Pushing Yourself to Power* provides you with everything you need to know to help your body achieve its natural, God-given strength and fitness potential. Whether your desire is simply to slim down and shape up, or to build your maximum all-around functional strength, athletic fitness, and *natural* muscularity, you will find complete training strategies specifically tailored to the achievement of your personal goals.

Profusely illustrated with 100s of clear, detailed photos showing every facet of every exercise, you'll never have to guess if you're doing it right again. You'll achieve the stamina you've always wanted in less time than it requires to drive to a gym and change into exercise clothes. Feel what it's like to have twice as much energy as you ever thought you'd have!

Unleash Your Greatness

AT BRONZE BOW PUBLISHING WE ARE COMMITTED to helping you achieve your **ultimate potential** in functional athletic strength, fitness, natural muscular development, and all-around superb health and youthfulness.

Our books, videos, newsletters, Web sites, and training seminars will bring you the very latest in scientifically validated information that has been carefully extracted and compiled from leading scientific, medical, health, nutritional, and fitness journals worldwide.

Our goal is to empower you! To arm you with the best possible knowledge in all facets of strength and personal development so that you can make the right choices that are appropriate for *you*.

Now, as always, **the difference between greatness and mediocrity** begins with a choice. It is said that knowledge is power. But that statement is a half truth. Knowledge is power only when it has been tested, proven, and applied to your life. At that point knowledge becomes wisdom, and in wisdom there truly is *power.* The power to help you choose wisely.

So join us as we bring you the finest in health-building information and natural strength-training strategies to help you reach your ultimate potential.

PG